D1612573

WITHDRAWN FROM
THE LIBRARY

UNIVERSITY OF
WINCHESTER

KA 0286269 7

Women, Social Leadership, and the Second World War

Women, Social Leadership, and the Second World War

Continuities of Class

JAMES HINTON

OXFORD

UNIVERSITY PRESS

OXFORD

UNIVERSITY PRESS

Great Clarendon Street, Oxford OX2 6DP

Oxford University Press is a department of the University of Oxford.
It furthers the University's objective of excellence in research, scholarship,
and education by publishing worldwide in

Oxford New York

Auckland Bangkok Buenos Aires Cape Town Chennai
Dar es Salaam Delhi Hong Kong Istanbul Karachi Kolkata
Kuala Lumpur Madrid Melbourne Mexico City Mumbai Nairobi
São Paulo Shanghai Taipei Tokyo Toronto

Oxford is a registered trade mark of Oxford University Press
in the UK and in certain other countries

Published in the United States
by Oxford University Press Inc., New York

© James Hinton 2002
The moral rights of the authors have been asserted
Database right Oxford University Press (maker)

First published 2002

All rights reserved. No part of this publication may be reproduced,
stored in a retrieval system, or transmitted, in any form or by any means,
without the prior permission in writing of Oxford University Press,
or as expressly permitted by law, or under terms agreed with the appropriate
reprographics rights organization. Enquiries concerning reproduction
outside the scope of the above should be sent to the Rights Department,
Oxford University Press, at the address above

You must not circulate this book in any other binding or cover
and you must impose this same condition on any acquirer

British Library Cataloguing in Publication Data
Data available

Library of Congress Cataloging in Publication Data
Data available
ISBN 0-19-924329-8

1 3 5 7 9 10 8 6 4 2

Typeset in 10/12pt Sabon by
Kolam Information Servies Pvt. Ltd., Pondicherry, India
Printed in Great Britain
on acid-free paper by
Biddles Ltd,
Guildford and King's Lynn

KING ALFRED'S COLLEGE
WINCHESTER

305.40942
HIN 02822697

For YVETTE

Preface

THIS BOOK HAS been a long time in gestation. More than fifteen years ago, fascinated by claims and counter-claims about the democratizing impact of the Second World War on British society, I set out to write a book comparing and contrasting the experience of two groups of people—male shop-floor workers in war industry and housewives thrust into unaccustomed public prominence by the centrality of austerity to the war effort. I had in mind a systematic comparison between the social relations of production and consumption within the corporatist economy of the war and its aftermath. As is the way of these things, the project was overambitious, spinning off in too many divergent directions to be held together within the confines of a single book. My work on shop-floor workers saw the light of day in 1994, as did the first fruits of my work on housewives. I will publish my findings about the politics of consumption and the gendered character of wartime corporatism in a forthcoming journal article. What is presented here is a spin-off from the original project. Gradually it became clear to me that questions about the potentially democratizing impact of the war on women's lives might be more fruitfully addressed not to their role as housewives (or as wartime wage earners where a good deal of work had already been done) but to their participation in voluntary work.

Paid employment was far from being the only route by which housewives were able to participate in a public sphere beyond the household. The early twentieth century had seen a rapid expansion of single-sex organizations catering for the associational life of women outside the home. During the war this female public sphere provided a basis for the mobilization of women into a vast range of part-time voluntary activities which made an essential contribution to Britain's war effort. One organization above all was responsible for organizing this work—Women's Voluntary Services (WVS). More or less by chance I came across the WVS archives, and these have provided the bedrock for this study, opening the way into a world of predominantly middle-class women's organizations which has been largely neglected by historians.

'In the second world war', wrote A. J. P. Taylor in 1965, 'the British people came of age.' Through their willing participation in the defence of Britain and the destruction of fascism, ordinary people took possession of the nation as never before—or, perhaps, since. Sixty years on, looking back over a century of unparalleled progress and destruction, the idea of the 'People's War' as an experience of social cohesion and democratic participation continues to fascinate both in popular memory and in academic history. In wartime Britain the language of democracy and of citizenship was pervasive. On the shop-floor this language, and the appeals to national unity which accompanied it, often had a deeply corrosive effect on established power structures. 'The people,' Angus Calder wrote in 1969, 'surged forward to fight their own war, forcing their masters into retreat'. This was the frame within which I cast my examination of wartime industrial relations, tracing the ways in which shop-floor citizens challenged autocracy in capitalist industry, as well as the mechanisms by which such pressures were frustrated and contained during and after the war. In line with Calder's approach I argued that the participatory democracy glimpsed in wartime held lessons for our futures, despite having been thwarted at the time.

Immersion in the WVS archive suggested a more pessimistic reading of the wartime experience. Fresh from the shop-floor I could not but be struck by the degree to which the social relations of voluntary work contributed to the continuities of upper- and middle-class power, contrasting sharply with the upsurge of democracy which I had charted in wartime factories. In the world of women's voluntary work wartime mobilization and its democratic rhetoric did more to provide opportunities for traditional social leaders to reinforce their authority than to stimulate radical challenges from below. Such challenges were not entirely absent, but in contrast to the shop-floor, their containment was never in doubt. By focusing on the wartime activity of WVS this book dwells more on continuity than on change, and it tends to lend support to the increasingly fashionable view that neither for women, nor for society in general, was the Second World War as transformative an event as has often been claimed. It was peacetime consumer capitalism, not total war, that was ultimately to render obsolete the structures of social authority analysed here.

Books have a life beyond the intentions of their authors. It may be that this study will reinforce the current tendency to dismiss the radical democratic potential of wartime mobilization. Certainly it helps to show what democrats were up against. Nevertheless, the Second World War, so central to the twentieth-century struggle for democracy, is likely to continue to provide a resource for historians concerned to uncover evidence of the capacity of ordinary people to take control of their collective destinies. For myself this quest remains open, and in future work I hope to demonstrate that, notwithstanding continuities of class like those traced in this book, democracy had more than a merely rhetorical relationship to the social relations of wartime Britain.

In the course of this work I have incurred many debts, none more important than that to Mrs Megan Keable who was in charge of the WRVS archives when I first consulted them in Brixton. When, in 1997, WRVS Headquarters moved to Abingdon there was no space for the archive and it was placed in temporary storage in a warehouse. I am extremely grateful to WRVS for allowing my work to continue by transferring the boxes I needed to the Modern Records Centre at Warwick, and to Christine Woodlands for facilitating this arrangement. I have visited a large number of other local and national archives in the course of this work and these are listed in the Bibliography. Thank you to all those who helped to make these visits pleasant and productive. I have learned much from responses to papers delivered to my colleagues at Warwick, to the 1999 Manchester conference on Mass Conservatism and to the Voluntary History Society in London. Successive generations of third-year Warwick undergraduates have been wonderfully stimulating, and I am grateful to them for allowing me to share my enthusiasm and forcing me to clarify my thinking. I owe particular thanks to Pat Thane for her careful reading of two drafts of the final text, to the other OUP reader, and to my first reader, at once the most critical and the most supportive, to whom this book is dedicated. The mistakes and misjudgements that remain are, of course, my own.

J H
WARWICK

Contents

Abbreviations

ARP	Air Raid Precautions
ATS	Auxiliary Territorial Service
BFBPW	British Federation of Business and Professional Women
BPW	Business and Professional Women
CPA	Conservative Party Archive
CSS	Council of Social Service
DMA	Durham Miners' Association
EAW	Electrical Association of Women
LCC	London County Council
MO	Mass Observation
NAHHO	National Association of Home Help Organisers
NCSRS	Nuffield College Social Reconstruction Survey
NCSS	National Council of Social Service
NCVO	National Council of Voluntary Organisations
NCW	National Council of Women
NIH	National Institute of Homeworkers
NUTG	National Union of Townswomen's Guilds
PAC	Public Assistance Committee
PEP	Political and Economic Planning
PRO	Public Record Office
PSL	Personal Service League
RDC	Rural District Council
RO	Record Office
SCWO	Standing Committee of Women's Organisations
SJC	Standing Joint Committee of Working Women's Organisations
TG	Townswomen's Guild
TUC	Trade Union Conference
WCA	Women Citizens' Association
WCG	Women's Co-operative Guild
WEA	Workers' Educational Association
WF	Women's Forum
WGPW	Women's Group for Public Welfare
WI	Women's Institute
WRVS	Women's Royal Voluntary Service
WVS	Women's Voluntary Services
YWCA	Young Women's Christian Association

I

Introduction

'It has been said that the middle classes are the backbone of England. I say that middle-age is the backbone of Women's Voluntary Service.'[1]

I

This book deals with a hitherto neglected group—publicly active middle-class and middle-aged women who proudly saw themselves during the war as the 'backbone of England'. Much has been written about British women and the Second World War, but the focus of attention has been disproportionately on the young and the working class. We know a good deal about working-class wives struggling to combine housewifery and motherhood with war work, and about young women finding their feet in war factories and the auxiliary services.[2] The wartime experiences of middle-aged women, and particularly middle-class ones, have attracted less attention from social historians. Some work has been done on the troubled history of middle-class domesticity during these years,[3] but the unpaid activities of middle-class women outside the home remain largely unexplored. Part of the reason for the relative neglect of the middle aged is that the social history of war has long been dominated by the pursuit of links between war and social change, and such links have been assumed to operate most forcefully in the experience of the young.[4] Increasingly, however, the debate on 'war and social change' has tended towards negative conclusions, particularly in the area of

---

[1] Mrs Boys, reported in cutting from *Lincolnshire Chronicle* (n.d., Apr. 1942?), in WRVS R3/5 Lincoln.

[2] Penny Summerfield, *Women Workers in the Second World War. Production and Patriarchy in Conflict* (London, 1984); ead., *Reconstructing Women's Wartime Lives* (Manchester, 1998); Richard Croucher, *Engineers at War* (London, 1982); D. Parkin, 'Women in the Armed Services, 1940–45', in R. Samuel (ed.), *Patriotism: The Making and Unmaking of British National Identity*, ii (London, 1989).

[3] Notably Elizabeth McCarty, 'Attitudes to Women and Domesticity in England, circa 1939–1955', Oxford D.Phil., 1994; Ina Zweiniger-Bargielowska, *Austerity in Britain. Rationing, Controls and Consumption, 1939–1955* (Oxford, 2000).

[4] Such experience also remains susceptible to the techniques of oral history, as is brilliantly demonstrated in Penny Summerfield, *Reconstructing Women's Wartime Lives*. But her illuminating discussion of wartime discourses about women and citizenship has nothing to say about the role of voluntary work. On the neglect of the middle aged see also John Benson, *Prime Time. A History of the Middle Aged in Twentieth-century Britain* (Harlow, 1997), 1–4.

gender relations. However important the wartime socialization of young women may have been in paving the way for fundamental shifts in women's expectations in the second half of the twentieth century, it now seems probable that the omnipresence of war in the first half of the century did at least as much to reinforce gendered discourses of 'warriors' and 'home-makers' as it did to advance the emancipation of women.[5] And what is true of gender may also be true of class. Summing up a brief survey of the wartime voluntary work undertaken by middle-aged and middle-class women, Martin Pugh remarked on the 'strong measure of continuity' linking these women's experience of the two world wars.[6] Rather than providing a reason to skip lightly over the territory, the existence of such continuities may itself be worth exploring. The primary argument of this book is that through their wartime voluntary work, middle-class women made a significant contribution to upholding the continuities of class.

The focus is on a detailed examination of one organization, Women's Voluntary Services (WVS), but that organization is considered throughout in relation to female associational life in general. Participation in women-only organizations, or in distinct women's sections of mixed organizations, played a significant role in the lives of hundreds of thousands of middle-class women. Such organizations had proliferated rapidly since the First World War and the granting of women's suffrage, and they all shared in a discourse about female citizenship which sought to foster the capacity of housewives to assert themselves in the public sphere but to do so in ways that did not threaten the overarching validation of marriage and motherhood as the primary sources of their identity. This vigorous female public sphere pro-vided middle-class women—most of them housewives, but also professional women and spinsters of independent means—with opportunities to meet and socialize outside the home, to educate and entertain themselves, to undertake charitable activity, to pursue campaigns around a wide and varied agenda of 'women's issues', and, in all this, to establish their places within the complex pecking-orders that characterized middle-class status; to assert a distinctive feminine presence in local civic life; and to exercise leadership over women less privileged than themselves.

Accounts of British social history in the 1940s abound with narratives of middle-class decline. Certainly the 1940s was not an easy decade for the middle classes. The collapse of appeasement discredited and marginalized

---

[5] M. R. J. Higonnet, *et al.*, *Behind the Lines. Gender and the Two World Wars* (New Haven, Conn., 1987); H. L. Smith, 'The Effect of the War on the Status of Women', in Smith (ed.), *War and Social Change. British Society in the Second World War* (Manchester, 1986); Jose Harris, 'War and Social History: Britain and the Home Front during the Second World War', *Contemporary European History*, 1 (1992).

[6] Martin Pugh, *Women and the Women's Movement in Britain, 1914–1959* (Basingstoke, 1992), 268.

the main vehicle of middle-class politics, the Conservative Party, which, to a much greater extent than its Labour rival, went into suspended animation at local level during the war years. The shifting balance of power within the war economy, together with a swing to the left among voters, opened the way for the first majority Labour government to direct the process of post-war reconstruction. Trade unionism returned from its inter-war wilderness to be acknowledged as an estate of the realm; and shop stewards were publicly wooed by Cabinet ministers. Full employment, austerity, and mildly egalitarian fiscal policies combined to produce a significant convergence of living standards, benefiting the less well off at the expense of an absolute decline in middle-class levels of consumption.[7] Cars without petrol, obsequious shopkeepers transformed by the rationing system into bullying autocrats, and labour market conditions that made it ever more difficult to find domestic servants—these and many other frustrations provided contemporary social commentators with ample evidence of middle-class decline. Even the revival of Conservative electoral fortunes in the late 1940s was built around an anti-socialist rhetoric which represented Britain's middle classes as profoundly damaged by a decade of egalitarianism.

And yet, somehow, the middle classes remained in control. Wartime national unity might have allowed an enhanced role for organized labour, symbolized by Ernest Bevin's position as the most powerful Home Front minister in the wartime coalition, but Bevin never threatened to replace Churchill, and the leadership of wartime Britain remained predominantly in the hands of those whose wealth, education, and social position were deemed to fit them for the task. Among these were the leaders of the women's public sphere in town and countryside whose capacity to mobilize the leisure time of middle-aged, middle-class womanhood proved indispensable to the war effort. After 1945, for all their reforming zeal, Attlee's ministers did little to attack the heartlands of upper middle-class power— inherited wealth, private enterprise, the public school system. Nor did Labour's 1945 victory spell sudden death to the capacity of middle-class women to exercise social leadership. Despite socialist traditions of hostility to the demeaning charity of Lady Bountiful, the Labour government, implementing ambitious welfare reforms in conditions of financial stringency and acute labour shortages, was keen to encourage voluntary work. Reconstruction, like the war itself, could be embraced by middle-class social leaders as one more opportunity to display their indispensability to the life of the community.

It was above all through their voluntary work that middle-class women made their contribution to the continuities of class. Men could wield

[7] Summerfield, 'The "Levelling of Class"', in Smith, *War and Social Change*; Zweiniger-Bargielowska, *Austerity*, 44–5.

enormous coercive power in economic life, or command the barely ques-
tioned deference owing to their professional expertise as, for example,
doctors, lawyers, or military leaders. Women, excluded by educational
disadvantage and the continued operation of the marriage bar in most
professional occupations, occupied few such positions in their own right.
Unable to rely either on coercive power or on the claims of trained expertise,
most female social leadership was a product of leisure dignified by 'character'. Upper-middle-class women remained 'natural' leaders both because they
had the time to devote to public life (households maintained by domestic
servants, children farmed out to public schools; or, for the spinsters, a
private income obviating the need for paid employment) and because they
possessed the 'character' to use their leisure not in the pursuit of frivolous,
hedonistic, or purely selfish ends, but in public service.[8] Historians of female
philanthropy have frequently pointed to the ambiguous relationship between Christian charity and social leadership: was she a humble servant of
other's needs or an arrogant mistress building her self-esteem by bullying the
poor?[9] While a persistent stereotype of 'posh ladies' from the WVS—
'poncey middle-class ladies ... going around ministering to the poor', as
one Labour Party supporter put it in the 1970s[10]—might lend support to
the latter interpretation, the willingness of comfortably-off leisured women
to render personal service to disadvantaged elderly people—the major area
of WVS activity since the 1950s—suggests a different story. These two
stories, however, had never been mutually exclusive. In voluntary work, as
elsewhere in life, motives are usually mixed. Historically the association
between charitable good works and claims to social leadership was at least
as old as the Evangelical revival, as was the accompanying contrast between
those dutiful women of the upper and middle classes who visited the poor
and their more frivolous, hedonistic sisters. By eschewing hedonism and
devoting themselves to good works, philanthropic ladies helped to cement
their social authority. It was in this tradition that WVS, during the Second
World War, served as a means by which leisured women sustained their
claims to social leadership. Through their activity in the public arena of

---

[8] Possession of a telephone, domestic servants, and a car were all cited by WVS administrators as critical to the capacity of individual women to undertake the duties of leadership at
local level. For the class correlation of these assets, see P. Massey, 'The Expenditure of 1,360
British Middle-class Households in 1938–39', *Journal of the Royal Statistical Society*, 3 (1942).
[9] Brian Harrison, 'Philanthropy and the Victorians', in Harrison, *Peaceable Kingdom.
Stability and Change in Modern Britain* (Oxford, 1982); Ross McKibbin, 'Class and Poverty
in Edwardian England', in McKibbin, *The Ideologies of Class: Social Relations in Britain,
1880–1950* (Oxford, 1990); Colin Jones, 'Some Recent Trends in the History of Charity', in
M. Daunton (ed.), *Charity, Self-interest and Welfare in the English Past* (London, 1996); A. J.
Kidd, 'Philanthropy and the "Social History Paradigm" ', *Social History*, 21 (1996); Diana Leat,
'Explaining Volunteering: A Sociological Perspective', in S. Hatch (ed.), *Volunteers: Patterns,
Meanings and Motives* (Berkhamstead, 1983), 54–6.
[10] Roger Sherrott, 'Fifty Volunteers', in Hatch, *Volunteers*, 118.

associational life these women simultaneously served the community and helped to uphold the authority of their class.

Voluntary work was concentrated among the higher-income groups. According to a wartime survey of housewives (see Table 1) nearly a quarter of all voluntary workers came from the wealthiest 5 per cent of the population. A further 38 per cent came from more modest middle-class homes. By contrast, the 75 per cent of housewives who were working class accounted for no more than 40 per cent of the total body of volunteers. Put another way, one in five upper-middle-class housewives was involved in voluntary work, compared with one in ten from the rest of the middle class, one in twenty-five among the better-off parts of the working class, and hardly any among the poor. The measurement of voluntary action is notoriously difficult,[11] and it seems probable that these figures, based on a house-to-house survey that disproportionately registered housebound women, substantially underestimate the proportion of women volunteering.[12] Moreover, as has often been noted, neighbourly informal mutual aid among working-class women is seldom classed by those who undertake it as 'volunteering' and is unlikely to have been reflected by the 1942 survey.[13] Despite this, however,

TABLE 1. *Housewives doing voluntary work, by income group (1942)*

Income group	Total	Number in voluntary work	Percentage in voluntary work	Percentage of voluntary workers
Class A	153	33	21.6	22.6
Class B	595	56	9.4	38.4
Class C	1,139	45	4.0	30.8
Class D	1,049	12	1.1	8.2
Totals	2,936	146	5.0	100.0

Source: Wartime Social Survey, *Workers and the War* (Aug. 1942), 7, 10, in PRO RG 23/16.

[11] Roger Tarling, 'Statistics on the Voluntary Sector in the UK', *Journal of the Royal Statistical Society* 163 (2000), 3

[12] The survey report points out this source of bias, and the following calculation suggests that the underestimate may be very substantial. In 1951 about two-thirds of the female population over the age of 14, or about 13.5 million people, were classified as not economically active. During the war the number of non-earning women would have been considerably lower: but even if we take 5% of the 1951 total then we only get 680,000 women volunteers, considerably less than the numbers claimed by WVS alone. So either the WVS figure is inflated (which seems unlikely) or the 1942 survey greatly underestimates the number of housewives involved in voluntary work.

[13] F. K. Prochaska, *Women and Philanthropy in Nineteenth-century England* (Oxford, 1980), 42; Leat, 'Explaining Volunteering', 53; Sherrott, 'Fifty Volunteers', 140 ff.

the survey is probably reliable as an indication of the relative propensity of housewives belonging to different income groups to join formal voluntary organizations. Broken down by age, the same survey showed that women in the age range 35–50 were more than twice as likely to be doing voluntary work than younger or older women. In the early 1950s it was estimated that about 60 per cent of WVS members were over 40 years of age, compared with 10 per cent under 25.[14]

II

During the war by far the largest group of female voluntary workers was to be found in WVS.[15] Set up at the request of the Home Office in June 1938 to recruit women to assist in local authority air raid precautions (ARP), WVS rapidly expanded its brief. After the danger of air raids receded in 1941, WVS became a maid-of-all-work filling gaps as they materialized at the behest both of local authorities and Whitehall departments. By 1943 membership had risen to close to one million and it remained at that level for the rest of the war. Twice as many women contributed to the war effort through WVS than joined any of the auxiliary services.[16] WVS was, from the outset, anxious to involve working-class women, and it succeeded in doing so to a degree unusual in the world of voluntary work. The manner of this involvement, however, did more to sustain social hierarchy than to democratize voluntary work. At all levels the leading personnel in WVS were drawn overwhelmingly from the upper layers of English society.

The fact that WVS was a newcomer to the women's public sphere, and in the eyes of many of the established organizations a rather unwelcome one, makes its history incomprehensible without placing it within that larger space inhabited by Women's Institutes, Townswomen's Guilds, the various organizations of business and professional women, the Conservative Party's women's sections, and a host of more specialist organizations. The concern with social leadership also dictates close attention to co-operation and conflict between WVS and women organized in the labour movement—the Women's Co-operative Guild and Labour Party women's sections. The WVS attempt to colonize and, to some degree, to control the established

[14] R. C. Chambers, 'A Study of Three Voluntary Organisations', in D. V. Glass (ed.), *Social Mobility in Britain,* (London, 1954), 388–9.
[15] Two histories of WVS have been published. Katherine Bentley Beauman, *Green Sleeves. The Story of WVS/WRVS* (London, 1977) provides a valuable survey of its various spheres of activity. The earlier history, Charles Graves, *Women in Green. The Story of the Women's Voluntary Service* (London, 1948), is less useful. None of the existing histories, however, seeks to place WVS in the wider social history, or to investigate its relationship with broader associational world of women. For my own first thoughts on the significance of WVS, some which have since been modified in the light of further research, see J. Hinton, 'Voluntarism and the Welfare/Warfare State. Women's Voluntary Services in the 1940s', *Twentieth Century British History,* 9 (1998).
[16] Summerfield, *Reconstructing Women's Wartime Lives,* 257

world of women's organizations generated reports and correspondence which provide the social historian with a unique window onto the mid-twentieth-century female public sphere. No other major women's organization preserved such extensive correspondence files, files which enable the historian to get behind the bureaucratic circular, the carefully fashioned public statement, or the aridity of committee minutes to glimpse these women with their hair down, speaking frankly to one another of their shared concerns. These papers might well not have survived. In 1946 the head of the Home Office civil defence registry visited WVS headquarters to inspect the archives with a view to moving them into Whitehall for weeding before their 'ultimate disposal in the Public Records Office'.[17] In the event the weeding appears to have been done by WVS staff in house.[18] Given the pre-occupation of Whitehall with the operations of central government it is highly unlikely that the wealth of detailed reports from, and correspondence with, local organizers would have survived had the original plan to move the records to the Public Record Office been implemented. Paradoxically, WVS officials felt obliged to preserve the papers intact partly because they saw WVS less as a voluntary organization than as an arm of the state and believed they had a duty to hold the records in trust for the national archives.[19]

By putting information drawn from WVS files alongside surviving local and national records of other women's organizations, the Conservative Party, studies of voluntary work carried out by the Nuffield College Social Reconstruction Survey, and by Mass Observation, local newspapers, and a variety of other sources, it has been possible to explore the mechanisms of female social leadership in a range of socio-economic settings in provincial England. In planning the research I considered whether a narrower focus on two or three places might produce more thoroughly grounded findings, and I have sometimes felt like one of WVS's own 'travelling administrators': just in town long enough to clear up the most obvious problems. Where this has led to mistakes or misjudgements my account will, I hope, be corrected by better-informed local historians. But too much would have been lost by narrowing the geographical focus, including the view from WVS headquarters and a sense of the variety of patterns of social leadership involved. The neglect of London, Scotland, Wales, and Northern Ireland is a result partly of a desire to keep the demands of local archival research under control, and partly of the relative weakness of the WVS archive for some of these areas.[20]

---

[17] WVS Chairman's Committee, Minutes, 21 Mar., 2 May 1946.
[18] Ibid., 10 Dec. 1947. Most files give the date on which they were weeded.
[19] A point clearly explained to me by Mrs Meagan Keable, who was in charge of the WRVS archives in the 1990s.
[20] Most surprisingly London, for which I was unable to locate the equivalent of the regional files that proved invaluable for the rest of England. Scottish records are located in Edinburgh and have not been used.

III

The 'middle class' whose associational life is explored in this book is not easy to define. At its upper edges it merged into the plutocracy of land and big business, whose womenfolk played a major role in the leadership of many of the middle-class women's organizations, including WVS. To avoid clumsy phraseology I have frequently used the terms 'upper-middle class' as a short hand for 'upper-middle and upper class', a usage whose meaning will be apparent in its context and can be justified by the permeability of this 'frontier zone' below the apex of the social hierarchy. Aristocratic ladies are easily placed, but where do the wives of retired lieutenant colonels belong, or those of bishops, colonial administrators, senior civil servants? The great bulk of middle-class people, of course, lived not on the fringes of plutocracy but in very much more humble circumstances. It was the rapid expansion of a 'new middle class' of white-collar workers, technicians, schoolteachers, and other lower professionals which captured the attention of contemporary commentators like Orwell and Priestley, and a good deal of recent historical work has positioned these groups in the vanguard of cultural change, pioneering life-style choices in the suburbs which paved the way towards later twentieth-century consumer culture.[21] Despite stereotypes of lonely housewives and 'the suburban neurosis', women's associational life flourished in the expanding suburbs, and many of the organizations examined here drew a substantial proportion of their members from these numerically dominant sections of the middle class. The women who ran these organizations, however, came predominantly from established urban and rural elites—the wives of businessmen, doctors, lawyers, bank managers, and gentry, or in some cases business and professional women themselves. It was the 5 per cent who undertook 23 per cent of organized voluntary work who supplied most of the leaders, and it is their voices that speak most clearly through the archives. By privileging these voices I am swimming somewhat against the tide of the growing historical literature on the history of the twentieth-century English middle class. Undoubtedly, as comfortably provided housewives, they did more than their share of consuming. At the same time, however, viewing them-

[21] Bernard Crick, *George Orwell. A Life* (Harmondsworth, 1982), 190, 371–2, 376, 406–7; John Blaxendale, ' "I had seen a lot of Englands": J. B. Priestley, Englishness and the People', *History Workshop Journal*, 51 (Spring 2001); Simon Gunn, 'The Public Sphere, Modernity and Consumption: New Perspectives on the History of the English Middle Class', in A. Kidd and D. Nicholls, *Gender, Civic Culture and Consumerism. Middle-class Identity in Britain, 1900–1940* (Manchester, 1999), 21–3; Tom Jeffery, 'A Place in the Nation', in R. Koshar (ed.), *Splintered Classes: Politics and the Lower Middle Classes in Inter-war Europe* (London, 1990); id., 'The Suburban Nation: Politics and Class in Lewisham', in G. S. Jones and D. Feldman, (eds.), *Metropolis London* (1989); Peter Bailey, 'White Collars, Grey Lives? The Lower Middle Class Revisited', *Journal of British Studies*, 38 (July 1999); McKibbin, *Classes and Cultures. England, 1918–1951* (Oxford, 1998).

selves as social leaders, they constructed an important part of their identities around a Victorian ethos of public service which, in some ways, stood at odds with the more individualistic sensibilities characteristic of the emerging consumer culture.

Much recent scholarship has been concerned to downgrade the explanatory power of the concept of class. Recent work on post-war party politics in Britain, for example, has tended to shift the explanatory focus from class to gender, arguing that Conservative success reflected a degree of sensitivity to issues of concern to women voters unmatched by their Labour competitors: in such accounts the issues that united women across class boundaries take on more salience than those which divided them.[22] In a similar vein the most recent historian of the Women's Institutes stresses their role in shaping a distinct (and in the author's view authentically feminist) gender identity while playing down the extent to which they operated as sites for the exercise of social leadership by the rural gentry.[23] My own reading of the social world inhabited by publicly active women suggests that the category of gender cannot usefully be given precedence over the category of class. In individual lives the formation of class and gender identities were inextricably interwoven, and if class was gendered, then gender was also 'classed'.[24] Class and gender worked together in constituting the style of social leadership practised by the women at the centre of this study. It is true that female social leaders often denied the salience of class in their public work, but this may well have been because they took the word 'class' as a sign for precisely that irreconcilable gulf of social antagonism which, through their social work, they sought to dissolve. As Margaret Stacey

[22] In this spirit, for example, Ina Zweiniger-Bargielowska has argued that Conservative anti-austerity campaigning was effective in shifting women voters disproportionately away from the Labour Party. The polling evidence makes it clear that, while women were indeed significantly more inclined than men to vote Tory throughout the post-war period, there was no significant *change* in the partisan gender gap between 1945 and 1955, apart from a blip in 1950 when it temporarily *narrowed* (Zweiniger-Bargielowska, *Austerity*, 253; ead., 'Explaining the Gender Gap: The Conservative Party and the Women's Vote, 1945–1964', in M. Francis and Zweiniger-Bargielowska (eds.), *The Conservatives and British Society, 1880–1990* (Cardiff, 1996), 201). Class breakdowns of the polling data show that the female swing to Labour in 1950 was exclusively a working-class phenomenon. Middle-class women did indeed respond to the anti-austerity message. Confronting the knee-jerk assumption that 'the women have let us down', Herbert Morrison pointed out at the time that the major cause of Labour's 1950 setback was the desertion of working-class *men* (Hinton, 'Women and the Labour Vote, 1945–50', *Labour History Review*, 57 (1993)). It is ironic that the chauvinist misinformation that Morrison sought to correct should now be in danger of becoming accepted as the conventional wisdom among historians concerned to blame, not women, but a 'masculinist' Labour Party for its failure to accommodate their presumed consumerism (Amy Black and Stephen Brooke, 'The Labour Party, Women, and the Problem of Gender, 1951–1966', *Journal of British Studies*, 36 (1997), 421–3).

[23] Maggie Andrews, *The Acceptable Face of Feminism. The Women's Institute as a Social Movement* (London, 1998).

[24] Joan Scott, *Gender and the Politics of History* (Oxford, 1988).

observed during her late 1940s research in Banbury, the more people were
concerned to defend the existing class system the less they liked talking
about it.[25] In reality, however, the shape of the female public sphere in
England was heavily determined by class.[26]

It is not, however, my intention to reassert a foundational concept of class
as a pre-discursive reality structuring social and political life. Ever since the
1960s the project of social history has thrived on pulling 'class' free from
simple objectivist definitions, and the recent deluge of theoretical debate
stimulated by post-modernism has served only to make this more explicit.[27]
Political historians, for example, have rightly insisted that parties do not
simply reflect interests or identities created elsewhere: they are active agents
in the construction of their own constituencies of support.[28] Popular notions
of 'class' may, sometimes, have more to do with the dynamics of contemporary political discourse—as has been persuasively argued in the case of the
early nineteenth-century invention of 'the middle class'—than with those
more material processes of class formation that social historians have often
taken as their primary object of investigation.[29] The history of 'class' is
as much a history of ways of imagining the social world as of tracking
changes in objectively existing patterns of social inequality. Class was,
among other things, a matter of identity, of the existence of imagined
communities whose power lay not in faithfully reflecting a pre-discursive
homogeneity of experience, but precisely in their capacity to transcend
individual, local, occupational, and gender difference. Equally important,
as David Cannadine has recently argued, 'class' describes not only a form of
identity, a way of imagining who 'we' are as against those who do not belong
to 'our' class, but also a means of imagining the shape of the social structure
as a whole—not only, 'where do we fit in?', but also, 'what is it that we fit
in to?'.[30]

Bipolar models of class played an important part in shaping middle-class
identities. The defence of property against a predatory imagined other, the
'enemy within', represented (however implausibly at times) by the political
and industrial rise of labour, was a central theme of Conservative Party
rhetoric both in the early 1920s and during the years of the post-war Labour

[25] M. Stacey, *Tradition and Change: A Study of Banbury* (Oxford, 1960), 145–6.
[26] Had Scotland been included this judgement might have been more nuanced. It would be
interesting to investigate whether class had a similar salience in the world of voluntary work in
Scotland.
[27] Marc W. Steinberg, 'Culturally Speaking: Finding a Commons Between Post-structuralism
and the Thompsonian Perspective', *Social History*, 21 (1996).
[28] J. Lawrence and M. Taylor (eds.), *Party, State and Society: Electoral Behaviour in Modern
Britain* (Aldershot, 1996); D. Cannadine, *Class in Britain* (London, 1998), 107.
[29] D. Wahrman, *Imagining the Middle Class. The Political Representation of Class in
Britain, c.1780–1840* (Cambridge, 1995).
[30] James Thompson, 'After the Fall: Class and Political Language in Britain, 1780–1900',
Historical Journal, 39 (1996); Cannadine, *Class in Britain*, 20 and *passim*.

Government.[31] This bipolar, anti-socialist model did not, however, exhaust the languages of class, even as deployed by Tory politicians. Throughout the period images of the enemy within jostled promiscuously with at least two older ways of addressing middle-class sensibilities. On the one hand, a confident self-assertion of the superior usefulness of the middling sort over those both below and above them in the social order continued to be deployed.[32] On the other hand, appeals were made to a hierarchical model of society. Raphael Samuel summarized the social imagery of the inter-war middle class as one which evoked 'less a class than a society of orders each with its own exclusion rituals and status ideology, jealously guarding a more or less self-contained existence, and exquisitely graded according to a hierarchy of ranks.'[33] Contemporary commentators often attributed an active role to women in sustaining middle-class identities, particularly through the exercise of their wifely duties both in facilitating sociability among families in the same social niche and in policing the boundaries of class.[34] Hierarchical models could be used, however, not only to shore up processes of social exclusion, but also as a basis for social integration. In her autobiography Mrs Thatcher evoked a social unity manifested in Rememberance Day celebrations involving the whole range of associational life in 1930s Grantham: 'the mayor, aldermen and councillors with robes and regalia' followed by 'the Brownies, Cubs, Boys Brigade, Boy Scouts, Girl Guides, Freemasons, Rotary, Chamber of Commerce, Working men's Clubs, trade unions, British Legion, soldiers, airmen, the Red Cross, the St John's Ambulance . . . representatives of every organisation that made up our rich civic life.' Such ways of imagining the social order held out the promise that existing social gulfs could be bridged though the exercise of leadership in associational life. In Mrs Thatcher's fondly remembered Grantham she had grown up believing 'that class was not important'.[35]

The stress placed by some political historians on anti-socialism as a key to middle-class identity may be overplayed. In the everyday life of the female public sphere, away from the hubbub of elections, hierarchical models of the class system which emphasized social harmony were probably more helpful

---

[31] McKibbin, *Classes and Cultures* 50–69; *id.*, 'Class and Conventional Wisdom: The Conservative Party and the "Public" in Inter-war Britain', in *The Ideologies of Class: Social Relations in Britain, 1880–1950* (Oxford, 1991); John Bonham, *The Middle Class Vote* (London, 1954), 19–20, 59–60, 181.

[32] Cannadine, *Class in Britain*, 151–2.

[33] R. Samuel, 'The Middle Class Between the Wars', Part I, *New Socialist* (Jan.–Feb. 1983), 30; Alan A. Jackson, *The Middle Classes, 1900–1950* (Nairn, 1991).

[34] R. Lewis and A. Maude, *The English Middle Classes* (London, 1953), 12–14; H. Pear, *English Social Differences* (London, 1955), 290; McCarty, 'Attitudes to Women and Domesticity in England', 27–9.

[35] M. Thatcher, *The Path to Power* (London, 1995), 20, 47.

to sustaining social leadership than embattled talk of the enemy within. The exercise of social leadership explored in this book involved relations of paternalism and deference right through the class and status structure. However useful anti-socialism might be as a means of whipping the voters into line at election time, its value for everyday social leadership was limited—especially during the 1940s when Labour was in government. Rather than confront the labour movement head on, representing it as predatory enemy of society, those with an eye to continuing social leadership chose more subtle ways of limiting the potential threat to their own prominence. Hierarchical images of class served to sustain elite power more surely than attempts to mobilize an anti-socialist nation, however well anti-socialism might serve in the confrontational world of electoral politics.

Individuals were free to employ different models of the class structure to make sense of different aspects of their experience. Thus a Tory woman who, at election time, saw herself as fighting to free the middle classes from socialist tyranny, might well at other times forgo bipolar models in favour of a hierarchical concept of class which allowed her to imagine herself, not as a victim, but as a responsible social leader whose indispensability to the life of the community would guarantee the continuing influence of her class no matter who held office at Westminster or the town hall. In the everyday exercise of social leadership, class (imagined in this non-confrontational way) played a more central role than party. While middle-class Labour women could and did participate comfortably in luncheon clubs dominated by Tories,[36] a working-class woman, whatever her politics, would have felt entirely out of place, even if she could find the time or the money to attend. There has been a tendency in some recent writing to exaggerate the creative agency of politics, writing the history of class identities too directly out of the discourse of political life itself.[37] Foregrounding the neglected history of non-partisan women's organizations suggests a more nuanced history of middle-class femininity than that provided by viewing it through the over-politicized lens of anti-socialism. Certainly the Conservative Party was aware of the political advantages to be gained from its members' involvement in non-partisan organizations, but publicly active middle-class women, including Conservatives, often saw the social leadership they exercised through their voluntary work as a more important signifier of social identity than anything derived from their political affiliations. Because class had a life beyond politics it can supply a richer and more fruitful conceptual

[36] For example, Dorothy Bates in Leicester or Pearl Hyde in Coventry (see Chapter 4, below).
[37] Duncan Tanner, 'Labour, 1910–31', in Lawrence and Taylor, *Party, State and Society*, 123. Cannadine, *Class in Britain*, invites this criticism. His assertion that party politics 'are as much about the attempt to create, manage and manipulate social identities as they are the direct expression of them' (p. 107) is helpful. But the suggestion that social identities fashioned by discourses other than those of party politics are 'unfathomable' (pp. 188, 168–9) is not.

framework for understanding mid-twentieth-century Britain than can be provided by privileging the noisy posturing of the partisan battle for votes.

IV

Part I of this book investigates the process of WVS mobilization. To a degree unusual among social institutions, WVS was the creation of a single individual—Lady Reading. For this reason Chapter 2 explores the beliefs and leadership style which enabled her to provide inspiration to so many women volunteers. It also outlines the structure of WVS as a national organization. The focus of attention in the chapters that follow is on the dynamics of mobilization at local rather than at national level. The history of twentieth-century Britain has often been written as a story of state expansion, in which local agency gives way progressively to a process of national centralization. In such narratives local history becomes unimportant: the vectors of historical change are to be found in the worlds of Westminster, Whitehall, the City, and the 'peak organizations' of the major organized interest groups.[38] Some historians have urged a focus on institutional history as a response to the tendency of social historians to neglect the state.[39] But crucial though these national sites of power became, they did not in fact strip out historical agency from more diffused social and cultural processes. It is an assumption of the present work that class, status, and social leadership were still largely fashioned at the local level, and that the towns and cities of provincial England should be seen not as backwaters, but as the source of deep currents underlying developments at national level that would otherwise be incomprehensible.

Chapter 3 describes the shape and nature of the urban female public sphere as it existed in the late 1930s. As WVS colonized this world, it took on many of its middle-class contours, in particular by seeking to build the new organization around the prestige of established female social leaders. At the same time, however, WVS recruited large numbers of working-class housewives, and Chapter 4 asks whether WVS did more to democratize the world of voluntary work or to consolidate middle-class leadership. Despite repeated overtures to the leaders of working-class organizations of housewives (the Women's Co-operative Guild and the Labour Party), Lady Reading was unable to break down the long-standing suspicion with which Labour women regarded the middle-class women's movement, and such co-operation as there was tended to be grudging and seen by the Labour women as a temporary wartime expedient. Chapter 5 explores the complex and

---

[38] Notably by Keith Middlemas in *Politics in Industrial Society* (London, 1979) and *Power Competition and the State* (3 vols., London, 1986, 1990, 1991).

[39] J. Zeitlin, 'From Labour History to the History of Industrial Relations', *Economic History Review*, 40 (1987).

ambiguous relationship between WVS and local government, in particular
probing the implications of Lady Reading's autocratic and hierarchical form
of organization for the capacity of local social leaders to resist the centralizing logic of state expansion. These three chapters deploy evidence from a
large number of towns and cities, but particular attention has been paid in
the research to the following places: Barrow-in-Furness, Blackpool, Coventry, Halifax, Hull, Guildford, Leicester, Nottingham, Portsmouth, Sheffield,
and Southampton. As well as representing a mixture of different kinds of
urban economy—a one-industry and several mixed industrial towns, a
seaside resort, a market town, three ports—these places were selected on
the basis of the richness of relevant sources in the WVS archive and local
record offices. The remaining two chapters in Part I deal with the position of
WVS in rural areas and in the Durham coalfield, areas where the social
leadership exercised by established elites found itself, respectively, exceptionally secure or facing its greatest challenges. In the shire counties WVS,
and the reception of evacuees with which it was mainly concerned, served to
reinforce existing social relations. In the pit villages of County Durham, on
the other hand, WVS became a site of open class struggle as Labour women
used it to challenge the paternalistic hold traditionally exercised by middle-
class social leaders over the associational life of the miners' wives. It is a
contrast that provides a useful reminder of how many different places mid-
twentieth-century Britain actually was.

Part II shifts the focus to the immediate post-war years, when the future of
WVS was in doubt. In 1945 most members expected the organization to
close down, and when it did not do so, they left. At the same time the
established women's organizations pressed the Attlee government to put
an end to an organization they perceived as an alien wartime growth
offensive to principles both of democracy and of voluntarism. Chapter 8
examines attitudes among the membership at the end of the war, and the
strategies employed by Lady Reading to make WVS indispensable to Whitehall by finding new work for tired hands. Chapter 9 returns to the wider
female associational world examining attempts to consolidate women's
organizations around a non-partisan reformist agenda which reflected
their conviction that, however extensively the state might or indeed should
intervene, ongoing social problems would continue to provide fertile soil for
middle-class social leadership. The ambition and self-assertiveness of this
non-partisan feminine reformism was limited both by the inability of women
to take on the male-dominated power of the political parties, and by the
growing marginalization of philanthropic forms of authority as social work
became increasingly professionalized in the welfare state. Chapter 10 looks
closely at one example of this process of marginalization—the establishment
of local authority Home Help services in the later 1940s, pioneered by the
Oxford WVS organizer in a failed attempt to sustain the authority of middle-

class social leaders in social work against the growing power of the professionals. Chapter 11 returns to the antagonism between WVS and the other
women's organizations, a relationship further embittered by an ill-conceived
government attempt to force an amalgamation of WVS with the National
Council of Social Services. WVS survived, largely owing to Lady Reading's
skill and determination, but the institutional continuity disguised significant
shifts in the social meaning of the organization. By the 1960s, when renewed
growth took the voluntary sector in new and more radical directions, the
continuing selfless work of middle-aged women delivering meals-on-wheels
or serving in hospital canteens embodied only an echo of WVS during its
Second World War prime. The story of the WVS adds weight to the view
that, despite the manifold crises of the first half of the century, it was not
until the full impact of consumer capitalism from the 1950s that values and
attitudes laid down in the late nineteenth century finally lost purchase on the
ways in which British society functioned.[40] Gareth Steadman Jones once
described the Attlee Government as the 'last and most glorious flowering of
late Victorian liberal philanthropy'.[41] In that display, Lady Reading's
'women in green' were indeed a prize bloom.

---

[40] Harris, *Private Lives, Public Spirit. A Social History of Britain, 1870–1914* (Oxford, 1993),
252–3; Francois Bedarida, *A Social History of England, 1851–1990* (London, 1991), 249–52.
[41] G. S. Jones, 'March into History?', *New Socialist* (Jan./Feb. 1982), 12.

Part I

2

Lady Reading and Women's Voluntary Services

In November 1947 Lady Reading appealed to her members not to allow austerity 'to lead us into temptation to dabble in the black market'.[1] While the echo of the Lord's Prayer was probably unconscious, it was none the less significant. Under-the-counter dealing was a threat not only to the fragile post-war economy but, more importantly, to the spiritual health of the community.[2] As chairman[3] of a committee of women's organizations established to advise the Government on its fuel economy campaign, Lady Reading fully understood the economic reasons why housewives should observe the disciplines of austerity. But the spiritual reasons were equally compelling. Britain, she claimed, was rich in two raw materials—'coal and character'. Both were rare and hard to come by: 'coal generated throughout the long space of time in the womb of Mother Earth and character formed in the deep consciousness of woman.'[4] For Lady Reading the central purpose of WVS, both during and after the war, was to cultivate and mobilize these reserves of feminine 'character'. For the middle-class housewives to whom she spoke responsible citizenship involved not only efficient and economical management of their households, but also active participation in public work undertaken on a voluntary basis.

I

WVS was the personal creation of Stella Reading, a woman of uncommon gifts. Born in 1894, she grew up in Constantinople where her father, of Huguenot descent, represented Britain in the Public Debt Administration established by western bankers to ensure that servicing foreign loans would

[1] *Cumberland News* (6 Nov. 1947), in WRVS, Press Cuttings. For the importance she attached to the black market as 'the cruel debaser that ruined countries and robbed individuals of their self-respect', see her 1947 Christmas Letter, WRVS, Chairman's Christmas Letters.
[2] C. K. Allen, 'The Pinpricked Life', *Spectator* (5 Nov. 1948), cited in Robert Hewison, *In Anger. Culture in the Cold War, 1945–60* (London, 1981), 20.
[3] This was the contemporary usage, and I have employed it throughout. WRVS, apparently impervious to late twentieth-century cultural change, still retains this usage.
[4] *Wren*, 186 (Jan. 1950), 3. For other versions of this metaphor see *Cumberland News* (6 Nov. 1947); *Edinburgh Evening Dispatch* (27 July 1948); *Wiltshire Gazette* (29 Sept. 1949).

remain the first priority of the Turkish state.[5] Forced by a weak spine to spend much of her adolescence lying in bed, she was not sent to school but educated at home by a priest.[6] The Christianity she imbibed in Constantinople had a touch of eastern mysticism about it. Wisdom, she wrote when she was 60, could be attained only by those who held part of themselves back from the world—'the old lady on the farm in the depths of the country, the mystic in retirement, the isolated human being in no-man's land'. Underlying the energetic, outgoing, and intensely practical skills that she brought to WVS was an ethical vision acquired and sustained through periods of contemplative inactivity: 'a thorough sorting of the rag-bag of one's mind...an ultimate tidying up of all views so that one reaches decisions on the general main points.'[7] Kathleen Halpin, who worked closely with Reading in WVS for over thirty years, felt that there was something unfathomable about her: 'she had the Eastern mind...always the philosophical strain running through it.'[8]

The outbreak of war in 1914 put an end to her father's job, and, back in England, Stella, after a short-lived foray into nursing—she could not stand the sight of blood—took a secretarial training. Following a variety of secretarial jobs in London, she went to India in 1925 as private secretary to the viceroy's wife, and subsequently to the viceroy, Lord Reading, himself. Born Rufus Isaacs, Lord Reading was a Liberal politician who as Attorney-General before the war had been involved with Lloyd George in the Marconi scandal, a stain on his character about which Stella was to remain defensive until the end of her life.[9] After their return from India in 1926, Stella became Reading's 'right-hand man', indispensable to his work as a leading opposition politician and, briefly, Foreign Secretary in MacDonald's national government in the autumn of 1931. In her capacity as his chief of staff, 'splendid Stella' rapidly established a reputation in political circles as an effective and knowledgeable woman of affairs.[10] 'Had she been born a man,' a friend remarked in 1931, 'the highest political offices might have been hers.'[11] Lord Reading's first wife

[5] H. Mongomery Hyde, *Lord Reading. The Life of Rufus Isaacs* (London, 1967), 389 n.; J. Cain and A. G. Hopkins, *British Imperialism. Innovation and Expansion, 1688–1914* (London, 1993), 405–6.

[6] *Sunday Chronicle* (1 Mar. 1936).

[7] Lady Reading, 'My Philosophy of Life' (1958), 6. Typescript in WRVS, Lady Reading (misc.).

[8] Interview with Halpin (1977), Brian Harrison Tapes.

[9] Sir Reader Bullard, *Stella Reading. Some Recollections by her Friends* (n.d., 1978), 5.

[10] *Star* (5 Aug. 1931); *London Evening News* (5 Aug. 1931); *Liverpool Evening Express* (6 Aug. 1931); Florence Van Gruisen to Lord Reading, (n.d., 1931), BL Add. MS EUR F 118/160; Montgomery Hyde, *Lord Reading*, 389, 398–9; Denis Judd, *Lord Reading* (London, 1982), 249; D. Cannadine, *The Decline and Fall of the British Aristocracy* (London, 1990), 590. She was one of the few women to be involved with PEP at its foundation in 1931 (J. Pinder (ed.), *Fifty years of Political and Economic Planning* (London, 1981), 14, 39).

[11] *Star* (5 Aug. 1931).

died early in 1930, and eighteen months later Stella married him, to the surprise of many of her friends, who had seen her as 'an inveterate "bachelor girl" '.[12] She was 37 and he was 70: he died four years later. During this short marriage Stella threw herself into the life of a society hostess.[13] She was quick to put her new social position to good use, playing a leading role in the organization of the Personal Service League in 1932 to raise funds from the upper classes to distribute clothes, boots, and blankets to the unemployed. Her talents flourished in this work and the League rapidly became one of the largest charitable organizations in the country, with depots and branches in every district.[14] By the later 1930s, Lady Reading had established herself as one of the great and good, appointed to a variety of public bodies (including advisory committees on migration within the empire and on the future of the BBC), holding figurehead positions in a variety of charities and women's organizations, and in demand as an entertaining speaker on the circuit of women's luncheon clubs.[15] It was therefore quite natural that the Home Secretary would turn to her when he decided, in May 1938, that a drive to recruit women to assist in Air Raid Precautions (ARP) would be a good way to ginger up local authorities who were refusing to take seriously the need to prepare for war.[16]

From the outset, Reading saw the provision of inspiration as central to her task: 'it is hopeless to call for effort from people and expect a response unless they can be shown the spark of the sublime which is within the scheme, and which must illumine the vision set before them.'[17] Her rallying calls to the membership addressed the 'great intangible things'[18] in a way that calls into question some recent accounts of the ethos of public life in 1940s Britain. 'We must go on building,' she wrote in December 1947, 'maybe with worn-out tools, maybe with backs that ache, but always with eyes that have seen something of the sublime . . . '. And two years later: 'I send you this Christmas an unusual wish and one which will call for much thought on your part . . . '. Working an elaborate metaphor of sumptuous, but hidden, possessions—'rich fabrics, beautiful silks, or yards of velvet'—Lady Reading

---

[12] *Newcastle Daily Journal* (6 Aug. 1931): 'she shared a flat with a friend and was not often seen with Lord Reading except when business threw them together.'

[13] Peggy Blampied, *Stella Reading. Recollections*, 8–9. There is a glimpse of her life during these years in her letters to 'The Prof.', Frederick Lindeman, in Cherwell Papers, Nuffield College, Oxford.

[14] A. S. Williams, *Ladies of Influence. Women of the Elite in Inter-war Britain* (Harmondsworth, 2000), 21–2, 167; Personal Service League, Leaflet (Nov. 1938), in MO TC Women, Box 4, File G; *Hull Daily Mail* (26 Nov. 1933); *Newcastle Sunday Sun* (25 June 1936); *Western Daily Mail* (15 Oct. 1936); Programme for Grand Charity Matinee, Empire Theatre, Newcastle (4 Dec. 1935), Durham RO D/He/188.

[15] Press cuttings from 1936 in BL Add. MS EUR F 118/134(o).

[16] Reading, Memo on Meeting with Gardiner, 29 Nov. 1938, PRO HO 186 569.

[17] Reading, 'My Philosophy of Life', 5

[18] Christmas Letter, Dec. 1947, WRVS Chairman's Christmas Letters.

sought to contrast the drabness of post-war austerity with the spiritual splendours earned by treading 'the hard path of self-denial' and devoting oneself to leadership in the service of others:

If you think on my wish you will discover that you posses a wondrous and a thrilling thing, unseen, uncatalogued, unpriced, but of so intrinsic a value that it far out-distances anything made of physical fabric, buyable for money, seeable by eyes, or touchable by mere hands... Think on my wish and realise that it is the depth of my feeling for you which emboldens me to write of things towards which we all yearn, but about which it is hard to speak.

Some recent historians have stressed the degree to which notions of citizen-ship in mid-twentieth-century Britain were cast in a cold, rational, unemo-tional language of classical republicanism which left little public space for displays of passion, desire, and affectivity. The tight-lipped unemotionality of Attlee and (most of) his ministers exemplifies this masculine discourse.[19] While the existence of such structures of feeling may help to explain why, for example, the uninhibited carnality of sexually active young women might be perceived as subversive of national unity,[20] the language with which Lady Reading mobilized her middle-aged followers certainly overspilled the con-fines of rationality. Physically large and deep-voiced, her imposing presence regularly swept audiences off their feet. A mystical Christianity, spirituality, and an appeal to distinctly feminine passions sustained a charisma which, according to one suffragette organizer who later became a close friend of Reading's, fully matched that of Emmeline Pankhurst.[21]

Not everyone, of course, responded well to this kind of thing. Mary Smieton, seconded from Whitehall to organize the WVS office and to keep an official eye on Lady Reading's impulsive improvisations, confessed that the blend of high sentiment and 'turgid expression' which characterized both the chairman's Christmas messages and her platform speeches 'roused in me nothing but distaste and discomfort'. Smieton also sharply rebuffed Reading's attempts to 'penetrate into my private life', perceiving her demands for intimacy as rooted in a compulsive need to recharge her own batteries by dominating the lives of others.[22] This was an unusual response. Reading's limitless capacity to interest herself in the details of other people's lives and problems made most of her organizers feel loved and cherished,

---

[19] Sonia Rose, 'Sex, Citizenship and the Nation in World War II Britain', *American Historical Review* (Oct. 1998), 1173–5; Martin Francis, 'The Labour Party: Modernisation and the Politics of Restraint', in Becky Conekin, Frank Mort, and Chris Waters (eds.), *Moments of Modernity. Reconstructing Britain, 1945–1964* (London, 1999).

[20] Rose, 'Sex, Citizenship and the Nation', 1175.

[21] Although, in other respects, she added, 'they were as different as chalk and cheese'. Interview with Olive Bartels, 1977, Brian Harrison Tapes.

[22] Dame Mary Smieton, *Stella Reading. Recollections*, 13; Interview with Mary Smieton (1977), Brian Harrison Tapes.

rather than invaded.[23] They were also captivated by her playful humour and moments of girlish gaiety.[24]

Gaiety, however, is often the mask worn by despair. Reading never spoke openly about her inner life, but she gave a glimpse of the self-discipline underlying her relentless public cheerfulness, in a piece she was persuaded to write about her philosophy of life in 1958:

Because life is so sad, and because everyone in turn has to carry... a heavy load of unhappiness, I have a firm conviction that... gaiety and a lightness of approach should be cultivated. Those who comfortably dismiss the superb efforts of others to create this atmosphere with the observation that they are fortunate in their happy disposition, are, for the most part, people of no understanding and without real power of observation. A sustained, happy outlook has its roots in the belief that it is right to generate happiness for others and therefore necessary to show happiness oneself.[25]

Being cheerful in the face of deeply distressing realities was a duty assumed by many women, particularly during the war. Nella Last, whose Mass Observation diary provides the most intimate picture we have of any WVS volunteer, spoke frequently of the contrast between public clowning and private distress: 'down at the WVS Centre they think I'm a "mental tonic", as old Mrs Waite put it. I must be a very good actress, for I don't feel gay often.'[26]

Mary Smieton's negative response to Lady Reading's leadership style probably reflected the fact that she was a career civil servant at home in a man's world. Most of the women whom Reading dealt with found her speeches inspiring, even those who found her Christmas messages impenetrable: 'she was as good an orator as she was bad a writer'.[27] While it might not always be too clear what exactly she was saying—'if you tried to take notes, you found she was saying practically nothing'[28]—her unrestrained

[23] A letter from Mrs MacDonald, the WVS organiser in Oxford, ill in bed but comforted by a solicitous note from her leader, gives some indication of the kind of devotion Lady Reading could inspire: 'I lay in bed & pondered just how typical it was of our chairman, in the midst of her own crowded programme, to give a thought to an insignificant little CB organiser who happened to be needing it badly... I wish I could convey to you just how much your words of commendation mean to me. When I think what WVS has done, under your inspiration, not merely for the country as a whole but for women themselves, I am filled with something much deeper than admiration. In your service I have found a long sought vocation. And I pledge you my loyalty in the months, years maybe, that lie ahead. May you too always find your heart's desire' (Mrs Macdonald (Oxford CB) to Lady Reading (23 Mar. 1944), WRVS, R6/6 Oxford).

[24] Smieton, *Stella Reading. Recollections*, 14.

[25] Reading, 'My Philosophy of Life', 4. See also Virginia Graham, *Stella Reading. Recollections*, 22.

[26] Richard Broad and Suzie Fleming (eds.), *Nella Last's War. A Mother's Diary, 1939–45* (Bristol, 1981), 22.

[27] Graham, *Stella Reading. Recollections*, 20.

[28] Lady Hamilton and Mrs James de Rothschild, *Stella Reading. Recollections by her Friends*, 26, 11; Interview with Halpin (1977), Brian Harrison Tapes; Williams, *Ladies of Influence.*, 164.

emotionalism spoke to a yearning among women who had, perhaps, good reason to fear that in the new low-key professional society some of the more mysterious sources of female influence (spirituality, moral authority) were in danger of marginalization. Some glimpse of the feelings evoked by Lady Reading's 'sublime power of leadership'[29] is provided by a tribute offered by the Surrey County Organizer in 1942:

I find it next to impossible to tell you what a joy it was to have you here yesterday. It is easy enough to write of what one doesn't feel too deeply but when that part of one which is guarded by every imaginable spiritual wall is touched by someone, words are quite useless . . . if anyone can perform miracles in these unimaginative days you can.[30]

One key to Reading's appeal was that she spoke particularly to a group of middle-aged women who had invested a good deal of their self-esteem in a style of voluntary service whose days, they had reason to suspect, might be numbered. Since the early years of the twentieth century the struggle to establish social work as a professional career for women had been seen as one strategy for recouping power lost as philanthropic forms of social authority declined. The transition, however, was neither unproblematic nor uncontested.[31] Women found it even more difficult to gain directing positions in the state welfare bureaucracy than had been the case previously in the voluntary sector.[32] And despite the Sex Disqualification (Removal) Act of 1919, the inter-war years saw a reinforcement of the marriage bar, forcing middle-class women to choose between marriage and a career in the civil service, teaching, or other professions.[33] Moreover, while some younger middle-class women might be eager to make the trade that professional society appeared to offer them—of moral for professional authority—this trade was seldom open to the women Lady Reading relied upon to lead WVS activity at local level. Even had they been so inclined the more established social leaders would have found it difficult to enter professional employment without severe loss of status. Stella Reading had been fortunate to be forced to earn her own living as a young woman, gaining professional secretarial

[29] Miss A. M. Day, Malvern Centre Organiser, to Halpin (17 Mar. 1947), WRVS, R9/5 Worcestershire.
[30] Mrs Charles Leach to Reading (28 Feb. 1942), WRVS, R12/4 Surrey
[31] For an excellent discussion of these tensions in context of the First World War, see Angela Woollacott, 'From Moral to Professional Authority: Secularism, Social Work, and Middle-Class Women's Self-Construction in World War I Britain', *Journal of Women's History* (Summer 1998). More generally, see Dorothy Thompson, 'Women, Work and Politics in Nineteenth-century England: The Problem of Authority', in J. Rendall (ed.), *Equal or Different. Women's Politics, 1800–1914* (Oxford, 1987); Jane Lewis, 'Gender, the Family and Women's Agency in the Building of "Welfare States": The British Case', *Social History*, 19 (1994).
[32] Lewis, 'Women's Agency', 40, 42–4.
[33] Martin Pugh, *Women and the Women's Movement in Britain, 1914–1959* (Basingstoke, 1992), 90, 116; Jane Lewis, *Women in England, 1870–1950* (Brighton, 1984), 77, 102–3, 199–200.

skills in the process.[34] But how many middle-aged social leaders would have voluntarily embarked on the social odyssey portrayed in Angus Wilson's 1958 novel of the prematurely widowed Mrs Eliot, plummeting from respected chairman of charitable committees to middle-aged student in a secretarial college?[35] Whatever possibilities might be open to younger women to acquire social authority through the acquisition of professional status, these were unlikely to appeal to the middle-aged housewives who made up the great bulk of Lady Reading's lieutenants. For these women professional training as social workers appeared a poor substitute for the social authority they derived from their husbands' positions, the women's public sphere in which they moved, and their own accumulated experience as movers and shakers within the local elite. With no easy way of reinventing themselves as salaried professionals, Lady Reading's followers were prepared to go to considerable lengths to demonstrate the continuing relevance to modern times of their Victorian ideal of service.

II

If middle-class social leadership rested, as Lady Reading believed, on leisure dignified by character, then the leisure was as much in need of protection as the character. In 1948 Beveridge identified the 'redistribution of leisure' away from those who had previously provided the mainstay of voluntary work as a major problem for the future of voluntary action.[36] A 1950 editorial in the journal of National Council for Social Services, for example, described those who could afford to work for nothing as 'survivors from a bygone age'. The relative decline of middle-class incomes undermined 'the great recruiting ground of earlier days, the middle-class wives and their daughters'... 'one finds the latter seeking mainly secretarial posts, while the former are often desperate for part-time work (frequently in the social services) with which to eke out an income that is no longer sufficient to maintain a customary standard of life.'[37] Even among those women who had no need to seek employment, post-war austerity increased the demands of shopping on their time, while the long-term decline of domestic service tied

[34] She herself laid rhetorical claim to having risen from lowly origins—'I have been a wage earner myself!'—and was not above citing the spectacular rise of her late husband who had 'started as a cabin boy and finished in the highest service' as evidence of 'the secret of democracy' in Britain (*Blackpool Gazette & Herald* (5 Nov. 1938); Lady Reading speech in Corn Exchange, Bedford (24 May 1939), WRVS, R4/1 Bedfordshire). In fact, as she well knew, Rufus Isaac's parents were wealthy merchants who had sent him to sea for a year as training for a trading career (*Hasting's Evening Argus* (7 Aug. 1931)).

[35] Angus Wilson, *The Middle-age of Mrs Eliot* (London, 1958).

[36] Lord Beveridge, *Voluntary Action. A Report on Methods of Social Advance* (London, 1948), 222.

[37] Editorial, *Social Service* (Sept.–Nov. 1950), 50.

Servent shortage (handwritten in left margin)

middle-class women more than ever before to the home. Between 1931 and 1951 the proportion of private households with live-in servants fell from 5 per cent to 1 per cent, and diaries kept by middle-class women suggest that the time they spent on household tasks nearly doubled in the quarter-century following 1937, reaching 7.5 hours per day by 1961.[38] To one WVS leader in 1950, the wife of a leading businessman, the future looked bleak: 'More and more the need will be for daily workers as the middle classes get poorer and poorer.'[39]

The growing unwillingness of women to work as domestic servants had long been a central motif in narratives of middle-class decline.[40] The inability of mistresses to impose discipline on the slovenly housemaid or to resist unreasonable demands from 'cook' whose threat to abandon the household to chaos was increasingly all too real, had provided endless material for social comedy in the inter-war years.[41] Mollie Panter-Downes' post-war novel, *One Fine Day*, revolved entirely around the inability of a middle-aged couple to cope with their servantless house and garden. For Lewis and Maude, documenting middle-class woes in the late 1940s, a future devoid of servants was a bleak one, no matter how much electric gadgets and collectivized provision might lighten the housewife's load. Civilized—'as against mechanized'—living, they believed, could not survive without servants.[42]

Many women agreed, refusing to reconcile themselves to a servantless future. During the inter-war years women's leaders had sought to involve both the state and the labour movement in campaigns to combat what everyone agreed was the basic problem, the low status of domestic service.[43] While unemployment drove many women back into domestic service, little progress was made in the quixotic mission to convince working-class girls

[38] Pamela Horn, *The Rise and Fall of the Victorian Servant* (Dublin, 1975), 167, 182; *Report on Post-War Organisation of Private Domestic Employment*, Cmd 6650, June 1945, 24; J. Gershuny, *Social Innovation and the Division of Labour* (Oxford, 1983), 149–51; S. Bowden and A. Offer, 'Household Appliances and the Use of Time: The United States and Britain since the 1920s', *Economic History Review*, 7 (1994), 734–5.

[39] Lady Gwendoline Schuster (whose husband was the National Liberal MP for Walsall and a director of many companies) was the WVS representative on the NIH advisory committee and much more enthusiastic for the NIH than most WVS leaders. Schuster to Johnson, 10 Feb. 1950, WRVS, V131/38 National Institute of Houseworkers.

[40] R. McKibbin, *Classes and Cultures. England, 1918–1951* (Oxford, 1998), 64–5; Horn, *Victorian Servant*; M. Glucksmann, *Women Assemble. Women Workers and the New Industries in Inter-war Britain* (London, 1990), 252–6; J. Giles, *Women, Identity and Private Life in Britain, 1900–50* (London, 1995), ch. 4.

[41] E. M. Delafield, *Diary of a Provincial Lady* (London, 1950); N. Beauman, *A Very Great Profession* (London, 1983); A. Light, *Forever England: Femininity, Literature and Conservatism between the Wars* (London, 1991).

[42] R. Lewis and A Maude, *The English Middle Classes* (London, 1953), 213.

[43] Horn, *Victorian Servant*, 167 ff.; Pugh, *Women's Movement*, 84; Elizabeth McCarty, 'Attitudes to Women and Domesticity in England, circa 1939–1955', Oxford D.Phil., 1994, 226–7. Women trade unionists were happy to co-operate in the establishment of training scheme and proposals for minimum wage levels.

that the life of a live-in servant, at the beck and call of an unaccountable mistress, was to be preferred to working in a factory.[44] During the war a report commissioned by Whitehall on the *Post-War Organisation of Private Domestic Employment* focused on the needs of middle-class women, stressing the loss to the community when 'an educated woman' capable of making 'a real contribution to the national life' was trapped in domesticity. Alongside means-tested emergency home helps for working-class wives, the report proposed tax breaks to enable middle class women engaged in paid or in voluntary work outside the home, or those with large families, to pay the going rate for regular daily help.[45] The evident class differentiation in this package was glossed over by a rhetoric unusual even in wartime discourse for its wilful evasion of the realities of social inequality:

The ideal of the good life for every citizen...is independent of the fleeting satisfactions of wealth or class...In a society which seeks however imperfectly to give expression to that ideal ['the worth and value of the individual'], domestic work will fall into its natural place as one of many functions necessary to the comfort and efficiency of a highly specialised community. 'I serve' is a princely motto, and it is through service from each to all in varying forms and ways that the true enrichment of life is found...[46]

It remained unclear how this appeal to a modernizing language of 'function' and 'efficiency' differed in substance from more ancient assumptions of hierarchy and deference. Indeed the authors of the report felt it appropriate to invoke Pauline authority for the proposition that superior persons—in this case the Apostles of the early church—could not be expected to wait at table, or to carry out God's work without 'daily ministrations' from their inferiors.[47] Remarkably, in a work whose declared purpose was to assimilate the status of private domestic work to that of the industrial worker, the report referred unselfconsciously throughout to 'mistresses' and their 'maids'.[48] Status is a zero-sum game, and the efforts of middle-class women to shore up crumbling hierarchies in the home by turning their servants into professionals was shot through with contradiction.[49] However

---

[44] *Post-War Organisation of Private Domestic Employment*, 4–11.

[45] Ibid., 7, 17–18.

[46] Ibid., 21.

[47] Ibid., 8.

[48] Elaine Burton, a left-wing campaigner for the reform of private domestic service who became a Labour MP in the 1950s, also approached the issue primarily from the standpoint of the professional woman. She took a similarly Utopian line on the terminology: 'Most people agree that the name of "servant" must be changed and the majority suggest "worker". It seems a good idea, but have you thought that nobody has ever put forward a suggestion that "Civil Servants" should be called "Civil Workers"' (Elain Burton, *Domestic Work. Britain's Largest Industry* (London, 1944), 16). See also ead., *What of the Women. A Study of Women in Wartime* (London, 1941).

[49] E. Wilson, *Only Halfway to Paradise. Women in Post-war Britain: 1945–1968* (London, 1980), 25–6.

'fleeting' they might be in the world of the spirit, wealth and class remained obstinately embedded in discussion of the servant problem. The report had been jointly drafted by Violet Markham, who had served on the Unemployment Assistance Board in the 1930s and had long been involved with efforts to improve the status of domestic work, and the trade unionist, Florence Hancock.[50] Markham freely confessed that she could not imagine her own life without servants,[51] and Hancock, like other leading Labour women, placed her concern to raise the status of domestic work ahead of any more radical critique of the mistress–servant relationship as such.[52] The main outcome of the Markham–Hancock report was the establishment in 1947 of a National Institute of Homeworkers intended to raise the status of domestic work by initiating training and certification of domestic workers and laying down model (but not statutory) wages and conditions. Its achievements were minimal.[53]

The early war years had seen a chorus of complaint from middle-class women who saw their own capacity for public service being destroyed by the loss of their remaining servants to the war factories.[54] In 1942 the WVS regional administrator in Wales complained bitterly about the attitude of Ministry of Labour officials, citing several instances in which her organizers had been forced to resign when their one remaining maid was called up for factory work.[55] The Derbyshire organizer reported that 'nearly all the Centre Organisers are women with homes to run and are suffering from

[50] Florence Hancock joined the Workers Union in 1913 and became the District Officer in Wiltshire in 1917; she was on the General Council of the TUC from 1935 and became National Woman's Officer for the Transport and General Worker's Union in 1942.

[51] H. Jones, *Duty and Citizenship. The Correspondence and Parliamentary Papers of Violet Markham, 1896–1953* (London, 1994), 3.

[52] Like almost everyone else who discussed the servant problem at this time, Lewis and Maude dismissed the possibility that a more equal sharing of domestic tasks between husband and wife might be provide part of the solution—with one intriguing exception: 'While washing-up may be positively beneficial to a university lecturer, there are some kinds of manual work which are not good for the hands of musicians and surgeons; and continually answering the door bell will drive a writer to drink' (Lewis and Maude, *English Middle Classes*, 213, 205). However Markham, while accepting that breadwinners at the end of a hard day could not be expected to do domestic work, did argue that boys should be expected to participate in the chores alongside their sisters (*Post-War Organisation of Private Domestic Employment*, 20).

[53] McCarty, 'Women and Domesticity', 250–68 gives a full account of the NIH. Overall, by the mid-1950s, about 1,500 women, mainly young, had received training, and a further 3,000 experienced domestic workers had been granted certificates by the Institute. Some of these women went into private residential service, while others joined NIH-run schemes designed, according to one account, to enable middle-class housewives to gain 'a little time for recreation' through the provision of regular daily help. Daily Houseworker's Services were established in a number of towns, reflecting the belief expressed in 1950 by a wealthy banker's wife active in WVS that 'more and more the need will be for daily workers as the middle classes get poorer and poorer' (Shuster to Johnson (10 Feb. 1950), WRVS, V131/38 National Institute of House-workers).

[54] McCarty, 'Women and Domesticity', 230–1.

[55] S. Vachell, 'Future of WVS' (n.d., 1941?), WRVS, R8 Wales.

lack of domestic help', a complaint echoed from Bradford where 'we are losing our members in a steady stream [partly] . . . because of home difficulties and the lack of maids.'[56] A particularly vivid illustration of the problem was given by the WVS organizer in Gainsborough, who had lost her maid to munitions work:

I have been maidless . . . for a year now, my only help a woman three afternoons a week, and I find it increasingly difficult to fit jobs in that can be left for some months but not for years. My husband is Managing Director of a firm on difficult Government work and whilst he helps me with the daily chores, there is a limit to what a man can do without impairing his own war work, and I very often feel most unhappy and uncomfortable at his efforts to aid me in doing, or trying to do, two people's work at one and the same time. I have done all I can to obtain a full time daily help, and have offered money in and out of reason without result. I am beginning to feel that I cannot indefinitely rise at 6.15 and do my household cooking and run this Centre, a full time job in itself; my reserve of physical energy is gradually being exhausted.[57]

In Cheshire, the blue-blooded regional administrator (daughter of the 14th Baron Dormer, wife of the vice-lieutenant of the country, president of the WI) struggled to cope with the demands of her stately home:

The staff in the house consists of one housemaid who was there before the war and it is more than she can do to try to keep the house from being permanently damaged by damp and moth, etc., and to keep the rooms clean which are actually being used. The evacuee does not live in the house but comes in every day and helps in cleaning the house, but cannot, or will not, help with the cooking. Mrs Eggerton-Warburton does the whole of the cooking so that in term time she is cooking for five people and the children are at home for eight weeks. This means that on days when she comes to the Regional Office she will have to do the cooking the day before, unless she succeeds in finding a cook.[58]

Such pressures figured among the difficulties confronted by WVS in attempting to revive the organization in the later 1940s. In Great Yarmouth, for example, the doctor's wife chosen to rebuild WVS refused at the last minute to take on the job because her daily help left to have a baby and the

---

[56] Holcombe to Reading (8 Apr. 1942), WRVS, R3/1 Derbyshire; Report of Northern Conference, Manchester (3 June 1942), WRVS, R10.

[57] Alice Ridely, Monthly Report (Aug. 1942), WRVS, R3. Tothill Street, well aware of the problem, urged the Ministry of Labour to extend exemption from conscription to girls working in the homes of full-time voluntary workers (Minute of meeting between Reading and Smieton (3 Dec. 1943), WRVS, H32 Home Helps Policy). Earlier, however, the WVS leadership had concluded that Ministry of Labour pressure was an insignificant cause of the scarcity of domestic servants, compared with the appeal of higher wages and better working conditions in munitions factories (WRVS, Chairman's Committee, Minutes (2 Oct. 1942)).

[58] Huxley, report on visit to region (10, 29 Nov. 1944), WRVS, R10 Regional Office. Huxley had added to the pressure by staying the night with Mrs Eggerton-Warburton. On the Eggerton-Warburton connection, see J. M. Lee, *Social Leaders and Public Persons. A Study of County Government in Cheshire since 1888* (Oxford, 1963), 20, 23, 32, 39, 101.

competition for domestic workers from the local guest houses made it impossible to replace her.[59]

Although WVS quietly lobbied Whitehall to exempt its organizers' domestic servants from conscription,[60] Lady Reading refused to lend her voice to the chorus of complaint about the servant problem and she was often unsympathetic to the conflicting pull of domestic and public duties experienced by many of her members. Shortly before D-Day, for example, a remark she made to a rally of WVS members in Surrey attracted widespread press coverage: 'Put first things first. Leave the beds undone: leave the house dirty; don't cook your husband's meal—let him jolly well get by with a piece of bread; but get on with the national job first!'[61] Some women may well have found such talk empowering. Nella Last, who had responded to the outbreak of war by getting her hair cut short in order to save time for her WVS work, cheerfully put 'nation before husband'. When her daily help left in 1941 she made no attempt to maintain domestic standards: 'a hurried dust and vac' was all she had time for between WVS commitments, surprising even herself with 'the slap-happy way I keep my home nowadays'.[62] Others, however, found Lady Reading's cavalier attitude to housework offensive.[63] In 1949 she provoked a storm of protest with an off-the-cuff remark to the effect that middle-class housewives should stop complaining about their domestic burdens and organize their time more effectively so that they could undertake voluntary work. The president of the National Council of Women, a doctor's wife, was particularly scathing, pointing out that Reading, who 'had never had to run a home and to bring up children without help' was hardly qualified to judge.[64] The leader of the North Oxford Townswomen's Guild responded by stressing that 'because we are members of the so-called middle classes we have to keep up an appearance' and that under contemporary conditions of servantless austerity this was duty enough for most middle-class women.[65] That, however, was to miss the point. For Lady Reading the responsibility of the middle- and upper-class woman to maintain the prestige of her class required her not only to keep up appearances at home but also to take an active public role.

[59] Report on visit to Great Yarmouth, 26–8 May 1948, WRVS, R 4/7 Great Yarmouth.
[60] Notes on a meeting at the Ministry of Labour with Mary Smieton (3 Dec. 1943), WRVS, H32 Home Helps Policy.
[61] *Surrey County Herald*, 2 June 1944, WRVS, Press Cuttings.
[62] *Nella Last's War*, 11, 131, 163, 174, 207.
[63] *The Daily Mirror* condemned her, upholding standards of working-class respectability against what it saw as ignorant remarks by an upper-class lady who had no inkling of the moral investment placed in housework by ordinary women and who had never done her own housework anyway. A. C. H. Smith, *Paper Voices. The Popular Press and Social Change, 1935–1965* (London, 1975), 114–15.
[64] *News Chronicle* (18, 19 Jan. 1949).
[65] *Oxford Mail* (19 Jan. 1949).

In practice this was not always as difficult as the rhetoric suggested. A 1948 survey found that 13 per cent of 'well-to-do' and 'middle-class' households still had live-in staff, while a further 47 per cent had daily helps. Figures for spending on servants as a percentage of income reveal how important this remained for the upper echelons of the middle class, rising from just over 1 per cent of income for families at the bottom end of the middle class to nearly 5 per cent of those on annual incomes of £700 or more.[66] However much they complained it is probable that most of Lady Reading's local leaders continued to employ servants after the war. Searching for a replacement for the centre organizer in South Shields in 1947, a senior WVS administrator remarked of her first approach to the favoured candidate: 'a maid answered the telephone which I thought was a good sign.'[67]

III

Lady Reading's conception of leadership was profoundly hierarchical. WVS, she always insisted, was 'a service not an organization', a reliable and disciplined handmaid for the statutory authorities whose businesslike methods she never tired of contrasting with the 'hit-and-miss old-world charitable voluntary service conception'.[68] WVS was constructed on entirely hierarchical lines. For each of the eleven civil defence regions in England and Wales, Reading appointed a volunteer administrator assisted by a paid regional organizer who supervised the work of voluntary 'centre' organizers in each locality.[69] Every one of the local organizers and their deputies held office by virtue of a personal letter of appointment from Lady Reading. The whole apparatus was co-ordinated from a London head office situated in Tothill Street (known to initiates as 'Totters'), in the heart of establishment London, half-way between Parliament Square and Buckingham Palace: it was a tall thin building equipped, someone once remarked, with a lavatory and a duchess on every floor.[70] Apart from Lady Reading herself, and, for the first two years, Mary Smieton, seconded from her civil service post to help get things started, the most important person at Tothill Street was

[66] Hulton Press, *Patterns of British Life* (London, 1950), 102, cited in D. L. North, 'Middle-Class Suburban Culture and Lifestyles in England, 1919–1939', Oxford D.Phil., 1989, 177.

[67] Rosamund Hornby, report on visit to South Shields (14 Jan. 1948), WRVS, R1/2 South Shields.

[68] Christmas Letter (Dec. 1950), WRVS, Chairman's Christmas Letters; Lady Reading to Chuter Ede (30 Sept. 1946), PRO, CAB 129 914.

[69] WVS, *Report on Twenty-five Years Work* (London, 1963), 3; R. C. Chambers, 'A Study of Three Voluntary Organisations', in D. V. Glass (ed.), *Social Mobility in Britain* (London, 1954), 387 ff. In some areas the centre 'organizers' were originally known as centre 'leaders', but head office, sensitive to reports that critics were using the German translation (*Führer*) decided to abandon the word 'leader' (WVS Executive Committee Minutes (16 Nov. 1938).) *Führer*, however, was what they meant!

[70] Elsa Dunbar, Memoir of Lady Reading (1990), 3, FL 7/yyy/2/2qq.

probably the Chief Regional Officer. From 1938 this post was held by Lindsay Huxley, a widow who had served for ten years as national treasurer of the Women's Institutes and had been secretary of the Land Settlement Association since 1935. She was succeeded in 1945 by Miss Kathleen Halpin, an active member of the Fawcett Society, who had been private secretary to Lord Simon (Lord Reading's successor as foreign secretary) in the early 1930s and, for several years before the war, organizing secretary of the Women's Gas Council. Many of the regional administrators and organizers had similar backgrounds in public work. As these examples suggest, Reading was able to assemble a core of upper-middle-class women, particularly widows and spinsters, with a range of experience in public life that fitted them well for leadership.

The 'volunteers' did not necessarily work without pay. In 1947 (when it had shrunk very considerably from its wartime peak) WVS employed 199 paid staff, mainly in Tothill Street and the Regional Offices, and gave some measure of financial assistance to a further 400 people, out of a total of about 5,400 centrally appointed staff.[71] Since the outbreak of war money had been allocated to help local organizers with their expenses (including paying for domestic help) and, 'in a limited class of case where owing to the necessity of the woman becoming the wage earner a small salary might be needed'.[72] In 1941, for example, the regional organizer in the northwest was prepared to pay £250 a year to secure the services of a widow in her early fifties who had previously worked as an organizer for various charities and had nothing to live on 'other than the rent of a house in Hert[fordshire] which has been bombed...'.[73] Six years later WVS courted as a borough organizer a spinster earning £500 a year as a factory welfare officer who wanted a less stressful job: 'she would need special expenses but she is not thinking in terms of £500!'[74] Such discretionary grants enabled WVS to draw on a considerably wider pool of talent than strict adherence to the voluntary principle would have done.[75] Nevertheless prevailing assumptions about the class composition of the WVS leadership were nicely illustrated by a Home Office decision to approve the payment of first-class rail fares to

[71] Statistics prepared for Beveridge Enquiry, WRVS, M456/40 Voluntary Social Service Enquiry; Reading to A. Whitley, WRVS, A1/38 File 6.
[72] WVS Executive Committee, Minutes (13 Sept. 1939), WRVS. By November over 80 WVS 'volunteers' were in receipt of at least £2 a week (Smieton to Dart (28 Nov. 1939), WRVS, R10 Regional Office).
[73] Dart to Huxley (19 Feb. 1941), WRVS, R10 Regional Office.
[74] Rosamund Hornby, report on visit to South Shields (14 Jan. 1948), WRVS, R1/2 South Shields, 202/5/6. In 1939 the regional administrator in the North West had insisted on offering some payment to her preferred candidate for the Manchester organizer, arguing that unless this could be done the woman concerned (an unmarried graduate) would go and work for the local authority (Dart to 'Dear Stella' (5 Sept. 1939), WRVS, R10/1 Regional Office).
[75] Although rumours as to who was paid and who was not sometimes created unrest and jealousy between centre leaders (Shawyer to Huxley (16 Sept. 1939), WRVS, R1 Regional Office).

full-time volunteers on the grounds that 'in private life they were accustomed to travel first class'.[76]

Some financial help was also given, again on a discretionary basis, for the
purchase of the WVS uniform—a green jacket, skirt, greatcoat, and a hat.
Much time was devoted to establishing exactly who was entitled to wear the
uniform, and it served to mark off the leadership cadre, full-time volunteers,
and those in front-line services dealing with the public from more humble
members who, where the work required it, were offered overalls.[77] Faced with
complaints that 'only the wives and daughters of rich men' could afford to buy
uniforms, Tothill Street eventually persuaded the Home Office to finance
discretionary subsidies, but it is unlikely that this opened up the privilege of
wearing a WVS uniform to significant numbers of working-class women.[78]
Lady Reading insisted, as a matter of democratic principle, that no distinctive
marks of rank were used on the uniform—'it is the job that carries the rank
and not the person'—but the equality involved was limited to an elite.[79]

The existence of a uniform symbolized the status of WVS as a disciplined
auxiliary service operating on very different principles from most established
voluntary organizations. Lady Reading's autocratic management style was
untempered by any kind of representative structure. There was an Advisory
Council made up of representatives of other women's organizations, and at
first Lady Reading trod carefully, aware of the need to win co-operation
from as wide a range of bodies as possible. As its name implied, however,
there was never any question of the Advisory Council having executive
powers, and it soon ceased to operate as anything other than an opportunity
for WVS to inform other organizations of its activities.[80] In 1938 a small
Executive Committee had been set up composed of Reading's senior staff
and leading women from the most important established women's organizations.[81] It rapidly became clear, however, that this committee was 'executive'
in nothing but name, and this was formally recognized in January 1940
when it was renamed and its status redefined as purely advisory.[82] When, a

---

[76] WVS Chairman's Committee, Minutes (5 Aug. 2 Sept. 1943), WRVS. Lady Reading protested that the Home Office would not extend the same privilege to the expenses of paid staff, and
succeeded in getting approval for the payment of first-class fares for 'a small officer class'.

[77] WVS Chairman's Committee, Minutes (3 Sept. 1941), WRVS. In 1941 around 72,000
people, perhaps 10% of the total membership, came into these categories. Allen to
McGregor (14 July 1941), PRO, MH 130 277.

[78] Letter from N. Kirkwood to *Staffordshire Chronicle* (Oct. 1940), in WRVS, R9 Regional
Office; WVS Regional Administrators Conference, Minutes (27 June 1941, 20 Mar., 15 May
1942), WRVS.

[79] Reading to Worsley (8 Nov. 1943), WRVS, R5 Kent.

[80] Halpin to Mrs Eugster (5 Dec. 1950), WRVS, R4 Eastern Regional Office.

[81] Including Lady Somers (Girl Guides), Miss Farrer (Women's Institutes), Caroline Haslett
(Electrical Association of Women), Eva Hubback (National Council for Equal Citizenship), Mrs
Patrick Ness (National Council of Women), and, later, Mary Sutherland (Labour Women).

[82] It became the General Purposes Committee of the much larger Advisory Council.

few months later, a new and rather important member of the committee—
Mary Sutherland, the Labour Party's Chief Woman Officer—queried its
precise status, Lady Reading asked the general secretary to draft a suitable
'prevarication on this theme'.[83] This was as close as Reading ever came to
acknowledging that there might be a legitimate argument for some check on
her own absolutism.

The rapid expansion of WVS activity after the outbreak of war resulted
in some confusion in Tothill Street and the departmental heads put forward
a proposal to establish a Chairman's Committee to improve office co-
ordination. The regular weekly meetings at which Reading gave 'instructions on policy' were designed to enable senior staff 'to gain a real knowledge of the policy aimed at by the Chairman' and thus to be competent,
when she was out of London, 'to carry on in an emergency knowing her
policy and views'. As if these phrases were not sufficiently deferential, the
draft terms of reference added: 'This suggestion of a Chairman's Committee
is not in any way put forward to divest the Chairman of any power, but
rather to strengthen her obvious duty to lead.'[84] That duty she was emi-
nently fitted to fulfil. Quite apart from her inspirational qualities, she was
extremely quick to grasp the many ways in which the spare time of housewives might be matched with local and national needs. Clear-headed and
forceful in negotiations with Whitehall, her practical imagination was indispensable both to the initial construction of WVS and to its post-war survival.
Kathleen Halpin remained thirty years later in awe of the strategic vision
Reading had displayed at the end of the war, recalling occasions when she
held her own against concerted advice from senior staff: 'I'm sorry I just
don't agree with you, you wait till six months time ... Nine times out of ten
she turned out to be right.'[85] Reading's authority in Tothill Street was further
enhanced by the fact that she spent much of her time touring the country
keeping in touch with local organizers and often picking up problems before
they reached her through the hierarchy. Leaving nothing to chance, she took
care to prevent the emergence of rival centres of power, even to the extent of
arranging dinners for regional administrators and organizers attending
monthly meetings in London in order to prevent them from 'ganging up'
independently of their chairman.[86] It was by such means that Reading
created a national machine capable not only of mobilizing hundreds of
thousands of women in voluntary work, but also of adapting traditions
of upper- and middle-class leadership to the challenges of the mid-twentieth
century.

[83] Sutherland to Reading (1 Mar. 1940), Reading to Smieton (2 Mar. 1940), WRVS, V/95/38
Standing Joint Committee of Working Women's Organisations.
[84] Office Memo (28 Nov. 1939), WRVS Chairman's Committee.
[85] Interview with Halpin (1977), Brian Harrison Tapes.
[86] Smieton, *Stella Reading. Recollections*, 15.

3

Colonizing the Urban Public Sphere

The public inauguration of WVS provided an opportunity for civic display. In Leicester, for example, one month after the Munich crisis, Lady Reading appealed to a meeting of 3,000 women to make 'a payment for the privilege of living in the best country in the world'. The event was organized to evoke not only patriotic sentiment with renditions of 'Land of Hope and Glory' ('chorus repeated,' the official programme instructed: 'all join in'), the national anthem, and a song entitled 'There's a land, a dear land', but also to celebrate a specifically feminine public culture with dancing 'by Miss Elsa Groocock and Pupils' and a display of exercises by the Women's League of Health and Beauty.[1] Leicester's first woman councillor took the chair, and the Lord Mayor fulfilled his normal role on such occasions, moving the vote of thanks and demonstrating, by his non-political presence, the symbolic unity of the local elite.[2] Variants of this scene were played out again and again during the autumn and winter of 1938 and by May 1939 WVS centres had been established in the great majority of English county boroughs.[3]

Behind such events lay a good deal of careful staff work. They were usually preceded by a meeting of women's organizations called by the mayor in order to consolidate support for establishing WVS locally and, in many cases, to approve the leaders selected by the WVS regional organizer. To set up these meetings, and prepare the ground for a fruitful outcome, WVS organizers had to secure allies from within two distinct worlds—the political and administrative cadre of local government (particularly the Mayor and the town clerk) and the leaders of local female associational life. Close attention to the process of WVS mobilization, therefore, can throw considerable light on the nature of urban social leadership in mid-twentieth Britain.

---

[1] *Leicester Mercury* (28 Oct. 1938); the printed Programme for the meeting is in WRVS, R3/2 Leicester.
[2] John Garrard, 'The Mayoralty Since 1835', in Alan O'Day, *Government and Institutions in the Post-1832 United Kingdom* (Lampeter, 1995), 6–7.
[3] M. Smieton to F. C. Johnson, 14 Mar. 1939, PRO, HO 186 569.

I

The dominant narrative in the existing literature on urban elites revolves around the withdrawal of the bourgeoisie from civic leadership since the later nineteenth-century. Not wishing to live in the muck that generated their brass, businessmen moved away to the countryside or the suburbs. The emergence of organized labour, the growth of a more self-assertive petty bourgeoisie increasingly influential in local government, the democratizing effects of the modern party system, and the growing importance of town hall bureaucrats all served to force traditional civic leaders into uncomfortable negotiation with rival centres of authority in the towns, inhibiting the free exercise of their patronage and power.[4] By 1939 Labour controlled 18 out of 79 country boroughs,[5] and the separation between non-Labour local polit-icians, mostly drawn from the butchers and builders of the local petty bourgeoisie, and the controllers of industry continued apace as family firms were gobbled up by national combines[6] and a growing range of local activities came to be run by highly educated professionals with mobile careers and few local roots.[7]

A study of the small Pennine town of Glossop published in 1959 places the changes of the mid-twentieth century in a historical trajectory subsequently elaborated by one of its authors—Harold Perkin—as 'the rise of professional society'. Once a shining example of civic-minded industrial feudalism, post-war Glossop was run politically by a Tory shopocracy despised by working-men and professional middle class alike. The geographically mobile profes-sional class had little interest in exercising either political or social leader-ship—of the eight principal Borough officials only one was a native of the town. The businessmen and professionals socialized with one another in the Rotary Club and the golf club, but they showed little interest in local politics and were alienated from the proletarian atmosphere of the Conserva-tive Club. Many of them did not live in the town, and even when they did they were a poor substitute for 'the old owner-managers of redoubtable charac-ters, independent opinions, and large resources' and 'the voluntary ladies

[4] Garrard, 'Urban Elites, 1850–1914: The Rule and Decline of a New Squirearchy?', *Albion*, 27 (1995), 583–621.

[5] National Executive Committee Report to Labour Party Annual Conference, 1939, 91.

[6] L. Hannah, *The Rise of the Corporate Economy* (London, 1976); M. J. Daunton, 'Payment and Participation: Welfare and State-formation in Britain, 1900–1951', *Past and Present*, 150 (1996), 201–2; F. Carr, 'Municipal Socialism; Labour's Rise to Power', in B. Lancaster and T. Mason (eds.), *Life and Labour in the Twentieth Century City: The Experience of Coventry* (Coventry, 1986); Mike Savage and A. Miles, *The Remaking of the British Working Class, 1840–1940* (London, 1994), 63–4.

[7] H. Perkin, *The Rise of Professional Society. England since 1880* (London, 1989); R. McKibbin, *Classes and Cultures. England, 1918–1951* (Oxford, 1998), 92; M. Stacey, *Tradition and Change: A Study of Banbury* (Oxford, 1960).

distributing charity'.[8] In sharp contrast to the professionals, the local working class were overwhelmingly native-born, and some at least among them looked back with nostalgia to the days when rival clans of owner-managers—and their ladies—had competed for power and prestige in the town.

Popular nostalgia for a paternalistic style of social leadership thought to have disappeared by the 1940s is noted in a number of social studies of the mid-century.[9] In some places, however, such nostalgia may have been premature. The withdrawal of urban elites from political life did not necessarily mean their withdrawal from social leadership. This point is strikingly illustrated by a study of elite society in 1950s Bristol where social leadership remained firmly in the hands of an urban commercial and industrial upper class of very long standing, men with public school and Oxbridge education who frequently visited London where they sat on the boards of companies or voluntary organizations.[10] A substantial proportion combined business and associational activity in the city with country living, opportunities for which were preserved conveniently close to the City Centre by the natural frontier of the Avon Gorge and accessible via Brunel's suspension bridge. The study, designed to discover why these notables—who devoted extensive time and energy to their leadership of Bristol's associational life—refused to participate in local politics, came up with answers that provide a sharp corrective to accounts of the voluntary sector which treat it unproblematically as a school of citizenship in a maturing democracy. On the contrary, in 1950s Bristol, associational life provided public spaces in which the economic elites could continue to behave as social leaders without compromising with the egalitarian implications of democracy. Asked to account for their preference for voluntary work over political engagement, the great and good of Bristol society made it clear that the central problem of politics was that one had to deal on terms of formal equality with one's social inferiors: 'I am used to a position of responsibility and getting obeyed—I should be driven mad if I had to argue the toss with a lot of half-wits.'[11] Contempt for the not-very-successful tradesmen who served as Tory councillors was matched by fear of the Labour professionals and trade unionists who had dominated the city council for most of the post-war period. In voluntary work, as in business, the elite faced no such systematic challenge to its right to rule. Rather than seeking to confront the challenge of democracy head on they preferred to

---

[8] A. H. Birch, *Small-Town Politics. A Study of Political Life in Glossop* (Oxford, 1959), 3–4, 30–1.

[9] P. Willmott and M. Young, *Family and Class in a London Suburb* (London, 1960), 6–7; D. E. G. Plowman, W. E. Minchinton, and M. Stacey, 'Local Social Status in England and Wales', *Sociological Review*, 10 (1962), 170.

[10] R. V. Clements, *Local Notables and the City Council* (London, 1969).

[11] Ibid., 39.

leave the council to get on with its (not terribly important) affairs and concentrate on exercising their own leadership in the more congenially hierarchical spheres of economic and associational life. Bristol may well be exceptional in the degree to which the local economic elite retained its civic commitment: this had certainly been J. B. Priestley's impression in the mid-1930s.[12] Until recently historians of twentieth-century urban society have been more interested in the rise of labour than in the continuities of middle-class power and we have no equivalent studies of the other main provincial cities.[13] Studies of some lesser cities, notably Norwich and Leicester, indicate the continued social leadership exercised by civic-minded economic elites well after they had ceased to be actively involved in local politics.[14]

The Bristol study was typical of much of the earlier work on urban elites in focusing almost exclusively on men.[15] In discussing the influx of successful Manchester professional men into the Peak District, the authors of the Glossop study remarked that they had no time or inclination for local activity, adding, as an unexplored aside, that 'only their wives' were active in the locality. Masculine maps of the social structure may tend to exaggerate the degree of middle-class withdrawal from social leadership. Since the later nineteenth century women had become increasingly prominent in philanthropic activity, and it may well be that the tendency of men to withdraw from public life was compensated to some degree by the efforts of their wives, daughters, and unmarried sisters: a feminization of paternalism.[16] Reflecting on evidence of inter-war social activism by the womenfolk of the Norwich business elite, Barry Doyle has recently remarked that the 'input from the wives, daughters and sisters of the "public men" has been greatly underestimated in accounts of the functioning of urban middle-class power in the period after 1900.'[17] Although it has been argued that the rise of state welfare in the twentieth century tended to deprive middle-class women of the kinds of authority that they had grown used to exercising in the philanthropic world,[18] it is easy to exaggerate the degree to which public

---

[12] J. B. Priestley, *English Journey* (Harmondsworth, 1987), 29–40; R. Trainor, 'Neither Metropolitan nor Provincial: The Inter-war Middle Class', in A. J. Kidd and D. Nicholls (eds.), *The Making of the British Middle Class? Studies of Regional and Cultural Diversity since the Eighteenth Century* (Stroud, 1998), 210.

[13] On the under-researched nature of this subject, see W. D. Rubinstein, 'Britain's Elites in the Inter-war Period, 1918–39', in Kidd and Nicholls, *Making of the British Middle Class?*, 186, 199.

[14] B. M. Doyle, 'The Structure of Elite Power in the Early Twentieth-century City: Norwich, 1900–35', *Urban History*, 24 (1997), 181; Peter Jones, *et al.*, 'Politics', in D. Nash and D. Reader (eds.), *Leicester in the Twentieth Century* (Leicester, 1993), 92–94.

[15] Only six of Clements' respondents were women.

[16] Garrard, 'Urban Elites', 609; F. K. Prochaska, *Women and Philanthropy in Nineteenth-century England* (Oxford, 1980).

[17] Doyle, 'Structure of Elite Power', 192.

[18] Jane Lewis, 'Gender, the Family and Women's Agency in the Building of "Welfare States": The British Case', in *Social History*, 19, (1994).

provision sidelined the voluntary sector. The inter-war years have been seen as the heyday of local social services.[19] Although local elective office remained overwhelmingly masculine—in 1937 only about 5 per cent of provincial local councillors were women and over a third of city and borough councils had no women members at all[20]—much welfare legislation involved local authorities in extending their partnerships with voluntary organizations, and significant numbers of women were co-opted onto council committees in recognition of their prominence as voluntary social workers.[21] Regretting the fact that the were only two women councillors in Blackpool by 1939, the Mayor suggested (with doubtful logic) that this must reflect a feminine disinclination for politics, since 'most of the charitable causes in this town are run by women and they raise the bulk of the money'.[22] In the late 1930s there were few cities in which the Town Clerk, when approached by a WVS organizer, could not identify a shortlist of middle-class women with the organizational skills and recognized place in local public life necessary for them to function as WVS leaders.

II

English provincial towns sustained a substantial and complex female public sphere in which social, educational, charitable, and political activities were promiscuously merged. The organized life of middle-class women revolved around luncheon clubs, whist drives, garden fetes, tours round local factories or coach outings to stately homes, teatime cafe meetings with improving talks, evening meetings of branch or committee, bring-and-buy sales, flag-days for the local hospital fund, administering charitable funds and hands-on personal service in the maternity and child welfare clinic, or providing leadership and moral guidance to young women in girls' clubs or the guides.[23] Philanthropy had long provided a means of empowerment for middle-class women,[24] and most women's organizations, whatever their primary purpose, had some involvement with charitable

[19] Mathew Thomson, *The Problem of Mental Deficiency, Eugenics, Democracy and Social Policy in Britain, c.1870–1959* (Oxford, 1998), 219. For details of local co-operation between statutory and voluntary agencies in the 1930s, see Political and Economic Planning, *Report on the British Social Services* (London, 1937), 105–6, 156–67, 172–5.

[20] Martin Pugh, *Women and the Women's Movement in Britain, 1914–1959* (Basingstoke, 1992), 57–8. In London the proportion of women was three times greater.

[21] Thomson, *Problem of Mental Deficiency*, 229–30.

[22] Undated press cutting in Lancashire RO, Preston Women's Citizens' Association, DDX 1749 Box 5.

[23] This list reflects activities recorded in the local Minute books listed in the Bibliography.

[24] K. D. McCarthy, 'Parallel Power Structures: Women and the Voluntary Sphere', in McCarthy (ed.), *Lady Bountiful Revisited: Women, Philanthropy, and Power* (Piscataway, NJ, 1990), 1, 11; Ann Summers, 'A Home from Home—Women's Philanthropic Work in the Nineteenth Century', in S. Burman (ed.), *Fit Work for Women* (London, 1979), 45.

activity if only through an annual distribution of surplus funds to local good causes.[25]

The points of entry into this world were many and various, and individual women might combine membership of several organizations. The largest women's organization was probably the Mothers' Union, an offshoot of the Anglican church which claimed half a million members in 1950.[26] Women had been active in political parties well before they got the vote, and during the inter-war years Conservative Women's Associations grew rapidly, raising funds for political and charitable activity while operating as social and educational clubs for middle-class housewives.[27] Many other male organizations had thriving women's auxiliaries—the Inner Wheel for the wives of Rotary Club businessmen, for example, and the women's sections of the British Legion, which, while not predominantly middle-class, provided an arena within which ex-army wives could continue to officer the rank and file.[28] Auxiliary medical organizations included Nursing Associations, whose main business was raising charitable funds to pay the salary of the District Nurse,[29] St John Ambulance, and the more fashionable Red Cross.[30]

The proliferation of women's organizations since the First World War was informed by the recent struggle for the vote, and a common objective was education for citizenship and the promotion of active participation in polit-ical life. The Women's Institute was the most successful of these bodies, but it only touched the fringes of the towns operating a self-denying ordinance not to recruit in townships with more than 4,000 inhabitants.[31] Its urban equivalent were the Townswomen's Guilds. Founded in 1929, the guilds had 54,000 members ten years later. During the war membership held up well and went on to double during the Attlee years, reaching a total of 114,000 by 1949.[32] 'Our programme', recalled Margery Corbett Ashby, a

[25] Examples of this in the local records examined are too numerous to list.

[26] Caitriona Beaumont, 'Women and Citizenship: A Study of Non-feminist Women's Societies and the Women's Movement in England, 1928–1950', Warwick Ph.D., 1996, 17; F. K. Prochaska, 'A Mothers Country: Mothers Meetings and Family Welfare in Britain, 1950–1950', *History*, 74 (1989).

[27] M. Pugh, *The Tories and the People, 1880–1935* (1985); Joni Lovenduski, Pippa Norris, and Catriona Burness, 'The Party and Women', in A. Seldon and S. Ball (eds.), *Conservative Century. The Conservative Party since 1900* (Oxford, 1994).

[28] Dr Roper Power, 'The Voluntary Social Services in Hertfordshire' (n.d., 1942), 12 NCSRS, E2/7; James McIntyre, Report on Voluntary Service in Devon (n.d., 1942), 33, NCSRS, E2/5

[29] Power, 'Hertfordshire', 6–7.

[30] For complaints about the snobbery associated with Red Cross see Power, 'Hertfordshire', 11; Walker, Weekly Report (18 June 1939), WRVS, R3 Regional Office; Report, 9 Oct. 1938, WRVS, R9 3 Wolverhapton; Lady Perrott to Lady Reading, 7 July 1938, WRVS, V32/38, St John's Ambulance.

[31] But this limit was not always respected: NUTG Executive Minutes, 22 Nov. 1938, 28 Nov. 1944.

[32] Elizabeth McCarty, 'Attitudes to Women and Domesticity in England, circa 1939–1955', Oxford D.Phil., 1994, 306. The number of branches also doubled to over 1,000 during the same period.

leading Liberal feminist and one of the moving spirits behind the foundation of the guilds, 'was...arts and crafts and citizenship.'[33] Arts and crafts commanded the greater part of members' attention, but from this basis the leaders of the National Union of Townswomen's Guilds (NUTG) pioneered methods of informal adult education designed to encourage housewives to take the first steps towards independent citizenship.[34] The Guilds, wrote their historian, 'threw open the doors of home, but they opened them into a safe, unthreatening world'.[35] The 'common meeting ground', open to women 'irrespective of creed or party', was intended to provide a protected terrain on which housewives could gain the confidence and learn the skills necessary to undertake political activity and voluntary work on their own account through whatever other organizations suited their individual needs and tastes.[36] Alice Franklin, the formidable upper-middle-class woman who ran the National Union from its foundation, combined a theoretical passion for democracy with a heavily paternalistic approach in practice. She and her close friend and assistant, Gertrude Horton, were both products of metro-politan liberal feminism, and they viewed the suburban housewives who made up the bulk of Guild members with some condescension: 'completely inexperienced people', 'people who did not know they wanted an education, the layer below the WEA'.[37] Fearing that these women lacked the political maturity necessary to sustain the 'common meeting ground' they kept a watchful eye on their activities and bombarded offending Guilds with in-structions to avoid any hint of political or religious partisanship. While they were conscientious in warning Guilds against succumbing to the lure of left-wing or explicitly feminist causes, the main thrust of their efforts was to prevent Guilds from taking on the Conservative, patriotic, and Anglican identities that came naturally to most of their members.[38] Already in

---

[33] M. Stott, *Organization Woman. The Story of the National Union of Townswomen's Guilds* (London, 1978), 101–3.

[34] Ibid., 101–3, 165–7; *Townswoman* (May 1945), 138–9; A. Franklin, 'Notes for a Talk to a Mass Meeting of...members' (Aug. 1944), in PRO, MAF 102 10.

[35] Stott, *Organisation Woman*, 20.

[36] Franklin, 'Notes', PRO, MAF 102 10.

[37] Interview with Gertrude Horton, 1977, Brian Harrison tapes; A. F. C. Bourdillon, note on interview with Horton and Franklin, 13 May 1942, NCSRS, E12/9. On Franklin and Horton's backgrounds see Stott, *Organization Woman*, 11, 14. On the NUTG attitude to suburban housewives, see D. L. North, 'Middle-Class Suburban Culture and Lifestyles in England, 1919–1939', Oxford D.Phil., 1989, 199 ff.

[38] Stott, *Organization Woman*, 44–5; 'The Common Meeting Ground of Ethical Belief', NUTG Circular, 9 Oct. 1944 in PRO, MAF 102 10. Guild choirs were not permitted to sing at Mothers Union meetings for fear of identifying the Guilds with the Church of England, and even donations to hospital funds were questionable since they might make Christian Scientists feel unwelcome (Franklin, 'Notes', PRO, MAF 102 10; NUTG Executive, Minutes, 28 Mar. 1939, 23 Jan. 1945). After some debate the Executive decided that nativity plays and carols might be performed by Guilds, so long as these were 'artistic performances' not associated with any religious service (NUTG Executive, Minutes, 27 July 1943).

1938–9, Franklin's resistance to any direct involvement of the Guilds with WVS work—on the grounds that pacifist women should not be alienated—was causing unrest among the membership and dividing the Executive.[39]

After the war this strict paternalistic regime backfired when Franklin's expansion plans triggered revolt among the parochially minded guild members who were asked to foot the bill for a national office whose policing of the 'common meeting ground' was seen as denying Guilds 'the freedom they wanted for their work'.[40] 'The National Union has trained us to think for ourselves,' declared one delegate, 'and we want to say that we do not approve' of the leadership's plans.[41] Despite rapid growth and plans for a significant democratization and decentralization of the organization, discontent continued to accumulate.[42] Franklin's assiduous visits to the Guilds may have done more harm than good: she did not suffer fools gladly and members were often left hurt and well aware of her low opinion of their competence.[43] Worried by growing discontent amongst those who, ultimately, paid their salaries the full-time organizers lost confidence in Franklin and accused her of being out of touch with the needs and desires of ordinary members.[44] At the end of 1948 the organizers gained the support of a majority on the executive and Franklin resigned, followed shortly afterwards by Horton. Something of their indignation at the 'impertinence' of 'the not well-educated, self-opinionated type that formed our executive committee' was reflected in the reported complaint of the president (a lady-in-waiting to Queen Mary), who also resigned, that 'we were being ruled from the coal face'.[45] Franklin and Horton's distress was, no doubt,

[39] NUTG Executive, Minutes, 28 Oct. 1938, 20 Feb. 1939, 28 Mar. 1939; *Townswomen* (Mar. 1939); Deeds to Shack, 28 Apr. 1939 in WF/E1.

[40] *Townswoman* (May 1945), 140; NUTG Executive, Minutes, 26 Sept., 1945. Horton acknowledged that some of the irritation felt by Guilds towards the National Union 'may be due to an ultra emphasis on detail and procedure' (Horton to Williams, 13 Apr. 1948, attached to NUTG Executive, Minutes, 5 Dec. 1948). Rumblings of revolt, particularly over the religious prohibitions of the common meeting ground, continued, and, to the alarm of the leadership, the 1946 AGM passed a resolution lifting many of the restrictions in this area (NUTG Executive, Minutes, 26 June, 1946).

[41] *Townswoman* (May 1945) (I have restored the speech, reported in the third person, to the first person—JH).

[42] By September 1945 the executive had agreed a schedule of constitutional change, though no final decisions were expected to be reached before 1948 (NUTG Executive, Minutes, 26 Sept. 1945). Alongside decentralization to regional federations it was planned to set up a representative Central Council to give the guilds more effective control of the National Union. Horton hoped that this would serve to dispel local Guild hostility to the centre and its financial demands on them (Horton to Williams, 13 Apr. 1948, attached to NUTG Executive, Minutes, 5 Dec. 1948; *Townswoman* (Dec. 1947), Apr. 1948).

[43] Interview with Mary Courtney, Brian Harrison tapes.

[44] Statement to Officers Meeting, 11 May 1948, attached to NUTG Executive, Minutes, 5 Dec. 1948. The organizers were also nervous about the implications of the decentralization plans (interview with Gertrude Horton, Brian Harrison tapes; Stott, *Organization Woman*, 120).

[45] Interviews with Gertrude Horton and Mary Courtney, Brian Harrison tapes.

reinforced by the thinly veiled disapproval of their presumed lesbianism displayed by some executive members.[46] Although both women had been due to retire in any case, the manner of their departure reflected deep tensions—generational, social, and, in the broadest sense, political—between the ex-suffrage 'prudent revolutionaries' who founded the Townswomen's Guilds as an experiment in education for citizenship, and the less radical but more representative provincial middle-class women who succeeded them.[47] Mary Courtney, the leader of the incoming regime, was a doctor's wife from Bristol, experienced nationally in the YWCA, and of an altogether more right-wing caste of mind than her predecessors.[48] The bitterness of this conflict fully exposed the internal contradictions inherent in Franklin's project of fostering the housewife-citizen, and it belies any simple construction of the women's movement as a school of democratic citizenship.

In 1950s Banbury women of the established local shopocracy joined the Townswomen's Guild, but better-educated incomers belonged to the Business and Professional Women's Club.[49] Started in 1938, these clubs were designed to cater for the same groups of women as the older Soroptimists, whose membership was restricted by adherence to the Rotarian principle of only allowing one representative of each of an elaborately drawn schedule of occupations to join any particular local club. The Business and Professional Women's Clubs were launched independently after the Soroptimists had refused to widen their brief, and membership grew rapidly from 900 in 24 clubs in 1940 to 6,500 in 109 clubs by 1945 and 14,500 in 240 clubs by 1951.[50] (The Soroptimists, by contrast, claimed no more than 3,500 members in the 1940s.[51]) At local level the two organizations usually worked closely together. Although small, the Soroptimists clubs could pull considerable punch. In some towns their annual dinners were civic occasions attended by the Mayor and other dignitaries and fully reported with appropriate photographs of bejewelled ladies in the local paper— 'giving the lie to that popular idea that working women are gawks and

---

[46] Interviews with Miss Hamilton Smith and Mary Courtney, Brian Harrison tapes.

[47] See Brian Harrison, *Prudent Revolutionaries. Portraits of British Feminists between the Wars* (Oxford, 1987) for the best account of the post-suffrage generation of activists of which Franklin was a distinguished member. Franklin's job would have disappeared with adoption of the constitutional changes in June 1949. Horton had already been talking about retirement in 1945 (NUTG Executive, Minutes, 14 Dec. 1948; *Townswoman* (May 1945), 139).

[48] In 1977 Courtney was not only dismissive of feminism, but appeared to equate Franklin's concern to prevent the Guilds from simply reinforcing existing social hierarchies as tantamount to communism! (interview with Mary Courtney, Brian Harrison tapes). In 1947 she chaired both the YWCA and the SCWO in Bristol (Warner to King, 4 June 1947, WF/K20 Bristol).

[49] Stacey, *Banbury*, 171.

[50] Dorothy Hall, *Making Things Happen* (London, 1963), 4–5, 265; Miss Gordon Holmes, *In Love with Life. A Pioneer Career Woman's Story* (London, 1944), 177.

[51] Bob Holman, *The Evacuation: A Very British Revolution* (Oxford, 1995).

frumps'.[52] Another organization appealing to educated middle-class women was the Electrical Association for Women. Founded in 1924 to channel female enthusiasm for the liberating force of the new power source and to promote the use of electricity in the home, it functioned not only to lobby business and government on electrical issues, but also as a social and educational club for its 9,000 or so local members. The Nottingham branch, for example, organized regular talks at luncheon meetings, outings, whist drives, and so on.[53] A number of towns sustained active Women's Citizen's Associations, which were particularly concerned with promoting women's candidacies in local elections.[54] The Mass Observer who attended a meeting of the WCA in Bolton in 1937 deduced from the number of fur coats in evidence that this must be an overwhelmingly middle-class organization.[55]

Alongside their social, educational, and philanthropic activities, these organizations often took on an active campaigning role—on women police and the moral welfare of young girls, nursery school provision, maternity and child welfare, housing, and other 'women's issues'.[56] While the housewives of the Townswomen's Guilds were sometimes reluctant to involve themselves in civic affairs,[57] the business and professional women intended

[52] Press reports of annual dinners of Soroptimist Club of Nottingham in 1938 and 1939, Nottingham RO, DDSO/2/2; Preston Soroptimist Club, Minutes, *passim*, in Lancashire RO, DDX 1139 1/1; press reports of annual dinners of Halifax Soroptimist Club in Calderdale RO, SOR/3/1. But by no means all Soroptimists were members of the urban elite. The membership of the Halifax Soroptmists included women in quite humble jobs—chiropodist, saleswoman, hairdresser, florist, fishmonger, etc. (Edith Cockcroft, *Silver Jubilee Poems* (Halifax, 1948), in Calderdale RO, SOR/4/24).
[53] S. Worden, 'Powerful Women: Electricity in the Home, 1919–1940', in J. Attfield and P. Kirkham, *A View from the Interior. Feminism, Women and Design* (London, 1989), 131–2, 141; C. Davidson, *A Woman's Work is Never Done. A History of Housework in the British Isles, 1650–1950* (London, 1982), 42–3; C. Pursell, 'Domesticating Modernity: The EAW, 1924–1986', *British Journal of the History of Science*, 32 (1999), 47–67; S. Bowden and A. Offer, 'The Technological Revolution that Never Was. Gender, Class and the Diffusion of Household Appliances in Inter-war England', in V. de Grazia (ed.), *The Sex of Things. Gender and Consumption in Historical Perspective* (Berkeley, Calif., 1996), 268; EAW Nottingham Branch, Minutes, *passim*, Nottingham RO, DD 1357\1\4\1.
[54] Anon, *The National Women Citizen's Association, 1918–1968* (London, 1968), copy in Preston Women's Citizens Association, Lancashire RO, DDX 1749 Box 5. In 1938 the NWCA had 30 branches, many with over 200 members, a few with 300–400 members (Dobbs to Smieton, 1 July 1938, in WRVS, V56/38, Women's Citizens Association).
[55] JW, Report of meeting of Women's Citizens Association, 25 Nov. 1937, in Mass Observation, Worktown, 44/1/C.
[56] Moral welfare and the linked issue of women police was a particularly prominent issue in the minutes I have consulted. The anxiety of Preston Soroptimists about 'the drunkenness and loose behaviour of young girls in company with soldiers' was exacerbated by the fact that some of these soldiers were 'coloured men' (Preston Soroptimists Executive, Minutes, 31 Aug. 1943 in Lancashire RO, DDX 1139 1/1). For an analysis of such anxieties, see Sonya O. Rose, 'Sex, Citizenship and the Nation in World War II Britain', *American Historical Review*, 103 (1998).
[57] See Chapter 9. The minutes of the St Albans guild, stored in the offices of the National Union of Townswomen's Guilds, illustrate the uphill struggle involved in trying to interest members in civic affairs during the war.

to be movers and shakers. The president of the Blackpool BPW club set an ambitious agenda: 'if our Club can hasten the day when men and women have equal opportunities for service I shall feel we have done something worthwhile.'[58] Established during the war, members had concentrated at first on self-education but they were not content to remain 'merely…a lecture Society' and were anxious to find ways of making themselves 'a vital force' in the town.[59] Similarly in Nottingham, the President of the Soroptimists insisted that they were not 'a luncheon club only and that we were called upon definitely to do something in the way of service.'[60] During the war the Soroptimists launched a major initiative to consolidate women's organizations at local level, the results of which are examined in Chapter 9. In some towns The National Council of Women (whose forerunner, the misleadingly named middle-class National Union of Women Workers, had been founded in the 1880s) already operated as a campaigns co-ordinator. But it was also a women's club in its own right with monthly speaker meetings, organized outings, etc.[61] Drawing on a similar middle-class constituency to the Soroptimists, but involving housewives as well as professional women, the NCW had 12,500 individual members in 1939 as well as affiliations from most of the other women's organizations.[62] Campaigning brought women's organizations together and members of the more elite organizations regularly attended each other's meetings.[63] From Stockton-on-Tees it was reported that the NCW, WCA and EAW were all 'largely supported by the same people'.[64] An active woman in Nottingham might find herself lunching at the Mikado Cafe several times a month under the auspices of a number of different organizations.[65] In Halifax the close association among leading personnel is clear from their frequent attendance at each others' annual dinners. The local newspaper ran a column throughout the 1940s entitled 'The Women's Sphere' in which the activities

[58] Blackpool Business and Professional Women's Club, Minutes, 7 July 1948, in Lancashire RO.
[59] Ibid., 7 Sept. 1946, 7 July 1948.
[60] Soroptimist Club of Nottingham, Minutes, 7 Feb. 1939, Nottingham RO, DDSO/2/2l.
[61] Coventry NCW Minutes, *passim*, Coventry RO, PA/1269; Halifax NCW, Minutes, *passim*, Calderdale RO, NCW/1; Pugh, *Women's Movement*, 69.
[62] Beaumont, 'Women and Citizenship', 264–5.
[63] Examples of such overlapping are legion in the minutes examined. When the national conference of the EAW was held in Nottingham in 1941, the local branch sought help in providing accommodation for delegates from the Soroptimists, the Inner Wheel, the BPW Club, the City Business Club, and the NCW (EAW, Nottingham Branch, Nottingham RO, DD 1357\1\4\1). Some sense of common identity across these organizations can be inferred from the EAW assumption that members of other organizations would be prepared to host strangers attending a conference.
[64] E. Moulsdale Williams (organizer of North East Area of the EAW) to Huxley, 1 July 1938, WRVS, R1/2, Durham County.
[65] In Nottingham, the Soroptimists, the NCW and the Women's Conservative Association all met at the Mikado.

KING ALFRED'S COLLEGE
LIBRARY

of all the local women's organizations were reported in detail every week. The editor's wife was herself a leading player in several of these organizations, and the range of her interests affords a glimpse of the world of these provincial public women. Daughter of an academic, and sister of Geoffrey Crowther, the editor of *The Economist*, Phyllis Ramsden held one of the first two Ph.D.s awarded to women by London University, for a doctorate on English social history. During the 1930s she helped to establish a Women's Welfare Clinic in Halifax and acted as the first secretary of the local National Council of Women. She chaired the Halifax Women's Luncheon Club, held honorary membership of the Inner Wheel, and gave historical talks to the Soroptimists. During the war she was asked to stand for election to the local council (presumably as a Liberal) but declined on the grounds that this would compromise the political independence of her husband's newspaper. She was, however, co-opted onto the borough education committee on which she served for nearly twenty years.[66] Alongside this active public life she pursued her historical interests, eventually immersing herself in the world of the early nineteenth-century Halifax businesswoman and traveller, Anne Lister, whose 6,000-page manuscript diary Ramsden was the first to explore.[67] Lister has since become something of an icon of independent womanhood, and Ramsden no doubt found in her diaries some inspiration for her own forceful presence in the public domain.[68]

Historical discussion of the mid-twentieth-century women's movement has been dominated by assumptions about the centrality of domesticity in women's lives. The deconstruction of 'the housewife' was initially driven by the need of 1970s feminism to construct a retrospective history of domestic slavery as a foil to its own emancipatory project: any 'affirmation of contentment with the housewife role', wrote the sociologist Ann Oakley, 'is actually a form of anti-feminism whatever the gender of the person who displays it.'[69] In attacking the legacy of domestic ideology, feminist historiography shone bright lights into many dark corners, but the construct of 'domestic ideology' itself tended, in turn, to obscure the sheer variety of ways in which non-earning women engaged with society beyond the home. Recent work on mid-century women's organization has challenged the view that they were sunk in the reproduction of domesticity and taken seriously

[66] Obituary in *Halifax Evening Courier*, 11 Sept. 1985; Halifax NCW Minutes, 9 July 1943, Calderdale RO, NCW/1; Halifax Inner Wheel Club Minutes, 8 July 1937, Calderdale RO, IW 2; Halifax Soroptimists Minutes, 20 Oct. 1938, Calderdale RO, SOR 3/19.

[67] M. Ramsden, 'Anne Lister's Journal, 1817–1840', *Halifax Antiquarian Society*, 1970; 'The two million word enigma', *Guardian* (17 Feb. 1984) (I am grateful to Jill Liddington for these references).

[68] Jill Liddington, *Female Fortune. Land, Gender and Authority. The Anne Lister Diaries, 1833–36* (London, 1998); Sarah Richardson, 'The Role of Women in Electoral Politics in Yorkshire during the 1830s', *Northern History*, 32 (1996).

[69] Ann Oakley, *Housewife* (1974), 233.

their common commitment to enabling women to move from the merely formal citizenship conferred by the right to vote to an active, participating citizenship that would complement, not contradict, their domestic roles.[70] Feminists like Winfred Holtby were not alone in deploring the tendency of women to define themselves solely as 'private persons' whose jobs lay entirely 'within four walls'.[71] Even the Mothers Union, the most conservative of women's organizations, entertained the view in the mid-1930s that: 'For a woman to give up all outside interests, to entirely merge her personality in that of another, is to help in producing husbands and fathers of the wrong type; the bully, the autocrat, the dictator. We have no use for the type today.'[72] In an era when the great majority of married women did not undertake work outside the home, there was a widespread belief that the non-working married woman, particularly as she emerged from the full-time burden of caring for young children, had a major voluntary contribution to make to the wider society beyond the home. This project of the housewife-citizen did not challenge the primacy of domesticity in women's lives. The home—and all that this ideologically loaded word signified (caring, intimacy, consumption, etc.)—was the centre of her being, but not the limit either of her contribution to society or her opportunities for self-development. The view expounded by the Conservative Women's Reform Group in 1945 would have been enthusiastically endorsed across the women's movement as a whole:

We hold the view that democracy will be better served if part of the mother's new freedom is spent helping to operate some of the local services from which her family benefits. A mother is not neglecting her child if she herself assists in cooking the school dinners and is more likely to take an intelligent interest in her local day-nursery if she sits on its committee of management. We believe that such opportunities for fuller citizenship will be welcome by women who have known the stimulus of war service. For, though still regarding the home as the centre of their well-being, they no longer regard it as their boundary.[73]

---

[70] Maggie Andrews, *The Acceptable Face of Feminism. The Women's Institute as a Social Movement* (London, 1998); McCarty, 'Women and Domesticity'; Beaumont, 'Women and Citizenship'. For an earlier treatment which stresses the degree to which women's organizations were swallowed up by an 'all-embracing domesticty', see Pugh, *Women's Movement*, 149.

[71] Quoted in C. Dyehouse, *Feminism and the Family in England, 1880–1939* (Oxford, 1989), 48.

[72] *Mother's Union Journal* (Sept. 1934), 11, cited in Beaumont, 'Women and Citizenship', 92.

[73] *When Peace Comes. A National Programme from the Standpoint of Women*, Conservative Women's Reform Group, Apr. 1944. For similar statements from a range of different standpoints see M. Corbett Ashby, *Women's Work and Position in the State*, Interim Report of Sub-committee of Women's Liberal Federation (London, 1943); M. Sutherland, 'The Work of Housewife and Mother', *Labour Woman* (Feb. 1944); Gertrude Williams, *Women and Work* (London, 1945), 126–7; Charlotte Luetkins, *Women and a New Society* (London, 1946), 122–3.

As wife and mother she serviced and fashioned the citizens of today and tomorrow, and she drew from this work a sense of self-worth. But she was also a citizen in her own right, and active participation in the wider life of the community was, for the millions of women who joined women's organizations in the mid-twentieth century, an important component of their identities.

In their anxiety to free women's organizations from the condescension of posterity some recent authors have, however, adopted a rather too optimistic view of the capacity of women to constitute themselves as fully-fledged democratic subjects in a society in which gender inequalities remained systemic.[74] The gendered division between public and private spheres lay at the root of masculine identity, and the project of the housewife-citizen ran into the sands to the extent that it posed a direct threat to that division.[75] Nor should the salience of class within the female public sphere be underestimated. The Mothers' Union provided tea and a gossip to women of all classes, but its inner life probably had more to do with reinforcing deference than dissolving class identities. The vicar's wife and her peers saw mothers' meetings as an opportunity to do good among more or less docile working women, a relationship sometimes even formalized into two classes of membership: ordinary Mothers and Lady-Mothers.[76] The Townswomen's Guilds maintained a low subscription and, during the 1930s, the National Federation used grants from leading charitable foundations to employ full-time organizers to establish guilds among the wives of unemployed men in the depressed areas.[77] It was reported from Hull that the guild 'includes women of widely varying social and economic position, yet in no case is there any suggestion that the policy of an individual guild is controlled by an unrepresentative clique.'[78] Other evidence however suggests that class was not so easily transcended within the organisation. One North London pub provided the meeting place for two separate guilds, one with members from the Watling council estate, the other from the neighbouring middle-class areas. Although they met in the same place their membership did not mix.[79] A Lancashire woman who moved to Exeter during the war found herself '*very* disappointed with the cold, unfriendly attitude of middle-class women to their working-class sisters in the Guild. So far all attempts to mix these

---

[74] Notably Andrews, *Acceptable Face*.

[75] See Hinton, 'The Tale of Sammy Spree: Gendering 1940s Corporatism', forthcoming.

[76] James McIntyre, Report on Voluntary Service in Devon (n.d., 1942), 55, NCSRS, E2/5; P. Hollis, *Women in Public. Documents of the Victorian Women's Movement, 1850–1900* (London, 1979), 276–7.

[77] NUTG Executive, Minutes, 1938–9, *passim*, and 25 May 1943.

[78] R. K. Kelsall, Report on Voluntary Social Service in Hull, Apr. 1942, 12, NCSRS, E2/8.

[79] Anon., 'Watling Revisted', *Planning*, 270, 15 Aug. 1947, 71.

sections in Guild life have broken down...'.[80] Similar anxieties were expressed in 1942 by leaders of the Liverpool federation.[81] Most Townswomen were middle class, and where the membership of individual guilds
was mixed the middle-class women occupied the leading positions.[82] As the
token working-class woman on the national executive put it in the 1930s:
'the Townswomen's Guilds would be very different if all the officers hadn't
got cooks.'[83] The EAW aspired to spread its vision of electrified modernity to
working-class housewives: in reality, however, the main impact of the inter-
war electrification on housework was to ease the transition from live-in
servants to daily helps, and working-class women were more likely to handle
vacuum cleaners as charwomen than in their own homes.[84] The gulfs in
everyday experience that continued to divide housewives on class lines were
simply too great to be bridged effectively in associational life. Amongst the
urban women's organizations most likely to answer Lady Reading's call for
volunteers working-class membership was very rare indeed.

III

As they went about colonizing the female public sphere, WVS organizers
accumulated a good deal of information about the structure of social leadership in mid-twentieth-century towns. Some of this can be quantified.
Details of the social status and associational affiliations of the 556 leaders
appointed during the WVS's first seven months were recorded in the executive Minute books, and this information is supplemented by a survey of 300
WVS leaders in the West Midlands compiled during 1942.[85] In the analysis
that follows, this quantified information is fleshed out with information
largely derived from the files on particular towns and regions compiled in
Tothill Street by the WVS Chief Regional Organizer, Mrs Huxley.

The rural upper class was not entirely absent from the towns. The small
businessmen and shopkeepers who ran the associational life of post-war
Banbury, for example, continued to look to upper-class people living in the
surrounding countryside to occupy the top positions in their voluntary

---

[80] McIntyre, Report on Voluntary Service in Devon, 19.

[81] NUTG Executive, Minutes, 30 Sept. 1942.

[82] Power, 'The Voluntary Social Services in Hertfordshire', 17; T. Bottomore, 'Social Stratification in Voluntary Organisations,' in D. V. Glass (ed.), *Social Mobility in Britain* (London,
1954), 363–4. In the Durham mining town of Birtley, the guild was run by the colliery managers'
wives (Stott, *Organisation Women*, 32–3).

[83] Interview with Miss E. Hamilton Smith, Brian Harrison tapes.

[84] Bowden and Offer, 'Gender, Class and the Diffusion of Household Appliances', 262–4,
268–9.

[85] Sample Analysis of Regional Appointments prepared by WVS for Mr Harry Hopkins,
special advisor to the President of USA, Jan. 1941, in WRVS, R3/3/38.

organizations even though they had neither an economic stake in the town nor any active involvement in its political life.[86] The role of such people was largely decorative: but in the theatre of social relations the observation of rituals of deference is likely to have real effects. One explanation for what was said to be the unusually democratic tone of the voluntary sector in Hull was 'that the proportion of "dead wood" in the Hull branches is appreciably less than in other parts of the country, possibly because there are fewer titled people resident here to monopolise the presidents' chairs and to encourage, by their presence, the wrong sort of charitable workers to become members.'[87] While WVS organizers were generally disinclined to appoint merely decorative leaders, they did occasionally seek help from the gentry to knock heads together among squabbling cliques of middle-class towns-women. Lincoln, for example, had a distinguished history of such infighting. At the outset progress had been blocked by the bitter rivalry of the elderly women of the Cathedral set—'the smart party'—who had run the Red Cross in the Great War and resented the newcomers in charge of WVS. It required national negotiations between WVS and the Red Cross to secure a truce.[88] In 1944, following years of 'bitter strife' under an ineffective leader, a travelling administrator sent in by Tothill Street was told by the Dean that WVS had failed locally because it had never had a leader with the social clout to rise above these petty quarrels. He proposed the appointment of a local aristo-crat. The Bishop of Grimsby offered similar advice: 'we needed someone who carried big guns to keep the ladies in order.' In the event the appoint-ment of the leader of the Cathedral party—the Bishop's wife—to act as President of the WVS seems to have been sufficient to calm things down.[89] In Burnley, where a feud between the WVS leader and the mayoress was disrupting WVS work, a proposal to use the local Bishop's wife to similar purpose failed because she was universally disliked. In desperation the regional organizer turned to Rachel Kay-Shuttleworth, spinster member of the leading county family in the area whose male relatives were scythed like corn in both world wars.[90] In the 1930s, operating from her father's stately home at Gawthorpe Hall, Kay-Shuttleworth had presided over a variety of Lancashire organizations, including the Girl Guides. She had

[86] Stacey, Banbury, 157; Plowman, Minchinton, and Stacey, 'Local Social Status', 176; and see more generally D. Cannadine, *The Decline and Fall of the British Aristocracy* (London, 1990), ch. 12.
[87] Kelsall, Voluntary Social Service in Hull, 1.
[88] Viscountess Falmouth to Lady Reading, 2 Nov. 1939; Reading to Falmouth, 6 Nov. 1939; Woodall to Reading, 20 Nov. 1939; Huxley to Hind, 6 Dec. 1939; Falmouth to Huxley, 8 Apr. 1940—all in WRVS, R3/5 Lincoln.
[89] Report on Lincoln, Nov. 1944, in WRVS, R3/5 Lincoln.
[90] Cannadine, *British Aristocracy*, 627; M. Hall, 'Voluntary Organisations in Burnley', in A. F. C. Bourdillon (ed.), *Voluntary Social Services. Their Place in the Modern State* (London, 1945), 264.

been instrumental in founding WVS in Burnley, but had withdrawn from public life following her father's death in 1939.[91] Convinced that 'we really should have someone of a little more standing who is above these quarrelling women', the regional organizer wrote to Kay-Shuttleworth begging her to take on the job of Chairman: 'the only person [the group leaders] want is The Hon Rachel.'[92] Rachel, however, declined.[93] Even where county ladies could be found to take on such roles, they were not necessarily what was needed. In Guildford, intervention by the local gentry helped to pacify warring middle-class factions, but it exacerbated difficulties with the Labour women.[94]

The great majority of WVS leaders in the towns were not gentry but members of the urban middle class. One elderly organizer, looking wearily back in 1939 over a life devoted to public service, felt that those who had borne the burden of social work in the Great War would have to do so again because the post-war generation 'were brain tired as well as bodily tired... having been encouraged to go in for careers for themselves...'.[95] In fact, many of the more effective WVS leaders were career women: headmistresses, doctors, businesswomen, or public officials. Sixty-five of the women appointed as WVS leaders by March 1939 had held full-time jobs. Of these nearly half were schoolteachers (twenty-nine, of whom ten were headmistresses); there were also seven businesswomen, five doctors, five civil servants, three solicitors, three journalists, and two librarians.[96] While most of these women had retired, some, like the manager at the local Labour Exchange in Jarrow, found time and energy to run WVS alongside a full-time job. A disproportionate number of the career women were single (including eight out of the ten headmistresses), but many had combined careers with marriage. Nevertheless experience of paid employment was not common among WVS leaders: 90 per cent of the married women appointed appear to

[91] WVS Executive, Minutes, 14 Dec. 1938; Vera Dart report on Burnley, 5 Dec. 1939, WRVS, R10/2 Burnley; Dart to Huxley, 24 Jan. 1940, WRVS, R10 Regional Office.

[92] Dart to Goldney, 12 July 1940, WRVS, R10 Regional Office; Foster Jeffery to Kay Shuttleworth, 3 July 1940, WRVS, R10/2 Burnley.

[93] Dart to Goldney, 12 July 1940; Dart to Huxley, 5 May 1940; Dart to Kay-Shuttleworth, 3 July 1940; Dart to Huxley, 2 July 1940; Dart to Huxley, 5 July 1940, all in WRVS, R10 Regional Office; Reports on Burnley by Vera Dart, 5 Dec. 1939, 14 May, 22 May, 15 July 1940; Report by Foster Jeffery on Burnley, 3 July 1940; Foster Jeffery to Kay Shuttleworth, 3 July 1940 all in WRVS, R10/2 Burnley.

[94] 'Housewives Section. Guildford Borough', 20 Nov. 1943, WRVS, R12/4 Surrey.

[95] Report of Regional Conference, Leicester, 16 Mar. 1939, WRVS, R3/2 Leicester.

[96] The great majority of the 145 single women appointed to run WVS centres before March 1939, details of whose backgrounds are recorded in the Executive minutes, appear not to have been in paid work, though almost all had some record in voluntary social work. Most of the 29 career women were current or former schoolteachers (19, of whom 8 were headmistresses). Of 392 married women appointed in the same period, only 36 are shown as having been employed. Although teachers are again the largest single group (10, of whom 2 were headmistresses), a variety of other occupations also make a showing.

have had no recent employment and, more surprisingly, the same is true of 80 per cent of the single women. Single women made up more than a quarter of the appointments and the fact that so many of them appear to have been women of independent means free to devote their time to voluntary service suggests how very important spinsters were to middle-class social leadership in the inter-war years.[97] There is, unfortunately, no data on the occupational status of their fathers or brothers.

Contemplating the social geography of her domain, the Warwickshire organizer remarked that, while the gentry were natural leaders in the rural south, the towns in the north of the county would require the 'semi-professional woman, the Doctor's wife for instance'. 'Semi-professional' is an interesting concept, implying that the public role undertaken by such women was an expected corollary of their husbands' professional role. Marriage to a vicar carried a similar obligation and the wives of bank managers, whose work often required intimate local knowledge,[98] also appear to have been pillars of the community. Among the 104 married women whose husbands' occupations were recorded in the Executive Minute book, by far the largest group were doctors' wives (29), followed by churchmen (10) and bank managers (5). Among other professional occupations the largest group were newspaper editors (3), town clerks (3), senior policemen (3), and headmasters (2). Apart from the wives of MPs (5), the other important group was businessmen's wives (8). The precise status of the husband's occupation could be critical to a woman's sense of her own fitness for leadership. In Sheffield, for example, where the wartime WVS had been run by the wife of a director of a steel firm, her reluctant successor was convinced that she lacked the necessary 'social standing' as her husband was 'only a Works Manager'. The wives of two senior public officials (the Medical Officer of Health and the Director of Social Services) would, she felt, have been more appropriate appointments.[99]

IV

High social status, though often considered necessary, was seldom a sufficient criterion for selection as a WVS leader. The establishment of WVS in the towns was essentially a process of colonization of existing associational networks. Thus the appointment of Lady Ethel Bowring to run the Bedford WVS owed less to the fact that her husband, a retired colonial administrator, had been knighted than to her chairmanship of the NCW: 'a very powerful

[97] 145 out of 392. Single women accounted for slightly less than one-fifth of the leaders in the West Midlands survey.
[98] M. Stacey, E. Batstone, C. Bell, and A. Murcott, *Power, Persistence and Change. A Second Study of Banbury* (Oxford, 1975), 29; McKibbin, *Classes and Cultures*, 519.
[99] Halpin to Reading, 16 Feb. 1946, WRVS, R2/2 Sheffield.

body of women in Bedford'.[100] What organizers were looking for were women known and respected for their public work: 'our experience throughout the country has shown that [the post of centre leader] should be filled by a woman of standing who is already an acknowledged leader of the Borough...'[101] Many WVS leaders held office in established women's organizations, often in more than one. The Tynemouth centre leader was said (not entirely convincingly) to be an active member of twenty-six of the thirty-one women's organizations in the town.[102] Other descriptions were less precise: 'secretary of many women's associations, and leader in civic work' (Preston); 'general leader in the town' (Middlesbrough); 'on all local committees' (Launceston); 'member of most charity committees' (Fleetwood); 'actively interested in all women's organizations' (Stourbridge); 'the most virile public woman in the town' (Kettering).[103] When the Blackburn centre leader became a JP in 1946 the local newspaper reported that she worked a seventy-hour week:

probably the busiest woman in Blackburn... Mrs Leach has led the town's WVS—a full time job in itself—since 1939. She is a keen worker for the Rotary movement; she takes an active interest in her husband's large business; she controls a not inconsiderable household; and she is at the beck and call of all charities.

When, four years later, she died after refusing medical orders to give up some of her work, her husband wrote to Lady Reading: 'She gave her life for the service of the people... It is a great consolation to know her work for the town of Blackburn has been appreciated and recognised by all shades of opinion, irrespective of politics and religion.'[104] The leading figures were not always so obvious. In Grimsby the regional organizer suspected that the gossip columnist on the local newspaper might prove to be the key to breaking though the general apathy and 'mak[ing] volunteering fashionable'. She had already founded both the local women's luncheon club and the Townswomen's Guild, and was later, on her own account, to take the lead in setting up the local Soroptimists.[105]

According to the appointments recorded in the Executive Minutes the major associational sources of WVS leadership were the Girl Guides (87) and the WI (65). As the largest women's organisation in the country, the predominance of the WI is unsurprising. The prominence of the Girl Guides reflects the fact not only that it was one of the largest voluntary organizations in Britain but also that at a national level the Guides, together with the

[100] Report by Mrs Reid-Jamieson, 18 Jan. 1939, in WRVS, R4/1 Bedfordshire.
[101] Huxley to Mayoress, 9 Oct. 1939, in WRVS, R6/4 Southampton.
[102] Hornby, Report on Visit to Tynemouth, 11 July 1945, WRVS, R1/2 Tynemouth.
[103] WVS Executive, Minutes, 7 June 1938, 15 Feb., 1 Mar. 1939.
[104] Jack Leach to Lady Reading, 23 Aug. 1950, R10/2 Blackburn.
[105] M. E. Walker, Report, 16 Jan. 1939, R/3 Eastern Regional Office; D. Clapham to Miss Warner, 25 Nov. 1943, WF/K29 Grimsby.

WI, had formed the third leg of Lady Reading's initial mobilizing committee for evacuation. It may also be the case that women drawn to Guide leadership felt a special affinity with WVS since both organizations involved uniforms and a quasi-military system of internal hierarchy and discipline. The next most prominent organization, out of all proportion to its size, was Lady Reading's Personal Service League (49): clearly she was making full use of the network she already controlled. The other major feeder organizations had specialist relevance to ARP work, the Red Cross and St John's Ambulance (39), the Nursing Associations (24), and, perhaps, the women's sections of the British Legion (21). The West Midlands survey of 1942 shows a similar predominance of the WI (33), the Girl Guides (13), and the Red Cross and St John's Ambulance (18), although the Personal Service League does not appear to have been significant in the region. According to both sets of figures the two specifically urban associations most likely to provide WVS leaders were the National Council of Women and the Townswomen's Guilds: but in both cases the numbers were insignificant compared with the organizations already listed.[106]

These figures, however, do not discriminate between urban and rural areas. My own database of information about local WVS leaders throughout the period, compiled from a variety of sources, contains some details of the associational affiliations of seventy leading individuals from forty of the largest towns in England and Wales. Figures from this source confirm the importance of the Girl Guides (8) and the PSL (6) as recruiting grounds for urban leaders, although the Red Cross and St John Ambulance (4) and, of course, the WI (2) were less prominent. In these towns, however, the NCW was the single most important source of WVS leaders (9), flanked by the Women Citizens' Association (4) and the Soroptimists (4). The prominence of the NCW reflects its role as a co-ordinating body, a place where the more forceful public women could become known to the leaders of the whole range of women's associational life in the town. The NCW was particularly important in Yorkshire where it was primarily responsible for initiating WVS in at least six towns: Bradford, Bridlington, Halifax, Harrogate, Hull, and Leeds.[107] In Birkenhead, unusually, the Women Citizens' Association performed a similar function.[108] In a number of towns, including Hull, Portsmouth, and Stoke-on-Trent, the commitment of NCW

---

[106] National survey: NCW (15) and TG (14). West Midlands survey: NCW (4) and TG (4).

[107] It is possible that the NCW's influence in some of these northern towns was partly a function of the fact that the local middle class remained politically divided between Conservative and Liberals in a way that had largely ceased to be the case in the south. In circumstances of political division, as has been argued for the nineteenth century (R. J. Morris, *Class, Sect and Party: The Making of the British Middle Class, Leeds 1820–1850* (Manchester, 1990), 165–9), voluntary organizations may have been especially useful as a vehicle for middle-class unity. In southern towns the Conservative Party could more easily play this role.

[108] WVS Executive, Minutes, 30 Nov. 1938; Homer to Watson, 26 Apr. 1948, WF/I4.

women to WVS work led to the virtual suspension of NCW activity for the duration of the war.[109]

One organization, equally important in urban and rural areas, has so far been neglected—the Conservative Party, which liked to think of itself as 'the largest Voluntary Movement in the country'.[110] Fifty-one of the first 556 WVS appointments made in 1938–9 held office in the Conservative Party, and most of the 57 local councillors not identified politically, were probably also Conservatives. A further 15 leaders were married to local councillors. By contrast only 7 Labour activists were identified. The 1942 West Midlands survey of 300 leading personnel showed 35 people as having been involved in local politics, and of these only 2 were identified as Labour activists.[111] In the sample of forty large towns Conservative activists appear among WVS leaders even more prominently than members of the NCW.[112] Conservative women played a central role in establishing WVS not only in Tory strongholds like Blackpool or Tunbridge Wells, but also in many more mixed localities (Southampton, Guildford, Scunthorpe) and in towns where Labour dominated the local council (Ipswich, Sheffield).

In many ways the WVS provided an ideal outlet for Conservative Party energies, providing activists with a means of strengthening their claims to social leadership in an arena stretching far beyond the contours of political partisanship. WVS was a natural home for women like the Tory councillor who was 'leader of all women's activities in Wednesbury', or the chairman of the Glamorganshire Women's Conservative Association who, despite her political affiliation, 'works a great deal with all Sections and [in 1938] undertook to help organize Cardiff Rural District [for the WVS] because she had so many links with the working women in outlying districts.'[113] Conservatives had always understood the political advantages of being involved with the broader associational world. In 1939 the party's Women's Advisory Council received regular reports from representatives on the National Council of Women, the Women's Advisory Housing Council, the

[109] Kelsall, Voluntary Social Service in Hull, 10–11; Portsmouth NCW, Minutes, 21 May 1940, 7 June 1944, Portsmouth RO, 1168A/1/1; Staffordshire WVS Advisory Council, Minutes, 16 Nov. 1939 in WRVS, R/9/3 Staffordshire.
[110] Marjorie Maxse, addressing the Eastern Area Women's Advisory Committee, Minutes, 8 Nov. 1945, CPA, ARE 7/11/2.
[111] Only 7 of the 35 individuals involved are recorded as Conservatives, but that reflects the Conservative practice of keeping explicit partisan politics out of local government elections (Sample Analysis of Regional Appointments prepared by WVS for Mr Harry Hopkins).
[112] On the other hand only two of the many Tory Party women organizers thrown out of work when the party closed down its political work at the outbreak of war became WVS organizers (Unionist Women Organizers, *Wartime Newsheet*, 1 (Jan. 1940), CPA, CCO 170/2/3/2). This probably reflects the fact that they were mainly young women whose role had been organizing within the party, not making contact with outside organizations. They also needed paid employment.
[113] WVS Executive, Minutes, 14 Dec. 1938; E. Wade, Report on Visit to Barry, 2 Dec. 1938, WRVS, R8/8 Glamorganshire.

Maternal Welfare Committee and the League of Nations Union—as well as the WVS.[114] At least a third of the fifty-one Conservative women recruited as WVS leaders in the early months also held office in other organizations. Six of them ran the local PSL, and the remainder were spread evenly between the WI, Red Cross and St John's Ambulance, British Legion, Nursing Associations, Girl Guides, and a variety of hospital charities. Conservative Women's branches, which subsisted on a staple diet of fund-raising spiced by the occasional more-or-less political talk, regularly gave money to local charities as well as to party funds.[115] The 1938–9 annual disbursement of funds by Stanley Ward women's branch in Blackpool included the following items: Victoria Hospital (3 guineas (£3.15)); Social Service (2 guineas); Chief Constable Fund (1 guinea); Sick Poor (1 guinea); Blackpool Women's' Unionist Association (2 guineas).[116] Whether this was the normal order of priorities in women's branches the present research does not reveal. Apart from the occasional ball or garden fete the majority of such funds were raised by that most popular of middle-class leisure pursuits: the whist drive. The formulaic minute entered by the Stanley Ward secretary for each AGM from 1938 to 1940 read, with slight variations: 'A light supper and whist drive followed, and this ended a very pleasant evening.'[117] In Portsmouth the secretary of a women's branch measured the party's wartime decline by the number of tables she could expect to fill at a whist drive.[118] A 1937 headline in the *Surrey Weekly Press* succinctly described the Tory women of Guildford: 'Conservatives at Whist'.[119]

When war came Tory women had little difficulty transferring their attention from politics to social work. For the women of Stanley Ward (Blackpool), September 1939 and the blackout 'curtailed activities for a short period...[but] after the first big shock, we soon got down to rearranging our lives according to the changed circumstances'. The 'rearrangement' was not extensive: 'it was decided to carry on with the whist drives as usual, the proceeds to buy wool for knitting comforts, such as socks, scarves, gloves, and mittens for H M Forces.'[120] The Chairman of one ward branch in Southampton urged a similar continuity, maintaining the whist drives 'to help members forget their troubles...in the difficult times we were passing

---

[114] Central Women's Advisory Committee, Minutes, *passim* in CPA, Central WAC, CCO 170/1/1/1.
[115] See, for example, the minutes of the Shirley Ward Women's Conservative Association, Southampton RO.
[116] Stanley Ward No 1, Women Unionists, Minutes, 23 Feb. 1939, Lancashire RO, PLC/5/12/1.
[117] Stanley Ward No 1, Women Unionists, Minutes, *passim*, Lancashire RO, LC/5/12/1.
[118] Interview with secretary of Women's Conservative Association (n.d., 1941), in MO, TC 17/D.
[119] *Surrey Weekly Press* (19 Nov. 1937).
[120] Stanley Ward No 1, Women Unionists, Minutes, 28 Sept. 1939, Lancashire RO, LC/5/12/1. They also decided to keep up payments to their usual charities.

through'.[121] Alongside knitting and occasional talks on home front activities this proved sufficient to keep the branch active: political talks, however, were suspended indefinitely.[122] The same pattern of whist drives, donations to war charities, and knitting comforts for the troops is apparent wherever information on the activities of wartime women's branches survives—Redhill, West Bridgeford, Sheffield, and throughout the North West. In Liverpool most of the party's forty or so women's branches were organized 'in a scheme of working parties for knitted wear...'.[123]

The prevalence of such activities did not mean that Tory women confined their war work to activities organized by the party: far from it. Many women threw themselves into WVS and other war-related voluntary work.[124] Already in June 1939 women Tory Party organizers in Wessex, several of whom had joined the ATS, remarked that 'when we are not trying to persuade our Divisions to take an interest in politics in the intervals of ARP work, we ourselves are busy "forming threes"'.[125] In Redhill the pressure of WVS work had even led to the suspension of afternoon whist drives.[126] While encouraging such activity, party leaders worried about its impact on the party. With men disappearing into the forces, the survival of the party on the ground depended largely on the women, and sustaining a healthy Conservative Party machine was vital, they believed, not only for the future but also for the health of the home front in wartime.[127] Although Conservatives took the wartime political truce seriously, the abandonment of political propaganda was not intended to lead to the dissolution of party activity altogether. In October 1940 the Blackpool Conservative Association felt impelled to issue a circular spelling out the position:

With the advent of War the work and activities of our Association became National rather than Party and this change has given the impression to some of our supporters that our work as Conservatives is at an end until the conclusion of the war. This is a

---

[121] Shirley Ward Women's Conservative Association, Minutes, 20 Sept. 1940, Southampton RO.

[122] Ibid., 3 Nov. 1941.

[123] Redhill Women's Conservative Association, Sussex RO, 353/5/6/1; West Bridgeford Conservative Association, Minute book, 1937–1948, Nottinghamshire RO, DD PP2; Park Division Conservative Association, Minute book, Sheffield RO, LD 2210; North West Women's Advisory Council, Reports of Divisional Activities, 24 Sept. 1940, CPA, ARE 3/11/3.

[124] North West Area Women's Advisory Committee, General Purposes Committee, Minutes, 23 May and 22 June 1939; North West Women's Advisory Council, Reports of Divisional Activities, 24 Sept. 1940, CPA, ARE 3/11/3; Women who resigned office to take on WVS work were encouraged to keep in contact (Unionist Women Organizers, *Wartime Newsheet*, 1 (Jan. 1940), CPA, CCO 170/2/3/2).

[125] Unionist Women Organizers, *Second Newsletter* (June 1939), CPA, CCO 170/2/3/2.

[126] Redhill Women's Conservative Association, Minutes, 6 July 1939, Sussex RO, 353/5/6/1.

[127] West Midlands Women Organizers, Minutes, 17 May 1940, CPA, ARE 6/25/1; North West Area Women's Advisory Committee, Annual Report, 4 June 1940, CPA, ARE 3/11/1; Eastern Area Women's Advisory Committee, Minutes, 9 Sept. 1939, 18 Jan. 1940, CPA, ARE 7/11/2; Park Division Conservative Association Annual Report, 1941, Sheffield RO, LD 2210.

complete misunderstanding of the true position. The Conservative Party through its principles and programme has a responsibility to the Nation, both in war and peace. To weaken the organisation would be as great a dis-service to the National effort as to renounce its principles.[128]

In some areas the message was well understood. Conservatives in the South East launched a fund for Prisoners of War with the explicit object of encouraging dormant branches to revive 'by giving them some definite object for which to work'.[129] In the West Midlands, at the outbreak of war, the Tory agent, had tried, unsuccessfully, to persuade WVS to devolve certain tasks exclusively to Conservative Party branches as a means of keeping them together and active.[130] Even the most mundane work could be bent to partisan purposes, as Salford Tories discovered when Labour women turned up at their knitting parties![131] In Blackpool itself, however, the Association's pleas appear to have fallen on deaf ears. The secretary of the Stanley Ward branch had closed the Minute book in March 1940 with the following entry: 'All political work was suspended and the officials and committee decided to carry on under the name of the Ladies Benevolent Fund.'[132] When she received the Association's circular in October she did not act on it. Rather, with a thrifty eye on the wartime paper shortage, she turned the glossy paper over and used the back to draft an appeal for furniture, sheets, and blankets for WVS volunteers staffing her local First Aid Post.

The enthusiasm with which Tory women threw themselves into WVS was sometimes an embarrassment. At the outset Lady Reading, anticipating complications with Labour, had tried to keep the Conservative Party at arm's length.[133] But the determination of Tory women to serve their country was not to be frustrated, particularly when Labour hostility to ARP preparations leant an added charge of partisanship to their patriotism.[134] Regional organizers were under instructions to avoid putting well-known Tories in charge, but found that this was frequently unavoidable since no one else could be found to do the job.[135] Conservatives were not always sensitive to

[128] Stanley Ward No. 1, Women Unionists, Minutes, Lancashire RO, LC/5/12/1. When war broke out the Association had urged branches not to disband but to carry on 'in such modified form as will preserve the organisation without indulging in any work of Party propaganda'.
[129] South East Area Women's Advisory Committee Executive Minutes, 30 Dec. 1941, 19 May 1942, CPA, ARE 9/11/4.
[130] Fletcher-Moulton to Huxley, 30 Oct. 1939, in WRVS, V/101/38, Conservative Party.
[131] North West Women's Advisory Council, Reports of Divisional Activities, 24 Sept. 1940, and Annual Report, June 1941 in CPA, ARE 3/11/4.
[132] Stanley Ward No 1, Women Unionists, Minutes, 7 Mar. 1940, Lancashire RO, LC/5/12/1.
[133] WVS, Executive Committee, Minutes, 27 June 1938, 6 July 1938; Lady Reading, memo dated 23 June 1938 WRVS, V95/38, SJCIWO; Middleton to Home Secretary, 24 June 1938, PRO, HO 45 17580.
[134] Park Division Women's Conservative Association Executive, Minutes, 23 May 1938, Sheffield RO, LD 2216.
[135] Myers to Smieton, Apr. 1939, WRVS, R1 Regional Office; Dart to Witton Town Clerk, 30 Apr. 1940, WRVS, R10 Cumberland.

the WVS need to present a non-partisan face. In working-class Scunthorpe, for example, all three of the original WVS leaders were Tory activists. Under pressure from Tothill Street to invite non-Tory women into the leadership they protested that 'they had always worked together and would find an outsider difficult.' They also produced a letter from the Mayor—a wealthy landed aristocrat and former Tory MP—saying that so far as he was concerned their politics were irrelevant![136] Once war broke out such claims were rather easier to sustain. So long as the political truce continued, it was argued, there need be no contradiction between the non-partisan stance of WVS and the leading roles adopted by Tory women. When, in 1944, questions were raised about the position of the Darlington deputy leader, who had doubled as agent for the local Conservative Party throughout the war, Tothill Street ruled that there was no incompatibility between the two roles since the agent's work was essentially non-partisan, limited to organizing social events and undertaking individual case-work on behalf of the Tory MP.[137] The Sunderland organizer who ran WVS from the local Tory Party offices throughout the war, successfully resisting all attempts to move her to less obviously partisan premises, was only taking the same doctrine to its logical conclusion.[138] It was difficult for some Conservatives to perceive any distinction between partisanship and patriotism.

V

The search for 'a woman of standing who is already an acknowledged leader of the Borough' necessarily involved WVS organizers in soliciting suggestions about suitable people from the major associations, and their choice was normally endorsed by a meeting of all the local women's organizations. This did not, however, mean that she was elected. In some cases organizers spoke loosely of the local women's organizations electing the WVS leader, but no contests or voting occurred and the only person these meetings had the option of 'electing' was the regional organizer's nominee. However much 'standing' she had locally, the centre leader and her deputies held their posts at the discretion of the WVS hierarchy: the power to appoint (and the, not infrequently

[136] Reading to Walker, 23 Nov. 1938; report by Fletcher-Moulton on Scunthorpe, 2 Dec. 1938, WRVS, R/3 Eastern Regional Office; Fletcher-Moulton to Howat, 25 Nov. 1938, R3/5 Scunthorpe. The mayor, Sir Berkley Sheffield, had been the MP for Brigg in the 1920s. He owned 40,000 acres and was director of two railway companies. Eventually the Scunthope women agreed to the establishment of an Advisory Committee consisting of the mayor's wife and two Labour women, one of them the wife of the man selected as Labour candidate to succeed the sitting Labour MP. Subsequently one of the Tory women stepped aside to allow the Labour candidate's wife to become the deputy Centre Organizer.
[137] Muriel Borron to Lady Reading, 27 Apr. 1944; Huxley to Boron, 1 May 1944, in WRVS, R/1/2 Darlington.
[138] Vera Dart, report on Sunderland, 8 May 1944 and regional administrator's report, 8 Feb. 1945, WRVS, R1/2 Sunderland.

used, power to dismiss) belonged ultimately to Lady Reading alone. The same organizational philosophy which gave absolute power to Lady Reading also gave autocratic authority to the centre leader over her subordinates. While leaders were encouraged to hold regular meetings of their senior staff, any suggestion that they were formally accountable to such meetings was firmly resisted: in WVS accountability operated upwards, never downwards.[139] Nor did it operate sideways: local WVS leaders were not formally accountable to the wider associational world within which their legitimacy as social leaders had been shaped. In colonizing that world WVS sought to annex the 'standing' of its leaders while resisting the more or less democratic processes through which that standing had been achieved in the first place. The meetings of women's organizations at which WVS was launched were usually the last such meeting to be called, and regional organizers worked hard to prevent these meetings from imposing an ongoing structure of lateral accountability. In the succinct words of the regional organizer in the North West, repeated in her reports on the establishment of WVS in towns across Lancashire: 'No Committee. All power invested in the Centre Leader.'[140]

Given the tension between the hierarchical principles of WVS organization and the democratic instincts of much of the wider women's movement it is not surprising that organizers were not always able to prevent the appointment of committees. In Barrow, for example, a committee representative of most of the women's organizations in the town met monthly and exercised significant authority. In 1941 a newly appointed centre leader explained that WVS policy did not permit committees to instruct her what to do, adding, somewhat ambiguously, that she 'hoped that the present Advisory Council would continue to function as ably as in the past, with special direction of policy towards local affairs'. Soon after this the Minutes cease, presumably because, stripped of its authority, the committee itself had faded out.[141] In Blackpool, while the centre leader was given full power to act in an emergency, it was decided that in normal times she should be responsible to a Board of Directors representing sixteen women's organizations meeting, under her own chairmanship, once a month with the town clerk and other officials.[142] Preston WVS had a Consultative Committee whose brief was to inform local associations of the work of the WVS.[143] In Derby the centre

---

[139] Regional Organizer to Leach, 30 Jan. 1940, WRVS, R12/4 Surrey; 'Points from speech made by Miss Dart . . . ', 20 Jan. 1942, WRVS, R10/1 Cheshire.
[140] Miss D. Foster Jeffery, Regional Report, 24 Sept. 1938, WRVS, R/10/1
[141] Barrow WVS Committee, Minutes, 26 June 1941 and *passim*, Barrow RO, BDso/27/1.
[142] Regional Report, 24 Sept. 1938, WRVS, R10 North West Regional Office.
[143] Foster Jeffery to Gouldney, 11 Mar. 1941, WRVS, R/10/2 Preston; Foster Jeffery to Huxley, 23 May 1941, WRVS, R10 North West Regional Office. In 1941 this committee consisted of the Centre Organizer and her staff, representatives of the three political parties, with an Alderman, Mrs Pimblett, in the chair. Following the Tothill Street suggestion (see below) that meetings be held with other local organizations, the committee was dissolved and replaced by a Council of Voluntary Organisations, meeting three times a year.

leader was proud of the fact that, breaking down initial resistance among local voluntary organizations, she had established regular monthly meetings with them by the autumn of 1942.[144] Occasionally, as in Southampton, committees representative of the main local interests were encouraged to take responsibility when weak leaders or powerful local rivalries were disrupting WVS work.[145]

Early in 1941, responding to resentment among established organizations about the cliquishness of some centres, WVS asked centre leaders to consider convening regular meetings with local branches of organizations represented on the national Advisory Council.[146] The response was minimal. From Lancashire Vera Dart, the regional administrator, reported that meetings of this kind called in Manchester and Liverpool had gone much more smoothly than anticipated—so much so that she referred to them, cattily, as 'purring parties'. Leaders of other organizations, however, had better things to do than to stroke the backs of WVS organizers.[147] Such tokenism could not address the main source of hostility to WVS—not that in some places it belonged to a particular clique, but that, everywhere, it represented the importation of an undemocratic and hierarchical form of organization alien to the norms of much of the established women's movement. Because this new organization claimed a privileged role in relation to the management of relations between the local authority and the voluntary sector existing organizations could not be indifferent to it. The resulting conflicts and hostilities will be examined at length in later chapters. However deeply WVS was rooted in the world of women's associations, it seldom fitted smoothly into that world.

IV

While WVS sought its leading personnel in the associational world of the middle class, it did not confine its recruitment to women already active in public life. A report on wartime voluntary work in Bury characterized WVS as 'an organisation which takes in part-time married women who have only spasmodically, if at all before, been concerned with public life, and who emerge from comfort to respond to a national emergency'.[148] A middle-class volunteer in Worcester who had never previously undertaken any public work confessed herself amazed at 'how much of this sort of work one can fit in'.[149] In Bristol, according to WVS organizers, most of the members had not

---

[144] Lochrane to Lady Reading, 5 Sept. 1942 in WRVS, R3/1 Derby.
[145] On Southampton, see Ch. 4.
[146] WVS National Advisory Committee, Minutes, 15 Jan. 1941; WVS, Regional Administrators Conference, Minutes, 17 Jan. 1941.
[147] Vera Dart to Lady Reading, 5 July 1941, WRVS, R10 North West Regional Office.
[148] Report on Bury (n.d.), NCSRS, E2/26.
[149] D. Atkinson Report, 17 June 1940, MO TC 21/F Worcester.

previously undertaken any kind of social work and had been 'prepared to give up the care of their homes and their personal interests ... [only] because their country needs them'.[150] Even a hostile critic conceded in 1942 that 'a great many women owe to the WVS their first experience of the satisfaction of public service'.[151] Patriotism, the urge to do one's bit, was heightened by a desire to club together in order to assuage the private fears and anxieties of wartime. Nella Last, the Mass Observation diarist in Barrow, 'thanked God ... that I could work at the centre and keep back the bogeys that wait to pounce on mothers and wives ... When my sewing machine is whirring it seems to wrap me round with a rhythm, as music sometimes does, and keeps me from thinking about my [son] Cliff in the Machine Gun Corps.'[152] Knitting and needlework, the activities most frequently cited by women when asked about their hobbies, had normally been carried on in the isolation of the home.[153] The wartime proliferation of knitting circles making comforts for the troops had little to do with maximizing the efficiency of women's labour— the work could just as well have been done at home—than with meeting the therapeutic needs of the knitters. As one centre leader put it, echoing pre-war anxieties about 'suburban neurosis' as a disease afflicting middle-class womanhood, 'the mental health of our women is important. If they have no such communal work in these dark days to cheer them, there is little for them to do but sit at home, and "measure out their graves" in solitude.'[154] The wartime cult of 'cheerfulness' in face of adversity may be seen, alongside all the purposeful planning and tireless leadership offered by WVS leaders, as one means of coping with the mayhem and madness of a world at war.

People who joined for therapeutic reasons were likely to be looking for fellowship with women from similar backgrounds to themselves.[155] Much of the inner life of the WVS operated as a middle-class club. A Mass Observer's record of conversation among WVS helpers in Worcester included remarks about the dinners being served in the canteen being 'better, more varied and well planned, than their own children get at boarding school';

[150] Gwyneth Pritchard, report on voluntary social service in Bristol, Sept. 1942, 36, NCSRS, E2/2.
[151] 'Draft Report on WVS', 1942, 7, NCSRS, File 169.
[152] Richard Broad and Suzie Fleming (eds.), *Nella Last's War. A Mother's Diary, 1939–45* (Bristol, 1981), 50, 18.
[153] T. Cauter and J. S. Downham, *The Communication of Ideas. A Study of Contemporary Influences on Urban Life* (London, 1954), 84–7. Contrast Prochaska's view that the Mothers' Union declined as sewing retreated into the home with the spread of the sewing machine (Prochaska, 'A Mothers' Country', 398–9).
[154] Beaty to Smieton, 17 Jan. 1940, WRVS, R10/1 Cheshire. The centre organizer in Leicester made a very similar point (Mary Woodall to Miss Huxley, 1 Oct. 1939, WRVS, R3/2 Leicester). On 'suburban neurosis' see Stephen Taylor's article in the Lancet (26 Mar. 1938), repr. in J. Giles and T. Middleton, *Writing Englishness, 1900–1950. An Introductory Source Book on National Identity* (London, 1995), 230–9.
[155] Willmott and Young, *Family and Class in a London Suburb*, 96–8.

discussion over mid-morning coffee of 'the difficulty of getting good maids or cleaning women, and how they eat up their employer's sugar and butter, grumbled about the food they were given and generally complained about everything'; and arrangements being made by one woman 'for her maid to meet one of the other women's cook, and for them to go cycling together'.[156] Clearly, this was not a place where a working-class woman would have felt at home. Class mixing inside WVS was difficult for financial as well as for cultural reasons: they were, as one small boy evacuated from London put it: 'The bloomin women wot werk fer nuffin.'[157] WVS women might be proud of the fact that all the work was done voluntarily, with no payment of incidental expenses (bus fares, sewing materials, soap, cups of tea, etc.), but even a middle-class woman like Nella Last, whose husband kept a tight rein on the housekeeping money, could feel embarrassed by the spending expected of her.[158] Requiring members entitled to wear uniforms to pay for them was a further obstacle to working-class participation, at least at a leadership level.[159] The situation was made worse by the widespread practice of fund-raising amongst the volunteers. WVS policy was that 'no-one ought to be asked for money while on duty' but, in practice, it proved impossible to prevent members from collecting for their favourite charities, and many centre leaders allowed work parties to charge subscriptions or to run regular raffles to cover the costs of materials.[160] As one centre leader explained: 'the trouble really is that most ... are members of political organisations ... Women's Institutes, Townswomen's Guilds etc., most of whom exist only by raising money, and the members have got this germ in their blood!'[161] Barrow WVS was involved in fund-raising to an unusual degree and the centre leader apologized 'for these departures from our fixed orbits' pleading that the members wanted to engage in fund-raising activities: 'otherwise apathy would have resulted.'[162] The national leadership was

[156] D. Atkinson reports, 17, 20 June, MO TC 21/F Worcester; D. Atkinson report, 31 July 1940, MO TC 32/4/ I WVS.

[157] Miss Margaret Batt, memoir of her WVS work in Oxfordshire (n.d.), in WRVS, Histories: Regional (Box 205).

[158] Maise Thacker, memoir of WVS work in Coventry, 2 Jan. 1968, in Coventry RO, PA 705; DH interview with F60c at Moore House, Bethnal Green, 10 Aug. 1947 in MO Beveridge Social Services Survey, Box 2, File D; Broad and Fleming, *Nella Last's War*, 37–8.

[159] Letter from N. Kirkwood to Staffordshire Chronicle, n.d, Oct. 1940, in WRVS, R 9 Regional Office; and see discussion of this point in Ch. 2.

[160] WVS Chairman's Committee, Minutes, 14 Dec. 1942; at the Conservative Party Central Women's Advisory Committee, Lady Hillingdon was asked about WVS fundraising and replied that 'WVS not supposed to raise funds but it was difficult to make local members keep the rule', Minutes, 6 Feb. 1940, CPA, CCO 170/1/1/2; Dorman to Woollcombe, 14 July 1940, WRVS, R1/ 5 North Riding. Nella Last wrote that, 'with bus fares, cups of tea and raffles ... and all my little sundries for sewing' WVS cost her 5s. a week (Broad and Fleming, *Nella Last's War*, 38–9, 92).

[161] Reid to Huxley, 11 Mar. 1940, WRVS, R1 Regional Office.

[162] M. Diss, Barrow Narrative Report, Oct. 1943, WRVS. Barrow WVS Committee, Minutes, 4 Sept. 1939, Barrow RO, BDso/27/1.

understanding: 'members should not be denied their "bit of fun" when they
wanted to have whist drives...the encouragement of a corporate spirit was
to be desired.' However much such activities fostered the corporate spirit,
they also effectively increased the costs of membership. As Nella Last
remarked, even whist drives could operate as occasions for conspicuous
consumption: 'There usually seem to be a lot of people at these 2/6d dos
who think they are "getting among such *nice* people", and come dressed up
like plush horses and smelling like an Eastern bazaar...'.[163]

Most local WVS leaders were not greatly worried about these informal
exclusions of class. Apathy among middle-class women—'people with leisure in hand [who] owe the State some of their time and services'[164]—was to
be deplored. J. B. Priestley's broadcast attacks on 'ladies doing nothing in
inland resorts' were echoed by the *Daily Mail*, which ran stories about the
idle rich who evacuated themselves to the Lake District, painted their nails,
and sat around all day gossiping in cafés.[165] Lady Worsley, the WVS regional
administrator in the South East, was infuriated by the antisocial behaviour
of 'the true-to-type people who settle down in sea-side towns and just won't
lift a finger to help their fellow creatures, or their country'. When, with
invasion threatening in the summer of 1940, these people fled inland,
abandoning the tasks they had volunteered to undertake, they undermined
not only their country, but also the claims to social leadership of their class:
'it dements me', Lady Worsley continued, with more passion than grammar,
'that they should place a stigma on those who are understood by the mass of
people to be the same "class" [as ourselves].'[166] By contrast, little surprise
was expressed about the reluctance of working-class women to get involved
in voluntary work, since it was generally understood that such women were
either fully occupied in the home or, for financial reasons, unable to forgo
wartime opportunities to go out to work for good wages.[167] Social work was

---

[163] Broad and Fleming, *Nella Last's War*, 135.

[164] Analysis of May 1947 Directive, in MO, Beveridge Social Services Survey, 1942–7, Box 3.

[165] Note for Lady Reading on visit to Kendall, 5 Dec. 1940. WRVS, R10 Westmoreland;
Penny Summerfield, *Reconstructing Women's Wartime Lives* (Manchester, 1998), 163. For
similar anxieties, see Violet Markham to Lady Reading, 10 Sept. 1941: 'I hear on many sides
a good deal of uneasiness expressed about the sluggish response of many women to take up war
work especially among the upper and upper-middle classes. The women who are working work
like blacks but others, I am told, are not pulling their weight...I do not come across these
people personally and can only speak of them second hand, But I am bound to say the shops of
Oxford Street crowded out by well-to-do women of all ages have filled me with speculation...',
cited in Helen Jones, *Duty and Citizenship. The Correspondence and Parliamentary Papers of
Violet Markham, 1896–1953* (London, 1994), 164.

[166] Lady Alexandra Worsley, report of tour of East Kent coastal towns, 7 June 1940, in
WRVS, R5 Kent.

[167] Florence Ogden to Lady Reading, 6 Jan. 1944, WRVS, R10/2 Burnley; Vera Dart report,
25 May 1944, WRVS R1/5 Middlesbrough. The lower-middle-class Nella Last, however, was
offended by the conspicuous consumption of the wives of high-earning shipyard workers, which
contrasted painfully with her own need to count the pennies (Broad and Fleming, *Nella Last's
War*, 93, 216, 227).

for leisured women, not for hard-pressed working-class wives who fulfilled their duties at home or in paid employment. The female public sphere was imagined as a space inhabited more-or-less exclusively by middle-class women.[168] As the centre leader in Poole explained in January 1939:

The large majority of women here are either the very poor (who are, of course, out of the question) or the next class, of respectable working people—eager to help, but without the time or the capacity of rendering services which would be of any real value to the State...As I understand it, the women whom the WVS wishes to reach are the unoccupied people of the educated middle and upper classes, whose brains and bodies are trained, whose time is not always fully occupied, and who could if they chose render really valuable services to their country...[169]

This was an unusually explicit statement, but such assumptions were probably widespread. Left to themselves most local WVS leaders would have made little effort to extend the organization beyond the middle-class world in which it originated. Lady Reading, however, never left anyone to themselves, and she was determined from the outset to integrate working-class housewives into her organization. The efforts made by WVS organizers to bridge the very separate worlds of middle-class and working-class women throw further light on the operations of class in mid-twentieth-century towns.

[168] Eileen and Stephen Yeo have commented acidly on the invisibility of working-class female networks, and the inability of middle-class observers to accord them any moral or spiritual status, until they were 'discovered' by Institute of Community Studies in the 1950s (Eileen Yeo and Stephen Yeo, 'On the Uses of "Community": from Owenism to the Present', in S. Yeo (ed.), *New Views of Co-operation* (London, 1988), 241–2).

[169] Bertha Devenish, OBE, to Lady Reading, 19 Jan. 1939, WRVS, R6/3, Dorset.

4

Integrating the Working Class

The first obstacle to Lady Reading's desire to involve working-class women in WVS was the open hostility of both major labour movement organizations recruiting among housewives—the Women's Co-operative Guild (WCG) and the women's sections of the Labour Party. Founded in 1883, the WCG had shared in the rapid growth of the inter-war women's movement, reaching a peak of 87,000 members in 1939.[1] During the same years twice as many women had joined the Labour Party, which claimed 178,000 women members by 1938, most of them organized in separate women's sections.[2] National co-ordination was provided by the Standing Joint Committee of Working Women's Organisations (SJC), which also represented the TUC Women's Advisory Committee, trade unions organizing women, and a variety of other organizations of the women's labour movement. With Mary Sutherland, the Labour Party's Chief Woman Officer, acting as its full-time secretary, the SJC operated effectively under Labour Party control.

Lady Reading originally intended to preserve the non-partisan stance of WVS by not involving any of the political parties on her Advisory Council, so she invited representation from the WCG and the TUC Women's Advisory Committee, but not the Labour Party.[3] In June 1938, however, the SJC let it be known that none of their affiliates would consider coming in unless the Government made a formal approach to the Labour Party. This forced Reading to invite the other political parties to co-operate formally as well.[4] The Labour women remained suspicious. Was WVS intended to ease the way to military conscription by drawing up lists of volunteers to fill the gaps? Would participation mean endorsing Government ARP policy— widely attacked for its failure to plan deep shelters for the civilian population? The major concern, however, lay with the implications of the new organization for the relations between voluntary work and the statutory

[1] Jean Gaffin and David Thoms, *Caring and Sharing. The Centenary History of the Co-operative Women's Guild* (Manchester, 1983), 89.
[2] Pamela M. Graves, *Labour Women. Women in British Working-class Politics, 1918–1939* (Cambridge, 1994), 212–13.
[3] 'A note on the approach by WVS to organisations representing working women', n.d. (1938), PRO, HO 45 17580.
[4] WVS, Executive Committee, Minutes, 27 June 1938, 6 July 1938; Lady Reading, memo dated 23 June 1938 WRVS, V95/38, SJC; Middleton to Home Secretary, 24 June 1938, PRO HO 45 17580.

authorities. If the Home Office was to fund the central apparatus of WVS, was the Home Secretary answerable in the House of Commons for its activities? Was WVS a voluntary organization or a quasi-governmental one? Was WVS simply going to recruit voluntary workers for ARP services organized by the local authorities, or would it take over some of the organizing itself? How was overlapping going to be avoided between local authority provision for ARP and the work of the WVS?[5]

Until WVS was up and running no one really knew the answers to these questions, and the constitutional issues were always to remain ambiguous. The Home Secretary, Samuel Hoare, meeting a deputation of Labour women in July 1938, offered what reassurances he could and pleaded for flexibility in allowing what was, after all, an improvisation to meet an emergency to find its own *modus vivendi* with the statutory authorities, local and national.[6] Unimpressed, the SJC finally decided on the eve of the Munich crisis to have nothing to do with WVS:

responsibility for ARP should be wholly with the Local Authorities which are subject to proper public control, and . . . the existence of a voluntary organisation with its own offices, staff, etc., . . . must lead to overlapping and confusion and perhaps to the transfer of functions, which should be the responsibility of a publicly elected authority, to a private organisation.[7]

Both Mary Agnes Hamilton and Barbara Ayrton Gould, leading middle-class Labour women sympathetic to WVS, told Lady Reading that the chief obstacle was the strong feeling among Labour women in northern industrial towns that local authorities, not voluntary organizations, were the proper agencies to deal with ARP.[8]

Beyond the constitutional matters, two deeper issues underlay the SJC decision. The foreign policy of the Chamberlain Government was widely detested in the labour movement. While few denied the need to make preparations to protect the civilian population against air raids, and the SJC advised Labour women to participate in local authority schemes,[9] any active co-operation with the Government could be seen as tacit endorsement of its wider policies. The decision on WVS was thus symptomatic of an

[5] Lady Reading, memo dated 13 June 1938 WRVS, V95/38, SJC; briefing note (unsigned), 13 July 1938, PRO, HO 45 17580; 'Report of Deputation to Home Secretary from the Labour Party Executive', 14 July 1938, in WRVS, V95/38, SJC; Women's Co-operative Guild, Central Committee, Minutes, 19 June 1938.
[6] 'Report of Deputation to Home Secretary from the Labour Party Executive', 14 July 1938 in WRVS, V95/38, SJC
[7] Sutherland to Hoare, 16 Sept. 1938, WRVS, V95/38, SJC. See also Herbert Morrison cited in T. J. Crosby, *The Impact of Civilian Evacuation in the Second World War* (London, 1986), 18.
[8] Hamilton to Reading, 24 Sept. 1938 and Ayrton Gould to Reading, 25 July 1939, WRVS, V95/38, SJC.
[9] Sutherland to Hoare, 16 Sept. 1938, WRVS, V95/38, SJC.

oppositional mentality that continued to prevent the labour movement from exploiting the political opportunities of participation in 'national unity' until war actually broke out.[10] Abstention prevented Labour women from having any input into shaping WVS during its formative months. However, it may well not have occurred to them that such an intervention was possible. Labour women, remarked one activist looking back from 1948, had been 'rightly suspicious of "voluntary work", which was [before the war] almost entirely carried on by those politically hostile to the Party and was largely exploited for their political ends.'[11] The refusal of the Labour Party in Sheffield to join WVS at its launch in March 1939 reflected not only hostility to the Chamberlain Government but also a rejection of the leadership claims of the middle-class women's organizations involved: 'we do not consider that any useful purpose can be served by appeals by people so completely divorced from the real life and interests of the working people'.[12] In pre-war Coventry WVS was seen by working women as 'a snob show': in Plymouth as 'a snob organization'.[13] Not yet ready to assert their own claims to leadership in a nation united by war, the SJC chose abstention as the best way of preserving the independence of their affiliated organizations, and of defending the autonomy of Labour local authorities against officious offers of help from political opponents thinly disguised (as the Labour women saw it) as disinterested volunteers. At the root of the SJC decision was an abiding hostility to Lady Bountiful, an identification of voluntary work as a strategy pursued by upper- and middle-class women, and by Tory women in particular, to sustain their social and political leadership. Such attitudes were reflected in the often hostile relationships between Labour councillors and the voluntary sector.[14]

Working women's organizations had good reason to avoid contact with the associational world of middle-class women. During the pre-1914 struggle for the suffrage the existence of a common feminist goal had sometimes made it possible for middle-class and working-class women to work together: there had even, briefly, been a formal alliance between the Labour Party and the predominantly middle-class women of the National Union of Women's Suffrage Societies.[15] Once the vote was won, however, feminist transcendence of class differences became more problematic. The collapse of the Liberal Party,

[10] Cf. J. Hinton, *Protests and Visions. Peace Politics in Twentieth-Century Britain* (London, 1989), 114–15.

[11] Joan Bourne, 'For the Community', *Labour Woman* (Feb. 1948).

[12] Mrs Florence Roebuck to WVS HQ, 9 Mar. 1939, WRVS, R 2/2, Sheffield.

[13] Fletcher Moulton, Report on Warwickshire, 8 July 1938, WRVS, R9 Midland's Regional Office; Tomkinson to Huxley, 10 Mar. 1939, WRVS, R 7/2 Plymouth.

[14] A. F. C. Bourdillon (ed.), *Voluntary Social Services. Their Place in the Modern State* (London, 1945), 19–20, 132, 256.

[15] S. Holton, *Feminism and Democracy: Women's Suffrage and Reform Politics in Britain, 1900–1918* (Cambridge, 1987); Graves, *Labour Women*, 7, 10–11.

the rise of a class-conscious Labour Party, and a Conservative electoral strategy which depended on representing Labour as the enemy within all served to reinforce the disinclination of Labour Women to co-operate with middle-class organizations. While Conservative women sought to reinforce their claims to social leadership by active participation in the burgeoning non-partisan women's movement, Labour women, by contrast, tended to pull up the drawbridge, pursuing political power through the expansion of numbers within strictly policed boundaries of party and class.[16] While rules laid down nationally against associating with middle-class organizations were sometimes disregarded at local level, the fundamental mismatch between the different ways of handling the relationship between partisan identity and associational life bedevilled attempts at co-ordination within the women's movement locally as well as nationally.

Reinforcing these party political developments, shifts in the discourse of feminism reduced its capacity to withstand the claims of class, as against gender, interests. The 'new feminism' of the post-war years played down issues of individual rights and patriarchal oppression within the family in favour of a stress on the need for the state to meet the welfare needs of mothers and children. During the 1920s Labour women had retreated from feminist demands on family allowances in the face of determined male opposition in the labour movement. Turning their backs on a sexual politics that might threaten the unity of the working-class movement, Labour women concentrated on pursuing the implementation of maternalist legislation, much of it permissive, by local authorities. Around such issues as maternity and infant welfare clinics, public baths and wash houses, libraries and secondary school scholarships women did much during the inter-war years to transform the Labour Party, adding a broad agenda of welfare reform to its pre-1914 origins in narrowly trade union concerns. By the 1930s Labour women had established a significant presence in local government, as elected councillors, co-optees on committees dealing with 'women's issues' or lobbyists for women's interests. Historians have disagreed both about the degree to which inter-war Labour women subordinated gender to class interests and about their wisdom in so doing. What is clear, however, is that the expansion of the female public sphere during these years was not accompanied by any significant narrowing of the gap between its middle-class and working-class component parts.[17]

[16] Graves, *Labour Women*, 120 and *passim*; Brian Harrison, *Prudent Revolutionaries. Portraits of British Feminists between the Wars* (Oxford, 1987), 146–9; Harold Smith, 'Sex vs Class: British Feminists and the Labour Movement, 1918–1939', *Historian*, 47 (1984); Gillian Scott, *Feminism and the Politics of Working Women. The Women's Co-operative Guild from the 1880s to the Second World War* (London, 1998).

[17] Graves, *Labour Women*; Scott, *Women's Co-operative Guild*; Susan Pedersen, *Family. Dependence and the Origins of the Welfare State. Britain and France, 1914–1945* (Cambridge, 1993); Olive Banks, *The Politics of British Feminism, 1918–1970* (Aldershot, 1993); Mike

The lines between working-class politics and middle-class feminism were never completely blocked. There were always a few (mainly middle-class) Labour women who worked with the advocates of equal rights feminism in Lady Rhondda's Six Points Group. From the late 1920s, however, bitter disagreement over the rights and wrongs of discriminatory legislation protecting women in the workplace had helped to turn 'feminism' into a derogatory term amongst Labour women.[18] Labour women's hostility was not confined to equal rights feminists. They were just as disinclined to co-operate with mass non-feminist organizations like the WI and the TG which broadly shared their maternalist outlook. As Brian Harrison has pointed out: 'no unbridgeable gulf on attitudes to women's family role separated the "welfare feminists" on the left from the more traditionalist attitudes to family on the right.'[19] It was class, not ideology, that divided them. The SJC's description of itself as the organization of 'working women', served to stigmatize the typical member of the middle-class organizations as an idle woman, freed by affluence and the labours of her domestic servants to interfere in lives which her very comfort prevented her from comprehending.

The refusal of Labour women to join the National Council of Women or to co-operate in broad campaigns initiated by middle-class women even when it shared their objectives reflected their determination to throw off the patronage of their middle-class 'sisters'.[20] Generations of working-class women had been subject to often arrogant interference from middle-class social workers.[21] The Labour MP Ellen Wilkinson cited 'vague but rather

Savage, *The Dynamics of Working-Class Politics. The Labour Movement in Preston, 1880–1940* (Cambridge, 1987); Martin Pugh, *Women and the Women's Movement in Britain, 1914–1959* (London, 1992); Pat Thane, 'Visions of Gender in the Making of the British Welfare State: The Case of women in the British Labour Party and Social Policy, 1906–1945', in G. Bock and P. Thane (eds.), *Maternity and Gender Politics. Women and the Rise of the European Welfare States, 1880s-1950s* (London, 1991), 93–118; Pat Thane, 'The Women of the British Labour Party and Feminism, 1906–1945', in H. L. Smith (ed.), *British Feminism in the Twentieth Century* (Aldershot, 1990); J. Mark-Lawson, M. Savage, and A. Warde, 'Gender and Local Politics: Struggles over Welfare, 1918–1939', in L. Murgatroyd, M. Savage, J. Urry, and S. Walby (eds.), *Localities, Class and Gender* (London, 1985).

[18] Graves, *Labour Women*, 138, 223; Banks, *Politics of British Feminism*, 120–1, 145, 147.
[19] Harrison, *Prudent Revolutionaries*, 149.
[20] Banks, *Politics of British Feminism*, 31; Pugh, *Women and the Women's Movement*, 69. In 1938, for example, the WCG refused a NCW request for help in campaigning over abortion (WCG Central Committee, Minutes, 19–20 Jan. 1938).
[21] Graves, *Labour Women*, 125; Ann Summers, 'A Home from Home—Women's Philanthropic Work in the Nineteenth Century', in S. Burman (ed.), *Fit Work for Women* (London, 1979); Ellen Ross, *Love and Toil. Motherhood in Outcast London, 1870–1918* (Oxford, 1993); ead., 'Good and Bad Mothers: Lady Philanthropists and London Housewives before the First World War', in K. D. McCarthy (ed.), *Lady Bountiful Revisited: Women, Philanthropy, and Power* (Piscotaway, NJ, 1990); Susan Pederson, 'Gender, Welfare and Citizenship in Britain during the Great War', *American Historical Review*, 94 (1990), 992–3; Jane Lewis, 'The Working-class Wife and Mother and State Intervention', in Lewis (ed.), *Labour and Love. Women's Experience of Home and Family, 1850–1940* (Oxford, 1986).

dreadful memories' of the activities of middle-class social workers during the First World War as one reason for her suspicion of WVS.[22] While many ordinary working-class women might be ready to accept charity at the price of being demeaned by its delivery, resistance to the operations of middle-class social leadership lay at the core of the political identity of working-class Labour activists. It is difficult to exaggerate the hatred with which Labour women viewed philanthropy and the *de haute en bas* condescension involved.[23] This is not to say that Labour women lacked philanthropic feelings of their own. The mutually supportive mechanisms of kinship and neighbourhood networks were central to the lives of working-class women, and Labour women might well explain their own socialism in essentially philanthropic terms.[24] In the WCG southern branches collected money and clothes for miners' families in the late 1920s, and occasionally Labour women even set up welfare organizations staffed by voluntary labour.[25] But 'voluntary work' was something else: along with 'feminism' it had come to be identified as the property of overbearing middle-class women whose claims to social leadership the women's labour movement existed to contest.

Working-class women entered this contest with many disadvantages, lacking not only the time and money available to their social superiors but also education and access to established networks of influence. There were, of course, some middle-class women within the labour movement, and they tended to fill a disproportionate number of leadership posts.[26] While Labour Party women officially expressed pride in their capacity to incorporate middle-class recruits, such recruits might well have to cope with currents of hostility to their incursions from working-class activists struggling to construct an autonomous public sphere in which they could develop their skills independent from middle-class tutelage.[27] Within the Labour Party such tutelage was not as yet a major threat: during the inter-war years the numbers of middle-class women prepared to identify with Labour remained

---

[22] 'Report of Deputation to Home Secretary from the Labour Party Executive', 14 July 1938, 16, WRVS, V95/38, SJC.

[23] Pederson, 'Gender, Welfare and Citizenship', 993–5; Brian Harrison, *Peaceable Kingdom* (Oxford, 1982), 247; R. Crossman, 'The Role of the Volunteer in the Modern Social Service', in A. H. Halsey (ed.), *Traditions of Social Policy: Essays in Honour of Violet Butler* (Oxford, 1976), 264; Margaret Brasnett, *Voluntary Social Action. A History of the National Council of Social Service, 1919–1969* (London, 1969), 53, 61–3.

[24] Graves, *Labour Women*, 46, 49, 54, 136. There are some suggestive remarks to this effect in R. Samuel, 'The Middle Class in Britain Between the Wars', *New Socialist* (Mar.–Apr. 1983), 32.

[25] Gaffin and Thoms, *Caring and Sharing*, 104; Thane, 'Visions of Gender', 101.

[26] A. H. Birch, *Small-Town Politics. A Study of Political Life in Glossop* (Oxford, 1959), 61, 67.

[27] Graves, *Labour Women*, 165, 57–9; M. Stacey, *Tradition and Change: A Study of Banbury* (Oxford, 1960), 161–2; Thane, 'Women of the British Labour Party', 126, 130–1.

Part I

small enough to prevent any significant encroachment on the autonomy of working-class activists. For the Women's Co-operative Guild, however, the erection of defensive walls against unwelcome intruders became a major concern. The achievement of the upper-middle-class founder of the WCG, Margaret Lewellyn Davis, in constructing a genuinely independent and self-regulating organization in which working-class women could socialize, educate themselves, and establish the basis for effective interventions in the wider society, owed much to her unusual combination of personal charisma and the sensitivity necessary to foster self-reliance among the working-class membership. Equally important to the ethos of the pre-1914 WCG, however, was the context of a wider feminist movement not yet fractured by the polarization of partisan identities on class lines. Davis' inter-war successors were working-class women, committed to linking the WCG firmly into the Labour Party's political advance. While membership remained open to any woman member of the retail co-operative movement, the rules were changed to exclude from office women who did not support the Labour or Co-operative Parties.[28] In some areas Conservatives had made concerted efforts to gain support in the WCG and enforcement of these rules in the late 1930s led to major ructions in Plymouth where Lady Astor had a substantial following in the Guild.[29] The leadership was equally suspicious of penetration by members of the non-partisan women's movement, deploring office-holding by members of the TG, WI, or the National Council of Women: to their regret the rules did not allow them to exclude these interlopers.[30] They were, however, able to invoke a rule first adopted in the 1920s excluding from office any woman whose husband's occupation (shopkeeper, insurance agent, etc.) placed him in competition with the local Co-operative Society—a vivid illustration of the precedence given to class over gender by some labour women in the inter-war years.[31] The degree to which the WCG held itself aloof is illustrated by the fact that in 1938 the Doncaster Guild felt it

---

[28] Scott, *Women's Co-operative Guild*, 193, 197.

[29] Blackpool Divisional Conservative and Unionist Association, Minutes, 2 June 1938, Lancashire RO, PLC 5/1/3; Meetings of Conservative Members of Blackpool Council, Minutes, 1 Apr. 1946, Lancashire RO, PLC 5/2/1.The enthusiasm with which the Tory agent for Bolton promoted this tactic inspired one of her fellow agents to verse: Mrs Kay | Has her own way | So the Bolton Co-op | Is her favourite shop (*Women Organisers Newsheet* (1939), CPA, CCO 170/2/3/2). During the war Mrs Kay became the local WVS organizer. On Plymouth, see Scott, *Women's Co-operative Guild*, 205; Gaffin and Thoms (1983), *Caring and Sharing*, 87.

[30] Scott, *Women's Co-operative Guild*, 203, 205, 208; WCG Central Committee, Minutes, 22 Jan. 1941, 16 Dec. 1941.

[31] Scott, *Women's Co-operative Guild*, 197 cites a contemporary protest that the WCG 'was not an organisation of employees wives, but a body of women who were free to work out their own destinies apart from their husbands'. The rule remained controversial and its enforcement became something of an embarrassment. Following a particularly difficult case in Hertfordshire, the Central Council agreed to suspend it for the duration of the war (WCG Central Committee, Minutes, 13 Aug. 1940, 11 Mar. 1941, 25 Sept. 1941).

necessary to ask whether it was permissible for them to participate in a local Cancer Campaign.[32]

The only issue sufficiently compelling in the 1930s to transcend these hardening boundaries of class was peace, a cause into which much of the energy of pre-1914 feminism had been channelled by the ghastly experiences of the Great War. In the League of Nations Union, in local Peace Committees, and in the pacifist Peace Pledge Union Labour women worked side-by side with middle-class campaigners, many of them Liberals.[33] The belief that women had a special role in resisting war transcended class and partisan divisions. This, however, was of little help to WVS in its efforts to mobilize women to cope with the effects of a new war. Sensitive to the identification between women and peace, WVS was keen to stress that making preparations to defend women and children against bombs and gas did not mean accepting the inevitability of war. Faced with pacifist opposition from the Labour women of Nelson, the local organizer was advised to stress 'that Air Raid Precautions are in no way opposed to Pacificism [sic]...the fact of the horrors of war being explained to the masses of the population should make people less anxious, not more anxious, to embark on war.'[34] In December 1938 the secretary of Watford WVS put up a large poster asking 'Which do you prefer? Panic, Ruin, Agony or Join the ARP and Retain Peace'.[35] On one occasion Lady Reading even went so far as to claim that: 'WVS came into being as an expression of the desire of women to preserve peace.'[36] Many found this message unconvincing. Dorothy Bates, who attended the inaugural rally of WVS in Leicester shortly after the Munich settlement, subsequently wrote to the local paper deploring the fact that women's energies should be diverted from preventing war into coping with its effects:

Do those splendid women who are giving of their time and energy to the organisation of the WVS really believe that England's greatness in the future will be reckoned by the number of bombs which her children are steeled to withstand?...I refuse to accept this...Where is the leader of the mass of women who would gladly sacrifice ...not just leisure but all they hold dear for peace?[37]

[32] WCG Central Committee, Minutes, 15 Mar. 1938.
[33] Graves, *Labour Women*, 120–1; Jill Liddington, *The Long Road to Greenham. Feminism and Anti-Militarism in Britain since 1820* (London, 1989), 152 ff.
[34] Vera Dart to Mrs Parker, 12 Jan. 1939, WRVS, R10/2 Lancashire.
[35] Photograph in WRVS, R4/4 Hertfordshire.
[36] Lady Reading, telegram to the King, 3 Sept. 1939, WRVS, R1 Regional Office. See also 'The Women's Side of ARP', WRVS, R3/2 Leicester.
[37] *Leicester Mercury* (29 Oct. 1938). This letter followed a similar line of argument to that presented by Women's International League of Peace and Freedom in leaflets handed out at WVS meetings, opposing ARP as an attempt 'to enrol the private citizen in the military machine in time of peace' which would 'squander the soul of a generation in a maze of ineffective air raid precautions', and lead a whole generation of children to assume that war was inevitable, thereby undermining the slow growth of genuine internationalism which alone could guarantee the preservation of peace in the long term. WRVS, R4/1 Bedfordshire.

Two years later, having, like so many pacifists, finally accepted that a repetition of the 1914–18 disaster could not be avoided, Mrs Bates was leading the WVS in Leicester. The fact that she was both a Labour Party activist and middle-class provides a clue to the ways in which WVS succeeded in overcoming some of the partisan and class divisions which had fractured the women's movement during the inter-war years.

II

Despite the SJC's 1938 decision not to co-operate, Lady Reading remained confident that the setback would only be temporary. The Labour leaders, she believed, did not speak for the mass of ordinary working-class women.[38] This view was confirmed by Sylvia Vachell, the South Wales organizer whose predecessor had resigned following the SJC decision not to co-operate on the grounds that without Labour support it would be impossible to build WVS in an area dominated by working-class institutions. In December 1938 Vachell reported from Glamorgan that: 'the trouble only arises with the executive officials; the women, for instance, in the co-operative guilds enrol with us and obviously cannot see why there need be this position.'[39] Although a few Labour women already involved in WVS found themselves under pressure to withdraw, the trend was clearly in the other direction.[40] As early as March 1939 it was reported that leading members of the SJC, aware that many local Labour Parties were co-operating with WVS, were already regretting their refusal to join the Advisory Council.[41] Once war broke out, bringing a further influx of Labour women into WVS, it was only a matter of time before the SJC regularized the position. By December 1939 Ellen Wilkinson had changed her mind (although she still objected to the rule of unpaid upper-class women at Tothill Street[42]) and in January 1940 the SJC agreed to come in. The WCG, however, continued to hold aloof.[43]

---

[38]   Smieton to Hutchinson, 19 Sept. 1938, WRVS, V/95/38 SJC.

[39]   Report on Glamorgan, Dec. 1938, WRVS, R8 Welsh Regional Office.

[40]   In December 1938, for example, the East Midlands organizer reported that she had spent the afternoon 'finishing up the conquest of the Women's Co-operative Guild' in Leicester, getting over 60 volunteers from the meeting (Walker, Report, 10 Dec. 1938, WRVS, R3 East Midlands Regional Office). For an example of Labour women being pressured to abandon WVS, see Wilson to Myers, 28 Mar. 1939, WRVS, R1 North East Regional Office.

[41]   Priscilla Norman reporting on a conversation with Mrs L'Estrange Malone on 22 Mar. 1939, WRVS, V/95/38 SJC.

[42]   Note on meeting between Lady Reading and Ellen Wilkinson, 2 Dec. 1939, WRVS, V/113/38 Ellen Wilkinson; WVS Chairman's Committee, Minutes, 6 Dec. 1939.

[43]   Sutherland to Reading, 18 Jan. 1940, Sutherland to Smieton, 1 Mar. 1940, WRVS, V/95/38 SJC; WVS Executive Committee, Minutes, 6 Mar. 1940; SJC Report to National Conference of Labour Women, Oct. 1940, TUC, 292 65.2/2; Sutherland in *Labour Woman* (Mar. 1941); WCG Central Committee, Minutes, 30 Apr. 1940.

During the late 1930s pacifism had become, for many of its leaders, the main *raison d'etre* of the WCG and they maintained a pacifist position throughout the Second World War.[44] While before the war pacifism acted, to some extent, as a bridge to the wider women's movement, in wartime pacifism and sectarianism worked together, isolating the WCG leadership not only from the wider movement but also from many of their own members. While not opposed to taking part in activities designed to protect the civilian population, the leadership's anxiety to defend the autonomy of the Guilds blocked full participation. Rather than attending classes organized by St John's Ambulance or the Red Cross, branches were instructed to arrange for First Aid Tutors to run special classes for their own members.[45] Already in February 1939 the Guild's refusal to nominate representatives to the regional evacuation committees was condemned by one dissident member as 'a policy of social suicide' which would cede opportunities for leadership to rival women's organizations.[46] Guild leaders responded to such complaints by establishing their own evacuation scheme, matching mothers who wanted to take their children out of the cities with potential hosts. Zealously embracing their own marginalization, they even discussed applying for official recognition under the same terms as had been granted to the Vegetarian Society. In practice only a handful of members responded, partly because many branches were already involved in the official scheme. When war broke out not a single evacuee was moved under Guild auspices.[47] During the war the abstentionist policy was eased and WCG members not only undertook their share of voluntary work but also served on many local emergency committees,[48] though participation in directly war-related activities like National Savings and Warship Weeks continued to be opposed.[49] So far as possible Guild autonomy was defended by setting up their own schemes—getting wool for knitting comforts for the troops directly from the Co-operative Wholesale Society for example, rather than through the WVS.[50] As late as October 1942 Mrs Cook, the General Secretary, advised Guild members running a Rest Centre in Stanwell not to enrol in WVS: 'The Guild can do its own public work.'[51] By that time, according to one estimate, 90 per cent of her members were 'furtively or

---

[44] Scott, *Women's Co-operative Guild*, 215–16, 220–3; Graves, *Labour Women*, 210–11; Liddington, *Long Road to Greenham*, 159–66; WCG Central Committee, Minutes, *passim*.

[45] WCG Central Committee, Minutes, 3 Apr. 1939.

[46] Scott, *Women's Co-operative Guild*, 220; WCG Central Committee, Minutes, 19 Sept. 1938. At same time Carlisle and Blackpool branches were refused permission to serve on local National Service committees (WCG Central Committee, Minutes, 11 Jan. 1939).

[47] WCG Central Committee, Minutes, 15 May 1939, 25 Sept. 1939.

[48] Ibid., 11 Mar. 1941, 23 Apr. 1941, 15 June 1941.

[49] Ibid., 15 June 1941, 11 Mar. 1942, 8 Mar. 1944.

[50] Ibid., 14 June 1944.

[51] Nanson to Sutherland, 15 Oct. 1942, WRVS, V/51/38 Women's Co-operative Guild.

openly engaged in some sort of war work', many of them in WVS.[52] Lady
Reading's policy of quietly waiting for circumstances to persuade Labour
women to come in was fully supported by Mary Sutherland, who advised
that, even had they wanted to, the WCG leadership would not have been
able to gain formal adhesion to WVS given the strength of pacifist feeling
within the Guilds.[53] By 1944 even the recalcitrant Mrs Cook was sitting on
the WVS Advisory Committee, although as a 'visitor' not a representative.[54]

In the London borough of Camberwell, where relations between the
Labour council and WVS had initially been frosty, a 1944 public meeting
cheered the Mayor's tribute to WVS: 'a crowd of interfering busy-bodies
who we are glad to have with us. The WVS has broken down nearly all the
class barriers of women's social strata.'[55] Glowing tributes of this kind—and
the example could easily be multiplied—indicate that the national unity of
wartime was a reality. Just as, in the 1930s, the anti-war movement could
mobilize emotions sufficiently powerful to overcome otherwise insuperable
differences, so the prosecution of war itself evoked deep currents of patriotism which united people across class and partisan boundaries. Patriotism,
however, is a protoplasmic thing. Its power lies not in displacing all other
agendas but precisely in its capacity to become the all-embracing discourse
within which sectional interests fight for influence. During the Second
World War abstention guaranteed marginality, but for those who participated, patriotism opened doors. Celebrations of wartime national unity, like
those voiced in Camberwell, should prompt in the historian not a weary
cynicism, but a dispassionate attempt to unpack the precise nature of the

---

[52] Scott, *Women's Co-operative Guild*, 221. It was reported from Staffordshire in 1942 that
most members of the WCG had either joined WVS or 'various working parties' (M. Forsyth
and M. Morris, Report on North Staffordshire, 30 May 1942, NCSRS, E2/34).

[53] Sutherland to Nanson, 19 Nov. 1942, WRVS, V/51/38 Women's Co-operative Guild.

[54] WVS Advisory Council, Minutes, 28 Jan. 1944. The WCG's most recent (and best)
historian has argued that the pacifist policy was largely responsible for the loss of 44% of the
membership between 1939 and 1943 (Scott, *Women's Co-operative Guild*, 222–3). This is what
the Communist Party, contesting the pacifist policy inside WCG from 1941, argued at the time
(Lesley Seyd, 'The Co-operative Women's Guild', *World News and Views* (16 June 1945)). Scott
(p. 220) exaggerates the democratic opportunity presented by WVS to WCG: 'It was envisaged
that women's groups would co-operate in the selection of representatives to work with the local
authorities in preparing [ARP] schemes . . .'. In fact Mary Sutherland may well have been closer
to the truth in telling WVS that the pacifist issue was so controversial within the WCG that a
more straightforward commitment to the war effort would have been at least as damaging
(Sutherland to Nanson, 19 Nov. 1942, WRVS, V/51/38 Women's Co-operative Guild). The
decline in membership was probably caused by the same wartime disruptions which undermined the Labour Party women's sections over this period, despite the Party's enthusiastic
embrace of the war effort (Labour Party, National Executive Committee, Minutes, 25 Mar.
1942, memo by the National Agent). Scott (pp. 5, 222) is misled in contrasting WCG decline
with 'mushroom growth' elsewhere. Far from growing, for example, the NUTG lost branches
during the first few years of the war (Elizabeth McCarty, 'Attitudes to Women and Domesticity
in England, circa 1939–1955', Oxford D.Phil., 1994, 305).

[55] *Elephant and Castle Gazette* (21 Jan. 1944), *South London Advertiser* (28 Jan. 1944), in
WRVS Press Cuttings.

compromises involved. Whatever transcendence had occurred it is evident that the 'class barriers of women's social strata' had not, in fact, disappeared. The primary question to ask about national unity is: 'national unity on whose terms'? Did the integration of working-class women into the world of voluntary work involve a democratizing shift towards a more equal citizenship? Or were working-class women brought in to WVS on terms which served more to sustain the social dominance of the middle class?

III

In 1942, according to Lady Reading, the vast majority of WVS members in the industrial areas were working-class wives.[56] Ten years later a sociological study concluded that working-class membership seldom exceeded 30 per cent.[57] Since middle-class membership probably held up better after the war, there is no necessary contradiction between these estimates.[58] While WVS were not permitted to encroach on the statutory duties of employers by organizing welfare or ARP work inside factories, many factory workers participated in WVS activities after work.[59] But it was among housewives that WVS was most successful in recruiting working-class women. Many volunteered to help out in rest centres for bombed-out people, to staff canteens or British Restaurants; to put in a few hours a week making camouflage netting. In many of these activities working-class and middle-class women worked alongside one another and, no doubt, many human lines were thrown across the class divide. Even hostile critics of WVS hierarchy sometimes conceded that 'there may in practice be a quite healthy democratic spirit present in the local unit.'[60] But friendliness was probably more commonly rooted in deference than in democracy. After the war Lady Reading assured the Labour Government that WVS enabled 'people of no substance...to contribute their mite alongside of the bigger gift with absolute equality'.[61] There is a telling tension here between the language of

[56] Lady Reading to Mrs Collingridge, 8 Dec. 1942, WRVS, R12/4 Surrey.
[57] R. C. Chambers, 'A Study of Three Voluntary Organisations', in D. V. Glass (ed.), *Social Mobility in Britain* (London, 1954), 392–3.
[58] Even in the 1950s the Home Office had to accept that WVS could never be used as a strike-breaking force because too many of the volunteers were married to trade unionists. Chief of Staff of Western Command to War Office, 3 Oct. 1952; Lady Reading, note on discussion with Home Secretary, 13 Jan. 1954, WRVS, A1/38.
[59] Charles Graves, *Women in Green. The Story of the Women's Voluntary Service* (London, 1948), 173. Industrial towns in which factory workers were active in WVS included Coventry, Leicester, St Helens, Warrington, Grimsby, Portsmouth, and Slough.
[60] Report on Leicester (n.d., 1942?), in NCSRS, E2/10.
[61] Lady Reading, 'Memo on Points Arising from Discussions between the NCSS and WVS' (n.d., late 1947), 3, WRVS AI/38, File 5; Chambers, 'Three Voluntary Organisations', 390; Reading to Perrot, 13 July 1938: 'As far as this organisation is concerned, we make no difference between East End and West End, between high and low, and we do not recognise any class distinction', WRVS, V32/38 St John's Ambulance.

social hierarchy ('no substance', 'their mite', 'the bigger gift') and a rather over-insistent egalitarianism ('absolute equality'). While Lady Reading argued, again somewhat patronizingly, that WVS was an emancipating experience for working-class women ('These small contributors gain self-reliance in time and become most worthwhile members of the community...'), Labour critics of WVS were often unconvinced. Before the war a heckler at a WVS meeting had complained about leading women 'who buzz around with an air of importance and are obviously going to be in a position to boss us around...'.[62] According to Labour women in Caerphilly, where WVS was run by middle-class Conservatives, such fears were fully realized during the war. They complained bitterly about the deference expected of them towards their social betters: 'if any of our Labour Women should join the WVS there is a spirit of antagonism against them unless they are prepared to accept a "Yes Attitude" toward the Leaders and this of course our women are not prepared to do.'[63] Many less politically conscious women were no doubt quite content to be 'yes women', accepting the patronage of their betters.

One response to proximity was informal segregation. In some canteens shift systems were organized so that friends could work together, allowing, as one participant noted, 'a subtle distinction of class... without any feelings being hurt.'[64] A more obvious segregation was recorded by a Mass Observer describing a WVS sewing party in an East Coast village:

About 15 women are knitting or sewing garments for the Forces. Ten of these are Class D... mostly the wives of fishermen... They are very neatly dressed... mostly in black or dark blue hats and coats... Nearly all have put on a necklace or bracelet. The ten Class D women are at a long table conversing in low voices. The remaining Class B members are at a smaller table. [*When the observer arrives the elderly vicar's wife who is in charge guides her to the smaller table.*] Two women from the long table go to make tea. They do so very quietly and bring round trays almost without speaking. [*At the end of the session*] 'class D are smiling warmly and walk out slowly all together in a bunch.' [*Meanwhile, Class B go off to find their cars.*][65]

---

[62] Graves, *Women in Green*, 28.
[63] Strutt to Reading, 3 Nov. 1945, WRVS, A1/38, File 4. In post-war Sidcup, however, it was a Labour candidate who used her position in the WVS to enhance her election prospects, appearing, much to Lady Reading's horror, on her election leaflet in her WVS uniform (Greaves to Reading, 19 Apr. 1948, Reading to George, 2 June 1948, WRVS R5/4).
[64] Kathleen Graham, 'A Survey of WVS and its Place in a Post-war World' (n.d.), 10, WRVS, Box 204: WVS Histories in Draft.
[65] Report by PC on WVS sewing party, 29 Aug. 1940, MO TC Women. Box 4, File 1. This was not a one-off: a later report on the same village (3 Oct. 1940) reads: 'As before there was a tendency for the B class members to make a group separately at a small table... tea was brought round by class D members walking soberly behind each other with tin trays.' In Dartford a separate ARP training course had to be set up in the autumn of 1938 because the well-to-do trades people—'the so-called "upper ten"'—refused to take classes alongside working women (Miss West, report on Soroptimists lunch at Dartford, 23 Sept. 1938, WRVS, R5 Kent).

In one case, it was alleged, WVS members were being sent to do private domestic work for friends of the organizer.[66]

The most effective way in which WVS brought working-class wives into voluntary work was through Housewives Service—a street-by-street organization designed to enable women to contribute without leaving their own homes. Working closely with the air raid wardens, Housewives undertook 'the detail work, work which does not come within the province of a man, but which is a woman's speciality.'[67] They provided first port of call for the homeless and the wounded; made tea for emergency workers; assisted elderly neighbours or the children of working mothers to the public shelter where they helped to allay panic by organizing community singing and children's games. As the blitz intensified in September 1940, WVS explained that through Housewives Service 'a woman can offer to the community all the gifts, experience, common-sense, which she has hitherto expended upon her home and family'. Even the housebound housewife could, in war conditions, fulfil the obligations of citizenship: 'The life of the Nation is distinctly the Housewife's province.'[68] Rather less portentously a Staffordshire member rhymed: 'H is the Housewife—let no one belittle her | She has her part to play in confounding Herr Hitler'.[69]

Many working-class housewives with neither the time nor the self-confidence to involve themselves in regular work outside the home could be coaxed to attend short training courses: although, it was reported from Salford, some 'hung back in the doorway', shy about appearing at a public lecture in their shawls.[70] WVS laid down a minimum training requirement of four ARP lectures, after which the Housewife qualified for membership of WVS and a blue card to display in the window of her house—'regarded as a national sign and valued as such'.[71] There was some confusion about the precise status of these 'members', and in some areas blue cards were issued without insisting on even the basic training.[72] Working-class housewives were often unhappy about signing the WVS enrolment form, which committed them 'to carry out whatever duties and instructions [they] might receive'.[73] Some boroughs

[66] Anonymous letter from Crawley (n.d., Mar. 1943?), WRVS, R12/3 West Sussex.
[67] 'Outline of WVS Housewives Service', 4 Sept. 1940, WRVS, Box File: Housewives Service.
[68] Ibid.
[69] *Venture* (July 1941), WRVS, R9/3 Staffordshire.
[70] 'WVS in the North West, Dec. 1940–Dec. 1941', typescript in WRVS, Box File, Housewives Service.
[71] 'Report of Housewives Section in Southampton', June 1943, WRVS, R6/4 Southampton; WVS Regional Administrators Conference, Minutes, 25 Sept. 1941.
[72] Notably in Lancashire where Tothill Street's expert on Housewives Sevice remarked in 1944 that 'I have seldom found such a lack of ability to interpret our guidelines on training' (Report by Mrs Creswick Atkinson, Apr. 1944, WRVS, R10/2 Lancashire County; Kay to Burkhardt, 30 Nov. 1943, WRVS, R10/2 Bolton).
[73] Reading to Scott, 1 Oct. 1943 WRVS, A1/38 File 4; Celia Fremlin, 'Note on Hampstead Housewives Service', 20 July 1940, MO TC 32/4/ I.

established effective street-level organization without formally enrolling any of their Housewives in WVS.[74] Nevertheless by 1943 Housewives Service accounted for up to 30 per cent of the total membership of WVS.[75] Since Housewives Service operated in most urban residential areas there is no way of knowing what proportion of these were working class.

In several towns the air raid wardens organized their own female auxiliaries without reference to WVS, and attempts by WVS to muscle in were often resisted. Thus it was reported from in Middlesbrough that the wardens preferred to make use of women's services without granting them 'any kind of standing... very much the North country man's attitude to women'.[76] A similar position existed in South Shields, Oldham, and Manchester, while in Guildford, where aggressive intervention by Tory ladies from the rural hinterland had created much bad feeling during the establishment of WVS before the war, neither the wardens nor their wives would have anything to do with the organization. Here it was issues of class rather than gender that blocked the establishment of Housewives Service, and this may also have played a role in the northern towns.[77] In some other places housewives' organizations originally formed by WVS were handed over to the wardens, who were not only better placed to know what help would be needed during raids, but also knew the working-class districts better than the middle-class ladies of the WVS.[78]

As the bombing receded, the WVS quickly found new functions for Housewives Service, providing information centres with details of local services, visiting the sick and the elderly, inviting neighbours in for first-aid training, talks by the local food adviser, war savings groups, make-do-and-mend sewing sessions, shopping for neighbours engaged in war work, minding

[74] Halifax WVS, for example, recruited 9,000 women for Housewives Service without enrolling any of them as members of WVS. Mrs Creswick Anderson, report on visit to West Riding, June 1943, WRVS, R2 Regional Office.

[75] The following figures are compiled from statistics available in the WRVS archive:

	Housewives Service	Total
Mar. 1943	199,526	776,552
June 1943	264,899	966,425
June 1944	300,162	998,317
Mar. 1945	296,231	968,242

[76] Reports by Vera Dart, 29 Feb. 1944, 25 May 1944, WRVS, R1/5 Middlesbrough.

[77] 'Report on Regional Administrator's Visit to South Shields', 14 Feb. 1944, WRVS, R1/2 South Shields; North West Regional Report, 24 Sept. 1938; Foster Jeffery to Dart, 28 Oct. 1938, WRVS, R10/1; Foster Jeffery, 'Report on Manchester', 24 Dec. 1943, WRVS, R10/2 Manchester; 'Housewives Section. Guildford Borough', 20 Nov. 1943, WRVS, R12/4 Surrey.

[78] Celia Fremlin, 'Note on Hampstead Housewives Service', 20 July 1940, MO, TC 32/4/ I; Butternick to Gretton, 11 May 1942, WRVS, R6/2 Buckinghamshire (Slough).

children of war workers, organizing the billeting of mobile industrial workers.[79] Where Housewives Service had previously been resisted by the wardens, more local authorities now came to recognize its value— although previous hostilities could, as in Manchester and Guildford, cast a long shadow.[80] In the feverish atmosphere of autumn 1940 WVS had proposed having 'one Key Housewife to every eight or ten houses, and through her, to form little street groups who can meet once a week in each other's homes, bringing their tea and sugar, and spending a happy social hour together.'[81] While organization seldom, if ever, reached that density, many housewives' groups did develop a social life of their own. In Liverpool, for example, 2,000 housewives were organized in sixty groups, most of which held regular weekly meetings and spawned bring- and-buy sales, whist drives and raffles to raise money for war charities, Christmas parties, programmes of Ministry of Information films and talks ranging from 'The Work of the WVS' to 'Town Planning', 'Religious Education in Schools', and 'The Life of Josephine Butler'.[82]

Reacting to a report on Housewives Service in July 1943, Mrs L'Estrang Malone, who had replaced Mary Sutherland as Labour Party representative on the General Purposes Committee, remarked: 'WVS had sown the seeds for much adult education by encouraging women who previously would never have thought of attending classes.'[83] This was optimistic. Lady Reading, anxious to prevent WVS taking on the educational characteristics of a peacetime women's organization, vetoed plans to issue notes for talks to housewives' groups.[84] Moreover the capacity of WVS to foster the potential for active citizenship among its working-class members was restricted by the hierarchical principles on which it was organized. The terminology differed from place to place, but the basic plan was for 'street housewives' to be

[79] Katherine Bentley Beauman, *Green Sleeves. The Story of WVS/WRVS* (London, 1977), 40–2; WVS Regional Circular, Apr. 1943, WRVS, Box File, Housewives Service; 'Points from a speech made by Vera Dart at Hoylake', 20 Jan. 1942, WRVS, R10/1 Cheshire; 'Report on Basic Training Conference', 24 Sept. 1942, WRVS, R1 Regional Office; 'Notes on Visit to Region 3', 17 Aug. 1942, WRVS, R3 Regional Office; Report on Housewives Service in the [West Midlands] Region, 5 Mar. 1942, WRVS, R9 Regional Office.
[80] In Manchester the WVS was unable to deliver on a local authority request to establish Housewives Service (Foster Jeffery, report on Manchester, 24 Dec. 1943; Foster Jeffery, report on interview with Manchester Town Clerk, 20 Jan. 1944; M. Goldney, 'Problem of Manchester', 24 Jan. 1944, WRVS, R10/2 Manchester). In Guildford the local authority asked WVS to help it establish its own Housewives Service while keeping in the background because WVS was so unpopular with local working-class activists. The Guildford WVS refused to help on these conditions (Diana Alexander, report on Housewives Service in Guildford, 20 Nov. 1943; Leach to Lady Worsley, 20 Nov. 1943; Lady Worsley to Leach, 24 Nov. 1943, WRVS, R12/4 Surrey).
[81] 'Outline of WVS Housewives Service', 4 Sept. 1940, WRVS, Box File: Housewives Service.
[82] 'Summary of the Liverpool WVS Housewives Service, Oct. 1940–Dec. 1941', 17 Jan. 1942, WRVS, R10/2 Liverpool. For similar developments in York, see Report on Yorkshire Area (n.d.) in NCSRS, E2/9.
[83] WVS Executive Committee, Minutes, 7 July 1943.
[84] WVS Chairman's Committee, Minutes, 24 Feb. 1944, 20 May 1943.

answerable to 'section housewives' responsible for several streets, with 'head housewives' at ward level.[85] In 1943 the Midlands' regional organizer attributed problems in the Rugby Housewives Service to the fact that 'the organisation was started in the street in the early days, instead of from the top...': things were now being put right, she reported.[86] Advice drawn up on the basis of wartime experience for centre leaders who were trying to re-establish Housewives Service in the early 1950s made the same point: 'to get the right people in' it was essential for organizers to pick them carefully, rather than ask for volunteers. Street housewives would normally belong to 'the prevalent class in the street', although where possible preference should be given to 'an obvious and recognised leader such as a vicar's wife...'. In the poorer areas section leaders were often middle-class outsiders: 'we found it was not possible to get someone accepted as Section Housewife without jealousy, and that then it was best (at any rate at the start) to have outside helpers who would come in to organise the section.'[87] Formally Housewives Service was as much a part of the centre leader's empire as any other aspect of WVS work, but occasionally 'the Housewives developed so much initiative that speculation arose as to whether perhaps the tail was wagging the dog.'[88] In Birmingham, where the woman responsible for Housewives Service acted quite independently of the not-very-effective WVS centre leader, the regional organizer warned of the danger that the Service would become 'the real WVS'.[89] More generally, Tothill Street warned that Housewives Service should not be allowed to take over functions belonging to the centre, like organizing canteens or rest centres.[90] Tensions between centre leaders and Housewives' organisers, however, were more likely to reflect power-struggles within the middle-class leadership than any stirring of democratic self-assertion by working-class housewives. In Darlington, for example, the ex-schoolteacher appointed to launch Housewives Service in 1944 ran it as a private empire, independently of both the wardens and the WVS centre leader. Her attitude to working-class self-assertion is apparent from her reaction to the appointment of the secretary, a working-class Labour woman, as centre leader after the war: 'she was nothing but a paid clerk'.[91]

[85] Mrs Cresswick Atkinson, memo prepared in 1951, in WRVS, Box File, Housewives Service.
[86] Report by Regional Organizer, 30 Mar. 1943, WRVS, R9/4 Warwickshire.
[87] Mrs Cresswick Atkinson, memo prepared in 1951, in WRVS, Box File, Housewives Service.
[88] Beauman, *Green Sleeves*, 41.
[89] Fletcher Moulton to Huxley, 31 Oct. 1940, WRVS, R9 Regional Office.
[90] 'Report on Basic Training Conference', 24 Sept. 1942, WRVS, R1 Regional Office.
[91] Chatfield to Halpin, 30 Apr. 1946, WRVS, R1 Regional Office; Vera Dart, reports on visits to Darlington, 9 and 13 Mar. 1944; Hilda Aspinall, report on visits to Darlington, 23–6 May 1944, WRVS, R 1/2 Darlington.

Housewives Service was sometimes criticized as an overly bureaucratic imposition on the spontaneous good neighbourliness evoked by the threat of air raids. In Stafford a dissident group within WVS publicly condemned 'the Best People ... of the County' for turning:

what ought to have been a simple local matter ... into a fearful and wonderful conglomeration of rules, regulations, forms, orders, counter orders, uniforms, badges and a few petrol coupons for the WVS to use in order to rush backwards and forwards on their Work of National Importance ...

These dissidents, who included a Lady Crawley Bovey, had been ousted from the leadership of WVS before the war, and were at least as upper-class as their successors.[92] A rather romantic belief in the popular capacity for self-organization was characteristic of the atmosphere of 1940.[93] Neighbours' Leagues suffused with radical democratic rhetoric sprang up in a number of cities, including Leicester where they gained local authority backing and worked in close association with the air raid wardens.[94] An enthusiastic *Times* leader welcomed these initiatives, and the democrats of the Nuffield reconstruction survey wondered whether they might have a long-term future as 'instruments of democratic local government which are more readily comprehensible by the ordinary citizen than the statutory machinery'.[95] Though not specifically a women's movement, the (male) co-ordinator of the Leicester leagues claimed that they offered women 'a special opportunity of War Service in their own streets and in their own homes ... perhaps ... the only opportunity of such service for most women.'[96] When, a year later, Leicester WVS contemplated taking over what was left of the Neighbours' Leagues as a basis for starting Housewives Service, they were clear that the Leagues' ethos of local autonomy would have to go, in particular their practice of weekly street collections to raise funds for helping bombed-out members.[97] Had WVS been challenged on the democratic issue, they might have responded with some justification that, for all the excitement about spontaneity and grass-roots democracy, it was precisely WVS *organisation* that gave staying power to the ephemeral upsurge of community feeling provoked by the blitz.

---

[92] Fletcher Moulton to Huxley, 1 Oct. 1940, enclosing cutting from *Staffordshire Chronicle*, WRVS, R9 Regional Office; *The Times* (19 and 20 Sept. 1940).

[93] R. Calder, articles in *New Statesman* (21 Sept. 1940, 8 Mar. 1941); R. Calder, *Carry on London* (London, 1941); J. Strachey, *Post D* (London, 1941); 'The New Pattern', *Planning*, 178 (30 Sept. 1941).

[94] Walter Thacker, 'Statement on the Beginnings and Development of the Movement in Leicester', 26 Oct. 1940, in NCSRS, E2/10; 'Statement on Neighbours League Centres', 15 July 1940; Neighbour's League, *Bulletin*, 1 (22 July 1940), WRVS, R3/2 Leicester.

[95] 'Voluntary Organizations in the City and County of Leicester', Aug. 1941, in NCSRS, E2/10. The *Manchester Guardian* (6 Sept. 1940) has a detailed report of a similar initiative in Hull.

[96] Walter Thacker, 'Statement on the Beginnings and Development of the Movement in Leicester', 26 Oct. 1940, in NCSRS, E2/10.

[97] 'Notes on Visit to Region 3', 17 Aug. 1942, WRVS, R3 Regional Office.

But the price of institutionalization tended to be middle-class leadership, whether in Housewives Service or in the WVS more generally. Bootle, the most proletarian town in Britain,[98] provided Tothill Street with its favourite example of successful organization amongst the working class. Run by a Labour council and predominantly inhabited by Irish dockers, Bootle was the kind of place that WVS organizers approached with trepidation. The initial WVS appointments were both wives of senior policemen,[99] but the woman who emerged as centre leader, Miss Cassady, was the Irish Catholic sister of a local doctor. Like most of the local middle class, Cassady herself lived outside the town.[100] Her inspired leadership of an almost entirely working-class membership was cited as evidence against the pessimism of the neighbouring Liverpool centre organizer about the possibility of recruiting dockers' wives for voluntary work.[101] Of 'irrepressible spirits and great good humour', she used her gifts as a musician and drama teacher to keep the members engaged in slack times, and the WVS choir frequently graced functions organized by the local authority.[102] The blitzing suffered by Bootle in 1941 was among the worst in Britain, reducing the population from 70,000 to 43,000 in six months as people fled the city. WVS came through with flying colours. 'The people are sound to the core, with no airs or affectations,' wrote Lady Reading after a visit to Bootle: 'They may be a bit uncouth, but they're the real thing.'[103] Miss Huxley was similarly impressed: 'There is a kind of ring about it which belongs only to the Bootle centre which may suffer from drawing its entire personnel from the Emerald Isle, but certainly has a character about it which is no-one else's.'[104] Sectarian divisions were sharp (in 1949 the local Conservative Women still had a clause excluding Roman Catholics from membership), and it is clear that the bonds of ethnicity provided one key to Cassady's success.[105]

In Salford, another overwhelmingly working-class Lancashire town where 'all the [WVS] workers are of the working-woman type', the centre leader was an ex-headmistress who had made a second career in voluntary

---

[98] Bootle was ranked bottom of the 157 towns with populations over 50,000 in Moser and Scott's 'social class index' based on the 1951 census, making it the most proletarian town in Britain (C. A. Moser and W. Scott, *British Towns: A Statistical Study of their Social and Economic Differences* (London, 1961), 124).

[99] WVS, Executive Committee, Minutes, 25 Oct. 1938, 20 Jan. 1939.

[100] Vera Dart, report on Bootle, 9 May 1941, WRVS, R 10/2 Bootle; Charles Cowen, report on Bootle (n.d., 1942) in NCSRS, E2/16; Rawcliffe, Report on Bootle, 11 July 1949 in CPA, CCO 1/7/102.

[101] Huxley to Nanson, 22 Feb. 1941, WRVS, R10/2 Bootle; Huxley, 'Report on Tour of Region 10', Nov. 1940, WRVS, R10 Regional Office.

[102] Dart to Smieton, 20 Nov. 1940; Mrs Doe, Report on Visit to Region 10, 5 Apr. 1940, WRVS, R10 Regional Office.

[103] Lady Reading, memo, 5 Nov. 1941, WRVS, R10/2 Bootle.

[104] Huxley to Maxse, 13 June 1941, WRVS, R 10/2 Bootle.

[105] Rawcliffe, Report on Bootle.

work.[106] Her husband was Deputy Chief Constable.[107] When Labour finally took control of Salford in 1945 they revenged themselves for years of exclusion by permanently excluding Conservatives from the mayoralty: 'It is high time ... that some of our people got a look-in at functions which have been a sort of "upper ten" preserve in the past, and that labour women had the chance to show that they too can organise successful charity dances, whist drives and socials.'[108] Labour's aspiration to wrest the rituals of social leadership from the 'upper ten' was not one which, in Salford, WVS had done anything to advance. In some other towns, as we shall see, WVS did provide an avenue for Labour women to acquire positions of social leadership. What is more difficult to determine is whether Labour women running charity dances—as aspiration or in reality—had a positive contribution to make to the democratization of Britain.

IV

From the outset Lady Reading had wanted to involve Labour women in the local leadership of WVS, and in some areas organizers succeeded in placing Labour women in leading roles ahead of the SJC's January 1940 decision to co-operate. Where Labour councils were resistant to WVS, organizers urged centre leaders to ease the way by recruiting Labour women into the leadership. 'I think I have collected one or two prominent socialist women who may be of use,' reported the centre leader in Derby in January 1939, adding cynically: 'even if they don't do much work they must perch on our platforms.'[109] Even in towns where Labour was not in control the involvement of Labour women in the leadership could become essential. In Southampton the authority of a WVS executive committee run by two leading political women was upheld by the regional administrator against successive inadequate centre leaders despite the fact that this arrangement flew in the face of the official anti-committee doctrine. One of these women, Mrs Thorneycroft Donaldson, was a leading figure in the local Conservative Party.[110] The other, Minnie Cutler, was the only Labour woman on the local council.[111] Cutler was disliked by several of the leading figures in the local WVS both

---

[106] Dart to Reading, 11 Jan. 1940, WRVS, R10 Northwest Regional Office; CV of Dorothy G. Rothwell, JP, 1944, in WRVS, R10/2 Salford. Salford was ranked 144th (out of 157) on the 'social class index', Moser and Scott, *British Towns*, 126–7.

[107] Dart to Lady Reading, 11 Jan. 1940, WRVS, R10/1 Northwest Regional Office, 138.

[108] John Garrard, 'The Mayoralty since 1835', in Alan O'Day (ed.), *Government and Institutions in the post-1832 United Kingdom* (Lampeter, 1995), 5.

[109] Lochrane to Fletcher Moulton, 24 Jan. 1939, WRVS, R3/1 Derby.

[110] Huxley to Reading, 18 July 1942, WRVS, R6/4 Southampton.

[111] Minnie Cutler (1890–1978), had secondary education, had been a teacher before she married a patternmaker. She was first elected to the council in 1935 (J. H. Mathews, Report on Southampton, Nov. 1942, in NCSRS, B3/16; *Southern Evening Echo* (21 Jan. 1978)).

for her politics and for what they saw as her aggressive manner. When, in 1942, Donaldson fell ill leaving Cutler in effective control this was more than they could bear, and the centre leader refused to accept her authority, conspiring with the mayor to have her removed. From her sick bed Donaldson insisted that she would resign if Cutler went, and this was sufficient to persuade the regional administrator to override major local protests and sack the centre leader instead.[112] Clearly Cutler's role was something more than decorative. The Donaldson/Cutler partnership embodied not only the political truce of the war years, but also—through their respective husbands—the industrial truce as well. Donaldson's husband was Managing Director of one of the city's main employers, Thorneycroft's shipyard, where he spent his life negotiating industrial peace with the unions.[113] His main partner in these negotiations, a patternmaker and the leading trade unionist in the shipyard, was Cutler's husband.[114] Many years later, reflecting on a long and successful career in local politics, Minie Cutler remarked that 'a lot of the stability of the country was due to the women, who were excellent managers'.[115] She was not the only Labour woman to play a significant role in maintaining social and political harmony in wartime Britain.

In at least two large towns, Leicester and Coventry, WVS was led by Labour women. In Leicester, the Labour ex-pacifist Dorothy Bates was appointed centre leader after the local authority complained in June 1940 that her predecessor was not up to the job. As in Southampton, the incumbent (a solicitor's wife) had a good deal of support inside WVS, and her pleasant middle-class manner was contrasted favourably with Bates' more aggressive style.[116] In Coventry WVS was run by Pearl Hyde, daughter of a North London publican. She joined the Labour Party in the 1920s, having gained her political education by sitting night after night in the Public Gallery of the Council Chamber. In 1937 she won a council seat.[117] Hyde involved herself in WVS from the outset, and her promotion reflected the WVS recognition that they would get nowhere in Coventry without the blessing of a Labour woman councillor.[118] According to her second-in-command, when Hyde took over as centre leader in Coventry shortly before the outbreak of war the WVS was 'a rather insipid friendly little "Tea

[112] The main sources for this row are 'Report on Southampton', 16 July 1942; Huxley to Reading, 18 July 1942; Tidpole to Reading, 22 July 1942, WRVS, R6/4 Southampton. But see also numerous other memos, reports, telegrams, and letters in the same file.

[113] K. C. Barnaby, *Thorneycrofts: 100 Years of Specialised Shipbuilding and Engineering* (London, 1964), 149, 11, 22, 45, 81.

[114] *Southern Evening Echo* (11 Mar. 1963).

[115] Ibid. (3 May 1967). She was Mayor of Southampton, 1951–2.

[116] Simpson to Woodall, 17 June 1940; Woodall, Report on Leicester, 13–17 June 1940, WRVS, R3/2 Leicester.

[117] *Coventry Evening Telegraph* (15 Apr. 1963).

[118] Fletcher Moulton, Report on Warwickshire, 8 July 1938, WRVS, R9 West Midlands Regional Office.

Party" affair'.[119] Though well supported by the middle-class women's organizations, it had cut no ice with the Labour council who were inclined to
dismiss it as 'a snob show'.[120] Hyde's decision to take on the leadership—
made in consultation with the Labour leader on the council—clearly marked
a change in the relations between WVS and the local authority and thereafter
WVS developed unusually good relations with the local labour movement.
In 1944 when local engineering trade unionists organized a dinner for their
elderly members, they did not hesitate to ask the WVS to prepare the room,
serve the dinner, and wash the dishes.[121]

The Coventry blitz, and Humphrey Jenning's documentary film 'Heart of
Britain' in which she features briefly, made Pearl Hyde into a celebrity.
While the camera lingers on a shot of WVS women getting tea from an urn,
Jenning's voice-over intones: 'Here, in Coventry, those everyday tasks of the
women came right through the fire and became heroic.' Speaking direct to
camera Hyde explains: 'You know you feel such fools standing there in a
crater with a mug of tea...until a man says "it washed the blood and dust
from my mouth" and you know you really have done something useful.'
Hyde was a large woman, and her 'charm and personality, heart and sympathy' were built to match her physical proportions.[122] Audiences cheered
her in neutral New York, and her own courage and indefatigable energy
trivialized complaints that she had exceeded her authority during the blitz.[123]

In Southampton, Leicester, and Coventry Labour women came to the fore
only after more conventional appointments had been tried and found
wanting. The same happened in Darlington after the war, when the regional
organizer overrode substantial local opposition to replace the incumbent
centre leader with her working-class secretary.[124] In her 1952 sociological
study of WVS, Rachel Chambers reported that the social composition of
the leadership was changing: 'more and more officers and leading members
are being chosen from the wives or female relatives of farmers, market
gardeners, minor public officials, small tradesmen, railwaymen and skilled
workers'.[125] This was an optimistic reading of the evidence. While a few

---

[119] Maisie Thacker to 'Dear Minnie', 2 Jan. 1968, Coventry RO PA 705. Hyde's predecessor
was a journalist and company secretary, wife of a well-known racing motorist, and 'influential
with the Church set' (WVS Executive Committee, Minutes, 25 Oct. 1938).
[120] Coventry National Council of Women, Minutes, 5 July 1938, Coventry RO, PA/1269;
Coventry Electrical Association of Women, Minutes, 18 July 1938, 16 Nov. 1938, Coventry RO;
Fletcher Moulton, Report on Warwickshire.
[121] WRVS, Narrative Reports, Coventry, Mar. 1945. Hyde herself was a member of the AEU.
[122] George Hodgkinson, *Sent to Coventry*. (London, 1970).
[123] Fletcher Moulton to Lady Reading, 7 Dec. 1940, WRVS, R9 West Midlands Regional
Office. See also various reports on the Coventry blitz in the same file.
[124] Houston, report on Darlington, 30 Apr. 1946; Houston to Halpin, 12 Aug. 1946;
Houston to Russell, 12 Aug. 1946; Cresswick Anderson, Report on Visit to Darlington, Nov.
1946, WRVS, R1 North-East Regional Office.
[125] Chambers, 'Three Voluntary Organisations', 385–6, 391.

working-class women held leadership positions—we could add Bedworth and Hebburn to the examples already cited in Southampton and Darlington—the advent of Labour women in control did not necessarily involve a change in the social class of the leadership. Pearl Hyde may have come from humble (though not working-class) origins, but one function played by WVS in her life was to help her entry into the local middle class. After the war, following a spell as a welfare officer in a car factory, she became a public relations executive, first for the tractor manufacturer Massey Fergusson and then, from 1960, for Associated Television. She played a leading role in local Labour politics, serving as Lord Mayor in 1957. By the early 1950s she was a prominent figure in charity work in Coventry, and she chaired the town's annual Music Festival. She also played an important role in the campaign to establish the city aerodrome. The guest list at her funeral in Coventry Cathedral in 1963—like her father before her she was killed in a car accident—reads like a roll call of Coventry's great and good.[126] In Leicester, Dorothy Bates, whose husband owned a small beer bottling business, was already a leading figure in the middle-class women's movement before taking over as WVS leader. Before the war she had combined membership of the Labour Party with the chairmanship of the National Council of Women. During the war she was able to maintain an unusually constructive link between WVS and the established women's movement, as well as taking a leading role in the local magistracy.[127] Elected to the Council in 1947 she went on to play a significant role in the establishment of the NHS in Leicester, wielding the kind of social authority as a member of the regional hospital board that, before the war, had belonged to women on the committees of voluntary hospitals. The arrival of Labour in municipal power in post-war Leicester coincided with an increase in business representation on the council. Two of Labour's leading politicians were themselves businessmen, and their politics had less to do with socialism than with using the Labour Party as a vehicle for public service in a way which 'in many respects conformed to the [ethos of] the old style "city father" municipal leaders'.[128]

The fact that some Labour women held leading positions in WVS was important to confirming the organization's non-partisan stance. But too much emphasis on the partisan issue may divert attention from the degree to which the tentacles of middle-class power were, by the 1940s, being extended into the Labour Party. Margaret Stacey noticed at the end of the decade that in Banbury some members of the professional middle class, denied access to the upper-class society of the rural hinterland and culturally alienated by the relatively uneducated milieu of the established middle-class

---

[126] *Coventry Evening Telegraph* (15 Apr. 1963).
[127] Bates to Reading, 6 Apr. 1945, WRVS, R3/2 Leicester; and see Ch. 9.
[128] Peter Jones, *et al.*, 'Politics', in D. Nash and D. Reader (eds.), *Leicester in the Twentieth Century* (Leicester, 1993), 92, 103.

social leaders, turned to the (disproportionately immigrant) Labour Party to provide them with outlets for participation and leadership.[129] In Newcastle-under-Lyme, by the 1950s, middle-class Labour Party members were behaving just as Conservatives had done in the past, combining political activism with the pursuit of a less partisan social leadership in voluntary organizations. (Meanwhile working-class activists remained as narrowly focused on trade union politics as ever.)[130] At national level the few Labour women who played leading roles in WVS were upper middle-class women who could deal with Lady Reading and her organizers on terms of something like social equality.[131] Where Labour women were in control of WVS this was often an indication more of the extent to which the middle-class had found a sphere of activity within the Labour movement than of any successful entry into the leadership of voluntary work by working-class women. Even in its engagement with Labour, WVS did more to consolidate middle-class social leadership than it did to provide working-class women with an avenue for democratic advance.

[129] Stacey, *Banbury*, 159–62.

[130] F. Bealey, J. Blondel, and W. P. McCann, *Constituency Politics: A Study of Newcastle-under-Lyme* (London, 1965), 398–400, 410–11. See also A. H. Birch, *Small-Town Politics. A Study of Political Life in Glossop* (Oxford, 1959), 61–71.

[131] e.g. Mary Agnes Hamilton, who served as a WVS vice-president, and Vera Dart, regional Administrator in, first, the North West and, later, the North East, who left WVS in 1945 to stand unsuccessfully as a Labour parliamentary candidate.

5

Discipline and Charm

Lady Reading saw WVS as a means of establishing a disciplined corps of volunteers ready to undertake tasks at the bidding of central and local government. She dismissed the local autonomy and independence prized by the leaders of most established voluntary organizations in favour of hierarchical structures designed to rescue voluntarism from—as she saw it—the 'whims' and unreliability of self-appointed cliques of local volunteers: 'there are no local committees', she explained to the Home Office, 'to delay matters'.[1] Reading's centralizing vision often sat uncomfortably alongside the practices of social leadership characteristic of the middle-class associational world which WVS had colonized. How could the women of standing that WVS had recruited be subordinated to the Tothill Street hierarchy without risking the independence and autonomy crucial to their status and identity as local social leaders?

In practice, the threat to their autonomy was less than it appeared. For one thing, the dual political accountability of WVS—both to the local authority and (via Tothill Street) to Whitehall—opened up spaces within which local WVS leaders could act with a degree of self-direction. From the outset WVS had been seen by the Home Office as a means of gingering up ARP preparations where local authorities were reluctant to act, and—especially in Labour-controlled areas—WVS had often been used by local social leaders as a means of asserting their authority in face of an unsympathetic council. Many of the women appointed to run local WVS centres perceived WVS as providing a platform from which they could reinforce their claims to social leadership. WVS leaders frequently outclassed the elected representatives and local government officials with whom they dealt, and one way in which WVS might function—as Labour women had feared when they refused to co-operate in 1938—was as a means by which well-to-do ladies were able to sustain social influence even when Labour was in control of local political power.

Some of the more thoughtful WVS leaders were puzzled by the potential conflict between the requirement to act simultaneously as handmaidens to the local authority and as a transmission belt for priorities handed down

---

[1] Reading to Chuter Ede, 11 Oct. 1946, PRO, CAB 129 914; Reading to Scott, 1 Oct. 1943, WRVS, A1/38, File 4.

from London. Tothill Street dealt with this ambiguity with a studied vagueness, rejecting tidy-minded attempts to clarify the precise lines of authority involved, while invoking, in their place, what were seen as the special capacities of women to overcome difficulties through the exercise of tact, patience, and practical improvisation. Within this gendered discourse virtues taken to be essentially female were understood to be more appropriate instruments for the exercise of effective social power than the disabling penchant for abstract theorizing attributed to over-educated bluestockings. Despite Reading's modernizing vision, WVS in practice was more inclined to encourage its members to pursue petticoat government through the exercise of charm, than to promote their disciplined subordination to the will of elected—and overwhelmingly male—local authorities.

Discipline was, nevertheless, an essential component of the WVS ethos. We have already seen how, in some towns, Tothill Street forced established social leaders to co-operate with Labour women or even to accept them as centre organizers. More generally, Regional Administrators were charged with dealing with inefficient local organizers, and WVS files bulge with details of the sacking—or attempted sacking—of centre organizers some of whom put up stiff resistance to what they perceived as illegitimate outside interference. The imposition of such outside discipline, however, painful though it was, might have done more to enhance than to diminish the authority of local social leaders. WVS had set out to recruit established social leaders, and if occasionally such women were found to be wanting then their unceremonious dismissal probably did more to reinforce than to undermine the leadership claims of their class. Whether the WVS colonization of middle-class associational life tended to strengthen the claims of the women involved to local social leadership, or to sap their autonomy and subordinate them to elected councillors and/or Tothill Street depended on the working out of a complex balance of local and national forces. As this chapter demonstrates, there were a variety of ways in which the triangular relationship between local authorities, WVS centres, and Tothill Street could impact on local structures of political and social power. In general, however, it was the marriage of charm (exercised by local social leaders) with discipline (imposed by the Tothill Street hierarchy) which provided WVS with its preferred technology of power.

I

In the interface between local government and the voluntary sector, WVS occupied a peculiar position. On the one hand it was a voluntary organization existing to serve the statutory authorities. WVS could not establish a centre without approval from the local authority; and, once established, the centre could undertake work only at the request of the local authority (or, from 1940, of a Government department).[2] It was not, unlike other voluntary organizations, free to set its own agenda. On the other hand, local authorities, whatever their attitude to co-operation with the voluntary sector in general, were under pressure to recognize the WVS. While not forced to do so, neither could they turn WVS down with impunity. In fulfilling their statutory requirement to undertake civil defence, local authorities needed the help of women volunteers. If they chose to recruit and organize volunteers without making use of WVS they were not eligible for Treasury grants towards the expenses incurred.[3] From the outset, Hoare had intended WVS as a means of gingering up the local authorities, making them take their ARP duties seriously.[4] While loudly proclaiming that WVS was the servant of the local authorities, WVS organizers gave short shrift to members who sought to justify disobedience to the centre organizer by claiming that they were carrying out instructions from the local authority.[5] As the Manchester organizer pointed out in 1939:

although WVS centres are instructed to act as desired by the local authority, a particular local authority has no guarantee that the circulars and instructions issued by WVS HQ (by which, according to their letters of appointment, the staff agree to be guided) will not run counter to its wishes.[6]

In practice, WVS was about transmitting government priorities to the local authorities as well as local authority priorities to the voluntary sector.

WVS leaders always resisted demands to spell out too precisely the relationships involved:

The WVS like all successful British institutions is something of an anomaly. Though officially recognised by the Government and under the control of the local authority, it retains its voluntary character and has won for itself its position in the life of the nation. More precise definition of its position would destroy much of its vitality.[7]

Such ambiguity came naturally to a nation without a written constitution. The genius of British democracy lay in nods and winks. By such means conflict could be smoothed away, principled confrontation lost in obscure manœuvres. If that is how men had generally run public life in Britain, the women of the WVS believed that they had a particular, gendered, aptitude

---

[2] Sir A. Salisbury MacNalty (ed.), *The Civilian Health and Medical Services*, i (London, 1953), 225.
[3] Dart to Goldney, 1 June 1941, WRVS, R10/1 Chester.
[4] Lady Reading, memo on meeting with Gardiner, 29 Nov. 1938, PRO, HO 186 569.
[5] Wynne to Jacob, 9 Dec. 1941; report of interview with two WVS officers, 16 Jan. 1942, both in WRVS, R10/1 Birkenhead; Dart to Reading, 15 Jan. 1942, WRVS, R10 North-west Region.
[6] Iris Scowby to Mrs Huxley, 2 Jan. 1940, WRVS, R10/2 Manchester.
[7] 'Note for letter to Miss Vachell re position of WVS' (n.d., Nov. 1939?), WRVS, R8/8 Glamorganshire.

for such work. They sought to cultivate a distinctive version of public-spirited femininity, laying great stress on the ability of women to exert their influence in non-confrontational ways. 'We are acting in the way of smoothing out difficulties', Lady Reading told the Labour deputation to the Home Office in June 1938.[8] A few days earlier some 'Hints on starting work in a Borough' issued to organizers spelled out the five main qualities to look for in potential centre organizers. TACT (in capital letters) was first, followed by patience, understanding and cheerfulness.[9] The relatively low ranking given by this document to 'intelligence', which came fifth, was characteristic of the WVS ethos: intelligence, however clearly it might be displayed by WVS women in practice, was deemed too masculine a virtue to prioritize. 'Purity of motive and steadfastness of purpose', Lady Reading explained on another occasion, was far more important to WVS than 'either... intelligence or... acumen'.[10]

Relations between WVS and local authorities were frequently difficult, especially in the early days. 'The real trouble', wrote Lady Reading, 'is that all this work must be done through the Local Authorities and if anyone with a super abundance of nervous energy gets going, they feel they are being bossed and immediately get bad tempered about it.'[11] A case in point was the West Sussex organizer, Evelyn Emmet, an energetic social worker and ambitious Conservative politician, who remarked of tensions with the local authorities on her patch: 'We women are becoming increasingly unpopular because we have been right all the time.'[12] Gender was often at the root of such problems, with local politicians finding it difficult to accept women in responsible roles in public life and fearing 'petticoat interference' in their work.[13] WVS leaders were usually sensitive to the fragility of male egos and aware of the need to handle them with care. Behind-the-scenes efficiency was the watchword, and centre organizers were encouraged not to seek press publicity for their activities: we 'must be prepared to be the tool of other

---

[8] Report of Deputation to Home Secretary from the Labour Party Executive, 14 July 1938,11, WRVS, V95 SJC.
   [9] 'Hints on Starting Work in a Borough', 30 June 1938, WRVS, R8/8 Cardiff.
   [10] Lady Reading, Letter to Members, June 1944, WRVS, R10.
   [11] Lady Reading to Fletcher-Moulton , 25 Nov. 1938, WRVS, V/101/38 Conservative Party. For early Home Office fears that WVS was tending to develop as a rival to local authority ARP services, see Hodsoll, memo on WVS, 25 Mar. 1939; Wood to Butler, 5 Apr. 1939, PRO, HO 186 107.
   [12] Evelyn Emmet to Lady Reading, 22 Sept. 1939, WRVS, R/12/3 West Sussex.
   [13] Anon., Report on Region Seven, 1938–44, WRVS, Histories—Regional, Box 205. The civil defence commissioner in the North East, Sir Arthur Lambert (a Newcastle retailer and Tory councillor, knighted in 1930 on the strength—it was said—of a game of golf with the Prince of Wales), was well known for his contempt for women's organizations. Although the WVS Regional Administrator was a fellow Tory and had known Lambert 'all her life' she could not persuade him to take WVS seriously. So far as he was concerned 'the best way we could occupy ourselves was in running sewing parties!' Reid to Reading, 29 Oct. 1939; Huxley to Reading, 8 Nov. 1939; Huxley to Smieton, 15 Jan. 1940, all in WRVS, R1 Northeast Region.

people, to do the work, but to let others get the praise'.[14] 'If we are to be trusted here', wrote the East Anglia organizer, 'we should work with absolute efficiency and yet very quietly.'[15] When local authorities were difficult the appropriate tactic was to cajole and persuade, cloaking impatience with unimaginative and obstructive males behind a veil of calculated charm. In the words of the chief regional administrator, Mrs Huxley:

I am sure that everyone in this room who before the war shared with me the experience of working with men in an organised team, or those of you who have had the experience of dealing with husbands, believe in the old and successful technique [of letting him think that your ideas are his own and then thanking him profusely for his advice].

One centre organizer explained that charm was more important than efficiency, since without the former one would not be invited to demonstrate the latter.[16] There were, of course, limits to the proper deployment of feminine charm. Vera Dart talked jokingly of 'vamping' a Liverpool alderman, and Lord Harlech, the regional civil defence commissioner, admitted to Lady Reading that he admired her Yorkshire administrator, Mary Aykroyd, partly because of his 'masculine prejudice toward an attractive feminine personality whom one finds it easy to click with'.[17] But a perfectly efficient centre organizer in the West Midlands town of Rowley Regis who allowed suspicion to grow unchecked that she was having an affair with the town clerk had to be sacked.[18]

Despite their reliance on feminine wiles there was nothing weak about Stella Reading's women. When, before the war, the Home Office put out civil defence posters depicting women as timid beings protected by their men folk, Lady Reading was furious and demanded that in future women should be involved in preparing materials.[19] But this kind of protest was rare, and WVS leaders normally tolerated the pervasive masculine discourse of feminine incapacity with good humour. Reflecting on a meeting of women's organizations in January 1940, one Mass Observer remarked on 'that freemasonry amongst women which treats ... men ... with a humorous forbearance which in no way destroys their determination to have things their own

[14] Mrs Rawnsley, Lindsay Organiser, at County Borough Organizers' Conference, 22 Apr. 1947, WRVS, CB Organizers' Conferences. See also Mrs Vachell, regional administrator for Wales: 'The wise Organiser avoids newspaper publicity as a danger and a possible cause of jealousy...', Quarterly Report, 30 Nov. 1943.

[15] Mrs Bragg to Miss Gray, 14 Jan. 1939, WRVS, R4/2 Cambridge.

[16] Minutes of a Brains Trust held at a WVS training school, Leeds, Mar. 1943, WRVS, R2 Yorkshire.

[17] Lord Harlech to Lady Reading, 24 Mar. 1941, WRVS, R2 Yorkshire; Dart to Reading, 5 July 1941, WRVS, R10 Northwest.

[18] Correspondence in April 1941 re Rowley Regis, WRVS, R9 West Midlands.

[19] WVS Executive Committee, Minutes, 20 Jan. 1939.

way...'[20] Amongst themselves WVS women could speak with uncurbed tongues. Following an 'appalling' meeting at which Mary Aykroyd, the Yorkshire administrator admired by Lord Harlech, entirely failed to 'click' with the retired general in charge of civil defence in the county, Lady Reading intervened to patch things up. After exchanging letters with the general, filled with soothing expressions of mutual esteem, she confided to Aykroyd:

I think now all is well and the little man has written to me by hand which means I think that he is ashamed of himself and is going to behave himself in the future, but I agree with you that it lowers him in one's estimation to know that he can loose his temper in such an abominable manner.[21]

One centre organizer remarked of her local authority that they behaved like 'children being given nasty medicine which they have to take for their own good'. For this woman, as no doubt for many others, this matriarchal sense of feminine superiority was reinforced by the class relations involved:

When you deal with the Local Authority you are dealing with men who have spent the first twenty years of their existence trying to persuade their Committees that they are worth £50 a year more. The Local Authority regard us as unpaid competition. Most of our volunteers are independent.[22]

Preparing for a difficult meeting with the authorities in Labour-controlled Nottingham, the regional organizer wrote:

I would suggest that you are your most placatory self, agreeing, smoothing out difficulties and being full of understanding ... I think the line of country best suited for the occasion would be intelligence held in curb to suit the wishes of the Moguls.[23]

To twenty-first-century ears such subterfuge may signify subordination. WVS women, however, could hold their own in gender warfare. Lilly Boys—vicar's wife, Girl Guide Commissioner, outspoken Tory activist, and a WVS organizer in rural Lincolnshire—was certainly no shrinking violet, and her clever turning of what was already in 1941 an established sexist put-down speaks volumes about the self-confidence of these public women: 'Rude men often say to me the WVS is like a woman driver. I think I know what they mean—that women look at an obstruction as a thing to be got over.'[24]

---

[20] S. Schofield, 'Report on Conference of Representatives of Women's Organisations on Women and War Conditions Now: The Status and Future of Women War Workers', 26 Jan. 1940, MO TC Women in Wartime 4/H.

[21] Reading to Aykroyd, 18 Aug. 1941, WRVS, R2 Yorkshire, Confidential Correspondence.

[22] Minutes of a Brains Trust held at a WVS training school, Leeds, Mar. 1943.

[23] Fletcher-Moulton, memo, 18 July 1938, WRVS, R3/7 Nottingham.

[24] Cutting from *Lincolnshire Chronicle* (n.d., Apr. 1942?), in R3/5 Lincoln.

The studied ambiguity in the lines of authority between WVS and local government was helpful to both sides in their search for a *modus vivendi*. Demands for greater clarity, on the other hand, could be counterproductive. Evelyn Emmet, worried by the vagueness of the WVS brief, irritated by the 'mixture of blarney and bluff' involved in establishing WVS as part of local power structures, and convinced that all the work involved in placing evacuees was better done by women than by men, proposed that the Government should instruct local authorities to devolve responsibility for evacuees entirely to WVS.[25] At Tothill Street the arguments against any such formalization of the relationships involved were too obvious to need reiteration.[26] The experience of Manchester fully confirmed their preference for ambiguity. The centre organizer, Miss Scowby, was impatient with a system that relied on the 'courtesy of individual Town Clerks and the tact of individual centre organisers'. Appointed soon after the outbreak of war she quickly reached a conclusion identical to the position adopted by the Labour women in June 1938: the existence of WVS as a national organization was a recipe for confusion and overlapping. Perhaps there had been some justification for this when reluctant local authorities needed gingering up into taking ARP work seriously, but now that war had come WVS should be dissolved and its organizers taken on as local government officials. Only when they were its paid employees, she believed, would women organizers be taken seriously by the local authority.[27] Although persuaded to carry on, it soon became clear that Scowby remained anxious about the ambiguities of the constitutional position: 'when a request comes to her... instead of getting on with the job... she has a mental argument as to whether it had come to her as WVS' or in her capacity as the local authority's Canteen Officer. Tothill Street attributed her unease to an academic and impractical turn of mind (she had a double first from Cambridge), although the fact that Manchester had from the start sought to minimize the role of the voluntary sector may have been more germane.[28] Scowby was resistant to instructions

---

[25] Evelyn Emmet, Report on Leadership, 8 Aug. 1939, WRVS, R/12/3 West Sussex.

[26] Marjorie Maxse forwarded to Lady Reading a subsequent missive from Emmet on similar lines commenting that 'it would not be advisable to go as far as she suggests for the obvious reasons'. Maxse to Reading , 4 Feb. 1941, WRVS, R/12/3 West Sussex. In July 1938, when Labour Party leaders had sought clarification from the Home Secretary about the precise lines of authority between himself, WVS, and the local authorities, Samuel Hoare had responded with studied and persistent vagueness (Report of Labour Party deputation to Home Secretary, 14 July 1938, 8, 16–18, WRVS, V95 SJC).

[27] Iris Scowby to Mrs Huxley, 2 Jan. 1940, WRVS, R10/2 Manchester.

[28] Huxley to Smieton, 5 Jan. 1940; Foster-Jeffery to Huxley, 7 May 1942, WRVS, R10/2 Manchester; Foster Jeffery to Goldney, 27 July 1939; Goldney to Huxley, 29 July 1939; Foster Jeffery to Goldney, 1 Aug. 1939; Smieton to Foster Jeffery, 3 Aug. 1939, WRVS, R10 North-west. Manchester was disinclined to co-operate with the Regional Commissioner and decided when war broke out not to rely on volunteers but to have all the emergency work done by paid

from the regional office or Tothill Street, preferring to see herself as answerable directly to the local authority—or, at least, to the handful of officers
'whose brains she admired'.[29] Eventually in 1942 matters came to a head
and agreement was reached for the local authority to hire Scowby as a full-
time civil defence worker while WVS found a new centre organizer.[30]
Scowby's desire for clarity led her out of WVS: it also contributed to the
failure of WVS to establish itself on a firm footing at any time during the war
in one of Britain's largest cities.[31] Events in Manchester served to justify the
Tothill Street belief that the key to WVS success lay not with the analytic
acuity of the academically trained mind, however brilliant, but the tact,
patience, and practical intelligence of women prepared to live with a certain
degree of ambiguity about who exactly was working for whom.

II

If feminine virtues were appropriate when dealing with male authority,
towards their own sex WVS leaders sometimes turned a harsher face. The
womanhood they offered to the public life of the community was 'womanhood on an organised basis', disciplined, efficient, and reliable.[32] In pursuit
of this they could be ruthless. In April 1944 Vera Dart, the Northeast
regional administrator, explained to an angry meeting of WVS women in
Darlington why she was determined to sack the incumbent centre organizer,
an amiable titled lady married to a retired Liberal MP who had run WVS in
Darlington from its inception.[33] Although popular with her helpers, in
Dart's view she lacked the strength of personality necessary to hold them
together as a disciplined force:

much as I like Lady Havelock-Allen, and charming as she has been to me (I would
imagine she would be particularly kind if anyone was unhappy or in trouble), her
personality is a little vague...It is not the person who is always gracious and

---

staff. The LEA adapted their well-developed school meals service to do the canteen work; the
UAB and the PAC deal with clothing for evacuated children; no one did much about comforts
for the troops (Huxley to Smieton, 5 Jan. 1940, WRVS, R10/2 Manchester).

[29] She did not suffer fools gladly and had quarrelled with most of the LA officers, as well as
alienating 'some of the leading women in Manchester' (Foster-Jeffery to Huxley, 7 May 1942,
WRVS, R10/2 Manchester).

[30] Foster-Jeffery to Huxley, 7 May 1942, WRVS, R10/2 Manchester.

[31] Report on Manchester, 29 June 1943; Goldney to Creswick Atkinson, 'Problem of Manchester', 24 Jan. 1944; Report on Manchester, 3 June 1951, WRVS, R10/2 Manchester.

[32] Lady Reading, reported in *Berkshire Chronicle* (11 Feb. 1944) Reading to Sir Harold
Scott, 1 Oct. 1943, WRVS, A1/38 Policy and Terms of Reference.

[33] Lady Pamela Havelock Allen was the third wife (1936) of Sir Henry Spencer Moreton
Havelock-Allen (baronetcy created in 1858), who had been a Liberal MP, 1910–18. Technically,
Dart was simply accepting her resignation, but it is clear that the resignation had been lightly
offered and rapidly withdrawn.

charming who would give the best advice and make quick decisions...A good organiser may be the type of person who is more difficult to live with.[34]

Dart proceeded to lecture her audience on WVS as a disciplined service, citing her own dismay at being forced to resign two years previously from the job of regional administrator in the North West (after the blitz Lady Reading had decided that Dart was exhausted and in need of a break). At the time this cut little ice with the local WVS leaders who were clearly fond of Lady Pamela and resentful of what they saw as Dart's 'gestapo methods'. Amongst people in the know, who included the businessmen husbands of several of the leading players, the row was the talk of the town.[35] But the sacking remained and within a few weeks all but a handful of Lady Pamela's supporters had accepted the inevitable, turning their fire on the ousted organizer for her temerity in continuing to protest.[36] During a stay of a few months in the Northeast, Dart, who had presumably been sent in to overhaul machinery which the previous administrator had allowed to sink into a comfortable apathy, sacked several other centre organizers including one in Gateshead who, Dart alleged, lacked the 'drive and push' to sort out problems with a difficult Labour local authority. In this case her rhetoric proved more immediately effective and a meeting which opened with the 'threat of wholesale resignations and demand for a public meeting of protest' ended with acquiescence.[37]

Two years earlier Dart had played a similarly disciplinarian role in the north-west. In Burnley a bitter personal—but public—row between the mayoress and the centre organizer (wife of a prominent local businessman) had created a situation in which the local authority refused to have anything to do with WVS. In May 1940 Dart intervened, meeting the mayoress behind the back of the centre organizer (which was normally seen as a quite inappropriate interference with the operational autonomy of the appointed leader) and, apparently, accepting her side of the story. Dart decided to get rid of the incumbent and replace her with a woman suggested by the town clerk, Mrs Ogden. When Ogden, who had no role in WVS at the time although she was well known to the local authority and sat on several council committees, pointed out that this would put her in an impossible position, Dart appointed her as 'co-ordinating officer' between WVS and the local authority,[38] hoping that 'when they have worked together for

[34] Report on Darlington, 25 Apr. 1944; minutes of a meeting in Darlington, 25 Apr. 1944, WRVS, R/1/2 Darlington.
[35] Report on Darlington, 23–6 May 1944, WRVS, R/1/2 Darlington.
[36] Report on Darlington Station Canteen, 3 July 1944, WRVS, R/1/2 Darlington.
[37] Dart to Egerton, 22 Apr. 1944; Report on Gateshead, 25 July 1939, WRVS, R1/2 Gateshead; Smieton to Bowerman, 15 July 1939, WRVS, R1 Northeast.
[38] Foster Jeffery, Report on Burnley, 3 July 1940, WRVS, R10/2 Burnley.

some time Mrs Ogden, who is by far the more capable woman' would take over.[39] With her successor breathing down her neck, it was the centre organizer who was placed in an impossible position and within two months she had resigned amidst well-cultivated rumours that she had been forced out by dubious means. Ogden, still reluctant because of the bitterness of local feeling, eventually agreed to take over and ran WVS effectively—if in a rather authoritarian way—for the next ten years.[40]

Vera Dart was by no means the only regional organizer to deploy such methods. When the Nottingham centre organizer was sacked without warning following complaints about the ineffectiveness of WVS from the local ARP controller (Lord Trent, the chairman of Boots), she was left with 'the dreadful feeling of being thrown out of the window with no opportunity of defence, with a crushing sense of failure and frustration and with no attempt on the part of my leaders to stand by me'.[41] 'Instead of justice and fair play', wrote a similarly aggrieved woman from the Wigan WVS, 'we were just thrown aside.'[42] 'Acting in the way of smoothing out difficulties' with the local authorities could involve the exercise of some pretty brutal disciplinary powers within WVS itself. Where internal rivalries were most acute, travelling administrators were sent in to run WVS until an acceptable centre organizer could be found. In one such incident, in Luton, the travelling administrator and the (sacked) centre organizer presented themselves simultaneously as head of the local WVS—'the situation was Gilbertian'.[43] By late 1942 rows over the dismissal of ineffective centre organizers— always formally done by Lady Reading who also rubber stamped all appointments—had become so much a part of normal operations that it was thought necessary to set up a formal appeals procedure (though one clearly designed to frustrate the appellant).[44]

[39] Vera Dart, Report on Regional Administrator's Visit to Burnley, 14 May 1940, WRVS, R10/2 Burnley.

[40] Dart to Huxley, 13 May 1940, WRVS, R10 Northwest; Dart, Report on Burnley, 14 May 1940; Dart, Report on Burnley, 22 May 1940; Dart to Shuttleworth, 3 July 1940; Foster Jeffery, Report on Burnley, 3 July 1940; Dart, Report on Burnley, 15 July 1940; Lancaster, *et al.*, to Lady Reading, 18 Dec. 1944; Report on Burnley, 4 Jan. 1945; Reading to Lancaster, 23 Jan. 1945, WRVS, R10/2 Burnley.

[41] The reason for WVS ineffectiveness in Nottingham may well have had less to do with any incompetence on the part of the organizer than with the fact that the Labour council had always been unenthusiastic about WVS and had never done more than tolerate its existence (Huxley to Nottingham Town Clerk, 15 Mar. 1939; Report on Nottingham, 2 Apr. 1940, WRVS, R3/7 Nottingham; Walker, Report for week ending 15 July 1939, WRVS, R3 Regional Office).

[42] Alstead to Reading, 23 May 1942, WRVS, R10/2 Wigan.

[43] Doe to Reading, Report on Luton, 12 Oct. 1941, WRVS, R4/1 Luton.

[44] WVS Chairman's Committee, Minutes, 31 Aug. 1942, 11 Sept. 1942, 24 Sept. 1942, 5 Nov. 1942; WVS General Purposes Committee, Minutes, 4 Oct. 1942.

III

In their zeal to create a disciplined service, regional organizers were some-times more critical of local centres than were the local authorities whose needs they existed, in theory, to serve. During the 1940–1 blitz the centre organizer in Chester, Mrs Knowles, refused to accept regional instructions to send support teams to the heavily bombed part of industrial Lancashire, preferring to make her own bilateral arrangements with particular towns. Summoned to Manchester for a private talking to, Knowles reported back indignantly to her officers who wrote a collective letter of protest to Vera Dart. When Dart came to Chester to confront the officers, Knowles, whose contempt for bureaucracy was one reason for her local popularity, made the mistake of accusing her rudely (and certainly unjustly) of being 'the type of amateur who flaps around and takes the kudos while the work is done by someone else'.[45] When Dart reported to Tothill Street it was agreed that Knowles would have to be 'terminated', and Lady Reading wrote a stern letter asking her to resign. The local reaction was first to close the office for a couple of days in protest, and then to reopen it declaring that 'they were taking no notice of Lady Reading, and were getting on very nicely'. The mayor, lobbied by Knowles and the town clerk (with whom she had a notoriously flirtatious relationship), was inclined to take her part, warning that Knowles, 'a member of many Associations in Chester', had the 'support of many women whom I know to be of sound judgement . . . If she goes 90% go with her'.[46] Chester WVS was now completely out of control and unavailable to Dart for support work during the Merseyside blitz.[47] For a time it seemed likely that Knowles would try to continue independently, but this became impossible after Dart convinced the mayor that this was not, as he suspected, just 'the usual women's quarrel' and reminded him that if the local authority tried to work with Knowles independently their expenses would not be eligible for Treasury grant. A travelling administrator was sent in, and after a difficult search—'Chester is full of people who are either suffering from bad hearts or are the petty gossiping type'[48]—a suitable woman was found. Subsequently all but two of Knowles' officers 'trickled back'. One of them, Dart reported to Lady Reading after a trip to Chester, 'was so frightened when I went into the office that she scuttled upstairs like a rabbit. However, she did nerve herself to come down eventually and con-gratulate me upon the honour. [*Dart had just been awarded the OBE for her services during the blitz.*] It is really comic the effect this has had in Chester. It just came at the psychological moment.'[49] Dart's stature as a respected

[45] Dart, Report on Meeting at the Queen's Hotel, 22 Apr. 1941, WRVS, R10/1 Chester.
[46] Huxley to Reading, 1 May 1941, WRVS, R10/1 Chester.
[47] Dart, Report on Meeting at the Queen's Hotel, 22 Apr. 1941.
[48] Dart to Goldney, 1 June 1941, WRVS, R10/1 Chester.
[49] Dart to Reading, 5 July 1941, WRVS, R10 Northwest.

figure in the regional response to the blitz had probably also been important in overcoming the mayor's parochial instinct to support Knowles against outside authority. According to one of her (admittedly devoted) assistants the mayor and town clerk backed off when they realized that they were 'up against...the whole standing of the WVS and...the personality of the Regional Administrator.'[50]

The outcome in Chester was not inevitable. A similar confrontation between the Yorkshire regional administrator, Mary Aykroyd, and the centre organizer in Hull ended quite differently. This crisis was precipitated in February 1942 by a Tothill Street decision to sack the East Riding administrator, Mary Ingham, thereby ending the anomaly of a region divided between two administrators working in parallel. Ingham refused to go quietly, and told all and sundry in the East Riding that she had been sacked to further the self-aggrandizement of Mary Aykroyd.[51] The centre organizers in York, Bridlington, and Hull declared that they could not work under Aykroyd's direction, accusing her of being 'dictatorial and bad tempered': the Hull centre organizer also hinted at a more personal objection, though the records do not reveal what this was.[52] Underlying all this was the historic antagonism of the East Riding to domination by the West.[53]

Aykroyd's response was to offer her own resignation, but this was refused by Lady Reading who demanded loyalty from the rebels. Most of the opposition quickly crumbled, but in Hull the centre organizer, Mrs Moreton Stewart, refused to attend regional conferences or to have anything to do with Aykroyd. Stewart had written to Reading threatening that if Aykroyd tried to interfere in Hull she would transfer her whole operation from WVS to the local authority. Reading's response to this 'poisonous' threat was blunt: since 'you do not feel the loyalty to WVS that is necessary for centre organisers...I sympathise with your suggestion that you should transfer from the WVS and become Officers of the Local Authority instead.'[54] Apparently spoiling for a fight, Reading wrote to Aykroyd: 'I am delighted to have a chance to come into the open and to tell them what I think.'[55] Although Reading's letter had demanded an immediate decision, there is no sign in the file that Stewart replied to the ultimatum. Instead, both the town clerk and Moreton Stewart came to London to see Reading, leaving

---

[50] Dart to Goldney, 1 June 1941, WRVS, R10/1 Chester.
[51] Lady Reading, Note on Visit from Town Clerk of Hull, 15 Apr. 1942, WRVS, R2 Yorkshire, Confidential Correspondence.
[52] '[T]here are family reasons why it is specially difficult for her to serve under Miss Aykroyd', Huxley, Report on Visit from Mrs Moreton Stewart, n.d., Feb. 1942; Aykroyd to Huxley, 24 July 1942, WRVS, R2 Yorkshire, Confidential Correspondence.
[53] Pritchard to Reading, 28 Aug. 1942, ibid.
[54] Reading to Moreton Stewart, 27 Mar. 1942, ibid.
[55] Reading to Aykroyd, 27 Mar. 1942, ibid.

her convinced that everything was sorted out. In fact the regime of non-co-operation with Aykroyd continued throughout the summer of 1942.

The relationship between WVS and the local authority in Hull was a particularly close one. Formed out of the NCW, and initially led by its secretary, the WVS acquitted itself well in the 1941 blitz and won the wholehearted approval of the town clerk and more or less exclusive control of all voluntary work sponsored by the local authority.[56] There may well have been a political affinity between the alliance of Conservatives and Independents which had won back control of the council from Labour just before the war, and the local WVS leaders who later developed ambitious and widely discussed plans to resist any post-war state take-over of welfare work traditionally undertaken by the voluntary sector.[57] Although some members of long-established social service organizations in the town were dismayed by the success of this undemocratic upstart organization, it was clear that Moreton Stewart, a doctor who had succeeded the original leader, had solid support among her own members.[58]

In July Aykroyd wrote to Reading complaining that 'with the present officers in control at Hull we shall never get the co-operation we want ... it becomes more and more evident that the leaders in Hull have no loyalty at all to Tothill Street or the Regional Office and they merely use them only when absolutely necessary, but really look upon themselves as a part of the Local Authority.'[59] At the same time, however, she acknowledged that any attempt to sack the leaders would produce 'wholesale resignation'. In September Reading made one more attempt at a decisive resolution to the stand-off, telling the town clerk that she would sack the leaders unless they came to heel immediately.[60] Again, however, the hunter was deprived of her prey. Dispatched to Hull to sort things out, Mrs Huxley returned with an agreement that left Moreton Stewart in undisputed control.[61] Whether Aykroyd subsequently got the co-operation she wanted is not apparent from the records. What is clear is that neither she, nor Lady Reading herself, was able to sack defiant local leaders where they enjoyed the full support not only of their own members but also of the local authority. Where a local authority stuck by its centre organizer, however much she defied the WVS

[56] Moseley, Report on Yorkshire, 13 Nov. 1939, WRVS, R2 Yorkshire; Ingham, Report on Visit to Hull, 7 Dec. 1939, WRVS, R2/1 East Riding; Pickard to Reading, 8 Mar. 1941, WRVS, R2/1 Hull; R. K. Kelsall, Report on Hull, 4 Apr. 1942, 3, 5, 10–12, 27–9, 40–5, in NCSRS, E2/8.

[57] Maxse to Capell, 19 Mar. 1943, WRVS, R2/1 Hull; R. K. Kelsall, Report on Hull, 4 Apr. 1942, 11; N. Tiratsoo, 'Labour and the Reconstruction of Hull', in Tiratsoo (ed.), *The Attlee Years* (London, 1991), 142 n. 11.

[58] Kelsall, op. cit., *passim*; Aykroyd to Reading, 21 July 1942, WRVS, R2 Yorkshire, Confidential Correspondence.

[59] Aykroyd to Reading, 21 July 1942, ibid.

[60] Reading to Pickard, 2 Sept. 1942; Reading to Huxley, 31 Aug. 1942, ibid.

[61] Huxley, Report on Meeting in Hull, 8 Sept. 1942, ibid.

chain of command, there was nothing that Tothill Street could do. For once Lady Reading was forced to swallow her pride.

Events in Hull remind us that power is never absolute and that WVS was not quite as disciplined a service as Lady Reading liked to pretend. There are other examples of this. In the summer of 1940 patriotic pressure from the membership forced Lady Reading, against her better judgement, to author-ize collections for the immensely popular local Spitfire Funds, one of the very few occasions when she admitted yielding to pressure from below.[62] In fact, as we have seen, fund-raising by local groups for war charities, though officially banned, was widespread. In a few cases the ability of WVS centres to fund their own activities without going cap in hand to the town hall allowed them to operate much like any other voluntary organization rather than as servants of the local authority. At Romsey, in Hampshire, following the resignation of the centre organizer, it emerged that she had been person-ally bankrolling WVS to the tune of £800 a year.[63] Similarly in Chester, one of the complaints against the sacked centre organizer, Mrs Knowles, was that she had used her own money to fund WVS and thus obviated the need to keep proper accounts.[64] In South Shields the centre organizer, Mrs Chap-man, kept on excellent terms with the Labour local authority (the wives of all the main local government officials were members of WVS, as were some Labour women), but, apart from staffing the rest centres, she ran WVS quite independently concentrating on knitting, sewing, and mending for the troops and the hospital, packing Red Cross parcels, and friendly visiting to servicemen's families, wounded sailors, etc. None of this involved local authority control and most of it was work usually undertaken by established voluntary organizations. Not only did Mrs Chapman install WVS headquar-ters rent-free in a house that she owned, she also appears to have raised almost all necessary finances by regular contributions from other voluntary organizations. The council, which was not interested in the establishment of Housewives Service since the wardens felt they already had effective support from housewives, was delighted that WVS cost it so little. Since everyone in South Shields was happy with these arrangements they did not come to the notice of the WVS regional office until after the war. When told that operating on the basis of subscriptions from other organizations was entirely contrary to WVS rules, Mrs Chapman blithely replied that 'they had always liked to feel independent in South Shields'.[65] A not dissimilar situation

[62] WVS Chairman's Committee, Minutes, 21 Aug. 1940; Huxley to Rothwell, 21 Aug. 1940, WRVS, R10/2 Salford.

[63] WVS Chairman's Committee, Minutes, 24 Mar. 1943.

[64] Minutes of Meeting at the Town Hall, Chester, 21 May 1941, WRVS, R10/1 Chester.

[65] Dart, Report of Visit to South Shields, 14 Feb. 1944; Hornby, Report of Interview with Town Clerk, 31 Oct. 1947; Hornby, Report of Interview with Mrs Chapman, 3 Oct. 1945, WRVS, R/1/2 South Shields.

existed in Middlesbrough, where WVS had been set up by the president of
the local NCW, Dr Levick, a retired consultant who was a leading figure in
the national federation of Townswomen's Guilds. Her three deputies were
all established middle-class leaders in the borough: a doctor's wife who ran
the local Red Cross, the secretary of the Guild of Help (who in 1938 ran a
flourishing women's luncheon club), and the chairman of the Townswomen's Guild who was described by the regional administrator as the 'general
leader' in the town. The close integration of the WVS leadership with the
other middle-class women's organizations was reinforced in the autumn of
1939 when the Guild of Help, whose secretary had helped to establish WVS
in the town, set up a war emergency committee for social service with Levick
on its executive.[66] As in South Shields, the local authority was not interested
in starting Housewives Service, and Dr Levick—'the professional woman
type who works quietly with a minimum of advertisement'—maintained
good relations with them while concentrating WVS work on knitting and
sewing parties and provision of emergency clothing.[67] When, in 1950, two
of the WVS wartime stalwarts were elected to the local council and put on its
Children's Committee, they made no attempt to involve the WVS: neither of
them knew that WVS had anything to do with the local authority.[68] These
two north-east towns serve to illustrate the capacity of middle-class women's
networks to sustain an independent local sphere of public activity and social
leadership during the war, and to use WVS, despite itself, to do this. In both
cases the local authority was happy to collude with such an arm's-length
arrangement, and everyone concerned remained blissfully unaware of Lady
Reading's mission to refashion voluntary work as a disciplined instrument of
the elected authorities.[69]

The impact of WVS on the urban middle-class world that it colonized was
far from uniform. Where the balance of local political power made it
essential to include Labour women in the local WVS leadership (Coventry,
Southampton), and where local authorities complained about WVS ineffi-
ciency (Nottingham, Leicester) Lady Reading's enforcers were able to oust
established local leaders and replace them. But the imposition of discipline

---

[66] Dart, Report on Middlesbrough, 25 May 1944; Levick to Reading, 6 Dec. 1939, WRVS,
R1/5 Middlesbrough; NUTG Executive, Minutes, *passim*; WVS Executive, Minutes, 7 June
1938, 14 Dec. 1938, 15 Feb. 1939; E. W. Fox, Report on Guild of Help, 5 Dec. 1938, NACVS,
Box 20.

[67] Dart, Report on Middlesbrough, 29 Feb. 1944, WRVS, R1/5 Middlesbrough.

[68] Stevenson, Report on Middlesbrough, 10 Jan. 1950, ibid.

[69] The only fly in the ointment was Lady Reading's chief enforcer in the north Vera Dart who,
during her spell as regional administrator in 1944, tried, unsuccessfully, to bully Middlesbrough
into starting Housewives Service (Dart, Reports on Middlesbrough, 25 May, 1944 1 June 1944,
WRVS, R1/5 Middlesbrough). In Tynemouth, a Tory stronghold in the North East (*Shields
Evening News* (2 Nov. 1945)), where a similar arm's-length arrangement seems to have existed,
Dart was more successful in putting things on an orthodox footing (WRVS, R1/2 Tynemouth,
passim). But even she did not spot what was going on in South Shields.

was not confined to such situations. Vera Dart was particularly vigorous when running WVS first in the north-west and later in the north-east in facing down protest in order to oust ineffective local leaders, even in the absence of any complaint from the local authority. In the case of Chester, the need to co-ordinate the WVS contribution to the emergency services in the Merseyside blitz served to legitimate sacking the parochially minded centre organizer, despite the fact that the local authority leaders were at first inclined to support her against Dart. But Lady Reading's vision of a disciplined national service did not carry all before it. In Hull, where the autonomy of the local WVS was backed by a friendly local authority, all attempts by regional and national WVS leadership to impose their authority proved futile. And there were probably many places like South Shields and Middlesbrough where, untouched by scandal or the attentions of zealous regional administrators, local centres quietly operated in ways which owed more to established traditions of voluntarism than to Lady Reading's modernizing vision.

It would, however, be misleading to view WVS simply through its urban operations. In the countryside, as we shall see in Chapter 7, WVS played a more unambiguously conservative role. And in the coalfields, one of which is the subject of the next chapter, the problem of balancing middle-class leadership in the female associational world with the self-assertion of Labour women could bring WVS to the point of disintegration.

6

Coalfield

Politically, County Durham belonged to the miners. First won by Labour in 1919, the county council had been under continuous Labour control since the mid-1920s.[1] Despite their crushing industrial victory in the 1926 lockout, the coal owners had largely abandoned the struggle for political hegemony in the county, leaving local Conservatives, regrouped with other anti-socialists as the Moderate Party in 1921, to soldier on as a permanent minority. 'There is literally no person of any standing who takes the slightest interest in politics on our side,' wrote Cuthbert Headlam, Tory MP for the marginal constituency of Barnard Castle, whose diaries record a stoic battle on behalf of an economic elite which he despised and whose eventual displacement by the nationalization of the mines he believed to be inevitable. 'Our forces are very weak,' he wrote in 1934, 'the people in this county are completely under the Socialist spell and most of the small ratepayers are too frightened to vote against the miners.'[2] In local elections reluctant Moderate Party candidates drawn from a tiny middle class of colliery managers, shop owners, and the occasional professional confronted officials of the Durham Miners' Association (DMA), a group of disciplined, self-educated labour leaders confident of their capacity to run the county on behalf of the miners. The DMA was no sectional trade union; rather it embraced the whole range of its members' interests both at work and in the pit villages, where union officials negotiated claims to company housing and made careers in the management of co-operative stores and working-men's clubs. 'Civil society', write the social historians of the early-twentieth-century coalfield, '[was] very largely regulated by a new layer of working-class committee men and officials.'[3] With the DMA so effectively leading local society, the Labour Party functioned merely as its shadow, having little independent existence.[4]

---

[1] W. R. Garside, *The Durham Miners, 1919–1960* (London, 1971), 325 ff.

[2] S. Ball (ed.), *Parliament and Politics in the Age of Baldwin and Macdonald. The Headlam Diaries, 1923–1935* (London, 1992), 111, 290, 9–10. On Headlam, see also Huw Beynon and Terry Austin, *Masters and Servants. Class and Patronage in the Making of a Labour Organisation. The Durham Miners and the English Political Tradition* (London, 1994), 314–28, 336–7.

[3] Beynon and Austin, *Masters and Servants*, 250.

[4] Ibid., 263. For complaints about the continuing subordination of the Easington Labour Party to the union apparatus in the 1980s, see H. Wainwright, *Labour. A Tale of Two Parties* (London, 1987), 171–3, 273–4.

It is a measure of the degree to which County Durham was dominated by the miners that it was the only place in England where Tothill Street completely lost control of a local WVS centre. The events in the mining villages of Easington Rural District, analysed in this chapter, represent the most extreme challenge mounted anywhere in England to the middle-class domination of wartime voluntary work. The fact that such a challenge needed to be made, however, points to the existence in these villages of middle-class women accustomed to the exercise of social leadership. Even where Labour, politically, was hegemonic, attention to the associational worlds of women reveals the continuities of class. What occurred in Easington between 1939 and 1942 was a contest between two radically different forms of social power. In some industrial towns, as we have seen, Tothill Street was instrumental in brokering an accommodation between middle-class social leadership and the institutions of the labour movement. This was also, eventually, the case in Easington, but only after a two-and-a-half year struggle in which rival women's organizations owing allegiance, respectively, to the Labour council and to middle-class social leaders fought a bitter war for the privilege of mobilizing voluntary war work among the miners' wives.

I

With 81,000 inhabitants Easington, a cluster of mining villages on the south-east edge of the Durham coalfield, was the largest Rural District in England. Two-thirds of the occupied population were miners, the next most significant groups being shop assistants, domestic servants, and employees of the local authority. Taken together, proprietors, professionals, and teachers— the core of the local middle class—constituted less than 5 per cent of the population.[5] On the social class criteria used in the 1951 census, Easington had the smallest upper class of any area in County Durham (0.7 per cent) and one of the smallest middle classes.[6] On the district council Labour members, most of them miners, held about three-quarters of the seats.[7] Together with the slightly more socially mixed town of Seaham Harbour to the north, Easington provided the Labour Party with one of its safest seats, occupied successively since the 1920s by Sidney Webb, Ramsay Mac-Donald, and, from 1935, Manny Shinwell, scourge of Churchill's wartime coalition and subsequently responsible as a minister in Attlee's post-war government for the nationalization of the mines.

---

[5] Census of England and Wales, 1931, Occupation Tables, Industry Tables; Durham County Council, Regional Civil Defence Organization, 1941, PRO, HO 186 657.
[6] Census of England and Wales, 1951.
[7] *Durham Chronicle* (23 Jan. 1942).

The main settlements—Easington Colliery, Horden, and Blackhall on the coast, Murton, Haswell, Shotton, and Wheatley Hill inland—were, to outsiders at least, grim places: 'the retort dreary is what I feel springing up, but [such a negative feeling] has to be crushed down' remarked a WVS travelling administrator on her first visit.[8] J. B. Priestley, who had no such need to control his feelings, left a vivid account of the awfulness of Shotton in 1935, 'a symbol of greedy, careless, cynical, barbaric industrialism':

Imagine then a village consisting of a few shops, a public-house, and a clutter of dirty little houses, all at the base of what looked at first like an active volcano...the notorious Shotton 'tip' [which] towered to the sky...its vast dark bulk, steaming and smoking at various levels, blotting out all the landscape at the back of the village... The atmosphere was thickened with ashes and sulphuric fumes; like that of Pompeii, as we are told, on the eve of its destruction...the whole village and everybody in it was buried in this thick reek, was smothered in ashes and sulphuric fumes. Wherever I stood they made me gasp and cough.[9]

The miners' cottages in Shotton were the most overcrowded in the district, and housing in Easington as a whole, with a 1931 average of 1.29 people per room, was among the worst anywhere in England and Wales.[10] At Easington Colliery, the dreary rows of cottages packed tight around the pithead spoke eloquently of the company's attitude to its workers: 'we were just fodder to be housed and sent down that bloody shaft.'[11]

Despite the domination of Labour politics by the Miners' Association, women were not excluded from political life. Three Labour women sat on the Easington district council, and they were to play a central part in the struggle for control of WVS. At county level the Labour Party Women's Advisory Committee was a well-established organization, promoting women's interests, nominating Labour women for co-option as magistrates or members of county council committees, and providing extensive educational programmes including competitive scholarships to take miners' wives to weekend schools. By 1939 the women's sections in the county had over 4,000 members, the great majority of them miners' wives.[12] During her tenure as the MP's wife in the 1920s, Beatrice Webb had been impressed by the 'moral refinement and perfect manners' of these Labour women, their capacity to rise above the dirt and endless labour of running a household in

---

[8] Shawyer to Wilson, 24 Aug. 1939, WRVS, R1, Regional Office.

[9] J. B. Priestley, *English Journey* (London, 1934), 336–7.

[10] Census of England and Wales, 1931; Women's Group for Public Welfare, *Our Towns. A Close Up* (Oxford, 1943), p. xii; Garside, *The Durham Miners*, 287.

[11] Beynon and Austin, *Masters and Servants*, 113.

[12] M. Callcott, 'The Making of a Labour Stronghold: Electoral Politics in County Durham between the Two World Wars', in M. Callcott and R. Challinor, *Working-class Politics in North East England* (Newcastle, 1983), 70–1; Durham Country Labour Women's Advisory Committee, Minutes, *passim*, Durham RO, D/X 1048/4.

a mining village. Attending a gathering of 400 Labour women in 1926 she remarked how much more 'jolly' and 'talkative' they were than their 'sullen' locked-out husbands: 'in their best dresses, and the prettily decorated tea tables, with piles of cake and bread-and-butter, it might have been a gathering of prosperous lower middle-class women...'[13] The miners' wives not only provided the practical intelligence—as Priestley called it, the 'gumption'—without which the pitmen's labour could not have been reproduced from day to day, but some of them also found the time to assert themselves beyond the household.[14] The wartime minutes of the Easington Colliery Women's Section reveal a group of miners' wives receiving regular reports from their local councillor, debating political questions, and engaged in serious educational work. These Labour women were certainly not confined to making the tea or, like their Tory counterparts, playing whist and raising party funds. The Easington meetings consisted of political discussion, talks, report backs from weekend schools, even occasionally sitting exams for the annual educational scholarship—although in 1945 they did resolve to 'rite' [sic] to the country women's organizer asking her to set simpler questions for the next scholarship test: the previous year's essay written in exam conditions on the basis of Labour Party pamphlets on either *Your Home* or *The Nation's Food* was considered 'too hard'. Whatever their educational deficiencies these were serious and independently minded women well aware of their gender interests—'we support Dr Edith Summerskill in her fight re wives savings, it caused good discussion'—and far from deferential towards their own county leadership. When, for example, it was reported that plans to celebrate the 1945 Silver Jubilee of the Women's Advisory Committee included the institution of a chain of office for the county secretary and the baking of a large cake, the branch protested that this 'was all against our principles as we did not like outward pomp and show and a large cake was ridiculous in these days of restriction'.[15]

It has been suggested that the Conservative Party in inter-war County Durham held considerable appeal for miners' wives frustrated by the labour movement's neglect of their interests.[16] While leading Conservatives certainly liked to present themselves as allies of the downtrodden working-class wife in her struggle against the male-centred politics of the miners' union, it is notable that this alliance did not extend to the fielding of women candidates in elections. The first female Conservative country councillor was elected in 1946: by which time the 'patriarchal' Labour Party had several

[13] M. Cole (ed.), *Beatrice Webb's Diaries* (London, 1956), 27, 123.

[14] Priestley, *English Journey*, 333–4.

[15] Easington Colliery Labour Party Women's Section, Minutes, 3 Dec. 1945, 20 Dec. 1943, 26 Feb. 1945, Durham RO, DX 1048/66.

[16] P. Lynn, 'The Influence of Class and Gender: Female Political Organisations in County Durham during the Inter-war Years', *North East History*, 31 (1997).

women on the council, some of them of long standing.[17] It is true that only a tiny proportion of Durham miners' wives were self-improvers active in Labour politics, and it is may well be that some of the others expressed their frustrations with domestic oppression by voting Tory in secret. In 1931 Labour men blamed the Easington wives for the fact that Ramsay MacDonald was able to retain the seat against the official Labour candidate, and with it his credibility as leader of a 'national' government. The continuing appeal of MacDonald's charisma among these women, however, may have had more to do with their growing political self-confidence than with any tendency to Conservatism: 'We know you have done your utmost for us, and you will have our loyal support no matter what the Seaham Labour Party may say,' wrote a defiant group of miners' wives from Easington Colliery to MacDonald during the election campaign.[18] Four years later, his reputation shattered by the National Government's regime of means tests and continuing mass unemployment, MacDonald saw a different face of the miners' wives: 'their eyes flamed and gleamed with hate & passion; their hair was dishevelled; their language filthy with oaths & some obscenity; they filled one with loathing fear just like French Revolution studies. Night after night their misery was upon me.' This, however, says more about MacDonald than it does about the women who, in meetings at Shotton and elsewhere in the constituency, had joined in shouting him down.[19]

Labour's influence among the miners' wives was contested not so much through party politics as by the capacity of middle-class women to sustain positions of social leadership in the villages. Take, for example, Mrs Jessie Dixon, a doctor, who not only ran the Mother and Child Welfare Centre in Horden, but also presided over the local Women's Institute, a thriving organization made up largely of miners' wives which held its 1940 annual general meeting in the Conservative Club Hall. Whatever tensions may have been caused by her sometimes patronizing manner, these appear to have been adequately dealt with by an annual 'topsy turvy' night on which the officers were temporarily displaced and the meeting closed with the singing of 'Jerusalem' in place of 'God Save the King'. (As usual both anthems were sung, one at the beginning and one at the end: but for 'topsy turvy' night the order was reversed—scarcely a revolutionary change in the order of precedence!)[20] The

[17] Moderate Party, Minutes, 19 Mar. 1946, Durham RO, D/MCF/174. In the 1949 local elections the number of Tory women on the Council increased to four (ibid., 11 Apr. 1949). In 1939 Labour had two women county councillors (Callcott, 'Labour Stronghold', 71), one of them Tamosin Todd.

[18] D. Marquand, *Ramsay MacDonald* (London, 1977), 653; Beynon and Austin, *Masters and Servants*, 340–1.

[19] Marquand, *MacDonald*, 781.

[20] Horden Women's Institute, Minutes, 12 Jan. 1943 and *passim*, Durham RO, D/WI/3/94/6; *Durham Chronicle* (20 Dec. 1940); Horden Child Welfare Centre Voluntary Committee, Minutes, *passim*, Durham RO, DX 1043/1; Kelly's Directory, County Durham, 1938.

WI had grown rapidly in the coalfield during the depression, and by 1939 it claimed over 12,000 members in County Durham—four times the number claimed by Labour Party women's sections—with about half the Institutes located in mining villages.[21] Durham's Labour leaders saw the WI as a dangerous rival, an 'avenue for the organisation of anti-Labour forces'.[22] Through their leadership of the WI the colliery manager's wife and her kind offered miners' wives ways of visualizing local society sharply at odds with the class rhetoric of the labour movement.[23] The depression years had also seen the establishment, under the patronage of the County Durham Council for Social Service, of Women's Social Service Clubs: by 1939 there were seventy-one clubs involving about 6,000 women, most of them miners' wives with young children.[24] The club life which developed among unemployed miners and their wives during the 1930s was seen by the philanthropists who fostered it as bringing civilization to a cultural desert: 'the first centres of general social and cultural activity that some places have had ... obviously the most import-ant social institution in the neighbourhood.'[25] Despite the political hegemony of the miners and the existence of a well-established network of Labour women, middle-class women active in the WI, the Women's Clubs, women's sections of the British Legion, and a host of more local institutions were serious contenders for social leadership in the Durham coalfield.

The 'thinness' of the Labour Party's presence in civil society has often been noted.[26] While local Conservative politicians networked assiduously in non-political associational life, their Labour counterparts seldom found time to engage seriously with organizations outside the labour movement. In the Durham coalfield assertive working-class women tended to concentrate their public activity on Labour politics, leaving positions of leadership in most local associations to middle-class women who, in any case, had the leisure and resources to undertake it. Only through the operation of univer-sal suffrage and the agency of the Labour Party were miners' wives able to challenge established social leadership even in their own villages. Amongst traditional social leaders the fact that these Labour women rested their claims to leadership merely on the fact that they had been democratically elected appeared little less than scandalous.

[21] Huxley to Heady, 20 Apr. 1939, WRVS, R1 Regional Office.
[22] J. W. Foster cited in P. Lynn, 'The Shaping of Political Allegiance: Class, Gender, Nation and Locality in Co. Durham, 1918–1945', Teeside Ph.D., 1999, 34, 40.
[23] Ibid., 35–7, 40, 70–1.
[24] Blanche E. Griffith, 'The Community Service Council for Durham County Ltd.', 10 Nov. 1938, WRVS, R1/2 Durham County.
[25] *Men Without Work. A Report Made to the Pilgrim Trust* (Cambridge, 1938), 312–33.
[26] M. Stacey, *Tradition and Change: A Study of Banbury* (Oxford, 1960), 49–53; F. Bealey, J. Blondel, and W. P. McCann, *Constituency Politics: A Study of Newcastle-under-Lyme* (London, 1965), 398–400, 410–11; Duncan Tanner, 'Labour and its Membership', in Tanner, P. Thane, and N. Tiratsoo (eds.), *Labour's First Century* (Cambridge, 2000), 252–3.

In Easington the anti-socialist resistance was led by Anthony Young, who served as head warden for the Easington Village Parish Council during the war.[27] He was secretary of the local ratepayers' association and, after the war—when the colliery manager was no longer willing to stand—the Moderate Party candidate in the county council elections.[28] Through the correspondence columns of the local newspaper he kept up a running fire, accusing Labour members of milking the public purse with excessive expenses claims and systematically favouring their friends and relatives in local authority employment.[29] A particular target for anti-socialists was the alleged nepotism exercised by some of the leading Labour families, and all three of the female Labour councillors involved in the struggle for control of WVS became targets of Young's attacks. Following her election to the Easington RDC, Florence Winter, wife of a council rent collector and Dixon's main rival for the leadership of women's voluntary effort in Horden, was accused of securing paid posts for her son successively in ARP and Food Control.[30] When E. F. Peart, a leading figure in the constituency Labour Party, resigned from the Council in 1938 to take up a local government post, his wife, another Florence, was elected for the vacancy. Two years later, when their son (who was also on the RDC) was called up, the father was co-opted back onto the council in his place.[31] Such behaviour appeared shocking to Young; and he was equally outraged by the fact that the senior minister in the Horden Methodist church (whose daughter, Mrs Nicholson, was the third woman Labour councillor) advocated socialism as practical Christianity from the pulpit.[32] To Young the moral was clear: 'The Socialists on Easington Rural District Council have shown outstandingly the truth "that the master of masters in tyranny is the working man in power".'[33] Young found it hard to accept the legitimacy of Labour's political hegemony. The kind of networking within leading political families which would have seemed perfectly natural among the gentry appeared positively corrupt when undertaken by people whose social prominence rested on nothing more substantial than democratic election. Such sentiments were, as we shall see, shared by some of the middle-class women who fought to wrest the local WVS from control by Labour councillors. Unable to challenge 'socialist tyranny' at the ballot box, it is clear that some

[27] *Northern Echo* (18 Oct., 2 Nov. 1940).
[28] Moderate Party, file on elections, Durham RO, D/MCF/26.
[29] *Northern Echo* (18 May 1938, 4 Feb. 1939). Allegations of nepotism were a staple of Conservative propaganda in the coalfield. Lynn, 'Shaping', 22.
[30] *Northern Echo* (8 and 11 Oct. 1940).
[31] Unidentified cutting, 4 Aug. 1938 in Moderate Party, Press Cuttings, Durham RO, D/MCF/71; Easington RDC ARP Committee, Minutes, 11 Apr. 1940, Durham RO, RD/EA/21; *Northern Echo* (8 and 12 Oct. 1940).
[32] *Northern Echo*, 22 Jan. 1939, 12, 17, 23, 29 Oct. 1940 ; *Durham Chronicle*, 20 Sept. 1940; Reid to Huxley, 28 Oct. 1940 enclosing cutting of letter to press from Hind who 'is the father of Cllr. Mrs Nicholson', WRVS, R1/2 Easington 1940–2.
[33] *Northern Echo* (18 Oct. 1940).

of those engaged in WVS saw their voluntary work as a means of sustaining a sphere of operation not subordinated to Labour's political hegemony.

II

Before the war the Chairman of the county council's National Service Committee saw no need for WVS; nor did the leading Labour women in the county, Tamosin Todd, who declared that miners' wives would not be interested in joining because they were all too aware that 'in a time of crisis they would have to do all the floor scrubbing' for the 'ladies' in charge. Nor, she asserted, would the various church sisterhoods support WVS if the Durham Miners' Association opposed it.[34] Despite this opposition, WVS claimed some success in persuading Labour women to participate, and by August 1940 Labour councillors were acting as WVS centre organizers in at least sixteen County Durham towns and villages.[35] Responding to allegations that Labour women were under-represented, Mrs Myers, the WVS Regional Organizer, reported that in the rural areas she always encouraged representative women's meetings to elect a small executive team rather than appointing a single leader: if Labour women remained under-represented this was a result of their own indifference.[36] Despite her claims to be 'wooing the labour element',[37] Myers was not unhappy about this outcome, remarking of complaints about the (Conservative) leader appointed in one solidly Labour mining village that she was 'the only suitable woman in this district, both because of her own and her husband's position and the respect that they command generally in the area in which they live.' Her deputies were the wives, respectively, of the colliery manager and a local doctor.[38] In Birtley, also solidly Labour, the colliery manager's wife, who was already president of both the Townswomen's Guild and the British Legion, took charge of WVS, making space in her own substantial house for the manufacture of hospital supplies. She too was assisted by a doctor's wife.[39]

[34] Memorandum from William Teeling, a Ministry of Labour official in Hull, 12 Apr. 1939, WRVS, R1.
[35] Wilson to Myers, 31 Mar. 1939; Huxley to Reading, 22 Nov. 1939, WRVS, R1; Huxley, 'Note on the Position in Easington', 8 Aug. 1940, WRVS, R1/2 Easington 1940–2.
[36] Myers to Wilson, 20 Mar. 1939; Myers to Smieton, 26 Apr. 1939, WRVS, R1.
[37] Smieton to Huxley, 26 May 1939, WRVS, R1.
[38] Myers to Smieton, 26 Apr. 1939, WRVS, R1; WVS Executive Committee, Minutes, 1 Mar. 1939; Moderate Party, File on Elections, Durham RO, D/MCF/26.
[39] Report by EJW, 16 Sept. 1939, WRVS, R1; Moderate Party, File on Elections, Durham RO, D/MCF/26. In Headlam's constituency of Barnard Castle the WVS committee was a thoroughly middle-class affair, including two representatives of the tennis club but none, as they were later to protest, of the Labour women (Barnard Castle UDC, File on WVS, Durham RO, UD/BC/186; Durham County Federation of Divisional Labour Parties, Minutes, 22 Feb., 12 Apr. 1941, Durham RO, D/sho/5b; Durham Country Labour Women's Advisory Committee, Minutes, 6 May 1941, Durham RO, D/X 1048/4).

However dominant Labour might be politically, some colliery managers still behaved, like the inter-war under-manager bitterly remembered by elderly miners in Easington, 'as if they owned the village and everyone in it'; and the public activity of their wives was central to such assumptions.[40]

Though vigorous in recruiting volunteers for ARP work before the war, the Easington district council was reluctant to accept WVS. The price extracted from Lady Reading's travelling administrator in the summer of 1939 was the appointment as centre organizer of Winfred Waring, wife of the left-wing clerk to the council and herself a committed Labour supporter. Balance was provided by the appointment as her deputies of two women whose sympathies lay with the middle-class resistance to the local Labour establishment.[41] One of them, Mrs Prior, was married to a Lieutenant Colonel who was the chief patron of Sunderland Football club, and the other, Mrs Martin, who as chair of the women's section of the British Legion in Horden worked closely with Jessie Dixon's husband, had been personally recommended by the Chief Constable of the county.[42] At the time WVS was established Mrs Waring was visiting the United States and before she returned in late September 1939, the deputies had already started to arrange for meetings in each village representative of all the local women's organizations. At least one such gathering had occurred in the village of Hetton attended by representatives of the Mother's Union, WI, British Legion, Primitive Methodist Sisterhood, an organization glorying in the title of Women's Bright Hour, the Labour Party, and the Conservatives (who, although in a minority, had enough support in the village regularly to field candidates in county council elections). The meeting, presided over by the vicar's wife, was enthusiastic to make a start.[43] Following Mrs Waring's return, however, the council ARP Committee accepted her husband's recommendation to abort this process on the grounds that 'the calling of a meeting of two representatives from every Women's Organisation in each Village was impracticable'. Instead the committee resolved that 'the [three] lady

[40] Beynon and Austin, *Masters and Servants*, 186. In Durham mining villages the Townswomen's Guild was frequently run by the wife of the colliery manager (M. Stott, *Organisation Woman. The Story of the National Union of Townswomen's Guilds* (London, 1978), 32–3).

[41] Smieton to Bowerman, 15 July 1939; Shawyer to Wilson, 24 Aug. 1939; Shawyer, Report on Meeting in Hetton, 25 Sept. 1939, WRVS, R1; *Northern Echo* (18 Mar. 1938).

[42] Huxley, 'Note on the Position in Easington', 8 Aug. 1940, WRVS, R1/2 Easington 1940–2; Kelly's Directory, County Durham, 1938. Both women lived in big houses: Tunstall Lodge, an eighteenth-century country seat on the Easington/Sunderland border and Mrs Martin of Yoden House, Horden.

[43] Shawyer, Report on Meeting in Hetton, 25 Sept. 1939, WRVS, R1; Moderate Party, File on Elections, Durham RO, D/MCF/26.

members of the Council be co-opted to the WVS Committee.'[44] This move, designed to place control with elected councillors, clearly reflected the Labour Party's preference for political and democratic sources of legitimacy over the non-partisan, middle-class dominated world of the women's associations. From the outset, therefore, the Easington WVS found itself embroiled in a bitter struggle for social leadership.

The WVS county organizer was Sabrina Gordon, the elderly widow of the Bishop of Jarrow, whose main qualification for the job was the role she had played in the Council for Social Service organizing women's clubs in the mining villages during the 1930s.[45] When, at the outbreak of war, the county Public Assistance Committee asked Gordon to set up a network of rest centres to be used by people rendered homeless in the event of bombing, she did this not directly through WVS, whose coverage was still patchy, but by working either through 'the best woman's organisation she found locally as the body to staff the Centre', or through individual women recommended by the police as 'responsible and respected'. In a number of areas this led to a curious situation in which the local WVS, deemed ineffective, was being sidelined by their own county organizer. In the case of Easington Mrs Gordon made no attempt to disguise her support for the deputies against their leader.[46] Mrs Prior, who found it impossible to work with Waring and quickly resigned, was reappointed in January 1940 to set up WVS in the neighbouring rural district of Sunderland, and Gordon, convinced that the Labour activists were intent on sabotaging WVS, subsequently faced down objections about the fact that Prior's substantial country house was (just) outside the Sunderland boundary.[47] For Mrs Martin, Gordon found a different solution, putting her in charge of plans for emergency rest centres throughout the Easington district and encouraging her to open a YMCA canteen for troops stationed in Horden, the village where she lived. When she heard about the canteen, Waring rushed to pre-empt Martin by setting up a rival WVS canteen in the village, while her husband used his powers as

[44] Easington RDC ARP Committee, Minutes, 23 Nov. 1939, Durham RO, RD/EA/21. Subsequently Mrs Waring claimed—somewhat ingenuously given her husband's role in the decision—that the presence of these three councillors was due to 'pressure from the local authority' (Waring to Lady Peele, 3 July 1941, WRVS, R1/2 Easington 1940–2).
[45] WVS Executive Committee, Minutes, 30 Nov. 1938; Hynes to the Warden of All Souls, 18 June 1943, NACVS, Box 5, Northumberland and Tyneside; Reid to Nanson, 14 Dec. 1941, WRVS, R1/2 Easington 1940–2.
[46] J. Foster, 'Organisation of Emergency Feeding and Sleeping Centres', 7 May 1941, Durham County Federation of Divisional Labour Parties, Durham RO, D/sho/5b; Durham Country Labour Women's Advisory Committee, Minutes, 6 May 1940, Durham RO, D/X 1048/4; Huxley, 'Note on the Position in Easington', 8 Aug. 1940, WRVS, R1/2 Easington 1940–2; Martin to Gordon, 7 Aug. 1940; Huxley to Nansen, 23 Aug. 1940, WRVS, R1/2 Durham County.
[47] 'Note on the Position in Easington', 8 Aug. 1940; Huxley to Smieton, 28 Aug. 1940, WRVS, R1/2 Easington 1940–2.

Food Controller to delay the opening of the YMCA canteen.[48] A similar unseemly competition to feed the troops was played out in Easington Village, where the council obstructed efforts by the Mother's Union to establish a canteen, while supporting a parallel WVS initiative.[49]

Given the hierarchical structures of WVS, senior staff would normally have sought to uphold the authority of the appointed centre organizer against rebellious deputies. In this case, however, Mrs Gordon made no secret of her support for the deputies against their leader. Waring responded by refusing to acknowledge the authority of the WVS hierarchy, or even to answer their letters. When Gordon or the regional organizer visited Easington, Waring either refused to meet them, or subjected them to torrents of abuse. This, of course, merely confirmed their view of her as 'an impertinent little beast' who, in cahoots with her husband and the Easington councillors, was out to undermine WVS and 'get things into their own hands'. By empowering the Labour women the council had 'made the name of WVS "stink in the nostrils" (forgive my vulgarity) of the very kind of people who want to help the Country and are willing to do so ... the name WVS in Easington is Mud ... ', and 'people in the neighbourhood who would be invaluable to WVS will have nothing to do with it'.[50] The regional administrator, a prominent Conservative, was no less forthright: 'She [Waring] is a clever, unscrupulous women (the truth is not in her!) and by making things too unpleasant for the better class of woman in the district, she has left herself only the type of illiterate working women whom she can influence.'[51] When Gordon learned that the WVS committee included all three women Labour councillors she bitterly condemned the 'an admirable Hitlerite plan [on which Waring] had organised her WVS.'[52] This was no mere hyperbole. The clash between the two versions of democracy involved—middle-class power exercised through associational life in civil society versus working-class power exercised through the ballot box—was, in Gordon's view, absolute and non-negotiable.[53]

[48] Martin to Gordon, 7 Aug. 1940; 'Note for Lady Iris Capell on the Position at Easington', n.d., WRVS, R1/2 Durham County.
[49] Easington RDC ARP Committee, Minutes, 15 and 29 Aug. 1940, Durham RO, RD/EA/21; *Durham Chronicle*, 27 Sept. 1940.
[50] Gordon to Huxley, 18 Aug. 1940, Reid to Goldney, 8 June 1940, WRVS, R1/2 Easington 1940–2; Gordon, Report on Visit to Easington Village WVS Branch, n.d.; 'Note for Lady Iris Capell on the Position at Easington', n.d.; Gordon to Huxley, 21 Aug. 1940, WRVS, R1/2 Durham County.
[51] Mrs Stewart Reid to Huxley, 5 June 1940, WRVS, R1/2 Easington 1940–2; Borron to Reading, 27 Apr. 1944, WRVS, R/1/2 Darlington.
[52] Gordon, Report on Visit to Easington Village WVS branch, n.d., WRVS, R1/2 Durham County. Such bitterness may have been intensified by the element of class treachery in Waring's behaviour: the Warings lived in the pleasant old hamlet of Little Thorpe, just outside Easington.
[53] Tory women saw working-class control of WVS as part of a more general offensive, including the take-over by the local authorities of mother and child welfare centres previously run by middle-class social leaders like Dr Jessie Dixon. Durham Country Labour Women's Advisory Committee, Minutes, 6 May 1941, Durham RO, D/X 1048/4.

With arrangements for the rest centres under the control of Martin's people, the main activity of Waring's 'illiterate working-class women' was knitting hospital supplies and comforts for the troops, visiting wounded soldiers, and collecting salvage. By September 1940 Waring claimed to have up to 5,000 women active in seventeen different working parties across the rural district.[54] The Easington WVS asserted a lively presence in the villages, mainly through a continuous round of dances, whist drives and other socials organized to raise funds for the purchase of the necessary materials. Raising or holding funds was not permitted under WVS rules, although Tothill Street had considerable difficulty in enforcing this rule and frequently turned a blind eye. Mrs Waring, however, claimed a high profile for her defiance of the rules, placing appeals for funds in the local press, and appointing outside Treasurers to guarantee the security of the funds for each of her village groups. When she appealed for funds to the women's organizations in Martin's home village of Horden, and organized a fund-raising dance in the Miners Hall, Martin was besieged by demands from her own helpers that they too should be permitted to raise money. Martin's attempts to explain that fund-raising was against WVS rules made her look, in her own words, 'a fool and a liar': since Waring's WVS was doing it, people said, it must be allowed. These activities also caused dissension in the neighbouring rural district of Sunderland, where Mrs Prior had a hard time explaining why she would not allow similar fund-raising. By July 1940, Gordon was seriously worried, convinced that Waring's continued defiance threatened her authority throughout County Durham:

> Mrs Waring is boasting of her independence . . . of the County, Regional and Headquarters Offices of the WVS, and persons of all types and interests throughout the County are losing their respect for the WVS, because we seem incapable of bringing a tiresome Officer to book.[55]

III

It was the first bombing raids on the north-east that brought matters to a head in Easington.[56] On 6 July seven bombs fell on Shotton, killing three

---

[54] *Durham Chronicle* (27 Sept. 1940).

[55] 'Note for Lady Iris Capell on the position at Easington', n.d.; Martin to Gordon, 7 Aug. 1940, WRVS, R1/2 Durham County; 'Note on the Position in Easington', 8 Aug. 1940, WRVS, R1/2 Easington 1940–2.

[56] Except where otherwise noted this paragraph and the subsequent one are based on the following sources: Martin to Gordon, 7 Aug. 1940; Gordon to Huxley, 21 Aug. 1940; Gordon, 'Report on Easington Emergency Feeding and Sleeping Centre', 22 Aug. 1940, WRVS, R1/2 Durham County; 'Note on the Position in Easington', 8 Aug. 1940; Huxley, Memo on Meeting with the Warings, 15 Aug. 1940, WRVS, R1/2 Easington 1940–2; Easington RDC ARP Committee, Minutes, 6 June 1940, 1 Aug. 1940, 26 Sept. 1940, Durham RO, RD/EA/21; County Durham PAC, Minutes, 25 July 1940, Durham RO, CC/A50/1/7 ff.

children and injuring thirteen other people. Otherwise the damage was minor and the few families whose houses were unsafe told the police that they were content to stay with friends and relatives in the village. As a result Mrs Martin decided not to open the local rest centre. A few weeks before this incident the Shotton Colliery WVS had protested to the council about their exclusion from the emergency preparations, and Waring seized on Martin's apparent inaction in the crisis to allege that she had abandoned sixty-four homeless people, a view endorsed by the Easington Council and the Shotton Lodge of the Durham Miners' Association. Protest meetings were held at which Martin was denounced, and, as Gordon put it: 'the people [were] harassed and frightened by being told nothing would be done for them in the event of [further] Enemy action.' Claiming support from 500 petitioners in Martin's home village of Horden, including leaders of the women's organizations, Waring called for her resignation. Gordon denied Waring's account of dissention in Martin's home town, insisting that 'the only Women's Organizations in Horden are working in fullest co-operation with the big Comforts Scheme Organisation...organised by men and women of the British Legion'. The comforts scheme was chaired by Jessie Dixon's doctor husband who worked closely with Martin in her capacity as chair of the British Legion women's section.[57] Martin offered to resign, but the county council backed her actions during the Shotton raid and she was persuaded to stay on. This, however, was only the first round.

On 15 August Easington Village was bombed and this time Martin did open the local feeding station, catering for about 180 homeless people from the cookery department of the local school. Unable, on this occasion, to attack Martin for doing nothing, Waring did her best to find fault with what she was doing. According to Gordon, Waring and some of her committee members:

walked into the Feeding Station and without a word of apology or explanation to the officers and ladies in charge went round the tables asking people if they were 'being well looked after' and if they 'had any complaints'!!... As the WVS have nothing to do with the Organisation of the Emergency Feeding and Sleeping Centres their presence and behaviour were superfluous (to say the least of it)...

At the same time, in breach of rules requiring that clothing be distributed only with the approval of the Public Assistance Committee, Waring asked anyone in need to apply direct to her. Eventually she was asked to leave by Alderman George Bloomfield who lived in Easington Colliery. Next morning John Waring turned up with a group of Labour councillors complaining on behalf of a number of families affected by the bombing who were said to have been refused food at the rest centre. Waring, Gordon reported, was very

[57] *Durham Chronicle* (14 Mar. 1941); Gordon to Huxley, 21 Aug. 1940, WRVS, R1/2 Durham County.

abusive, declaring that 'my ladies had no right [to be] there', and threatening to use his authority as clerk to the council to close the centre down. Again Bloomfield came to Martin's defence, going to the houses of those allegedly refused food and satisfying himself that the allegations were without foundation. Subsequently, the Easington council established a supplementary feeding centre under its own control, and resolved to set up a parallel organization 'for the feeding of the people in case of similar air raids' throughout the district to be run by ward and parish councillors in co-operation 'with any Women's organisations in the Parish'.[58]

The part played in these events by George Bloomfield, who had been Ramsay MacDonald's agent in Seaham and was now chair of the county council Public Assistance Committee (PAC) under whose auspices Martin's rest centres were organized, indicates that the county Labour Party was far from happy with the confrontational strategy being pursued by the Easington councillors. Although some members of the PAC remained deeply suspicious of WVS, they were unanimous in dismissing the Warings' complaints against Martin as unfounded.[59] Relations between Bloomfield and the Easington councillors were further strained during the autumn of 1940 by the enthusiasm with which the latter embraced a Communist-led campaign for the construction of deep air raid shelters. Ever since the Munich crisis Easington had been pressing the regional authorities for greater provision of shelters. Shortly after the Shotton raid, John Waring and the chair of the RDC attended the founding conference of the 'Northumberland and Durham ARP Co-ordinating Committee'—the first of its kind in the country—and the RDC subsequently agreed to affiliate. Waring was, in fact, a leading figure in the new organization, heading its deputation to the Regional Civil Defence Commissioner in August accompanied by, among others, Mrs Nicholson.[60] Subsequently Waring put himself at the head of the public agitation for the construction of deep shelters in Easington, working closely with Shinwell who arranged for him to meet the Home Secretary in London. By October the agitation had succeeded in persuading the Home Office to approve the construction, by unemployed miners, of a tunnel shelter capable of holding up to 4,000 people in a disused limestone quarry in Easington Colliery.[61] In the autumn of 1940 Waring briefly became, in the eyes of the Communist Party, a working-class hero, personally congratulated by the local branch, and singled out by the head of the

[58] Easington RDC ARP Committee, Minutes, 22 Aug. 1940, Durham RO, RD/EA/21.
[59] County Durham PAC, Minutes, 25 July 1940, Durham RO, CC/A50/1/7 ff.; Durham County Federation of Divisional Labour Parties, Minutes, 12 Apr. 1941 Durham RO, D/sho/5b.
[60] *Northern Echo* (8 July 1940); *Daily Worker* (26 and 31 Aug. 1940); Easington RDC ARP Committee, Minutes, 15 Aug. 1940, Durham RO, RD/EA/21.
[61] *Durham Chronicle* (20 Sept. 1940, 18 Oct. 1940); *Daily Worker* (7, 15, and 21 Oct. 1940); Nanson to Reading, 23 Sept. 1940, WRVS, R1/2 Easington 1940–2; Easington RDC ARP Committee, Minutes, 26 Sept. 1940, 11 Oct. 1940, Durham RO, RD/EA/21.

Party's north-east district, in an article on the leader page of the *Daily Worker* as the 'quiet spoken, but resolute' man who had led the 'ceaseless agitation' of the Easington miners and their wives to a victory that set an example to the whole country.[62] Resentful Easington ratepayers joked that the canteens that Mrs Waring was busy opening, with the support of the council but in competition with Mrs Martin's efforts must in reality be camouflaged entrances to her husband's deep shelters![63]

No one in Tothill Street seems to have read the *Daily Worker*, but had they done so the enthusiasm of the Communist Party for the husband of their most troublesome centre organizer would certainly have confirmed their view that no solution could be found to the problems in Easington so long as Mrs Waring remained at her post. As early as June WVS leaders had concluded that the only way to resolve the conflict in Easington was to rid themselves of Mrs Waring, but they were puzzled about how exactly to proceed. Normally, when a centre organizer was found wanting, the regional staff would explain things to the clerk of the local council, force her to resign, and, in consultation with the local authority, appoint a replacement. The situation in Easington, however, left them with no option but to close the centre altogether. Mrs Huxley, head of the WVS Regional Department, fearing that Shinwell would ask questions in Parliament, was concerned to secure the agreement of the County Council before taking such a drastic step.[64]

Three days after the August bombing Mrs Waring went to London with her husband and met Huxley, who urged her to resign. John Waring, not at all the Communists' 'quiet spoken' hero, was, according to Huxley, 'extremely cross and very abusive', threatening to go to the High Court for an injunction to prevent his wife's dismissal. They both put the blame entirely on Mrs Gordon and the regional staff and demanded their dismissal. They also insisted 'that the whole matter was a question of party politics', and John Waring said he was going to the House of Commons about it that afternoon. Throughout the interview Waring—who had been described by the regional administrator as 'a lawyer [with] a very astute bitter mind...' —wrote down everything that Huxley said. He was, however, taken aback when Huxley remarked that his account of the meeting would not stand up in court since a wife could not be a witness: 'My God,' he said, 'you're a business woman and weren't born yesterday!' After that the tone of the

[62] *Daily Worker* (21 Oct. 1940); Easington RDC ARP Committee, Minutes, 26 Sept. 1940, Durham RO, RD/EA/21. On the wider Communist campaign, see K. Morgan, *Against Fascism and War. Ruptures and Continuities in British Communist Politics* (Manchester, 1989), 288 ff.
[63] *Northern Echo* (23 Oct. 1940).
[64] Reid to Huxley, 5 June 1940, WRVS, R1/2 Easington 1940–2; 'Note for Lady Iris Capell on the Position at Easington', n.d., WRVS, R1/2 Durham County; 'Note on the Position in Easington', 8 Aug. 1940, WRVS, R1/2 Easington 1940–2.

meeting changed, and the Warings proposed a round table meeting in Easington to sort things out. Huxley stalled, saying that she had no authority to agree but that they would consider the idea carefully if he made it in an official letter. In fact her face-to-face encounter with the Warings only confirmed her view that they had 'no intention of co-operating with the WVS and their only object is to bring it down in the Country of Durham.' Tothill Street, she concluded, should lose no time in moving to close the centre.[65]

By 2 September Gordon was close to cracking. She had already threatened resignation ten days earlier, and now she wrote to Huxley demanding action:

there is more talk and unpleasantness and injury to WVS created by the Easington behaviour than is endurable, and if something is not done soon, will you mind if some of your most active and helpful WVS leaders (including myself) resign in a body?[66]

Ten days later Reading told the regional administrator that the centre would be closed, and on 26 September she wrote to both the Warings officially to this effect.[67]

IV

The decision to close down the Easington centre registered the inability of the WVS hierarchy to negotiate the clash between the established structures of female social leadership in the mining villages and the political hegemony of the Labour Party. It did nothing, however, to resolve the conflict. The district council responded, as Huxley had expected, by declaring that it intended 'to continue to recognise the existing organisation which is fully representative of the whole of the women in the Easington area...the greater majority of whom are working amicably and smoothly together in harmony in Civil Defence matters.' Seizing the high moral ground, John Waring expressed surprise that Lady Reading should have made such a decision at 'a time of great national stress... when every possible effort of good will... is necessary for the common cause'. Challenged by Labour moderates in Easington, the decision to sustain WVS was subsequently endorsed by a vote of 13 to 5 on the ARP committee, which also supported the clerk's demand to be given access to the reports on which Lady Reading had based her decision, and his threat of legal action when this was refused.

---

[65] Reid to Goldney, 8 June 1940; Huxley, Memo on Meeting with the Warings, 15 Aug. 1940.
[66] Gordon to Huxley, 2 Sept. 1940; Gordon to Huxley, 21 Aug. 1940, WRVS, R1/2 Durham County.
[67] Huxley to Reid, 12 Sept. 1940, WRVS, R1; Reading to Waring, 26 Sept. 1940, WRVS, R1/2 Easington 1940-2.

Tothill Street countered with demands that his wife should stop claiming the title of WVS, and return papers, badges, and other WVS property.[68]

In the villages the contest for leadership continued. Anthony Young, leader of the Easington Ratepayers, wrote to the local paper praising the spirit of those women who 'have always been ready to do what was necessary' for the war effort but would not 'meekly submit' to Waring's socialist tyranny. He singled out the Mothers' Union, the WI, and the Primitive Methodist Sisterhood for special praise.[69] A woman from Wheatley Hill expressed alarm about the 'party spirit' invading voluntary work, remarking that 'a great many people think that unless a man or woman is Labour they have not a right to help in any way'.[70] Many people, no doubt, found themselves caught up in the crossfire of a battle they did not comprehend. In Easington Village, the parish council, having debated the matter, decided not to withdraw recognition from the WVS working party.[71] Members of the working party, however, were reported by the local vicar to be greatly distressed that their activities were no longer officially recognized: 'it came as a thunderbolt when the members were informed that the branch had been closed down. They had not been concerned nor connected with the causes which led to their suppression...'. Although the working party decided to continue its work so as not to deprive troops of the comforts they were knitting, 'they do not want to work in this way, but as part of the WVS and recognised as such by your Ladyship.' Tothill Street had been well aware that the closure would deprive 'large numbers of loyal WVS members... of their opportunity of continuing in the Service', but Reading's reply to the vicar did little to clarify the position in which such loyalists now found themselves:

I am glad to know that the working party to which you refer is continuing, and I am only sorry that it is not possible at the moment for them to be officially recognised by WVS HQ, particularly as I appreciated that the individual members were not lacking in their loyalty to HQ.[72]

Since WVS could only operate officially in any area with the approval of the local authority, Tothill Street now had even less scope than Martin and Gordon had enjoyed before the closure to promote any rival to Waring's WVS. Many war comforts groups continued to operate on a purely local

---

[68] Easington RDC ARP Committee, Minutes, 3 Oct. 1940, 5 Dec. 1940, Durham RO, RD/EA/21; Reid to Waring, 15 Oct. 1940; Waring to Reading, 16 Oct. 1940; Waring to Nanson, 7 Nov. 1940 WRVS, R1/2 Easington 1940–2; 'Note for Lady Iris Capell on the Position at Easington'.

[69] *Northern Echo* (25 Oct. 1940).

[70] Ibid. (28 Oct. 1940).

[71] Ibid. (2 Nov. 1940).

[72] Algernon West to Reading, 13 Nov. 1940; Reading to Algernon West, 22 Nov. 1940; Note on Advice from Home Office Legal Department, 26 Oct. 1940, WRVS, R1/2 Easington 1940–2; 'Note for Lady Iris Capell on the Position at Easington'.

basis without claiming affiliation to WVS, although this did not prevent Mrs Martin from describing herself as the WVS leader in the district.[73] As the struggle in the villages developed the food sub-committee of the district council, run by Mrs Peart, set out to rival Martin's emergency centres with cash-and-carry feeding centres designed, not for emergencies, but for every-day use. 'Women', she declared, 'have been cooks and butlers far too long, and these centres will give them a little relief from their household duties.'[74]

The WVS hierarchy was only one of the enemies that now bore down upon the Warings and their supporters. In August the Durham county council had refused to sanction Mrs Waring's take over of an unused prop-erty in Easington as her headquarters. When the RDC countered by provid-ing her with a building of their own, local Conservatives protested about the misuse of ratepayers' money to support an organization which was no longer recognized by either WVS or the county civil defence authorities.[75] In September John Waring and the Easington councillors were summoned by the county council to account for their actions during the bombing raids. After several extensive meetings, the Emergency Committee resolved to dismiss Waring from his (voluntary) post as District Controller.[76] By twelve votes to two the Easington ARP committee refused to accept Waring's removal or to nominate a successor; forbad any council employee to accept the appointment; declined to recognize the man eventually appointed in his place; and called for a Home Office enquiry into the handling of the August bombing raid.[77] Faced with open rebellion, the Durham Labour leaders, who certainly did read the *Daily Worker*, launched a full-scale attack on Waring's flirtation with the Communists. The county council had already written to all local authorities warning them against associating with the ARP Co-ordinating Committee, and, responding to a TUC circular in Octo-ber, the Durham Federation of Labour Parties also instructed local parties to boycott preparations for the Communist-inspired People's Convention.[78] In November the local newspaper led with a story derived from an unnamed Labour Party source attacking Waring—thinly disguised as 'the clerk of one

[73] *Durham Chronicle* (13 Dec. 1940, 10 Jan. 1941, 21 Feb. 1941).

[74] Ibid. (27 June 1941, 4 July 1941, 11 July 1941, 9 Jan. 1942).

[75] *Northern Echo* (23, 25, and 31 Oct. 1940, 1 and 5 Nov. 1940).

[76] Durham County Council Emergency Commitee, Minutes, 16 and 18 Oct. 1940, Durham RO CC A55/1. Mrs Waring later claimed that her husband was dismissed because Mrs Gordon 'got round the County Chief Constable', which no doubt she did, but the main actors here were Alderman Bloomfield and his fellow county councillors (Waring to Lady Peele, 3 July 1941, WRVS, R1/2 Easington 1940–2).

[77] Easington RDC ARP Committee, Minutes, 24, 25, and 31 Oct. 1940, 7 Nov. 1940, Durham RO, RD/EA/21; *Durham Chronicle* (1 Nov. 1940).

[78] Easington RDC ARP Committee, Minutes, 26 Sept. 1940, Durham RO, RD/EA/21; Durham County Federation of Divisional Labour Parties, Minutes, 26 Oct. 1940, Durham RO, D/sho/5b; Durham Country Labour Women's Advisory Committee, Minutes (1 Nov. 1940), Durham RO, D/X 1048/4.

district authority in Durham County' who was leading a campaign for deep shelters—as 'contributing materially and assisting officially in the work of the Communist Party'. Alderman Bloomfield (probably himself the un- named source) placed himself at the head of a concerted campaign to see off Communist attempts to use the shelter issue to expand their not very extensive support within the Miners' Association.[79] So long as the Warings had the support of the Easington councillors they could defy Tothill Street with impunity. But the enmity of the County Durham Labour leadership was more difficult to deal with.

V

Tothill Street understood that the reconstruction of their authority in Easing- ton would be impossible without support from within the Labour Party. They were also well aware that the situation in Easington was not all of Waring's making and that Gordon was also at fault.[80] Shortly before the closure decision, Huxley agreed to approach Mary Sutherland, national secretary of Labour's women's advisory committee, 'to see whether it would be possible for her to quite unofficially speak a good word for WVS in the North East.'[81] It was not only the Easington councillors who resented Gordon. There was widespread discontent among Labour women in other parts of the county over the way in which they had been excluded from the rest centre scheme. Despite their initial reluctance to involve themselves in WVS, by early 1941 Labour women in both Chester-le-Street and Barnard Castle were protesting that they had been 'passed over to do this work... It is supposed to be non-political but the leaders... always voted Tory and usually canvassed against Labour candidates.' They predicted, with some bitterness, that in the event of bombing the menial work involved in provid- ing food and beds for the homeless would be likely to fall on miners' wives, while those in charge would consider themselves 'too nice to handle this sort of thing'.[82] Although the PAC, after investigation, dismissed these com- plaints, Tamosin Todd, the leading Labour woman in the county and a member of the PAC, assured Labour delegates that the chair of the commit- tee, Alderman Bloomfield, was himself unhappy about the position and 'had agreed to go out to any place to form another local committee where it was

[79] *Durham Chronicle* (8 Nov. 1940).

[80] Even the Regional Organizer, who loathed Mrs Waring, felt constrained to tell Mrs Gordon that her own behaviour was partly to blame for the conflict. Reid to Gordon, 8 June 1940, WRVS, R1/2 Easington 1940–2.

[81] Smieton to Huxley, 28 Aug. 1940, WRVS, R1/2 Easington 1940–2.

[82] Durham County Federation of Divisional Labour Parties, Minutes, 22 Feb., 29 Mar. 1941, Durham RO, D/sho/5b; County Durham PAC Minutes, 27 Feb. 1941, 27 Mar. 1941, 24 Apr. 1941, Durham RO CC/A50/1/7 ff.; Brandon and Byshottles UDC Minutes, 3 Feb. 1941, 3 June 1941, Durham RO UD/BB/26–7.

found that the WVS was keeping our women out of it.'[83] Even John Waring's most determined Labour opponent in Easington was forthright in condemning the rest centre scheme on the grounds that Mrs Martin had set it up without consulting the council.[84]

Any solution to the Easington problem would require WVS to demonstrate a rather less dismissive approach to the Labour women than that adopted by Mrs Gordon. When the Easington RDC appealed to Ellen Wilkinson, Parliamentary Secretary at the Home Office, against both the closure and Waring's sacking as District Controller, she endorsed Reading's view that 'no good purpose would be served by' Whitehall intervention.[85] Before the war Wilkinson, who was MP for Jarrow, had been extremely critical of WVS as a bastion of arrogant upper-class ladies—no doubt she was acquainted with the Bishop's widow.[86] Now, however, she adopted a more supportive attitude, as did Jack Lawson, the Labour MP for Chester-le-Street, who served as deputy to the Regional Commissioner for Civil Defence during the war, and claimed to have been instrumental in persuading Labour women to overcome their initial reluctance to participate in WVS.[87] Shinwell, Easington's own MP, was less helpful to Tothill Street, pressing Waring's demand for a round-table conference to sort things out and restore official recognition for the local WVS. In February 1941 Lawson advised Reading not to accede to this request.[88] Shinwell's efforts to get the Home Office to intervene were further obstructed by John Waring's decision to launch legal actions, one seeking an injunction to prevent the new civil defence District Controller from taking up his post, the other an action for libel against the Chief Warden in Easington. He lost the first case in April and the second in June and was ordered to pay the defendants' costs on both counts.[89]

[83] J. Foster, 'Organisation of Emergency Feeding and Sleeping Centres', 7 May 1941, Durham County Federation of Divisional Labour Parties, Durham RO, D/sho/5b; Durham County Federation of Divisional Labour Parties minutes, 29 March 1941, Durham RO, D/sho/5b.

[84] E. Cain moved a motion to this effect on the Easington Guardian's Committee in Nov. 1940 (*Durham Chronicle* (15 Nov. 1940)). Earlier he had led the move to accept the closure of the WVS centre (Easington RDC ARP Committee, Minutes, 3 Oct. 1940, Durham RO, RD/EA/21), and, in February 1942, he was to lead the move to sack Waring.

[85] Wilkinson to Reading, 26 Nov. 1940; *Durham Chronicle* (29 Nov. 1940).

[86] Verbatim report of deputation from Labour Party Executive, 14 July 1938, WRVS, V/95/38 SJC. For the softening of Wilkinson's attitude, and Lady Reading's solicitous wooing of her, see WRVS, V/113/38 Ellen Wilkinson.

[87] Reading to Reid, 8 Feb. 1941, WRVS, R1.

[88] Lawson to Reading, 31 Jan. 1941, WRVS, R1/2 Easington 1940–2; WVS, Chairman's Committee, Minutes, 23 Jan. 1941, 20 Feb. 1941; Reading to Reid, 8 Feb. 1941, WRVS, R1/2 Durham County; Easington RDC ARP Committee, Minutes, 31 Jan. 1941, 13 Mar. 1941, 10 Apr. 1941, Durham RO, RD/EA/21.

[89] Easington RDC ARP Committee, Minutes, 27 Mar. 1941, 10 Apr. 1941, Durham RO, RD/EA/21; County Durham Emergency Committee, Minutes, 9 Jan. 1941, 21 Mar. 1941, 16 Apr. 1941, 5 June 1941, Durham RO CC A55/1; *Durham Chronicle* (11 Apr. 1941).

A few days after Waring's application for an injunction was refused, Shinwell, who had talked things over with Tothill Street as well as the Home Office, wrote to the Council indicating that a new request for a conference might now meet a more favourable response. The Home Office rebuffed an attempt by the Easington councillors to link the WVS question to their continuing demand for Waring's reappointment as District Controller, and they were plainly told by Tothill Street that there could be no question of reopening the centre so long as Mrs Waring remained at her post. Finally, in July 1941 the ARP committee decided by fifteen votes to eight to accept Reading's condition, and in October the regional administrator, Mrs Steward Reid, met the Easington councillors.[90] Despite her responsibility as county organizer, Mrs Gordon was instructed not to attend, a clear acknowledgment that she had been partly to blame for the conflict.[91] Acting on the advice of Jack Lawson, Reid also avoided consulting Alderman Bloomfield about a possible successor to Mrs Waring since his own role in the conflict meant that anyone he suggested would be unacceptable to the Easington councillors.[92] Rather than herself conducting consultations and proposing a new centre leader (the normal WVS practice), Reid accepted a two-stage procedure involving each of the thirteen existing WVS working parties nominating a candidate for the post of centre organizer, to be followed by a meeting of the nominated candidates to decide which one of them should take over. Mrs Waring continued to protest, threatening legal action over alleged irregularities in her dismissal unless Reid agreed not only to put her name on the ballot but also to support her election. By this stage, however, even her most loyal supporters had accepted the inevitable, and only one of the working parties refused to participate in the ballot on the grounds that Waring was not allowed to stand. In the event the meeting of candidates could not agree on a leader and a second ballot of the working parties was held among the three most favoured candidates.[93] One of them, Mrs Peart, a member of the most prominent Labour family in Thornley, had been one of the councillors on Mrs Waring's executive, and had earlier had her own run-in with the county civil defence authorities. She remained a faithful ally of the Warings throughout.[94] Another, Mrs Liddle from Shotton, had served as Waring's deputy leader.[95] Between them, however, they appear to have split the pro-Labour vote, and the woman who was

[90] Easington RDC ARP Committee, Minutes, 15 May, 31 July, 28 Aug., 12 and 25 Sept. 1941, Durham RO, RD/EA/21; Reading to Waring, 25 July 1941, WRVS, R1 Regional Office.
[91] Reid to Reading, 8 Aug. 1941, WRVS, R1 Regional Office.
[92] Reid to Nansen, 20 Aug. 1941, ibid.
[93] Easington RDC ARP Committee, Minutes, 9 Oct., 31 Dec. 1941, 26 Feb. 1942 Durham RO, RD/EA/21; Reid to Nansen, 14 Dec. 1941, WRVS, R1/2 Easington 1940–2.
[94] Easington RDC ARP Committee, Minutes, 25 Apr., 30 May, 5 June 1940, 9 Apr. 1942 Durham RO, RD/EA/21.
[95] *Durham Chronicle* (27 Sept. 1940).

finally elected, Miss Hutchinson from Wheatley Hill, had earlier been appointed by Mrs Martin to run the local rest centre.[96] This outcome may have done something to heal the rifts which had divided the local women's organizations since the beginning of the war. In Easington Colliery, where a meeting of women's organizations had been held to discuss the reconstruction of WVS, WI members, who had previously held aloof, voted to join the new WVS; the leader of the Easington Village Women's Working Party, which had remained aloof from Waring's WVS, was appointed to office under Hutchinson; and in Horden, Mrs Dixon, the paternalistic local doctor, encouraged her WI followers to join the Labour women in making WVS a success.[97]

The chances of success were greatly enhanced by the departure of the Warings. By the time Hutchinson's appointment was confirmed, in May 1942, John Waring had finally lost the support of the Easington councillors. Early in January Tothill Street learned that 'there was great agitation going on at Easington because Mr Waring was asking for an increase of salary and his opponents on the Council were hoping to make this an opportunity for parting with his services.'[98] The row split the Labour group, and in a noisy public confrontation during which the chairman of the council threatened to call the police to prevent Waring's supporters from breaking up the meeting Labour dissidents joined with the Moderates to reverse an earlier decision to give Waring his pay rise. A month later, accusing Waring (probably unfairly) of appropriating payments made to him as Food Controller which should have been returned to the council, the Labour rebels narrowly secured a majority for the clerk's dismissal.[99] Once again Waring threatened legal action, and the majority of Labour councillors who supported him (including both Mrs Peart and Mrs Nicholson) stuck by him until the expiry of his three-months' notice in May when it was announced that he had been appointed deputy town clerk in Bootle.[100] A month later the new WVS held its inaugural public meeting, addressed by both Todd and Gordon as well as the WVS regional officials and Mrs Councillor Nicholson.[101]

The reconstruction of the Easington centre depended on co-operation between Tothill Street and the Labour leadership in County Durham. No attempt was made to summon village meetings of all the women's organizations—the procedure favoured by Gordon and Martin in 1939 and aborted

[96] Easington RDC ARP Committee, Minutes, 14 May 1942 Durham RO, RD/EA/21.
[97] *Durham Chronicle* (12 June 1942); Horden WI, Minutes, 14 July 1942, Durham RO D/WI/3/94/6; Easington Colliery WI, Minutes, 19 May 1942, Durham RO D/WI 3/92/2.
[98] Nansen to Reading, 6 Jan. 1942, WRVS, R1/2 Durham County.
[99] *Durham Chronicle* (23 Jan., 20 Feb. 1942).
[100] Easington RDC ARP Committee, Minutes, 9 Apr., 14 May 1942 Durham RO, RD/EA/21 Bootle may have appealed to the Warings because the council was not only, like Easington, overwhelmingly proletarian and solidly Labour, but also, like themselves, Catholic.
[101] *Durham Chronicle* (19 June 1942).

by the Easington councillors who rightly feared that it would tend to confirm existing middle-class social leadership. Those groupings which had remained aloof from Waring's WVS, like a War Comforts Committee in Easington Colliery which claimed to represent 25 voluntary organizations and was led by a WI stalwart, were told that they had no right to nominate.[102] The members of Martin's rest centre organizations were not invited to participate in the process either, and when they lobbied the county council in the autumn of 1941, it was explicitly to Todd—recently appointed Gordon's deputy—that the PAC looked to sort out any 'lack of harmony' on the ground.[103]

In 1939 WVS had been warned that they would not be able to establish themselves in Durham without Todd's support, and that she was not a woman who would be fobbed off with a token position of deputy to the county organizer.[104] Todd had initially opposed WVS and she always remained deeply suspicious of its hierarchy. Lady Reading, she explained to a county Labour Party meeting a few months before her appointment as Gordon's deputy, was 'politically against us' and the bishop's widow 'could only work through the ... supposedly non-political bodies of women ... with which she was acquainted'. Nevertheless Todd had quickly reached the conclusion that if WVS was going to be set up, Labour women should participate as she herself did in Seaham, where she ran a WVS committee which included representatives of the Townswomen's Guild and the British Legion alongside the Women's Co-operative Guild. 'I had made up my mind', she said, ' . . . that supposedly non-political women [like Mrs Gordon] were not going to rule in Seaham'.[105] Her agreement to become Gordon's deputy in the summer of 1941 served to cement the accommodation between Tothill Street and the dominant forces in the Durham Labour Party and to complete the isolation of the Warings and their allies on the Easington Council. When, in April 1943, Hutchinson invited local councillors to a WVS rally in Easington it was Todd, not her notional superior, Mrs Gordon, who was billed as the star speaker.[106]

In order to align with moderate Labour against the Warings, Tothill Street was prepared to take the risk of alienating 'the better class of woman in the district' whose support had seemed so essential to Gordon, Martin, and the regional administrator, Mrs Stewart Reid. From the outset, Lady Reading had understood that Durham was not Norfolk or Cumberland and could not

---

[102] Easington RDC ARP Committee, Minutes, 31 Dec. 1941, Durham RO, RD/EA/21.

[103] County Durham PAC, Minutes, 30 Oct. 1941, Durham RO, CC/A50/1/7 ff.

[104] Memorandum from William Teeling, a Ministry of Labour official in Hull, 12 Apr. 1939, WRVS, R1.

[105] Durham County Federation of Divisional Labour Parties, Minutes, 29 Mar. 1941, Durham RO, D/sho/5b; County Durham PAC, Minutes, 16 Oct. 1940, Durham RO, CC/A50/1/7 ff.; *Durham Chronicle* (1 Nov. 1940).

[106] Easington RDC ARP Committee, Minutes, 4 Apr. 1943, Durham RO RD/EA/21.

be worked effectively through the traditional elites. It was normal for WVS administrators to make their initial approach to the Lord Lieutenant of the county, in this case Lord Londonderry, a major local coal owner, and an undistinguished Tory politician, who, it was said, had used his wife's status as Ramsay MacDonald's favourite duchess, to 'cater his way into the cabinet'.[107] Despite the fact that Reading had worked closely with Lady Londonderry in the Personal Service League, when it came to setting up WVS in the north-east she had given strict instructions to the regional organizer that she should make no contact with the Lord Lieutenant.[108] Reading's understanding that he represented a dying breed may have owed less to the contempt in which he was held by the Durham miners, than to his own very public admiration for Hitler: as the widow of a leading member of Anglo-Jewry, Lady Reading had no time for the pro-Nazi views of sections of the British upper class.[109] When, in 1942, Londonderry learned that Reading had given the deputy county leadership to one of his political enemies in Seaham he wrote her a furious letter, complaining that this would undermine his long-standing refusal to accept Todd's appointment as a magistrate, and thereby jeopardize his efforts to resist the advancing tide of socialism: 'You will understand the difficult position I am in now, when you give her a very responsible position in your organisation when, at the same time, the Committee over which I preside . . . is unwilling to make her a Magistrate.' Reading's dismissive reply gave no quarter, simply pointing out that 'it is an advantage to have all points of view represented, particularly in a county where a number of our most faithful workers come from mining homes.'[110] Within the year Todd had indeed become a magistrate and two years later she was awarded the MBE.[111]

The accommodation of WVS with the Durham labour movement should not be understood as involving a genuine convergence between middle-class social leaders and Labour women. Tamosin Todd agreed to serve in the county for the same reason as she had earlier agreed to serve in Seaham—to take power from middle-class hands. Working as Gordon's deputy, however, did nothing to enhance her opinion of the vicars', doctors' and colliery managers' wives with whom Gordon had tried to construct WVS in the

---

[107] D. Cannadine, *The Decline and Fall of the British Aristocracy* (London, 1990), 219, 352–3, 344; J. C. C. Davidson, *Memoirs of a Conservative* (London, 1969), 405; Beynon and Austin, *Masters and Servants*, 154, 203–4, 305.

[108] Wilson to Myers, 31 Mar. 1939, WRVS, R1; Smieton to Reading, 21 May 1938, WRVS, A 3/38 Advisory Council General Correspondence.

[109] In the 1930s Londonderry and his wife were besotted with Hitler and active in the Anglo-German Fellowship (Cannadine, *Aristocracy*, 549; A. S. Williams, *Ladies of Influence. Women of the Elite in Inter-war Britain* (Harmondsworth, 2000), 14, 36).

[110] Londonderry to Reading, 28 July 1941, 2 Aug. 1941; Reading to Londonderry, 30 July 1941, WRVS, R1/2 Durham County.

[111] Durham Country Labour Women's Advisory Committee, Minutes, 8 Apr. 1942, 17 Jan. 1944, Durham RO D/X 1048/4.

coalfield. Shortly before the 1945 election Todd was asked by the regional administrator to attend a national meeting called by Lady Reading to discuss the WVS stance in the election. Ahead of the meeting she wrote anxiously to Mary Sutherland at Labour Party headquarters: 'Naturally I am very suspicious, and this looks like the parting of the ways to me, but before I go I feel I want to know all about their little schemes.' Todd feared that regulations designed to keep WVS above the electoral battle might be used 'as a pretext for silencing a large number of women and depriving them of their citizen rights': i.e. to prevent WVS office holders like herself from campaigning in the election. The promotion of WVS as a 'non-political' focus for social leadership appeared to Todd both contemptible and potentially dangerous. 'Most of the dear ladies', she wrote, 'have found themselves in public work for the first time and aim to use WVS to keep them in the limelight.' 'Non-political . . . ?', she added, querying a concept of which she had every reason to be suspicious. It was, after all, only by bringing 'politics' into local affairs that the labour movement had been able to counter the 'non-political' power of established social leaders. After the London meeting, and reassured by its practical tone, Todd wrote again to Sutherland reporting that 'nothing sinister' had been under discussion after all. With the danger past, these two powerful Labour women could comfortably share their contempt for what they saw as the ignorance of the 'dear ladies'. Having been sent a Questions and Answers circular designed to instruct WVS officers how to avoid any improper overlap between electioneering and their social work, Sutherland confided to Todd:

some of [the questions] are so naive and silly and the answers so obvious that it hardly seems worthwhile putting them down. I have, however, constantly to remind myself that Lady Reading is not dealing with such a highly educated section of the female population as I am dealing with from day to day, and therefore these elementary instructions may be necessary . . . [112]

In articulating such pride of class Sutherland spoke for all those Labour women who struggled without benefit of secondary education to acquire the knowledge necessary to transform their lives. What neither Sutherland nor Todd understood, however, was that politics, which for a working-class woman lay necessarily at the centre of her public life and provided the main basis from which she could aspire to exercise social leadership—as a magistrate, perhaps, or an organizer of voluntary work—was not necessarily of the same salience for middle-class women. Todd was first and foremost a Labour woman and her exercise of social leadership was consequent on her political engagement. By contrast middle-class women, even those who were active in Conservative Party politics, normally thought of their voluntary

[112] Todd to Sutherland, 9 Apr. 1945, Sutherland to Todd, 17 Apr., 2 May 1945, Labour Party Archives, Mary Sutherland Papers, S23 WVS.

work as non-political. It is not to be wondered that Labour women and established social leaders had a hard time understanding one another: the basis of their social power was so different.

The Warings may well have been difficult individuals. John went to law at the drop of a hat, and Winifred does not appear to have conducted herself with much dignity, either in the aftermath of the Easington bombing or, a year later, when she tried to blame the whole affair on religious bigotry: the reason the Anglican bishop's widow hated her, she alleged, was because she and her husband were Catholics.[113] Although officials in London were probably right to dismiss this as bluster—'having failed to get what they want through political channels, the Warings are now turning to religion!'— it is possible that the contempt shown by the bishop's widow to Waring and her supporters had a religious component. There was a significant Catholic presence among the miners and their wives, many of them of Irish descent.[114] Certainly Mrs Gordon was an unfortunate choice as Durham county organizer. 'A delightful and amusing personality', was the travelling administrator's verdict in 1939, but at the same time dreadfully 'vague' and lacking in organizational imagination: 'one is worn out with exercising tact over her...'.[115] Playing lady bountiful in the 1930s with her Women's Clubs for the wives of unemployed miners may have suited her temperament, but facilitating an accommodation between middle-class social leaders and elected Labour councillors determined to rule on their own patch was clearly beyond her capacities. Faced with working-class militancy she could see only 'Hitlerite plans' and, as the Tory regional administrator put it, the 'impertinence' of people making claims beyond their station. Nevertheless, however inept the individuals concerned, the drama played out in Easington represented something more than a clash of personalities. The self-assertion of the Labour women, backed by male colleagues on the council, exposed very clearly the clash between established notions of social leadership exercised by middle-class women operating through the associational life of voluntary organizations, and the determination of working-class women to use the power bestowed by universal suffrage to organize a counter-hegemony on the terrain of local government politics. The compromise eventually engineered patched things up for the remainder of the war and allowed Tothill Street to reclaim the formal authority that it had, for more than a year, been forced to abandon in Easington. But the underlying class conflict remained, with all its suspicions, fears, hatreds, and contempts. An unusual balance of class forces made these negative sentiments more visible than elsewhere in England in what the Tory diarist Cuthbert Headlam called 'the miserable

[113] Waring to Lady Peele, 3 July 1941, WRVS, R1/2 Easington 1940–2.
[114] Reid to Nansen, 20 July 1941, Simpson to Nanson, 23 July 1941, WRVS, R1/2 Easington 1940–2. On the Catholic presence, see Lynn, 'Shaping', 42, 85, 93.
[115] Shawyer to Wilson, 24 Aug. 1939, WRVS, R1 Regional Office.

miner-led County of Durham',[116] but one wonders how much more generally they existed, an undercurrent of potential unpleasantness among
women, kept at bay by the constant repetition of that class-coded mantra
most favoured, after 'character', by WVS organizers: the quality of 'nice-
ness'.

[116] Cited in Beynon and Austin, *Masters and Servants*, 314.

7

Rural England

The mobilization of WVS in the towns involved striking a balance between colonizing the middle-class women's associations and incorporating the very distinct world of Labour women. Once mobilized, WVS often acted to subordinate middle-class local autonomy to the needs of the war effort. In rural areas, where social relations were simpler and more transparent, WVS played a more consistently conservative role. As in the towns it built on already established women's networks, in particular the Women's Institutes. In the absence of any rural equivalent to the challenge represented by the urban labour movement, the WVS hierarchy had little need to intervene in established structures of authority in the countryside. Where WVS organizers attempted to impose outside discipline on local social leaders they generally failed. Traditional modes of social leadership in the countryside came through the war unscathed, even strengthened. The major rural trauma of wartime, the invasion of evacuees from the towns, tended to reinforce existing assumptions, shared across class boundaries, about the distinctness of rural life. In handling the problems thrown up by evacuation, established social leaders, working partly though the WVS, reaffirmed their right to speak on behalf of country folk as a whole. Whatever class resentments simmered below the surface, the need to defend the rural community against the depredations threatened by the urban invasion provided, in the traumatic autumns of 1939 and 1940, powerful new cement for the old social order.

I

Over much of the English countryside aristocrats and substantial gentry continued to hold sway and the 'big house' remained the seat of local leadership. The sources of upper-class wealth had long since ceased to be predominantly agricultural. The entry of the industrial and commercial bourgeoisie into the rural upper-class, commonplace throughout the nineteenth century, had been accelerated by the collapse of the great aristocratic estates in the early twentieth century.[1] These rural immigrants took over the

---

[1] F. M. L. Thompson, 'English Landed Society in the Twentieth Century. ii, New Poor and New Rich', *Transactions of the Royal Historical Society*, 6th ser., 1 (1991), 16–18.

gentry's social role with their houses—quite literally in Ely where, in 1948, the first choice for the succession as WVS centre organizer fell on a woman who had moved into the big house previously inhabited by the Cambridge-shire county organizer.[2] In Hertfordshire the continued vitality of Lady Bountiful was explained by the 'constant succession of *nouveaux riches* aspirants (mainly from London) to the ranks of the gentry [who] have kept something of the feudal pattern alive, but subsidising it with fortunes made elsewhere.'[3] The influx of large numbers of retired officers of the military and colonial services supplemented the ranks of those 'leisured persons of independent means' who provided the backbone of social service in the villages.[4] In 1950s Gosforth—a rural parish in West Cumbria, adjacent to the yet-to-be notorious seaside town of Windscale (Sellafield)—all the upper-class people were first-generation immigrants. They effortlessly accumulated chairmanships and presidencies in local associations, their leadership as unquestioned as if they had been lords of the manor for centuries. At meetings in the town the front row was always left vacant for members of the 'upper ten', and people even made way for them in the local shops—a remarkable persistence of deference after the years of queuing.[5] A hostile account of the world of voluntary work in wartime Devon characterized these incomers as 'semi-gentry... worthy, if often dull people... possessed with a strong caste-spirit'. The men 'suffer from the defects of the English Public School education, and... the women from the grave defects of the well-known exclusive girls' schools'. They knew nothing of international affairs and had little social awareness apart from a vague sense that it was their duty to be 'kind to the poor'.[6]

Upper-class identity was fashioned not primarily in local sociability, but at national level.[7] Taken aback by a retired colonel's wife living in an Oxford-shire village who regretted the absence of any neighbours with young children, Margaret Stacey realized that a 'neighbour' in this vocabulary was a member of the same class living within a radius of about thirty miles. The upper class, Stacey argued, was the one truly national class—

---

[2] Memo by Country Organizer on Cambridgeshire Centre Organizers (n.d., 1948?), WRVS, R4/2 Cambridgeshire. Nine years earlier the regional organizer had felt it necessary to reassure the country organizer that she was not being appointed merely because of the size of her house (Bragg to Tharp, 25 Apr. 1939, WRVS, R4/2 Cambridgeshire).

[3] Dr Roper Power, 'The Voluntary Social Services in Hertfordshire' (n.d., 1942), NCSRS, E2/7.

[4] E. M. Foster, Report on East Sussex (n.d., 1942), NCSRS, E2/4.

[5] W. M. Williams, *The Sociology of an English Village: Gosforth* (London, 1956), 104.

[6] James McIntyre, 'Voluntary Service in Devon' (n.d., 1942), 4–5, 21, 35, 46, NCSRS, E2/5.

[7] This was also increasingly true of the provincial urban upper middle class: R. Trainor, 'Neither Metropolitan nor Provincial: The Inter-war Middle Class', in A. Kidd and Nicholls O. (eds.), *The Making of the British Middle Class?* (Manchester, 1998).

'something akin to a national status group'—united by common and separate education in the public schools and ancient universities (and the instantly recognizable dialect thus inculcated); and by the ongoing associational life of the metropolis where many of the men and some of the more publicly active women spent all or part of their working weeks. 'Their local paper is *The Times* and the West End of London their Town Centre'.[8] The fact that children spent much of the year away at boarding school enabled even the younger married women of the upper class to play leading roles in voluntary work. Upper-class people did not have to be long-established residents in a locality to be recognized as leaders. They brought their lineage with them, in their accents, attitudes and acquaintances, as well as in their bank balances. The assumption of authority by such incomers did occasionally cause offence, particularly among local aspirants to upper-class status who lacked the cultural entry tickets. 'More breeding than sense...' remarked one such social climber in Gosforth about these arrogant incomers: 'because they talk like a BBC announcer and their great-grandfather was a tuppenny-ha'penny baronet, they think they own the place'.[9] But, in effect, they did.

Evelyn Emmet, WVS organizer for West Sussex, reported that, in the rural parts of the county, leadership 'went unquestioned to the right type'.[10] As the daughter of a City baron who had inherited Amberly Castle from her late husband, Emmet would have had little difficulty in knowing who 'the right type' were. If in doubt, she could always turn for help to her sister-in-law, the 1950s satirist of the distinction between 'U' (upper and upper-middle class) and 'non-U' speech and behaviour.[11] Southern region was particularly rich in blue blood.[12] Lady Emma Northampton, the WVS administrator, had all the lineage anyone could hope for. She grew up at Longleat, daughter of the fifth Marquis of Bath who combined the chairmanship of the Wiltshire County Council over forty years (1904–1945) with the Lord Lieutenancy of the neighbouring county of Somerset (1899–1945). In 1921 she married the sixth Marquis of Northampton who, despite a big sell-off in 1919, still owned 10,000 acres in 1945. Although David Cannadine cites Bath as an example of the twentieth-century decline of aristocratic power—his public

[8] M. Stacey, *Tradition and Change: A Study of Banbury* (Oxford, 1960), 151–2, 162–3, 188, 195.
[9] Williams, *Gosforth*, 90–1, 104, 107.
[10] E. Emmet, Memo on Leadership, 8 Aug. 1939, WRVS, R/12/3 West Sussex.
[11] Emmet was the daughter of Lord Rennell of Rood (1st Baron. cr. 1933)—and sister-in-law of Nancy Mitford (D. Cannadine, *The Decline and Fall of the British Aristocracy* (London, 1990), 399–400). The political sympathies of the Mitford sisters famously ranged from Stalin to Hitler. Another of Emmet's sisters-in-law—Lady Rennell—helped to finance the far-right British Housewives' League after the war.
[12] Unless otherwise noted the genealogical information in this paragraph is derived from *Who's Who, Who Was Who,* and *Debrett*.

role was, it seems, more decorative than effective—there was nothing decorative about his daughter's role in WVS.[13] Most of the county organizers who served under her were members of the same aristocratic elite. Lady Stavordale, Dorset county organizer, was married to the heir to the earldom created in the mid-eighteenth century.[14] In Buckinghamshire Lady Dashwood, wife of the ninth baronet, was succeeded as country organizer by the Countess of Courtown, wife of the seventh earl and herself of aristocratic lineage. In Hampshire Lady Malmesbury, daughter of the sixth Lord Calthorpe and wife of the fifth earl (who had chaired the county council for eleven years until 1938, owned 4,000 acres in the county, and had Canalettos hanging on the wall of his stately home) ran WVS with the help of two other aristocratic ladies.[15] In Wiltshire, appropriately enough, the county organizer was Lady Lansdowne, with whose family the regional organizer's father (the marquis of Bath) had traditionally shared power in the county.[16] While in Hampshire this aristocratic regime gave way to rather less blue-blooded leadership in the course of the war, in Norfolk, where Lady Diana Albemarle, wife of the ninth earl, had recruited the great majority of centre leaders from old county families, the aristocratic grip proved, as we shall see, much more tenacious.[17] Other aristocratic strongholds included Cumberland, Westmoreland—where the forebears of the county organizer, The Hon Mary Hornyold-Strickland of Kendall, had been members of parliament in the thirteenth century—and parts of rural Lancashire.

Even in the south, not all the leading positions were filled by aristocrats. While the existence of *Who's Who* and *Debretts*, themselves important instruments of elite cohesion, makes it easy to trace the lineage of titled ladies, it is much more difficult to track down the precise social location of non-titled WVS leaders. In the more rural parts of the West Midlands it was clear to the regional organizer that WVS 'must be led by members of the gentry'.[18] Where the private addresses of county organizers are available

[13] Cannadine, *Aristocracy*, 71, 111, 155, 162, 167. In 1942 she divorced her husband. A year later she was given the OBE. Her younger sister, Mary, sat on the WVS national General Purposes Committee. She married the third baron of Nunburnholme (Eton, army, wounded at El Alamein).

[14] His father, who sat on the boards of both the British Museum and the National Portrait Gallery, had sold off land and a Rembrandt in the early 1920s (Cannadine, *Aristocracy*, 111, 115, 579).

[15] Lady Congelton, Assistant County Organizer, was married to old aristocracy (and was herself of aristocratic birth). Lady Portal, Assistant County Organizer in North Hampshire, was married to a business baron (Eton and Oxford) from a titled—but not ancient—aristocratic family.

[16] Lady Lansdowne (née Elizabeth Hope), whose husband died in 1936, remarried in 1940. Her second husband was Lord Colum Crichton-Stuart, a Tory peer whose son was selected as Liberal Candidate for Northwich in 1922—though the family had no connections at all with Cheshire (J. M. Lee, *Social Leaders and Public Persons. A Study of County Government in Cheshire since 1888* (Oxford, 1963), 97).

[17] Lawson Johnson to Miss Halpin, 21 July 1950, WRVS, R4/2 Cambridgeshire.

[18] Fletcher Moulton, Report on Shropshire, 8 July 1938, WRVS, R9 West Midlands.

they generally indicate a big house.[19] The wives of landowners, business-men, retired generals, and admirals figured prominently in the county lead-ership. Upper-class ladies, titled or otherwise, did not run WVS unaided. At village level the manor house shared leadership with the rural middle class. The 'semi-professional' wives of clergymen, doctors, and bank managers bulked as prominently among village centre leaders as they did in the towns. So did spinsters of independent means. They were joined by some more specifically rural figures—notably, in Lancashire, Mrs Long, the wife of Lord Derby's land agent, 'most of [whose] division belongs to Lord Derby and she knows every village'.[20] As this example suggests, however, the rural middle-class was not generally inclined to resent aristocratic or gentry leadership, and most were happy to accept the subordinate role assumed by the com-ment of one of Gosforth's 'upper ten' on the value of the local professionals: 'very handy when you have about a dozen village organisations to see to'.[21]

It would be wrong to suggest that class relations within the rural WVS were entirely harmonious. Aristocratic condescension was sometimes resented by middle class women, as in the case of a Mass Observation diarist in Dorset:

Went up to the WVS Centre Organiser's house as usual to do typing and odd jobs in the morning. It would be so much better for both of us if the aristocracy had a business training. Mrs A is the best type of aristocrat no doubt, public-spirited, conscientious and very gracious but we waste most of the morning in civilities.[22]

Some rural women with professional experience were anxious to distinguish themselves from the presumed incompetence of the seriously idle rich. Thus the centre organizer in Churt (Surrey), feeling looked down upon as an ignorant housewife by Tothill Street, angrily listed the reasons why her opinions should be treated more respectfully, reasons which included the fact that she had run a large estate for twenty-five years, been trustee for the sale of a well-known bank, and chairman of the board of directors of a colliery—not to mention running the finances of the Girl Guides' first world camp.[23] More succinctly, Eleanor Ritchie of Malmesbury pointed out that—having worked as a company secretary before the First World War—'I am not "County" too awful...'. Ritchie was bitterly hostile to the leadership of the Wiltshire WVS, characterized by a friend of her daughter as just 'another institution to enable you to shake hands with Lady Lansdowne', and she wrote to Lady Reading complaining that 'you are giving all this work to one

[19] Margaret Stacey reckoned the extent of the upper class in late 1940s rural Oxfordshire partly by counting the number of entries for 'The Hall' or its equivalent in the telephone book (M. Stacey, *Banbury*, 151).

[20] WVS Executive, Minutes, 14 Dec. 1938.

[21] Williams, *Gosforth*, 107.

[22] Mrs P. C. Walther, diary entry, 12 May 1941, MO Diarist, W5454.

[23] Bowers to HQ, 9 Oct. 1939, WRVS, R12/4 Surrey.

class of woman and not trying to enlist the professional woman who might be of so much use.' The last straw was the appointment of a wealthy 70-year-old spinster as her local centre organizer. Although this woman had a distinguished record of public work, 70 ('an age to retire to bed with hot water bottles') was too old for anyone to take on a major new job. Someone younger and less upper class could surely have been found to take over among the twenty or so ladies in the rural district whose commitment and experience of other public work qualified them for leadership. The county ladies running WVS, however, had refused to look beyond their own elderly clique.[24] Tothill Street was unsympathetic to Ritchie's complaints, eventually writing her off as a troublemaker 'on the verge of a nervous breakdown . . . I think she is just a little deranged through the strain of the war.'[25]

Some challenges to the rule of the 'county' came from within the WVS hierarchy, but they were hardly more successful. In 1943 the East Anglia regional administrator, Mary Gray, was troubled by the ineffectiveness of the old county families who ran WVS in Norfolk: disinclined to widen involvement, they preferred to rely 'on their own particular circle of friends or acquaintances'. Nothing was done. Although Gray felt that 'perhaps I've been a bit of a coward', the influence of the aristocratic leader, Lady Albemarle, with the County Council made it very difficult to contemplate replacing her.[26] As late as 1950 the regional organizer, fearful that the Norfolk WVS would sink gently into oblivion with the elderly ladies who still ran it, confessed that she was 'at a loss to know how to replace them'.[27] The set-up in Cumberland was not dissimilar. Lady Mable Howard, the county organizer, ran everything that moved and quite a lot that did not. She was senior alderman of the county council, chair of its public health and public assistance committees, chair of the county WI, and a leading figure in the Nursing Association, the Personal Service League and the Girl Guides.[28] Not surprisingly the regional organizer, Vera Dart, remarked that 'we could not stir without her'. Dart, however, became increasingly critical of Lady Mable's influence. Local organizers, particularly those in the industrial towns on the coast, complained of neglect because she never visited them, leaving this work to the regional office which was too far away to do it effectively. Most of her nominees as WVS organizers turned out to be ineffective. By January 1941 Dart had concluded that the only real value of Lady Howard lay in her good relations with the County Council and even this was a dubious asset.

[24] Ritchie to Reading, 7 Mar. 1939; Ritchie to Wade, 27 Sept. 1939; Ritchie to Reading, 21 May 1940; Ritchie to Lady Colum Crichton Stuart, 22 May 1940, WRVS, R7/5 Wiltshire.
[25] Huxley to Reading, 23 May 1940; Huxley to Smieton, 29 May 1940; Smieton to Whetworth, 31 May 1940, WRVS, R 7/5 Wiltshire.
[26] Gray to Huxley, 5 June 1943, WRVS, R4 Eastern.
[27] Lawson Johnson to Miss Halpin, 21 July 1950, WRVS, R4/2 Cambridgeshire.
[28] Lady Mable Howard, of Greystoke (nr. Penrith).

The County officials might, as Lady Reading put it, 'eat out of Lady Mable's hand', but they were a 'trying' bunch headed by a County Clerk 'so ancient and gaga that the local [Town] clerks cannot be bothered with him'. Vera Dart was prepared to defy Lady Reading herself in order to force Lady Howard into a background, presidential role. But, after several bungled attempts to find a successor, Dart ended up appointing a woman from Lady Howard's own circle and the 'county' domination of the Cumberland organization continued.[29] In this case there was no question of cowardice. Dart, as we have seen, had no hesitation in taking on inefficient leaders in the towns of both the north-west and the north-east where she played a significant role in forcing the middle-class establishment to come to terms with changing times and new social forces. In the countryside, however, upper-class rule faced no equivalent challenges and even the most determined WVS apparatchik was unable to break the county grip.

Like the urban bourgeoisie, members of the rural upper class tended to withdraw from active participation in local government during the early twentieth century, a process well documented in J. M. Lee's 1963 study of Cheshire county council.[30] Upper-class social leaders, most of them wealthy commuters from Manchester and Liverpool who bought big houses and estates in the Cheshire countryside, were being replaced as county councillors by 'public persons'—men and women who built social esteem exclusively through political work, rather than dignifying politics with the reflected glory of a pre-existing social leadership. Lee's focus, however, was on politics and he had little to say about the extent to which the rural upper class, despite having opted out of elective office, continue to act as social leaders in associational life. While there is, to my knowledge, no rural equivalent of Clements' study of post-war Bristol, the social origins of WVS organizers in rural England strongly suggest that, at least among the women, it would be premature in the 1940s to talk of any widespread upper-class withdrawal from social leadership. No doubt many upper-class people gave themselves up to an idle and hedonistic lifestyle, embracing the pleasures of country living without taking on the responsibilities of the traditional landowning classes. While it was understandable that older people found the emerging alliance between upper-class glamour and the popular press distasteful, it would be difficult to think of a time when theatrical displays of affluence had not been part of the repertory of upper-class rule.[31] And

---

[29] Dart to Huxley, 9 Jan. 1941; Reading to Dart, 24 Jan. 1941; Dart to Reading, 25 Jan. 1941; Dart to Reading, 27 Jan. 1941; Huxley to Dart, 5 Feb. 1941; Dart to Huxley, 19 Feb. 1941, WRVS, R10 Northwest.
[30] Lee, *Social Leaders and Public Persons*.
[31] Ross McKibbin, *Classes and Cultures. England, 1918–1951* (Oxford, 1998), 22–37; R. Williams, *The Country and the City* (St Albans, 1975); D. Hay, 'Property, Authority and the Criminal Law', in D. Hay (ed.), *Albion's Fatal Tree* (London, 1975).

upper-class hegemony had for centuries been accompanied by denunciations of the new rich as 'too vulgar to use the opportunities of [their] position for anything but self-indulgence'.[32] Far from establishing that upper-class social leadership was withering away, the very existence of such jeremiads can be seen as evidence of its continuing appeal. Those who uttered them believed in the continuing viability of a *normal* rural regime in which social leadership belonged 'unquestioned', as Emmet put it, to the upper class.

There were, of course, places where gentry leadership had broken down. Many of Lee's Cheshire notables retired to the South Coast ('the monuments of Manchester cotton are to be found among the tombstones of Bournemouth'), or, unable to keep up residences in both Cheshire and London, chose to preserve their access to the metropolitan heartbeat of upper-class life by deserting the rural hinterland of the industrial north for the squire-cluttered home counties.[33] Some WVS leaders sought to explain local difficulties precisely by such desertions. In the small East Anglian town of Chatteris, for example, the reception of evacuees was handled with such exceptional clumsiness by the local authority that the regional administrator sent her assistant, Joan Fryer, to investigate. Related by marriage to the gentry family that had been lords of the manor in Chatteris since the sixteenth century, Fryer had no doubt where the root of the problem lay. The departure of the Fryers in the early 1930s, after 400 years in the area, left a vacuum: 'So tragic there is no one else now to give them a lead ... no one whom the whole place will follow and respect. Some may have made money and risen in the world [*she had in mind several of the leading figures on the local council*], but Chatteris people would not look up to them ...'[34] Elsewhere the selling off of country houses for institutional use—25 per cent of the larger houses within a ten-mile radius of Hertford had been disposed of in this way during the interwar years—led to a situation where many villages were 'without even a titular squire'. The author of a wartime survey of social work in Hertfordshire noted, however, that 'aspirants on the distaff side' among incoming middle-class commuters from London were, in such cases, quick to lay their own claims to social leadership: 'in the place of the "lady bountiful" a select body of "ladies" of the village comes into being. Their status is not so defined, nor yet their order of precedence, but they are none the less significant for that.'[35] As Raphael Samuel suggested: 'leadership in girl guides, chairing of

[32] Lee, *Social Leaders and Public Persons*, 25, 41–2.
[33] Ibid., 95
[34] Fryer to Miss Gray, 9 June 1940, WRVS, R4 East Anglia; Thursfield to Mrs Gibbs, 5 June 1940, WRVS, R4/6 Isle of Ely. Mrs Gibbs, the WVS organizer, was an ex-teacher, and a newcomer to the town: 'as a Bank Manager's wife she is sure to be free of politics and sect' (Report on Chatteris, 14 Feb. 1939, WRVS, R4/6 Isle of Ely). The latter was particularly important in Chatteris where spirituality thrived in 'little religious sects ... chapels, Salvation Army, Plymouth Brothers, etc., etc.'.
[35] Power, 'The Voluntary Social Services in Hertfordshire'.

meetings of the WI, activity in the Red Cross or the WVS' provided middle-class women with a substitute for the parish work and cottage visiting traditionally associated with Lady Bountiful, something recognizably modern and progressive, but equally suffused with condescension to those beneath them in the social order.[36]

Lee suggested that in the Home Counties geographical proximity to London may have made it possible for the upper class to combine participation in rural affairs with metropolitan life in a way not available to the Cheshire gentry.[37] Certainly many of the women working at Tothill Street lived in the country, and during the 1940 blitz Reading proposed that senior civil servants who had petrol for their cars should bring their wives up to town two or three days a week to join WVS working parties.[38] Caroline Haig, North Oxfordshire WVS volunteer and Mass Observation diarist, sustained an upper-class lifestyle which included regular trips 'to town' (where she stayed the night at Claridges) throughout the war years.[39] Evelyn Emmet, most of whose pre-war public activity had been in London, had always kept a hand on local matters and was able to shift effortlessly from her work as an elected councillor on the LCC into organizing the West Sussex WVS from her country seat in Amberly. Similarly, in Leighton Buzzard, according to the town clerk, the two most prestigious women in the area were 'powerful in the neighbourhood if they are at home'.[40] Other upper-class women, who spent half the year in London and the other half abroad, were not present often enough in their country houses to hold more than merely decorative office in local associations, a practice which some WI leaders had attempted, unsuccessfully, to ban during the inter-war years.[41] Some of the upper-class ladies recruited to organize WVS found themselves starting virtually from scratch. In the East Kent rural district of Sandwich, the well-to-do people spent most of their time in London, using their country houses only at weekends and having no local contacts outside 'a tiny groove'. Appointed WVS organizer, Lady Hambro (of the banking dynasty) found herself in May 1941 'working like a black' to get to know the locals and build the 'trust and confidence' necessary for the exercise of social leadership.[42] A similar situation existed in Hertfordshire where improved transport made daily commuting to

[36] R. Samuel, 'The Middle Class in Britain Between the Wars', *New Socialist* (Jan.–Feb. 1983), 31

[37] Lee, *Social Leaders and Public Persons*, 225.

[38] WVS Chairman's Committee, Minutes, 12 Nov. 1940.

[39] Alan Howkins, 'Mass Observation and Rural England, 1939–45', *Rural History*, 9 (1998), 85

[40] Mrs Reid Jamieson, Report, 20 Jan. 1939, WRVS, R4/1 Bedfordshire.

[41] Maggie Andrews, *The Acceptable Face of Feminism. The Women's Institute as a Social Movement* (London, 1998), 62.

[42] Lady Worsely, Report on Visit to Sandwich, 8–9 May 1941, WRVS, R5 Kent.

London possible so that 'the wealthy no longer need a "town house" '. The result was that 'local loyalties become weakened and confused and the gentry tend to become but a class of superior dormitory residents'.[43]

II

In the towns women's associational life was clearly demarcated along class lines. In the villages the major development of the inter-war years, the growth of the WI, involved women of all classes. Founded in 1915, the WI was easily the most successful of the new mass women's organizations, gaining a membership of 331,600 by 1940. Limiting itself to recruiting in communities of no more than 4,000 people, the great majority of WI members lived in villages, although it also built a significant presence in some of the new middle-class suburbs. The WI established, for the first time, a public space for village women, taking over the pub once a month, or building their own hall which then served as the village hall under female management.[44] Alongside the everyday rhythms of social and educational activity, the inter-war WI also campaigned around issues of practical concern to rural women—the extension of piped water and sewage facilities, improved housing, phone boxes, libraries, maternity and child welfare clinics, etc. By such means the WI rapidly established itself as the main representative body for rural women, fostering a feminine rural identity which to some extent transcended class divisions.[45] 'In the WI,' wrote one usually sceptical witness, 'the gentry and the labourer's wife, the farmer and the school teacher together practise quilting or help to preserve jam, make hats or learn how to feed bees.'[46]

The WI had a democratic constitution and, in the person of the Liberal aristocrat Lady Denman, a national leader committed to developing citizenship skills among all sections of the membership. How this worked in practice depended on local circumstances. Eleanor Ritchie, the anti-'county' troublemaker from Malmesbury, had refused to serve as president of her local WI, believing that the village folk were 'best left to their own pig clubs and village "does" as long as you subscribe'. Subsequently she 'observe[d] with approval that the women themselves have made [the WI] a really going and successful concern'.[47] But this was unusual. A report on voluntary organizations in the East Riding of Yorkshire remarked that while 'some of the individual institutions are democratically run, in others (where there is

[43] Power, 'The Voluntary Social Services in Hertfordshire'.

[44] Martin Pugh, *Women and the Women's Movement in Britain, 1914–1959* (Basingstoke, 1992), 14–15, 227; Andrews, *Acceptable Face of Feminism*, 66 and *passim*.

[45] Maggie Andrews, ' "For Home and Country": Feminism and Englishness in the Women's Institute Movement, 1930–1960', in R. Weight and A. Beach (eds.), *The Right to Belong. Citzenship and National Identity in Britain, 1930–1960* (London, 1998), 116–17, 119.

[46] Bourdillon, draft note on WI, 29 June 1942, NCSRS, E12/8 WI.

[47] Ritchie to Reading, 7 Mar. 1939, WRVS, R 7/5 Wiltshire.

a local "lady of the manor" in effective existence) they are run, in practice, on very undemocratic lines. It entirely depends on local village circumstances...'[48] In Oxfordshire the election of a 'village woman' to office in the WI could still cause amazement among the gentry in the late 1940s, while in Hertfordshire, where the WI officials were 'invariably women whom education and social standing in the village made the "obvious" leaders', the election of a farmer's wife as President in one Institute was seen as risky experiment.[49] In Devon the local 'great lady' was invariably elected president: and even when, like Eleanor Ritchie in Wiltshire, she would have preferred to take a back seat, the village women insisted on deferring if only to avoid the problems of sorting out an order of precedence among themselves.[50] Noting that village women participated actively and enthusiastically in WI activities, the Hertfordshire report at the same time regretted that they showed no desire for self-government and no inclination to challenge the upper-class leadership described by one woman as 'right, natural and satisfactory'.[51] A similar combination of attitudes was noted by other frustrated democrats reporting for the Nuffield Reconstruction Survey from Devon and Sussex—a sturdy independence among the village folk coexisting unproblematically with deference to their 'natural' superiors.[52] Much the same conclusion was drawn by the sociologist Rosalind Chambers in her 1954 study of women's organizations. Whatever the democratic aspirations of its leaders, the WI could not buck the feudal spirit infusing social relations in much of the English countryside. E. M. Delafield's fictional 'provincial lady' had commented aptly on the contrast between democratic rhetoric and hierarchical reality in the WI in the late 1920s:

Have occasional misgivings at recollections of rousing speeches made by various speakers from our National Federation, to the effect that all WI members enjoy equal responsibilities and equal privileges... Can only hope than none of them will ever have occasion to enter more fully into the inner workings of our Monthly Committee Meetings.[53]

It was, as Chambers noted, in the middle-class suburban areas that the WI functioned most democratically.[54]

Writing in 1937, the first historian of the WI described it as an uprising of country women in the tradition of Joseph Arch.[55] But this is precisely what it

[48] R. K. Kelsall, Report on Hull, 4 Apr. 1942, 25, NCSRS, E2/8.
[49] Stacey, *Banbury*, 162; Power, 'The Voluntary Social Services in Hertfordshire'.
[50] James McIntyre, 'Voluntary Service in Devon' (n.d., 1942), NCSRS, E2/5.
[51] Power, 'The Voluntary Social Services in Hertfordshire', 5, 13 NCSRS, E2/7; 121/1/13.
[52] McIntyre, 'Voluntary Service in Devon' Foster, Report on East Sussex.
[53] E. M. Delafield, *Diary of a Provincial Lady* (London, 1950), 205.
[54] R. C. Chambers, 'A Study of Three Voluntary Organisations', in D. V. Glass (ed.), *Social Mobility in Britain* (London, 1954), 395, 398.
[55] Andrews, *Acceptable Face of Feminism*, 51.

was not. Arch's agricultural trade unionism, building on the non-conformist identity that provided the main source of alternative values to the Tory Anglicanism underpinning gentry rule, brought class struggle to rural England.[56] The WI, though formally both non-denominational and non-partisan, was frequently run by the vicar's wife and well-integrated with both the church and the Tory Party.[57] While there is no doubt that the inter-war WI constituted a significant pressure group speaking for the interests of rural women, and while it may well have done something, as its most recent historian has argued, to strengthen a female sub-culture resistant to the cruder manifestations of patriarchy, the identity it fostered was that of country versus town, not village women versus lady of the manor.[58] If there were any places where the WI was used by plebeian women to challenge gentry power, these were vastly outnumbered by the villages in which it provided women of the upper class with a forum within which to renew their claims to social leadership. At national level, despite positive attempts to involve working-class women, all but two of the sixteen executive members in 1942 were of aristocratic or gentry extraction. One member was married to a farmer: none to a farm labourer.[59]

Given the dominance of the WI in village life, the process of WVS mobilization in the countryside necessarily revolved around the relations between the two organizations. In some countries the WVS was initially seen as an irrelevance, since the WI itself could undertake any necessary emergency work. Thus in Huntingdon the WI, anxious not 'to open the field up for other organisations', were backed by the clerk to the County Council who saw no need for WVS interference in his existing relationship with the WI.[60] Similarly in Northumberland, the County Council showed no interest in WVS, organizing the 1939 evacuation without any help from them, and in the North Riding of Yorkshire it was the WI, not WVS, which took the lead in organizing the reception of evacuees. Lady Reading's response was to point to the need for co-ordination with other organizations operating in the

---

[56] Alan Howkins, *Reshaping Rural England. A Social History, 1850–1925* (London, 1991), 185–94; J. P. D. Dunbabin, ' "The Revolt of the Field": The Agricultural Labourers' Movement in the 1870s', *Past and Present*, 26 (1963).

[57] Despite denying Labour allegations that the WI was a Tory preserve (Committee on Evacuation, Minutes, 21 July 1938, PRO, HO 45 17635), Lady Denham defended the WI ban on political and religious discussion on the grounds that 'many villages still consist of people who are in the main members of the Church of England and of the Conservative party' (Denman to the Master of Balliol, 24 Aug. 1942, in NCSRS, E12/8 WI).

[58] The most recent historian of the WI claims, rather extravagantly, that 'through the formation of a female sub-culture within rural villages they provided a space for women to fight the internalization of male domination and to adopt an alternative value system... [providing] a significant site for the development of gyn-affection...a form of female-run counter culture...' (Andrews, *Acceptable Face of Feminism*, 11).

[59] Bourdillon, draft note on WI, 29 June 1942, 3–4 in NCSRS, E12/8 WI; Andrews, *Acceptable Face of Feminism*, 22–3.

[60] Reid Jamieson, diary, 3 Jan. 1939, WRVS, R4 East Anglia.

countryside, though in many cases informal co-ordination already existed in the overlap of committee membership between organizations like the Girl Guides or the Red Cross and the WI.[61] A more convincing argument for the need for WVS was the reluctance of the WI national leadership, in deference to the sensibilities of Quaker members, to involve the organization in ARP preparations or to take the lead in devising arrangements for receiving evacuees from the towns.[62] Explaining the WI stance to the official committee on evacuation in the summer of 1938, Lady Denman hinted at an additional reason for this reluctance—the preservation of WI as a genuinely independent voluntary association rather than a servant of the state. Too much involvement in war preparations, she said, would jeopardize social activities and undermine the capacity of the WI to function as 'as a centre of tranquillity and cheerfulness in a troubled world'.[63]

Not everybody in the Institutes welcomed this less-than-wholehearted attitude to the war effort. Although the WI eventually developed its own very effective war work—above all jam making—some of the membership protested that 'they did not want to have lectures in glove making, bottling fruit, etc.... but would much rather be doing Hospital Supplies or knitting for the WVS.'[64] In one group of Yorkshire villages the WI decided to suspend its activities entirely for the duration 'and be only WVS'.[65] The decline of WI membership during the war—from 331,600 in 1940 to 288,000 at the end of 1944—may have owed something to transfer of members into WVS.[66] Where WVS did take off as a mass membership organization in the villages, relations between rival local leaders could be bitter. A report from Devon spoke of 'a state of siege in some villages between the WI and the WVS. The former as the old established body are wildly jealous of the powers invested in the WVS and refuse absolutely to co-operate.' Some of these cases reflected personal rivalries which pre-dated WVS: disappointed aspirants to the local WI presidency had seized the opportunity provided by

[61] Huxley, note on visit to Region I, 22 Nov. 1939, WRVS, R1 Northeast; Committee on Evacuation, Minutes, 21 July 1938, PRO, HO 45 17635; Power, 'The Voluntary Social Services in Hertfordshire', 5–6, NCSRS, E2/7.

[62] Lady Reading reported that the WI 'were very chary and did not want to do any work at all in regard to WVS because they were afraid it would mean nothing but ARP'. (Committee on Evacuation, Minutes, 21 July 1938, PRO, HO 45 17635). On WI obstruction to ARP work, see Foster Jeffery to Huxley, 21 July 1938, WRVS, R10 Regional Office. The national executive of the WI, sensitive to sensibilities of Quaker members, refused to allow the organization to participate in activities that directly contributed to preparation for or prosecution of war (Andrews, 'Home and Country', 121). See also Stella Schofield, Interview with Miss Farrer, 7 Nov. 1939, MO, TC Women in Wartime 32/4/G/WI.

[63] Committee on Evacuation, Minutes, 21 July 1938, PRO, HO 45 17635. The WI was very decentralized and placed high value on local autonomy: 'We're a community working together with no orders from anybody but ourselves' (Andrews, 'Home and Country', 123).

[64] 'The Voluntary Social Services in Yorkshire', 1942, NCSRS, E2/9.

[65] Ingham, Report of Visit to East Riding, 4–8 Dec. 1939, WRVS, R2/1 East Riding.

[66] Andrews, *Acceptable Face of Feminism*, 53.

war preparations to set up a rival organization.[67] In Staffordshire, where the WI ran evacuation until the WVS took over at the end of 1940, there was a good deal of resentment of the 'over-publicised activities of the WVS, and its uniform-wearing proclivities'.[68]

But such conflicts were rare. More usually the WI protected its autonomy as a voluntary organization precisely by colonizing the WVS hierarchy. A large proportion of WVS leaders in the countryside were recruited from the leadership of the WI, which contributed a larger number of the first wave of WVS appointments than any other organization apart from the Girl Guides.[69] A close interpenetration of WVS and WI leadership was reported from many rural areas.[70] The following report from Hertfordshire is probably representative of the WVS/WI relationship in most parts of the country:

Since the outbreak of the war the WVS has, of course, made itself felt in the villages as elsewhere. But it has mainly affected the 'ladies' of the village, and where wider support for particular ventures has been needed it has worked largely through the WI. Relations with the WI have invariably been good, owing to the fact that WI leaders and WVS are very often synonymous.[71]

In so far as WVS was run by WI leaders they could ensure both that the wartime arrangements did not threaten the long-term hegemony of the WI in the villages, and that WVS did not interfere too much with elite local autonomy in the meantime. Thus the WVS county organizer in Oxfordshire was never wholly convinced of the need for WVS in rural districts, but she took on the job to make sure that whatever happened WVS did not interfere with the work of the WI which she was 'determined at all costs to maintain unscathed by the war'.[72] One reason for Mary Gray's inability to bring Lady Albemarle to heel in Norfolk was that she doubled as president of the county federation of WIs. Since the county ladies, through the WI, had effective control of any possible mobilization of women volunteers at village level, Gray's desire to outflank them by using Housewives Service

<hr/>

[67] McIntyre, 'Voluntary Service in Devon'.
[68] M. Forsyth and M. Morris, Report on North Staffordshire, 30 May 1942, 5, NCSRS, E2/34. Such mean motives are also attested in Hampshire, where, according to one observer, village organizations tended to be run by local ladies-of-the-manor who were more concerned to see their names on headed notepaper than to look to effective co-ordination over evacuation between rival organizations (Katherine Furse to Tom Harrison, 13 Aug. 1940, MO, TC Women in Wartime 32/4/A). Even the humble jumble sale was a potential source of rivalry between the two organizations: 'It wasn't right the WI having their jumble sale two days before ours. I didn't go of course. They said they got £5. But I don't like the spirit' (PC, report on WVS sewing party in an East coast village, 3 Oct. 1940, MO, TC 32/4/ I).
[69] WVS Executive Committee, Minutes, 1938–9, *passim*. 65 of the first 556 appointments were WI activists.
[70] Including the East Anglia, rural Lancashire, East Sussex, Cumberland, and Oxfordshire.
[71] Power, 'The Voluntary Social Services in Hertfordshire'.
[72] Huxley, Report on Visit to Region 6, 6 June 1941, WRVS, R6 Regional Office.

to give WVS an independent membership base in the villages was a non-starter.[73] Vera Dart's problems in Cumberland were similarly underwritten by the fact that among her many other offices Lady Howard controlled the county WI. During the 1939 evacuation she used her position as WVS organizer to ensure that the welfare work should be left to the WI and other established local organizations.[74] In both Norfolk and Cumberland aristocratic WVS leaders were thus able to concert their influence in the WI and the county council to resist undue WVS penetration. In the Hertford-shire village of Redbourn, such was the zeal of the 'upper ten' for self-determination that they were able to keep the county council at bay as well. The local WI leader took over WVS (after an attempt to organize it separately had failed) and mobilized her upper-class friends to cope energet-ically with difficult evacuation problems: but she did so 'with a degree of independence that has made co-operation with County Council welfare schemes extremely difficult'. The independence so effectively defended was, as the author of the Hertfordshire report sourly pointed out: 'the independence of an oligarchy and not a community'.[75]

III

The work organized by WVS in the countryside included most of the activities common in the towns, but its central rural concern was with the reception of evacuees. The upheavals involved in evacuation made high demands on the skills of rural social leaders. In the towns bombing threatened life, limb, and the destruction of property, but the source of the threat was external and its impact, by and large, was socially unifying. In the countryside the threat was not from German bombers but from British refugees, mothers and children moved out from the cities in the autumn of 1939 and again, a year later, when the bombing started in earnest. These evacuee invasions might threaten no more than inconvenience and discom-fort for country folk, but being forced to share your home with people from very different social backgrounds promoted social antagonisms in a way that losing your home altogether to German bombs did not. Settling evacuees in the countryside involved the negotiation of profound cultural differences, not only between town and country but also between class and class.[76] Evacuation clearly worked best where the class gulf was narrowest. Familiar tales of East End children amazed to discover that milk came out of cows and distressed by the absence of fish and chip shops, are less important

[73] Gray to Huxley, 5 June 1943, WRVS, R6 East Anglia.
[74] Dart, Report on Visit to Cumberland, 9–10 Oct. 1939; Dart, Report on Tour of Cumber-land, Feb. 1940, WRVS, R10 Cumberland.
[75] Power, 'The Voluntary Social Services in Hertfordshire' 13, NCSRS, E2/7.
[76] Tom Harrison, *War Begins at Home* (London, 1940), 306, 313, 324, 329, 331.

here than the undisguised disgust felt by well-to-do hosts at the sanitary
habits and the ingratitude of their working-class guests, or the equally
passionate resentments aroused among evacuees auctioned like cattle to
fastidious householders, or expected to keep out of their hosts' way by
roaming lifeless village streets for long hours of the day. After two months
of war, Mass Observation wryly observed, there were more atrocity stories
circulating about the treatment of hosts by evacuees—and vice versa—than
about German behaviour in Poland.[77] The fact that most of these stories
were either untrue or grossly exaggerated, and that kindness and understanding between evacuees and their hosts existed alongside open conflict
and dull resentment, should not obscure the function of atrocity stories in
giving vent to profound currents of social fear and anxiety. Many of the first
wave of evacuees quickly returned home, having concluded that the risks of
bombing were negligible compared with the miseries of living as unwelcome
guests in other people's houses: the culture clash was at least as difficult for
uprooted working-class mothers as it was for their hosts.[78] As things settled
down antagonism subsided, but the rifts and chasms in Britain's social fabric
revealed by the early experience of evacuation had long-term consequences
for both working-class and middle-class perceptions of the causes of social
inequality.[79]

The reception of evacuees, the vast majority of them women and children,
was perceived as women's work.[80] In the summer of 1938 Lady Reading had
taken the initiative in making contingency plans, convening a committee
with the main women's organizations likely to be involved.[81] From then on
WVS played a central role, working with local authorities on the reception
and billeting of evacuees, organizing the supply of clothing and footwear to
evacuated children, and setting up canteens, mother's clubs, and other
facilities for evacuees in the villages.[82] WVS pioneered provision for pre-
school children and lobbied Whitehall effectively to meet the costs.[83] They

---

[77] Ibid., 312–13, 299–301, 367; R. Titmuss, *Problems of Social Policy* (London, 1950), 180;
T. J. Crosby, *The Impact of Civilian Evacuation in the Second World War* (London, 1986),
passim.
[78] Harrison, *War Begins at Home*, 322.
[79] Crosby, *Civilian Evacuation*, 9–10, 148–55.
[80] Sir A. Salisbury MacNalty (ed.), *The Civilian Health and Medical Services*, i (London,
1953), 225.
[81] WVS Evacuation Committee, Minutes, WRVS, E9; Evacuation—pre-Munich Plans,
July—Sept. 1938, WRVS, E1.
[82] Titmuss, *Problems,* 373–6; Susan Isaacs, *The Cambridge Evacuation Survey* (London,
1941), 30–2; Katherine Bentley Beauman, *Green Sleeves. The Story of WVS/WRVS*
(London, 1977), 28–9; John Welshman, 'Evacuation and Social Policy During World War
Two: Myth and Reality', *Twentieth Century British History*, 9 1 (1998) suggests a (slow and
uneven) shift in official attitudes to provision of footwear and clothing to evacuated children—
from insistence on voluntarism in 1938 towards acceptance of the need for public provision
(managed by the WVS) on universalistic lines.
[83] Beauman, *Green Sleeves*, 23–6.

took a similar leading role in pressing for improved medical services in reception areas.[84] Through these practical activities WVS leaders did much both to meet the needs of evacuees and to assuage the terrors of their hosts.

These terrors ran deep. In February 1939, long before any evacuees actually arrived, a vicar's wife and daughter in Elmstead, a village near Godalming (Surrey), organized a petition against compulsory billeting under the heading 'Your Home is Threatened'. In an accompanying memorandum they conjured nightmare visions of barbarian invasion:

Our homes are built up gradually through patient contriving and loving care, and are paid for by the fruits of honest toil. They are our most sacred possession, and from their roots grow our patriotism and our spiritual life. The material goods which comprise them have often a sentimental value which could never be replaced: and we regard it as the most TERRIBLE INJUSTICE that our property should not be regarded as sacred.

Evacuees, they feared, would smash treasured household goods or—'a terror with many people'—set fire to the house, and even if the refugees 'were in every way as nice as ourselves [!], they would still inevitably wear things out'. The reaction to compulsory billeting from 'inoffensive citizens loyal to the Government' would, they predicted, be extreme: 'Strangers in MY kitchen!! I'd clout them over the head ... NO ONE WOULD STAND IT, THERE WOULD BE A REVOLUTION'. The local WVS organizer's anxieties about the likely effects of this agitation on her efforts to complete the billeting survey were intensified by a sense of class shame that 'two "ladies" of breeding and education' should lend themselves to such irresponsible scare mongering.[85] But the fears articulated by the Elmstead ladies were widespread. In Kent, early in 1939, two WVS centre organizers joined with thirty-one other leading local women to petition the Home Secretary demanding that no adult evacuees would be billeted in private houses and that great care should be taken to billet children only on households where they would receive adequate care.[86] From West Sussex it was reported that elderly spinsters were living in terror at the thought of having to take in

[84] Titmuss, *Problems*, 229 n.

[85] Fitzwilliam to Halpin, 6 Feb. 1939, enclosing 'Memorandum from the Elmstead Women's Social Club', WRVS, R12/4 Surrey (capitals in original).

[86] Petition to Home Secretary (n.d., Jan. 1939?), WRVS, R5 Kent. In October 1938 the WI in one of the petitioning towns (Westerham) had demanded that both adults and schoolchildren should only be billeted in public buildings or hutments on the grounds that, unlike billeted soldiers, such people would be neither employed nor under effective supervision and that 'the continuous daily discomfort and menace to health is more certain to undermine the morale of the civilian population than the occasional risk of physical danger' (from bombing?) (Text of Resolution, in WRVS, R5 Kent.). In October 1938 a far-right organization run by John Mitchell and T. H. Story, the United Ratepayers Advisory Association, had set out to organize concerted local actions against billeting ('No Billeting Campaign. Preliminary Directions on Organising Local Campaigns', 26 Oct. 1938, WRVS, R6/1 Berkshire).

children: 'children appear to them as a cross between a poltergeist and a wild beast.'[87] Where fears about billeting were running high, the WVS mission to enable women to 'defend their homes in the time of war' could take on a double meaning.[88] The solution generally favoured was the construction of special hutments to house the refugees. If hutments 'are good enough for our relations when serving in the Forces, and the nobility,' wrote the Elmstead ladies, then 'we consider they are equally suitable for town refugees', and, like many others who demanded the establishment of camps, they protested their willingness to give voluntary service to the needs of evacuees so accommodated, provided the sanctity of their own homes was preserved.

When evacuation actually happened on the outbreak of war the fear of taking in children seems to have been largely overcome. Many of them might arrive verminous, dirty, and badly house-trained, but rescuing the next generation from the culture of the slums (as well as from German bombs) was a cause for which many rural women were prepared to put themselves out.[89] The mothers, on the other hand, were considered simply impossible— 'rude, dirty, discontented', 'the low, slum type ... dirty ... idle and unwilling to work or pull their weight ...'.[90] 'There is one generalisation which one can safely make', wrote Evelyn Emmett, 'children are billetable but adults (except under some form of military discipline) are not and it does not matter a bit how strongly the London end deprecate the return of the unbilletable evacuee, back she will go as sure as God made little apples.' From Lincolnshire the county organizer Lilly Boys suggested that 'if the Government is anxious to save the lives of the mothers ... for the purpose of the next generation' (they were hardly worth saving for themselves, she implied) then they should be put into camps or hostels where they can 'live dirtily (and happily) together and be a nuisance to no-one but themselves'.[91] 'They like to be herded together', remarked the WVS organizer in Petworth (Sussex), adding that her helpers would refuse to receive any more mothers unless hostels were available for them.[92] From Dorset it was reported that, while most evacuees had settled down well, 'complaints have been received by us of vermin, drunkenness, fighting; of furniture and crockery broken, and carpets being soiled by children who are untrained and uncontrolled (not only infants)'. The troublesome minority should be put in Army camps

[87] Report on West Sussex, 18 Feb. 1939, WRVS, R/12/3 West Sussex.
[88] Mrs Farrer, speaking at a public meeting to launch WVS in Guildford, 17 Jan. 1939, WRVS, R12/4 Surrey.
[89] Lily Boys, 'Preliminary report on Evacuation', 11 Sept. 1939, WRVS, R3/5 Linconshire/Lindsey; Lady Reading to Mrs Morris, 5 Nov. 1940, WRVS, R4/2 Cambridgeshire.
[90] Report on Evacuation, Sept. 1939, WRVS, R/12/3 West Sussex; Lily Boys, 'Preliminary Report on Evacuation'.
[91] Lily Boys, 'Preliminary Report on Evacuation'.
[92] Report on Evacuation, Sept. 1939.

with the children under appropriate supervision.[93] In September 1939 Vera Dart, normally a woman of progressive views, reported from the north-west that:

stories of the reception of filthy evacuees continue to pour in. This Region is certainly unfortunate in having to cope with the Liverpool Irish who are all verminous and unpleasant in every possible way. A lot of them have gone home leaving destruction in their wake and men in Cheshire have said that they would much rather go to prison than that their wives should have to put up with them again. The only sensible thing to do with people who are a lower type of civilisation altogether is to put them into huts.[94]

The omnipresence of these stories of barbarian invasion bear witness to the trauma confronting rural social leaders, but they should not be treated as accurate accounts of the behaviour of the refugees themselves. A process of stereotyping was clearly at work. In one village a group of evacuated mothers and children billeted in an empty house quickly struck up a friendly relationship with the spinster sisters living next door, one of whom happened to be a Mass Observer. They did not, however, get on so well with the gardener (who was looking after the property on behalf of its absent owners), and he called in the Evacuation Officer. In relating what happened next the Mass Observer made no attempt to disguise her own feelings, and there may even be an element of counter-stereotyping going on. Nevertheless the account is worth quoting at length as a rare insight into how the social relations of evacuation might appear to a bystander:

About the fifth day we heard the harsh, strident voice of a managing, self-satisfied woman suddenly upraised next door, and listening through the hedge, heard the [Evacuation] Officer... pouring abuse and insult on these three mothers. She said, 'I have worked in the slums of Lambeth all my life, and I have never seen such filthy people as you are' (!). She accused them of stealing the vegetables and ruining the house. They showed immense self-control and presence of mind, and instead of curbing her, kept quiet and tried to explain. She would have no excuses and ordered them to be ready to start in half an hour, when she would take them to a camp, 'which is the only place you are fit for'—I was boiling with rage and went round to help... The husband of... one arrived on a visit as the whole household were being bundled off, and faced up to the billeting officer's second in command, who had come to fetch them. 'She said my wife was dirty,' he said. 'Well, I can tell you she isn't, and I'm very particular.' They all got off eventually, and were taken to a parish hall, where they lay on sacks on the floor and were looked after by Guides. The next day two of them brought the children walking right across the fields hoping to thank my sister and me.

[93] Sylvia Mansel to Lady Stavordale, 9 Sept. 1939, WRVS, R7 West Country.
[94] Dart to Reading, 17 Sept. 1939, WRVS, R10 Northwest. These attitudes to the Liverpool Irish were reinforced by later evacuations. In 1941 Dart wrote: 'they are destroying houses... as they did in Cheshire in 1939' (Dart to Reading, 8 June 1941, WRVS, R10/2 Liverpool).

They were cheerful and philosophical and managing their overwhelming families amazingly. Each besides her three toddlers had brought a friend's child away too.[95]

While rejecting alarmist accounts of the impossibility of persuading people to take in refugees, Lady Reading pressed the authorities to do what they could to provide communal accommodation for evacuees.[96] Interestingly she was supported in this by representatives of the evacuees themselves who disliked the idea of living as unwelcome guests just as much as their potential hosts feared the invasion of their homes.[97] But both the scarcity of labour for building hutments and the danger that any such camps would themselves become targets for enemy bombers ruled out any such solution, and Reading was forced to explain to her members that, for the great majority of evacuees, there was no alternative to billeting in private homes.[98] However, provision of welfare services, clubs' canteens, and nurseries could do much to defuse the tensions festering in the unsupported cohabitation of refugee and reluctant host, a point well made by Lilly Boys in September 1939 alongside her contemptuous characterization of urban working-class mothers.[99] The mission to re-educate the slum children in their own homes was the practical end of a larger reformist response to the experience of evacuation among rural social leaders. According to Mass Observation a minority of upper-class women had 'turned horror into pity, and . . . determined that the appalling conditions which the evacuee children reflect shall be swept away, and very soon.'[100] These sentiments were channelled through a new organization established in the autumn of 1939, the Women's Group for Public Welfare, whose most significant intervention was the wartime publication of a widely discussed account of the social lessons of evacuation, *Our Towns*. These developments will be fully discussed in Chapter 9. In line with its avoidance of public lobbying or speculation about future social arrangements, WVS was happy to leave this reformist response to evacuation to the Women's Group, and referred those of its staff who were inclined to pursue the larger issues to that quarter.[101]

Billeting brought out the best and the worst in rural social leaders. Some WVS leaders combined their voluntary work with more than their share of

[95] Harrison, *War Begins at Home*, 318.
[96] WVS, Executive Committee, Minutes, 15 Feb., 1 Mar., 15 Mar., 3 May 1939; WVS Chairman's Committee, Minutes, 29 Oct. 1940.
[97] Davie to Dart, 15 May 1939, WRVS, R10/2 Liverpool; Women's Co-operative Guild Central Committee, Minutes, 25–7 September 1939; Lily Boys, 'Preliminary Report on Evacuation'.
[98] Lady Reading to Mrs Morris, 5 Nov. 1940, WRVS, R4/2 Cambridgeshire.
[99] Lily Boys, 'Preliminary Report on Evacuation'; ead., letter to *The Times*, 2 Oct. 1939.
[100] Harrison, *War Begins at Home*, 336.
[101] Dart to Reading, 10 Nov. 1939; Reading to Dart, 16 Nov. 1939; Smieton to Dart, 20 Nov. 1939; Huxley to Dart, 23 Nov. 1939, WRVS, R10 Northwest.

evacuees. In October 1939 the district organizer in Cleveland was coping with a household of sixteen including several 12-year-old boys and their mothers.[102] The organizer of Basingstoke rural district had a sick-bay for evacuee children in the top of her house.[103] A Gloucestershire centre organizer was looking after four evacuees as well as an elderly friend and her own two little girls. When, in 1942, the last two servants departed leaving only an elderly cook housekeeper the WVS was bound to suffer.[104] If the servants could be retained, on the other hand, upper class women could transfer to them much of the burden. One of Eleanor Ritchie's grievances against the incoming centre organizer was that she knew nothing of the hardships suffered by less well-provided women:

What can a good lady with a large household of maids—and in this part of the world there are many people who still live in the manner of before the last War—a large car and has never cooked a meal in her life or bathed a child or known a moment's discomfort know of the work taking evacuees means. There is no handing over to the second footman or the parlour maid or, as was said to me: 'It of course makes no difference to us, the maids do it all.'[105]

The ability of the rich to protect themselves against the inconvenience of hosting evacuees was widely attested. After the Munich crisis the Liberal representative on the WVS Advisory Committee remarked that 'the willingness to co-operate and to receive refugees seems to have been in inverse ratio to the wealth, social position, and discomfort involved to the householder'.[106] The selfishness of the well-to-do was amply confirmed in the wartime evacuation, and Lady Reading was prepared to take the matter up in Whitehall to see if more could be done to force owners of large houses to take their fair share of the burden.[107] She was not, however, keen to encourage over-zealousness in this direction amongst her own staff. A local billeting officer in Haslemere (Surrey) who had the temerity to challenge the transparent excuses for refusing to take evacuees into her sixteen-roomed

---

[102] Mrs Charles Dorman to Davidson, 4 Oct. 1939, WRVS, R1/5 North Riding.

[103] Lady Reading, Report of Visit to Region 6, 5 Mar. 1941, WRVS, R6 Region.

[104] Olive Hirtzel to Mrs Colchester-Wemyss, 6 July 1942, WRVS, R7/3 Gloucestershire. Mass Observation cites several well-to-do households in Surrey complaining that servants were quitting because of the extra burden of looking after evacuees (Harrison, *War Begins at Home*, 329–30).

[105] Ritchie to Reading, 21 May 1940, WRVS, R 7/5 Wiltshire.

[106] Mrs Helen Argenti to Lady Reading, 22 Dec. 1938, WRVS, V102/38 Women's Liberal Federation.

[107] WVS Chairman's Committee, Minutes, 12 Feb. 1941. The selfishness of the rich is well attested. E. M. Delafield, *Diary of a Provincial Lady* (London, 1950), 378, 382–3, 459, is eloquent on the topic, and Crosby, *Civilian Evacuation*, cites ample evidence (pp. 50–1, 57), including the following statement by a WVS Regional Administrator (p. 47): 'We find over and over again that it is the really poor people who are willing to take evacuees and that the sort of bridge playing set who live at such places as Chorley Wood are terribly difficult about it all' (p. 60).

house offered by the wife of the local MP, Sir John Wardlaw-Milne, was firmly told that it was no part of her WVS role to mount class-conscious attacks on important Tory MPs (Wardlaw-Milne was chairman of the Public Accounts Committee).[108]

While WVS rejected the selfish and irresponsible opposition to billeting represented by the Wardlaw-Milnes or the Elmstead ladies, they were not interested in rooting out upper-class privilege in the name of equality of sacrifice. In the country, as in the towns, their role was to 'smooth out difficulties', seeking practical solutions to immediate problems and there is no doubt that they contributed constructively both to reconciling county people to evacuation and to improving the conditions of the evacuees themselves. Despite their own material privilege, WVS leaders frequently articulated the grievances of ordinary cottagers and the whole experience of evacuation was one which encouraged the rural community to count its blessings.[109] Occasional attempts by WVS organizers to push traditional social leaders to one side were unsuccessful, and, after the war, as we shall see, the rural WVS in most areas quickly dissolved back into the WI. Overall, it seems safe to conclude that the work undertaken by WVS in the country-side during the war served to enhance the legitimacy of established social leaders in the eyes of country folk.[110]

[108] She had written to the MP pointing out that: 'It places an intolerable burden on the willing half of the community if some of the large house owners refuse to do their share' (Janet Lawson (WVS deputy to Chief Billeting Officer, Halesmere, Surrey) to Sir John Wardlaw-Milne, 23 Sept. 1939; Wardlaw-Milne to Lawson 26 Sept. 1939; Report on Haslemere, 3 Oct. 1939, WRVS, R6 Region). Lawson had a long-running feud with the local centre organizer, and in 1943 she resigned after a sharp confrontation over the undemocratic running of WVS. Lawson may have been a Labour woman, since the Regional Administrator felt it necessary to explain the reasons for her resignation to the Labour Party's WVS vice-president, Mary Agnes Hamilton (Collingridge to Leach, 26 Oct. 1942; Leach to Collingridge, 3 Nov. 1942; Collingridge to Leach, 5 Nov. 1942; Reading to Collingridge, 8 Dec. 1942; Worsely to Hamilton, 16 Apr. 1943, WRVS, R12/4 Surrey).
[109] 'Generally the war has made ordinary folk of the villages more conscious of their importance in the general scheme of things, and of their good fortune, and less conscious of the superiority of town life' (R. K. Kelsall, Report on Hull, 4 Apr. 1942, 22, NCSRS, E2/8). Examples of WVS leaders articulating rural working-class grievances include: Report on Evacuation, Sept. 1939, WRVS, R/12/3 West Sussex; Huxley to Wrigley, 18 Sept. 1939, WRVS, E3 Evacuation, Sept.–Dec. 1939; Cannon to Reading, 30 Mar. 1940, WRVS, R4/7 Norfolk.
[110] Howkins, 'Mass Observation', 92 draws a similar conclusion.

Part II

8

Uncertain Future

The first part of this book examined the process by which WVS colonized the world of organized middle-class womanhood. I have argued that the wartime WVS provides a window through which we can observe wider currents in the public world of women, in particular the continuities of class embodied in the social leadership exercised by middle-class housewives. At the end of the war, as the present chapter relates, many of its members expected WVS to close down, and when it did not, most of them resigned anyway. Colonization gave way to a battle for survival, and the establishment of WVS on a long-term basis involved re-inventing the organization not as an occupying power but as one among a plethora of groups offering voluntary social service in the welfare state. The 200,000-strong organization that had emerged by 1950 stood in a very different relationship to the women's movement as a whole than Lady Reading's wartime directorate of a million volunteers. If the war had provided something of an Indian Summer for Lady Bountiful, by the late 1940s leisured middle-class women were being forced to come to terms with a world in which their claims to social leadership were becoming increasingly difficult to sustain. The ongoing professionalization of social work in the welfare state placed a question mark over the continuing relevance of the kind of voluntary work traditionally undertaken by middle-class housewives. At the same time, under the Labour Government, the reconstruction of anti-socialism around the politicization of post-war austerity offered middle-class housewives an aggrieved and self-interested identity potentially corrosive of older traditions of service. The women to whom Lady Reading spoke after the war defined themselves apart from, and to a significant degree in opposition to, both professionalization and anti-socialist consumerism. By looking at the world through the eyes of such women the second half of this book offers an interpretation of the dynamics of class and gender during Britain's post-war reconstruction significantly different from those currently prevailing in the historical literature on the period.[1]

---

[1] Contrast, for example, Ross McKibbin, *Classes and Cultures. England, 1918–1951* (Oxford, 1998); Ina Zweiniger-Bargielowska, *Austerity in Britain. Rationing, Controls and Consumption, 1939–1955* (Oxford, 2000).

Despite the re-mobilization of the Conservative Party in the later 1940s around a stridently anti-socialist rhetoric, the ethos of non-partisanship continued to play a central role in the efforts of organized middle-class women to maintain and extend their influence. In the towns a reformist current of opinion focused by the wartime publication *Our Towns* helped to inform the post-war consolidation of the middle-class female associational world. Although the practically minded housewives who formed the bulk of WVS local leadership took little part in these developments, Chapter 9 treats them in some detail as evidence of the continuing appeal of non-partisanship among middle-class women, in this case under the leadership of organizations catering for professional women. But the painful adjustment of WVS to the accelerated post-war rise of professional society is best illustrated by its role, documented in Chapter 10, in the provision of home helps for housebound people after the war. In this instance middle-class housewives were unable to sustain their claims to social leadership in face of democratic and bureaucratic rationales for the establishment of professionally organized services under local authority control. Lady Reading was mistaken in assuming that the forms of co-operation that she was pioneering between statutory and voluntary agencies would become central to the future of the social services in Britain. Her success in finding a place for WVS in the post-war world, analysed in the final two chapters, represented a rather more modest, but nevertheless significant, achievement: providing a route by which middle-class housewives who continued to identify with the old order could make a constructive, if relatively humble, contribution to a world in which social leadership had passed into other hands.

I

Since its foundation WVS had been prone to what today might be known as 'mission creep'. Initially intended simply to facilitate the *recruitment* of women for civil defence work, the organization quickly took on responsibilities for organizing the work of the volunteers. By 1940 WVS expansion into a whole range of activities bearing no direct relation to civil defence was recognized by government, and by the end of the war, in addition to its work for local authorities, WVS was working for at least twenty different Whitehall ministries.[2] 'A large patch-work quilt' was one of Lady Reading's more homely descriptions, simultaneously evoking her members' craft skills and their capacity for improvisation: 'a valuable covering made up of odd pieces'.[3] A deliberate vagueness about the precise scope of the organization

[2] A. Macdonald, Report on WVS for Beveridge, Apr. 1947, chs. 2, 3, WRVS Histories in Draft (Box 204); Sir A. Salisbury MacNalty (ed.), *The Civilian Health and Medical Services*, i (London, 1953), 234–9.
[3] Lady Reading reported in *Derbyshire Advertiser* (29 June 1945), WRVS, Press Cuttings.

was reflected in the habit of WVS leaders (followed throughout this book) in referring to their organization without the definite article. They liked to think of 'women's voluntary service' as a potentially limitless ongoing activity rather than as a proper name describing an organization with a limited brief. Official recognition of its expanding functions had been granted after the fact. Whitehall anxiety about the irregular and improvised nature of its relationships with this protean organization had been overridden by its obvious usefulness.[4] As peace approached, however, Lady Reading lobbied for some official guarantee that WVS would not disappear with the emergency that had spawned it. Prior to the 1945 election she secured no more than a statement that WVS work would continue 'for some time to come'.[5] The incoming Labour Government was prepared to be slightly less vague. After consulting departments making use of WVS, several of which felt that discontinuance of WVS would cause serious difficulties for them, the Government announced in September 1945 'that there will be many tasks for the WVS to perform in the transitional period following the end of the war, possibly for two years, and that the organisation should therefore be continued in operation'.[6] This effectively postponed the need to make any decision about the long-term future of WVS, a decision which the Labour Government expected to be difficult and controversial.[7]

Certainly the question of the post-war future of WVS was controversial within the organization itself. Already in 1942 plans being formulated by other voluntary organizations, notably the Red Cross with which WVS had close relations, stimulated calls for similar discussions within WVS.[8] In Hull the independent WVS leader, Mrs Morton Stewart, laid out plans to use her partnership with the local Tory council as a basis of resistance to further state encroachment in the voluntary sector after the war.[9] Lady Reading did her best to rule out such speculation, insisting that the post-war role of WVS would be decided by Government when the time came.[10] She was irritated by the draft report on WVS written for the Nuffield Reconstruction Survey, which criticized the lack of internal democracy, and she refused an invitation

[4] W. W. Simpson to N C Rowland, 27 July 1940, PRO, MH 130 277.
[5] A. Macdonald, Report on WVS for Beveridge, Apr. 1947, chs. 2, 7, WRVS Histories in Draft (Box 204).
[6] Id., 'Note on Views of Departments not Represented at Tomorrow's Meeting', 30 Aug. 1945, PRO, CAB 129 914. Herbert Morrison had already, in September 1944, called on WVS to stay on during the transition period and 'finish the job', Morrison to Reading, 28 Sept. 1944, WRVS, A1/38 Outline of Policy and Terms of Reference.
[7] Chuter Ede, 'Future of the WVS', 28 Aug. 1945, PRO, CAB 71 21; Lord President's Committee, Minutes, 7 Sept. 1945, PRO, CAB 71 19.
[8] WVS Chairman's Committee, Minutes, 24 Sept. 1942, 8 Aug. 1944; Field Marshal Sir Philip Chetwode to Lady Reading, 9 Dec. 1941, WRVS, M 146/40 Red Cross and St John's Emergency Committee.
[9] Maxse to Capell, 19 Mar. 1943, WRVS, R2 /1 Hull.
[10] WVS Chairman's Committee, Minutes, 24 Sept. 1942, 10 Dec. 1942, 19 Mar. 1943.

to respond to a piece by the director of the Nuffield project, G. D. H. Cole, in the Red Cross journal.[11] Asked whether a WVS advisory committee in Derby could extend its brief to talk about post-war reconstruction, Reading replied in fine Churchillian style: 'It seems to me too many people are trying to escape through peace talk ... and are diverting energy which ought to be devoted to aggressive war waging.'[12] In 1943 the Chairman's Committee firmly quashed a suggestion that Tothill Street should issue speakers' notes' for talks on post-war issues.[13]

After D-Day, with the end of the war in sight, it was impossible to prevent internal discussion.[14] Evelyn Emmet, the Conservative WVS leader in West Sussex, was worried about Lady Reading's attempts to broaden the scope of WVS work beyond war-related issues to general welfare matters which were likely to be of continuing importance after the war.[15] The regional organizer in the South West, reporting on a wide-ranging discussion of the issues at a meeting of centre organizers in Somerset in April 1945, made a similar point: while her members were prepared to 'finish the job' during the transition period after the war, they were 'anxious lest new work be taken on of a gradually altering character so that imperceptibly the purpose of WVS may change'. This was a perceptive description of Lady Reading's tactic of mission creep, but the organizer warned that any such underhand attempt to turn WVS into a permanent social service body would result in mass resignations from members who 'had not enrolled for this sort of thing' and would prefer to undertake any peacetime voluntary social work through the established organizations from which many of them had been recruited.[16] Shortly after the war Ruth Balfour, announcing her intention of resigning the WVS leadership in Scotland, rehearsed the same arguments, pointing out that peacetime welfare work would be better done through the established voluntary organizations: 'the aim should be for diversity not uniformity and for freedom of voluntary societies from Government control'.[17] Far from believ-

---

[11] WVS Chairman's Committee, Minutes, 20 Aug. 1942, 29 Oct. 1942; Editor of BRCS Journal to Lady Reading, 25 Feb. 1943 and Reading's reply on 2 Mar. 1943, WRVS V20/38 British Red Cross Society.

[12] Reading to Baird, 27 Oct. 1942 WRVS, R3 East Midlands. In July 1943 Reading asked the Regional Administrators to come to the next meeting with ideas about the post-war role of WVS. But she stressed that they should not consult widely about this, for fear of triggering unhealthy speculation in the ranks (Reading to Regional Administrators, 22 July 1943, WRVS Confidential Correspondence between Lady Reading and Lady Ruth Balfour).

[13] WVS Chairman's Committee, Minutes, 20 May 1943.

[14] WVS Regional Administrator's Conference, Minutes, 29 Sept. 1944; Foster Jeffery to Reading, 14 Sept. 1944, WRVS, R10 Northwest.

[15] WVS Meeting at County Hall, Chichester, 25 May 1945 Minutes, WRVS, R/12/3 West Sussex.

[16] Godfrey, 'Views on the Future of WVS', Apr. 1945, WRVS, R7 West Country.

[17] Balfour to Reading, 23 Nov. 1945, WRVS Confidential Correspondence between Lady Reading and Lady Ruth Balfour. This echoed concerns expressed by several of the Nuffield reports: 'Probably after the war there will be useful work for the WVS acting as agents of the

ing that WVS had pioneered a model for future relations between the state and the voluntary sector, these women saw its centralization, lack of internal democracy, and tendency to subordinate the voluntary sector to the needs of the state as temporary evils necessitated by war.

In line with such views many WVS leaders called for a date to be set for a formal stand down so that instead of just 'fizzling out' members could properly celebrate their wartime work and 'go out in a blaze of glory'.[18] Early in May 1945, in a misjudged attempt to head off such demands, Lady Reading wrote to members asking them to reaffirm their undertaking to do whatever work was required of them by their superiors: 'I cannot tell you yet exactly how you are going to work, but WVS will continue as a national service in order to serve the need of the community through the Local Authority, both in the months of the prelude of peace and in the post-war era.'[19] This statement went far beyond anything authorized by government, and in asking members to sign a blank cheque committing them to post-war activities that were as yet unknown Reading overstretched the loyalty to her own person that had been so important a part of the WVS ethos during the war.[20] In September 1944 Reading, while urging the case for a significant post-war extension of WVS activity, had told the regional administrators that 'we must be careful not to exaggerate the importance of the WVS, or to hold on to it for personal reasons'.[21] But that was precisely what she now appeared to many members to be doing. Evelyn Emmet's fiefdom in West Sussex was particularly troublesome. Already at the end of 1944 Reading had been alarmed by reports of discussions of post-war prospects in the district, and in March 1945 she went to Chichester to appeal directly to the assembled centre organizers. They were unconvinced, one of them writing to the regional administrator: 'One did not want to argue with Lady Reading, she looked so tired, but WVS couldn't go on the same basis. It's quite undemocratic and unlike the WI which works from the bottom upwards...'[22] The terms of the May letter turned sorrow to anger and the West Sussex organizers made it clear that they would refuse to pledge themselves to do whatever work Lady Reading thought desirable: 'in other words', the minutes of their

local authorities, but care must be taken that the independent voluntary organisations with power to criticise all and sundry must not be pushed aside in favour of a more pliant body like the WVS.' Report on Preston, n.d., 1942?, NCSRS, E2/29.

[18] Margaret Spicer to Lady Worsley, 6 Mar. 1945, WRVS, R5 Kent; WVS Chairman's Committee, Minutes, 27 Apr. 1945.

[19] Lady Reading, letter to members, 4 May 1945, WRVS, A1/38 Outline of Policy and Terms of Reference.

[20] Wright Brown to Eggerton-Warburton, 5 June 1945, WRVS, R10 Cumberland.

[21] WVS Regional Administrator's Conference, Minutes, 29 Sept. 1944; Reading to WVS leaders ('Not For Publication') 18 Sept. 1944, WRVS, R10 Northwest.

[22] Margaret Spicer to Lady Worsley, 6 Mar. 1945, WRVS, R5 Kent; WVS meeting at County Hall, Chichester, 25 May 1945, Minutes, WRVS, R/12/3 West Sussex; Worsley to Huxley 12 Dec. 1944, WRVS, R12/3 West Sussex.

meeting defiantly concluded, ' "the determination to be Free" is strong in our race'.[23] The regional administrator, worn out by 'the great strain of swimming against the tide', reported in June that, in the absence of any demand for WVS services from the local authorities in the region, it 'would be extremely difficult if not impossible to try and harness goodwill which will have gone back to the Guides, WI, British Legion, and other organisations from whom we took many of our best members in the early years of the War.'[24] Lady Davidson, a centre organizer in rural Sussex and, like Emmet, a leading Conservative, had been prepared to give Lady Reading the benefit of the doubt in March, but by June she had decided to join the other centre organizers in the district in resigning *en bloc*: 'so many of us feel that we must now be free to go forward to the many jobs waiting to be done.' WVS, she implied, had no monopoly on patriotism and whatever activity they chose—Davidson listed citizen's advice bureaux, community centres, WI, clinics, Mothers' Union, youth work, moral welfare, housing—they would be 'the same women, imbued with the same spirit of wishing to take part in the great battle against evil, fighting for God, King and Country'.[25] Nor, many argued, should the patriotism of those who wanted to give up their WVS work in order to devote themselves to domestic and family concerns be denied. As a resigning centre organizer in Lancashire put it: 'we women with families, who have had to do without us so much during their formative years, can best serve our dear country, by getting back into our homes and again exercising our individuality, which has been stifled for so long.'[26]

Such feelings were widespread. In Scotland Lady Reading's May 1945 letter precipitated widespread resignations as members sought 'to protect themselves against being forced to undertake unspecified commitments... without end.'[27] The Lancashire county organizer, Mrs Birley, summed up the general feeling as being in favour of a dignified stand down. Similar views were reported from Cumberland, Leeds, and the South West.[28] Lady Reading's attempt to pull things around with a rally in Manchester certainly misfired with one member who wrote her a bitter letter:

I have heard you speak on four different occasions: on three occasions I have looked up to and been inspired by you: the last time I knew you were just trying to talk down to me... I left that meeting feeling that my idol had feet of clay...

[23] WVS meeting at County Hall, Chichester, 25 May 1945, Minutes, WRVS, R /12/3 West Sussex.

[24] Worsley to Huxley, 7 June 1945, WRVS, R5 Kent.

[25] Iris Davidson to Lady Worsley, 18 July 1945, WRVS, R12/3 West Sussex.

[26] Catherine Taylor to Lady Reading, 29 June 1945, WRVS, R10/2 Lancashire.

[27] Balfour to Reading, 23 July 1945, WRVS Confidential Correspondence between Lady Reading and Lady Ruth Balfour.

[28] Wright Brown to Eggerton-Warburton, 5 June 1945, WRVS, R10 Cumberland; Report of Meeting of Divisional Representatives at Lancashire County Hall, 31 May 1945, WRVS, R10/2 Lancashire County.

By calling so lightly for a continuing commitment Reading revealed that she had no real understanding of the sacrifices involved for women with family responsibilities—'how could you, whose life is so different?'. Offering neither an 'honourable stand down' nor any valid reasons for continuing, Reading had contented herself with what this listener clearly saw as empty rhetoric about the supposed identity between WVS and responsible womanhood:

I think you devoted more time to...the category of womanhood...than anything else: for my own part—I want praise from no one for being womanly and, of all things, we do not need to be harnessed to WVS to possess the virtue of womanliness![29]

A year later a meeting of centre organizers in Surrey expressed a similar indignation about attempts to blackmail them into supporting the continued existence of WVS by appealing to their sense of civic responsibility. WVS leaders, they insisted, had been recruited from people who had 'already shown that they had the welfare of their fellow-citizens at heart' and who did not need official positions in WVS to continue to behave as active citizens in the future.[30]

There were some exceptions to the general tide. On VE Day the Midlands regional office staff signed the kind of loyal message that Reading's 2 May letter invited: 'We know that immense post-war work lies in waiting...With you to lead and inspire us we look forward with confidence to the future and whatever it may hold.'[31] In Tynemouth the members were reported to be 'thoroughly welfare and social minded' and eager to carry on.[32] In July, reporting on a recent visit to Essex, Lady Reading asserted that 'all but two of the centre organisers had been anxious to carry on.'[33] Where another leader might have bowed to the weight of opinion favouring a close down, Lady Reading, looking on the bright side, told the new Home Secretary in August 1945 that a surprising number of her members wanted to go on.[34]

The return of party politics was particularly problematic for WVS. Leading Conservatives who had put partisan activity to one side during

---

[29] Lillian Tomlinson to Lady Reading, 5 July 1945, WRVS, R10/2 Lancashire County. This woman was not alone in her disappointment. Her own centre organizer had earlier written to Lady Reading expressing her dismay after the Manchester meeting: 'You took from me in one hour, all the enthusiasm and ideals which had been built up in six years of work with over 500 of the finest women I have ever known' (Catherine Taylor to Lady Reading, 29 June 1945, WRVS, R10/2 Lancashire County).

[30] Mrs A. Macfarlane, Report of Meeting of Surrey Centre Organizers, 6 July 1946, WRVS, R12/4 Surrey.

[31] WRVS, R9 West Midlands.

[32] Hornby, Report on Visit to Tynemouth, 11 July 1945, WRVS, R1/2 Tynemouth.

[33] WVS Chairman's Committee, Minutes, 26 July 1945.

[34] Chuter Ede, 'Future of the WVS', 28 Aug. 1945, Lord President's Committee, PRO, CAB 71 21.

the war, now wished to return to the political fray. Marjorie Maxse departed at the end of 1944 to take responsibility for rebuilding the Conservative Women's Associations, and other leading Tories found it increasingly difficult to juggle WVS responsibilities with the reviving demands of political commitment.[35] In April 1945 Lady Reading, worried about possible abuses,[36] convened a meeting of regional representatives to agree guidelines that would allow WVS leaders to participate in the forthcoming general election without resigning their posts.[37] The main provisions were that where WVS was using premises belonging to a political party they should move as soon as possible; that members should not exploit the prestige of WVS by wearing their uniforms while campaigning; and that candidates (or candidates' wives) should be asked to step down temporarily during the election.[38] This policy worked well, and Tothill Street knew of only one town in which the centre organizer had continued in office despite acting as election agent.[39]

The outcome of the election, however, posed much more serious problems. Nella Last recorded the immediate impact on the leadership of WVS in Barrow:

At the Centre... we got a real shock when we heard our Conservative member had been beaten by 12,000—we simply could not believe it... Everyone who came in this afternoon spoke of 'the complete slide'. I'd the feeling that it was beyond our handling, that it was fate... Mrs Higham said, 'You take things very calmly. Don't you realise we may be on the brink of revolution?' And then Mrs Lord [*organizer of the Centre*] came in... flushed and upset... She *personally* feared riots and uprising in the civil population, and so on, with her poor old voice rising in hysterics.[40]

Mrs Lord was eventually calmed down with the aid of two aspirins and the dregs of a bottle of sherry. Such apocalyptic reactions were short-lived, but

[35] WVS General Purposes Committee, Minutes, 1 Nov. 1944. Maxse had assumed that WVS would close down at the end of the war: WGPW Executive Committee, Minutes, 15 June 1943 WF A1. Other Tory WVS leaders who experience a growing incompatibility between their political and social work commitments in the closing months of the war included Lady Lloyd (Brecon) (Vachell to Huxley, 15 Dec. 1944; Huxley to Vachell, 18 Dec. 1944, WRVS, R8 Wales); Evelyn Emmet (Worsley to Huxley, 12 Dec. 1944, WRVS, R/12/3 West Sussex; Mrs Weston (Chelmsford), Huxley, Report on Tour of Region Four, 12 Feb. 1945, WRVS, R4 East Anglia).
[36] WVS Chairman's Committee, Minutes, 21 Feb. 1945. At this meeting Hamilton said that 'once party activity had been revived it would be extremely difficult to control'. Huxley 'drew attention to the danger of the use of the Street Organisation for political purposes'.
[37] The issue had already been discussed in relation to local elections (WVS Chairman's Committee, Minutes, 21 Oct. 1943).
[38] Agenda for WVS conference on political work, 18 Apr. 1945, Labour Party Archives, Mary Sutherland papers, S23, WVS; WVS General Purposes Committee, Minutes, 5 May 1945; WVS Advisory Council, Minutes, 25 May 1945.
[39] WVS Chairman's Committee, Minutes, 14 June 1945.
[40] Richard Broad and Suzie Fleming (eds.), *Nella Last's War. A Mother's Diary, 1939–45* (Bristol, 1981), 297–8.

over the next eighteen months the unexpected return of a Labour Government served to accelerate the downward trend in WVS membership.

WVS had flourished in conditions of political truce. As Evelyn Emmet had pointed out in May 1945, after the election some members were going to find themselves being asked to carry out work for a Government with whose policies they disagreed.[41] Few members reacted like the Wimbledon women who were said to have taken a collective decision to abandon voluntary work altogether so long as Labour remained in office: 'they frankly admitted that they hoped things would go wrong and that the public would suffer inconvenience and distress', leading to the return of a Conservative Government.[42] This kind of fanaticism was unusual, but the desire to rejoin established voluntary organizations working at arm's length from Government was certainly enhanced by the Labour victory. Some of the rapid post-war growth of the WI, TG, WCG—not to mention the Conservative Party—can probably be explained by the re-engagement of members who had spent the war years in WVS.[43] A year after the war ended centre organizers in rural Nottinghamshire demanded the formal closure of WVS, citing all the normal reasons—a desire to spend more time looking after their families; to give any time they could spare to peacetime organizations; and 'a strong feeling against working for the present Government'.[44] In the summer of 1947 the county organizer was still unconvinced that there any role for WVS that could not be fulfilled by the WI.[45] In November 1946 the county organizer in East Suffolk proposed formal acknowledgement of the fact that WVS now had a purely dormant existence. She thought that the centre organizers, who had all threatened to resign, might agree to remain as nominal heads if Tothill Street made it clear that they would only be called on in emergencies.[46] Even one of the staunchest supporters of WVS as a major innovation in relations between the state and the voluntary sector believed in early 1947 that most of the membership would never provide more than a reserve of volunteers willing to undertake emergency work.[47]

---

[41] WVS Meeting at County Hall, Chichester, 25 May 1945, Minutes, WRVS, R /12/3 West Sussex. Incoming Labour ministers were well aware of this danger and of the need to tread carefully so that WVS was not seen as an arm of partisan policies (Chuter Ede, 'Future of the WVS', 28 Aug. 1945, Lord President's Committee, PRO, CAB 71 21; Lord President's Committee, Minutes, 7 Sept. 1945, PRO, CAB 71 19).
[42] Sybil Howard to Lady Reading, 20 Nov. 1947, WRVS, A1/38.
[43] After the war Franklin urged an ambitious expansion programme, noting that members of WVS Housewives Service, distressed at loss of opportunity represented by wartime civil defence work, 'clamour for Guilds when they hear of them' (*Townswoman* (May 1945), 139).
[44] Thursfield to Halpin, 26 Aug. 1946 R3 East Midlands.
[45] WVS County Borough Organisers' Conference Minutes, 22 Apr. 1947.
[46] Lady Yoland Eddis to Halpin, 8 Nov. 1946; Halpin, memo on Ipswich meeting, 15 Oct. 1946, WRVS, R4/8 East Suffolk.
[47] A. Macdonald, Report on WVS for Beveridge, Apr. 1947, chs. 4, 3, WRVS Histories in Draft (Box 204).

At the end of the war Tothill Street stopped requiring centre organizers to send in membership figures.[48] There is, therefore, no way of estimating the scale of the overall decline. The low point was reached during 1947. As late as February 1951, however, after several years of strenuous rebuilding, the membership claimed was no more than 200,000, one-fifth of wartime levels.[49] In many areas WVS virtually ceased to exist. In Kent the whole organization closed down in the autumn of 1945 and remained inactive until the summer of 1947.[50] The only active groups in Surrey, by the spring of 1946, were those where a paid member of staff had kept things going.[51] In Great Yarmouth, where the centre organizer had left to start up a branch of the TG, members of the Inner Wheel did their best to kill attempts to revive WVS in 1948 because they feared that it would seek to 'muscle in' on work already being done by other organizations in the town.[52] The centre organizer in Luton, who had initially been an enthusiastic supporter of the post-war continuance of WVS, resigned at the end of 1946 convinced that any work WVS might undertake was already being carried out by established voluntary organizations which were co-ordinating their efforts under her own leadership.[53] The close-down was particularly acute in rural areas where WVS tended to dissolved back into the WI. In Cumberland, for example, the 3,000 rest centre workers had all been members of the WI, and, for them, the WVS had never been more than a commitment to work in an emergency that never, in practice, arose.[54] A similar situation was reported from rural parts of Scotland, Wales, Yorkshire, Oxfordshire, and Hampshire.[55] In many of these areas the WVS leaders had always intended to close WVS down at the end of the war, and had to this end ensured, during the war, that WVS had never really consisted of anything but its officials.[56]

[48] WVS Regional Administrators Conference, Minutes, 12 Oct. 1945.

[49] Chuter Ede to Morrison, 9 Feb. 1951, PRO, CAB 124 914. Beveridge was surely mistaken in reporting that WVS still had 900,000 members in 1948: Lord Beveridge, *Voluntary Action. A Report on Methods of Social Advance* (London, 1948), 137.

[50] Briefing for Lady Reading's visit to Kent, 11 July 1947; Tonbridge Rural District Centre: Christmas Bulletin, 1948, WRVS, R5 Kent.

[51] Mrs A. Macfarlane, Report of Meeting of Surrey Centre Organizers, 6 July 1946, WRVS, R12/4 Surrey.

[52] Anon., Report on Visit to Great Yarmouth, 26–8 May, 1948; Mrs Long to Mrs Darling, 8 Oct. 1948, WRVS, R4 Great Yarmouth.

[53] Huxley, Report on Tour of Region 4, 12 Feb. 1945; Halpin to Darling, 23 Feb. 1950, WRVS, R4 Cambridge Regional Office; Barker to Halpin, 25 Nov. 1946; Darling to Halpin, 7 Dec. 1946, WRVS, R4/1 Luton. It was not until May 1948 that a new leader was found (Reading to Mrs Anderson, 22 May 1948, WRVS, R4/1 Luton).

[54] Wright Brown to Eggerton-Warburton, 5 June 1945, WRVS, R10 Cumberland.

[55] Balfour to Reading, 23 July 1945; Balfour to Reading 23 Nov. 1945, WRVS Confidential Correspondence between Lady Reading and Lady Ruth Balfour; Vachell, Report on Wales Region, Nov. 1945 to Apr. 1946, WRVS Regional Reports, Wales; Regional Administrator's Report, 11 July 1945, WRVS, R1/5 North Riding; Minutes of County Organizers Meeting, Reading, 20 May 1947, WRVS, R6 Region.

[56] See discussion of wartime relationships between WVS and the WI, in Ch. 7.

In many areas WVS survived only in skeleton form.[57] In Blackpool, for example, the Conservative clique that controlled the local WVS successfully resisted all attempts to revive it until the early 1950s. In 1947 the centre organizer had offered her resignation on the grounds that 'as I am actively interested in politics as a Conservative, and as the WVS works directly with a Socialist Government' she was not the person to get things moving again. In fact she remained in control of a purely nominal organization until 1951, when her successor, wife of a leading Tory councillor, took an equally negative view—refusing to undertake any active work and insisting that 'there were too many Associations in Blackpool anyhow and there was no need for WVS.'[58] In this case the main purpose of running WVS seems to have been to ensure its inactivity. As late as March 1949 Sylvia Vachell, the Welsh regional administrator, who shared Reading's distaste for party politics and had looked forward in wartime to long-term co-operation among her 'band of workers . . . of all religious and political views', was close to despair: 'Those of us who would make our service "a rock of salvation in a drifting world"—she was quoting from a speech of Churchill's seven years earlier— find our resolution sorely tried' by the 'excuses and evasions' offered by women approached to re-launch derelict centres. Where once a sense of public duty had reigned there was now only 'apathy, greed and irresponsibility. . . a tendency to slither. . . a horrid fluidity'.[59] Against this background, Lady Reading showed remarkable powers of leadership in not only keeping WVS going but also offering its services to the Government as, among other things, an agent of the austerity policies necessary to postwar reconstruction.

II

Because of its national coverage and the depth of its social penetration via the street-level organization of Housewives Service, WVS could offer more to Whitehall departments anxious to preach austerity to ordinary housewives

---

[57] WRVS, R7 South West, *passim*.

[58] Mrs Daisy Baird to HQ, 16 June 1947, WRVS, R10/2 Blackpool. Baird's predecessor as Centre Organizer, Mrs Leonard Thompson, was the daughter of one Tory alderman and the wife of another, and she chaired the Women's Unionist Association. As managing director of the pleasure beach, her husband was also one of the town's leading businessmen. Mrs Thompson ran the centre with the help of Mrs Grime, who was married to the editor of the local newspaper, a Conservative, and a leading figure in the organization of voluntary work in the town. Despite serious doubts about Thompson's performance during the Munich crisis (Grimes was much more effective and consideration was given to putting her in charge—a move favoured by the Town Clerk), this cosy set-up continued undisturbed throughout the war (WRVS, R10/2 Blackpool, *passim;* Blackpool Divisional Conservative and Unionist Association, Minutes, *passim*, LRO PLC 5/1/3).

[59] S. Vachell, Wales Regional Report, Mar. 1949, WRVS, Regional Reports; Vachell to Wade, 9 Nov. 1938, WRVS, R8/8 Glamorganshire.

than any other women's organization. The WVS role in the realms of food education and of fuel economy played an important part in Lady Reading's strategy for convincing the Attlee Government that her organization had a vital role to play in post-war reconstruction.

In the field of food education, WVS had been largely responsibly for inventing the 'food leader' scheme, under which volunteer housewives undertook to disseminate by word of mouth information sent out in a monthly bulletin from the Ministry of Food on economical ways of providing nutritious meals. In some areas food leaders also played a role in the distribution of welfare foods and the staffing of local food advice centres.[60] The scheme had originated in 1942 in an experiment run by the Birmingham WVS, looking for new ways to employ its Housewives, in co-operation with the local officials and other women's organizations.[61] Impressed by the effectiveness of the Birmingham experiment, the Ministry of Food asked the voluntary organizations to join the WVS in proliferating such schemes throughout the country, and subsequently produced window posters and badges for distribution to those who had attended training courses.[62] After the war the scheme continued to spread, especially in London where war-time efforts to launch it had failed. By the end of 1947 the number of food leaders throughout the UK had grown to 23,567.[63]

By no means all the food leaders were WVS members. Other women's organizations had been involved from the start in Birmingham, and across the country the scheme was actively promoted by other housewives' organizations including the WI, the NUTG, and, particularly after the 1945 election, the Women's Co-operative Guilds.[64] Despite this, Lady Reading attempted to assert the right of WVS to run the scheme nationally, claiming that her women understood better than the experts in Whitehall how to appeal to ordinary housewives. Although by 1946 about two-thirds of the

[60] 'What is a Food Leader?' (n.d., 1944), in WRVS, F1/3 Food leaders.
[61] 'Food Leadership. An Achievement in Democracy', *Labour Woman*, Apr. 1948; M. Forrester, 'Report to Meeting of Women's Organisations', 14 Nov. 1946, in PRO, MAF 102 20.
[62] WGPW circular to SCWOs, Dec. 1943, in WF I/3; M. Forrester, 'Report to Meeting of Women's Organisations', 14 Nov. 1946, in MAF 102 20.
[63] WVS Advisory Council, Minutes, 27 Mar. 1946; WVS, General Purposes Committee, Minutes, 9 Jan., 6 Mar., 3 July 1946; M. Forrester, Report to Meeting of Women's Organisations, 14 Nov. 1946, in MAF 102 20; Tomkin, Report to Food Adviser Organisers Conference, Jan. 1948, PRO, MAF 102 24; *Labour Woman* (Apr. 1948): 'Growth has been steady rather than spectacular, and it is highly encouraging that while many wartime organisations, not unnaturally, weakened with the secession of hostilities, the Food Leader Scheme continues to add to its numerical strength and its geographical spread.'
[64] WGPW circular, Dec. 1943, in WF I3; WGPW Sub-committee on SCWOs, Minutes, 11 Nov. 1943, 18 June 1945; WGPW Executive, Minutes, 1 May 1944; Report of Meeting of Women's Organisations on Future of the Food Leader Scheme, 14 Nov. 1946, PRO, MAF 102 20; SJC Annual Report, Jan.–Dec. 1945, in TUC 62.14/1; WCG, 64th Annual Report, May 1947; 65th Annual Report, May 1948; both in TUC 63/3; Joan Bourne, 'For the Community', *Labour Woman* (Feb. 1948).

food leaders had received some minimal training (a course of three lectures), WVS placed little emphasis on this, seeing the job mainly as one of passing on easily assimilated 'food facts'. The suitability of WVS Housewives for this task lay not in their expertise, but in their access to a wide range of contacts.[65] According to the founder of the Birmingham scheme, word of mouth was the key to effective food leadership and each leader developed her own technique, not only speaking to friends and neighbours (whose houses she might well already be visiting in her capacity as WVS street leader, salvage or national savings collector), but also to women wherever they could be found in groups (whist drives, sewing parties, etc.) or, in the case of one woman endowed with an exceptionally loud voice, addressing 'whoever sat next to her in a bus, knowing full well that a number of others round about were bound to overhear'.[66]

Not everyone was impressed by such an approach. The experts in the Ministry of Food were irritated by what they saw as the arrogance of WVS leaders and their amateurism about nutritional issues.[67] In 1946, following a row over a leaflet produced by WVS to explain why women should cooperate in the controversial introduction of bread rationing, Reading demanded increased control over the bulletin and the general administration of the scheme.[68] Resisting any privileged role for WVS, Ministry officials stressed the advantages of the decentralized nature of the scheme and the involvement of other organizations to whose reservations about being implicated in an unpopular Government policy WVS was, they believed, insufficiently sensitive.[69] As austerity began to ease the Government decided to close down local Food Advice Centres and hand over responsibility for any continuing work on food education to be run locally under the auspices of the Board of Education. WVS again responded by trying to take the national administration of the food leader scheme into its own hands, but the scheme remained dependent on Food Ministry producing and distributing its monthly Food Bulletin. With a declining circulation, the Bulletin became a prime target for Treasury cuts and, despite resistance from both the WVS and the WCG, it was eventually discontinued in July 1951.[70]

[65] Foster Jeffery, Report on Food Leader Scheme, 24 Sept. 1943, WRVS, R10 West Midlands Region; WRVS, F1/3 Food Leaders, *passim*; PRO, MAF 102 12, *passim*.
[66] WVS Advisory Council, Minutes, 17 July 1945.
[67] Alison Rowe, Report on Meeting with Walker, 2 Oct. 1943; PRO, MAF 102 12, *passim*.
[68] WVS Chairman's Committee, Minutes, 25 July 1946; Chatfield to Hillingdon, 18 Nov. 1946, WRVS, F1/3 Food Leaders.
[69] Walker, Report of Meeting with Lady Reading, 9 Aug. 1946; A. Wilson, Record of Interview with Lady Hillingdon, 17 Oct. 1946; Report of a Meeting on the Future of the Food Leader Scheme, 14 Nov. 1946, PRO, MAF 102 20; Ruth Abrahams, Report of Meeting at Ministry of Food, 15 Nov. 1946, WRVS, F1/3 Food Leaders.
[70] WVS, Chairman's Committee, Minutes, 14 and 21 Oct. 1948, 17 and 24 Feb. 1949, 16 and 30 June 1949, 13 Oct. 1949; Notes of Meeting of the Economic Information Unit, 31 May 1949, Sheldon-Smith to Hillingdon, 10 July 1951, WRVS, F1/3 Food Leaders.

The fuel crisis of 1947 provided WVS with a second opportunity to re-mobilize its street-level organization. Even in a normal winter the run-down state of Britain's undermanned coal industry would have led to severe problems in the early months of 1947. But the arrival, in January, of the worst winter weather of the twentieth century turned a difficult situation into a catastrophe. Power stations ran out of coal, large parts of industry closed down, unemployment reached slump proportions, and all households were subject to electricity cuts for five hours each day. Emanuel Shinwell, the fuel minister, now joined John Strachey, author of bread rationing the previous summer, in the pantheon of Tory hate-figures: 'Starve with Stra-chey, Shiver with Shinwell'. In fact most of the public blamed the weather more than they did the Government.[71]

While the immediate crisis would be resolved as the weather improved, politicians and officials debated the options for conserving coal stocks during the summer in order to prevent a repetition of the disaster in the following winter. Amongst these options economy in domestic fuel use took pride of place. During the war a scheme had been drawn up for fuel rationing though it was never in fact implemented. These plans were now dusted off and updated.[72] At the same time preparations were made for an educational campaign to be implemented either as a supplement to rationing or as a substitute for it. By early April the Ministry of Fuel and Power was moving away from rationing in favour of a compulsory ban on the use of gas or electricity for space heating during the summer months, together with a campaign for housewives to make a voluntary reduction to achieve standard targets for fuel consumption set by the Ministry.[73] Aware that the effective-ness of any campaign would depend to a great extent on the degree to which the women's organizations were prepared to co-operate, the Ministry invited them to a meeting to discuss the details of the scheme before it was launched. Lady Reading effectively took control, subsequently chairing a small sub-committee elected to decide between absolute consumption targets based on a calculation of household needs, initially supported by the Labour women on grounds of equity, and the alternative of a percentage reduction which Reading herself preferred because of its simplicity. After two days of meet-ings and detailed briefings from the gas and electricity suppliers, Reading's committee recommended a target reduction of 25 per cent, though in defer-ence to the argument of equity they thought that individual household targets should also be issued.[74] In the event the Government accepted the percentage approach and plans to issue standardized targets were scrapped.

[71] A. J. Robertson, *The Bleak Midwinter: 1947* (Manchester, 1987), 158–9 and *passim*.
[72] G. L. Watkinson, 'Domestic Fuel Rationing: Draft Proposals', 13 Feb. 1947, PRO, T 273 305.
[73] Robertson, *Bleak Midwinter*, 136–7.
[74] Second Meeting of the Sub-Committee of Women's Organisations at the Ministry of Fuel and Power, Minutes, 17 Apr. 1947, in WF B12.

In order to keep within the target housewives would have to be persuaded to monitor their consumption by reading their fuel meters regularly and making comparison with the relevant period in the previous summer. To inculcate such 'fuel awareness', leaflets and press advertising were to be supplemented so far as possible by personal visits. As with bread rationing the previous summer, the WVS quickly got out its own leaflet (superior in the opinion of the Central Office of Information to that produced by the advertising agency) and mobilized its own members to join a 'sales force' of volunteers prepared to make house-to-house visits. During the next three months, Lady Reading spoke at ninety-eight meetings up and down the country, using her oratorical skills to rally the constructive energies of the membership.[75] A duplicated leaflet put out by the WVS in Burton-on-Trent nicely caught the tone of this mundane patriotism, pointing out that by learning to balance three saucepans one on top of the other (potatoes, soup—which 'gets quite hot'—and milk for junket) the conscientious housewife could make her contribution to Britain's continued ability to play the role of 'bridge between Europe and America. Both watch our efforts, and though we are weakened we are still great and *can* by our actions inspire hope and "the will to live" in Europe and an example of courage and sacrifice to America.'[76] To paraphrase a more recent slogan: 'think imperially, act domestically.'

In practice the campaign seems to have had little impact. In the absence of compulsory rationing women were unlikely radically to alter their domestic routines. A sample survey conducted in August 1947 showed that only 2 per cent of housewives were reading their meters once a week (the basic goal of the campaign), while 85–90 per cent never read them at all. Less than one-fifth of respondents thought that the 25 per cent target was feasible, while over a third insisted that they were already using as little as possible.[77] So far as the personal visiting was concerned it soon became apparent that Lady Reading's enthusiasm was not always matched by that of her members: coverage was patchy and 'nobody could see any reliable way of finding out how quickly [the volunteers] were in fact making personal contact with housewives ... One had to hope for the best.'[78] This comment, by the official report on the scheme, throws light on the extent to which Reading's disciplined wartime organization had decayed by 1947. Perhaps compulsory

---

[75] 'The Domestic Fuels Saving Campaign', PRO, INF 2 135; David Ginsburg, 'Meter Reading and the Fuel Target', 1947, PRO, RG 23/126A; Robertson, *Bleak Midwinter*, 138; Meeting of Women's Organisations at Ministry of Fuel and Power, 26 Sept. 1947 minutes, in TUC 292 183.24/4; WVS Advisory Council, Minutes, 24 Sept. 1947.

[76] Cyclostyled leaflet written by the centre organizer written for the benefit of the 'not so well informed WVS members in our town', Payton to HQ (n.d., 1947), WRVS, R 9/3 Burton on Trent.

[77] David Ginsburg, 'Meter Reading and the Fuel Target', 1947, PRO, RG 23/126A.

[78] 'The Domestic Fuels Saving Campaign', PRO, INF 2 135.

rationing would have persuaded women to seek advice about reading their meters (as the advertising company in charge suggested) and have enabled WVS to remobilize its street-level organization. In September 1947 Communist representatives at a meeting of women's organizations convened at the fuel ministry urged the adoption of street (as well as household) targets, to be policed, no doubt, by Stakhanovite street leaders on the model of shop steward productivism in the factories.[79] The authorities, however, had no need to move in this direction, since the summer weather, as exceptionally hot as the winter had been cold, had enabled the required savings to be made despite the minimal impact of their campaign. Instead the ministry responded by scrapping talk of targets altogether in favour of more general advice about how to use equipment economically. At the same time door-to-door visiting was abandoned in place of a drive to set up representative local Fuel Economy Committees with a general educational brief.[80] However ineffective the 1947 economy campaign had been in practice, it had served to establish Lady Reading as the chief representative of the women's organizations in matters concerning fuel economy, a role which she continued to fill for the rest of the life of the Labour Government.[81]

The shift from targets and talk of street fuel wardens to locally co-ordinated general education mirrored the trajectory of food advice during these post-war years. By 1951, when the food leader scheme was effectively closed down, it was clear that 'street leadership' as originally envisaged by the wartime WVS was a thing of the past. As one regional organizer pointed out, her members no longer saw any point in a scheme which simply duplicated food education messages more effectively communicated via radio and press advertising.[82] This was in flat contradiction to the WVS' original rationale for the scheme which was that while the working-class housewife was generally unresponsive to press campaigns, she could be reached by 'direct leadership given to her in the atmosphere of the home . . .'.[83] The shift in emphasis both in food and fuel education is probably best understood as an indication of the declining acceptability of the intrusion of Whitehall and its agents into

[79] Meeting of Women's Organisations at Ministry of Fuel and Power, 26 Sept. 1947 Minutes, in TUC 292 183.24/4. On productivism in the factories, see J. Hinton, *Shop-Floor Citizens. Engineering Democracy in 1940s Britain* (Aldershot, 1994). There was talk of using shop-floor Fuel Saving Committees in the factories as the channel through which to introduce 'fuel awareness' into the home. G. H. Norton, memo, 12 Mar. 1947, PRO, INF 2 135.

[80] Robertson, *Bleak Midwinter*, 170–1; Meeting of Women's Organisations at Ministry of Fuel and Power, 26 Sept. 1947, Minutes, in TUC 292 183.24/4; 'The Domestic Fuels Saving Campaign', PRO, INF 2 135.

[81] Standing Committee of WVS Advisory Council, Minutes, 3 Sept. 1947; WVS, County Borough Organisers Conference, Minutes, 12 May 1948; WVS Chairman's Committee, 4 and 11 Jan. 1951, WRVS; Robertson, *Bleak Midwinter*, 161, 176–8.

[82] Stevenson to Clift, 13 July 1950, WRVS, F1/3 Food leaders.

[83] Report of Meeting at Ministry of Food, 11 Aug. 1942, WRVS, F1/3 Food leaders. There is probably no way of determining which of these approaches was more effective. Mass

the private sphere of the home as the atmosphere of wartime emergency receded. It was in relation to food education that Douglas Jay had originally made his much-quoted remark that 'the gentleman in Whitehall really does know better what is good for the people than the people know themselves',[84] and libertarians worried about the totalitarian implications of empowering experts and bureaucrats to instruct housewives though networks of interfering volunteers how to arrange things in their own kitchens. Responding to the publication of Hayck's *Road to Serfdom* in 1944, one of the leaders of the centrist think-tank, Political and Economic Planning, asserted that 'the real question is: do you place abolition of malnutrition higher than the freedom of the housewife to buy bad food and cook it badly?'[85] The answer to this question changed as conditions of scarcity declined, and with them the probability that deregulation would produce widespread malnutrition. By the early 1950s freeing the private sphere from state intervention appeared more desirable than continued rationing, or the further elaboration of an intrusive machinery of street leadership originally designed to cope with the disruptive effects of bombing. Improving visits from the busybody WVS street leader might be acceptable in wartime—although it is improbable that being shouted at by a loud-mouthed know-all on the bus had ever inspired economical food habits. In 1944 the WVS organizer in Yorkshire had looked forward to the post-war extension of Housewives Service to provide a comprehensive machinery of enlightenment and organized good neighbourliness throughout the community.[86] By 1950, such thinking had lost its appeal and street leadership did not figure in many people's vision of the good society.

III

Lady Reading had emerged as the leader of the fuel economy drive in April 1947 not only because the WVS appeared to have the machinery necessary to implement any campaign, but also because, unlike many of the leaders of the other women's organizations being consulted, she went straight to the point and wasted no time grumbling about this further twist to the screw of austerity.[87] Delivering patriotic co-operation with Labour's austerity programme was central to her strategy for establishing the long-term future of the WVS as a recognized arm of the state. 'Austerity', she told her

Observation believed that attitudes to food were far too deeply rooted to be influenced significantly by any kind of propaganda (Mass Observation, *An Enquiry into People's Homes* (London, 1943), 91).

[84] Douglas Jay, *The Socialist Case* (London, 1947), 258.

[85] PEP, Notes on Executive Meeting, 18 July 1944, in PEP A 13/4.

[86] Aykroyd to Huxley (enclosing memorandum on post-war policy for WVS), 20 Sept. 1944, WRVS, R2 Yorkshire Region.

[87] Meeting Between Ministry of Fuel and Women's Organizations, 15 Apr. 1947, WF B/12.

members in December 1945, 'is the first tool at our disposal with which to meet the problems of peace, and with this painful weapon we will fashion the re-entry to prosperity.'[88] As austerity tightened in the new year she urged members to 'look at the situation in an unbiased and humanitarian way; we must be clearing our minds of the difference between party politics and national dilemmas which are the natural aftermath of war...'.[89] At the height of the fuel crisis she rallied her regional administrators to combat 'the apathy and disintegration which was everywhere apparent', stressing that 'the next few months were going to be very difficult and the influence of people thinking on broad lines would be needed'.[90] Informing local leaders of the Government's decision in April 1947 to extend the life of the WVS she struck a positively heroic note:

Like every other woman I had hoped that 'emergencies' and 'bad days' were only insurance terms and that we might be facing a world less tragic in its grim austerity, less demanding in its personal discipline. That hope has gone. Serious thinking people know that the days and months and even years ahead will demand of every member of this country the greatest contribution he or she can give, mentally, physically and spiritually...[91]

In May 1948 she praised centre organizers for the way they 'had subjugated political feelings and had understood the necessity of looking at broad issues and avoiding political bias'.[92] Sixteen months later, with the devaluation of the pound triggering a rising volume of criticism of the Labour Government, she again appealed to her members to resist the temptation to make political capital out of the crisis, urging them to place 'our national conscience... in front of our political conscience' and to practise retrenchment in their own domestic lives.[93]

Such talk made enemies. The assumption in these statements was that most WVS personnel were political opponents of the Labour Government. Not all of them were happy with the extent of Reading's loyalty to embattled ministers. When, in the summer of 1946, the WVS instructed food leaders to explain details of the bread rationing scheme, significant numbers refused

---

[88] Lady Reading, Christmas Letter, Dec. 1945, WRVS, A1/38 File 5.
[89] Speech at County and County Borough's Organizers Conference, 6 Feb. 1946, WRVS, R6 Regional Office.
[90] 14 Feb. 1947, Regional Administrators Conference.
[91] Printed letter from Reading to WVS organizers, Apr. 1947, WRVS, A1/38 File 5.
[92] County Borough Organizers Conference, Minutes, 11 May 1948.
[93] *Lowestoft Journal* (25 Nov. 1949); see also WVS Regional Administrators' Conference, Minutes, 23 Sept. 1949. She had used a similar language earlier: 'whilst constantly avowing the value of political consciousness, we urge our individual members to recognise the dictates of their national conscience and to know the difference between the two, and act accordingly' (Reading, Draft Statement on WVS, 30 Sept. 1947, WRVS, WVS Histories in Draft, Box 204). She made a similar remark in October 1948: 'there were those who did not like the political flavour of the day, but they could see the problem of the recovery as something much bigger than politics' (*Midlands Daily Telegraph* (6 Oct. 1948), WRVS Press Cuttings).

to take part, and an irate Conservative Central Office subsequently extracted guarantees that more care would be taken in future to prevent 'party political propaganda' from creeping into literature distributed to the food leaders.[94] A few months later an incautious remark by Lady Reading about a WVS member 'who, though an ardent Conservative, was nevertheless anxious to do everything possible to help production' led to protests from Central Office about the implied slur on the patriotism of Tory womanhood in general.[95] Lady Reading's attempts, during the fuel economy campaign, to reassure Conservative women by privately attacking Whitehall bureaucrats for failing to practise in their own offices the austerity that they preached to the public may have done something to allay fears that she was acting simply as a government propagandist.[96] But suspicions remained, and in 1949 members of the south-eastern Conservative women's advisory committee condemned WVS as 'Government stooges' being used 'to cover up the deficiencies of the Socialist administration'.[97] Other women's organizations were resistant to the close co-operation with austerity measures embraced by WVS, notably the WI, which distanced itself from both the food leader and the fuel economy campaigns.[98] The emergence of the 'militant housewife' from 1946 had increased the strain, and WVS organizers cast around for ways to 'strengthen the arm of our Food Leaders against the ration-cuts protesting housewives' of the British Housewives League.[99] In Sheffield, where several WVS members, including the woman—now a Tory councillor—who had led WVS during the war openly identified with the militants, the centre organizer was careful to remove Housewife League members from the register of local food leaders.[100] More remarkably, in Tynemouth, the WVS organizer—a formidable woman who ran more or less anything that moved in the town—appears to have persuaded the local Housewives' League to work under WVS supervision.[101]

[94] Salisbury MacNalty (ed.), *Civilian Health*, 232; Conservative Party Central Women's Advisory Committee Minutes, 11 July 1946, CPA, CCO 170/1/1; National Federation of Women's Institutes to E. Walker, 8 July 1946, PRO, MAF 102 20.
[95] WVS Advisory Council, Minutes, 24 Sept. 1947, 10 Dec. 1947; Marjorie to Stella, 22 Oct. 1947; Stella to Marjorie, 28 Oct. 1947, WRVS, V/101/38, Conservative Party.
[96] Reading to Ward, 5 June 1947, WRVS, V/101/38 Conservative Party. See also Lady Reading's remarks on the same issue at Meeting Between Ministry of Fuel and Women's Organizations, 15 Apr. 1947, WF B/12.
[97] South-Eastern Women's Advisory Committee Minutes, 24 Feb. 1949, CPA, ARE 9/11/5.
[98] Ruth Abrahams, Report of Meeting at Ministry of Food, 15 Nov. 1946; Notes of Meeting of the Economic Information Unit, 31 May 1949, WRVS, F1/3 Food Leaders; NFWI to Walker, 8 July 1946, PRO, MAF 102 20; W. Crofts, *Coercion or Persuasion? Propaganda in Britain after 1945* (London, 1989), 20.
[99] Doris Derrington (Yorkshire Regional Food Organizer) to Miss Russell, 26 Feb. 1946, WRVS, R2/3. On the militants see J. Hinton, 'Militant Housewives: The British Housewives' League and the Attlee Government', *History Workshop Journal*, 38 (1994).
[100] Report on WVS in Sheffield, June 1947, WRVS, A1/38 File 5.
[101] Reports on Visits to Tynemouth, 11 July 1945, 23 Jan. 1947, WRVS, R1/2.

Lady Reading's willingness to collaborate with the Attlee Government's management of austerity sits uncomfortably with established pictures of late 1940s middle-class womanhood. Certainly it alienated many of her wartime supporters, and she was swimming against a tide which, by 1950, had buried wartime discourses of heroic self-sacrifice and threatened to make the very word 'housewife' synonymous with individualistic resistance to the disciplines of austerity.[102] Nevertheless, the fact that WVS survived at all bears witness to the continuing relevance of traditions of non-partisanship in the female associational world. If many housewives looked to the revival of the electoral fortunes of the Conservative Party to deliver them from socialist oppression, there were others—including many Conservative voters—for whom Lady Reading's call to engage constructively with a process of national reconstruction directed by a Labour Government held a positive appeal. Had this not been the case it is unlikely that Lady Reading would have succeeded in establishing WVS on a permanent basis.

---

[102] By the end of the decade the WVS leaders responsible for re-establishing Housewives Service hesitated to use the word 'housewife' on the grounds that it 'is sometimes associated with...the Housewives League and other like organisations' (Cresswick Anderson, typescript (n.d., 1950?) in WRVS Box File, Housewives Service).

9

Our Towns

Oh Lord, thought Mrs Miniver... I'm sick and tired of being offered nothing but that same old choice. Left wing... Right wing... it's so limited; why doesn't it ever occur to any of them that what one is really longing for is the wishbone?[1]

Our discussion of the dynamics of urban social leadership has so far focused on WVS colonization of the established women's movement. WVS, however, was not the only innovation of the war years, which also saw both a limited revival of feminist campaigning and, more importantly, the establishment of a new co-ordinating body, the Women's Group on Public Welfare (WGPW), which did much to consolidate a broad non-partisan current of social engagement among middle-class women. In the later 1940s the WGPW was to become the major focus of opposition to the post-war continuation of WVS. The bitterness of that conflict, examined in detail in Chapter 11, should not obscure the affinities between the two organizations: indeed it was the degree to which their objectives overlapped that provided the occasion for conflict. Even while they denied the right of the upstart WVS to exist at all, leaders of the WGPW were fostering among middle-class women precisely that commitment to non-partisan engagement with social issues that, in the event, served to sustain Lady Reading's creation.

The WGPW originated from a meeting, convened by the National Council of Social Service in November 1939 (at the instigation of the WI and Townswomen's Guilds), to discuss 'the challenge to the civic conscience' caused by evacuation.[2] An enquiry into slum conditions was launched immediately, but it was not until the following June that the provisional executive, which had at one point considered adding 'middle class distress in town and country' to the Group's agenda, agreed on a longer-term aim for the new organization: 'to bring the experience of its constituent organisations to bear on questions of public welfare, more especially those affecting women and children'.[3] The

---

[1] Jan Struthers, *Mrs Miniver* (London, 1989), 101.
[2] An additional challenge to the established women's groups—the challenge represented by WVS—may also have been instrumental in the establishment of the WGPW. Gertrude Horton remarked to the NUTG Executive in April 1940 that the original purpose of the WGPW had been 'to safeguard those organizations of a permanent nature that might be affected by the evacuation of adults'. NUTG Executive, Minutes, 23 Apr. 1940.
[3] Women's Problems Arising from Evacuation, Minutes, 30 Nov. 1939, 17, 16 May 1940, 2 July 1940, WF A1.

NCSS contributed most of the Women's Group's running expenses, and seconded its chief woman officer, Miss Letty Harford, to work more or less full-time for the Group.[4] The Women's Group established itself as the recognized co-ordinating body for what the Townswomen's Guild described as 'all the women's organisations of repute'.[5] By the end of the war forty-six national organizations had affiliated, including the women's sections of the mainstream political parties.[6] Non-partisanship was symbolized by the co-operation between the chair and vice-chair, respectively Margaret Bondfield,[7] who had been the first woman Cabinet Minister in the Labour Government of 1929–31, and Priscilla Norman, wife of the Governor of the Bank of England widely held responsible for the fall of that Government.

Although the establishment of the WGPW probably owed something to the desire of the WI and NUTG to defend their spheres of operation against the burgeoning activity of WVS, Lady Reading did not initially view the new organization as a threat.[8] Aware that the response of some of her more imaginative organizers to the horrors exposed by evacuation was to look for ambitious schemes of social reconstruction, she welcomed the Women's Group as a place where such initiatives could be pursued without dragging WVS into politically charged territory. Like Mrs Miniver, who believed that 'some of us are more suited by nature to be Palliators, or Patchers, and others to be Rebuilders',[9] Lady Reading insisted that the practical amelioration of suffering offered by WVS should not be mixed up with discussion of

---

[4] WGPW, Minutes, 19 Oct. 1942, WF A14; A. F. C. Bourdillon (ed.), *Voluntary Social Services. Their Place in the Modern State* (London, 1945), 190. Before joining NCSS head office Harford had worked for many years in Chesterfield where co-operation between the voluntary sector and the local authority was particularly well developed between the wars. Margoret Brasnett, *Voluntary Social Action. A History of the National Council of Social Service, 1919–1969* (London, 1969), 164; 'Memorandum on Urban Work', Aug. 1940, Nottinghamshire RO MS 396/31.

[5] *Townswoman* (Apr. 1944), 106, May 1943, 114. Affiliates included all the main generalist women's organizations (WI, NUTG, BFBPW, Soroptimists, NCW, Women Citizens, WCG, SJC), a wide range of more specialist groupings (EAW, Women's Gas Council, Toc H, British Legion, Friends Service League, Personal Service Group, British Association of Residential Settlements, Educational Settlements Association, British Institute of Adult Education, National Council for Maternity and Child Welfare, National Society of Children's Nurseries, Nursery Schools Association, Mental Health Emergency Committee), and various professional organizations (College of Midwives, Royal College of Nursing, Hospital Almoners Association, Women's Public Health Officers Association, National Union of Teachers, Association of Teachers of Domestic Subjects, British Federation of Social Workers).

[6] Report of National Women's Advisory Committee to the TUC, 1945–6, 13, TUC 292 66/3.

[7] It is unlikely that Bondfield's presence did much to reconcile Labour women to the middle-class organizations. Her reputation in Labour circles never recovered from her unimpressive performance as Minister of Labour in MacDonald's government (J. M. Bellamy and J. Saville, *Dictionary of Labour Biography*, ii (London, 1974), 39–44).

[8] NUTG Executive Committee, Minutes, 23 Apr. 1940. WVS was represented from the outset on the WGPW Executive by its general secretary. Norman also played a leading role in the early years of WVS, but resigned her WVS vice-chairmanship in January 1941.

[9] Struther, *Mrs Miniver*, 144–5.

large-scale social reform. The practical ladies of WVS had quite enough to do sorting out immediate problems; those of a more speculative cast of mind could be referred to the WGPW.[10]

The best-known initiative taken by the WGPW was the publication, in 1943, of a study of the urban poverty revealed by evacuation, *Our Towns. A Close-Up*. This text has provoked a good deal of recent debate, but its ambiguities are difficult to unravel without attention to the main intended audience—the leaders of middle-class women's organizations in Britain's towns. The WGPW served these women not only by providing a non-partisan social reformism tailored to their concerns, but also by offering through local Standing Committees of Women's Organisations (SCWOs), established from 1943, an institutional framework within which urban social leaders could co-ordinate their activity and enhance their influence. Analysis of SCWO activity throws particular light on two aspects of urban social leadership in the period: tensions between professional women and organized housewives, and (despite Margaret Bondfield) the continuing hostility of Labour women to the middle-class organizations in general.

I

The war years saw a modest revival of feminism, and some diminution of the clash between equal rights and maternalist demands which had been so debilitating for feminism between the wars. The major equal rights agitation was provoked by the flagrantly discriminatory provisions of the scheme introduced to compensate civilian victims of bombing. Fearing that any concession would open the floodgates to disruptive pressures for equal pay in industry, the Government held out against equal compensation for over three years until it was finally forced to concede by the threat of a backbench revolt in April 1943. The demand had overwhelming public support and the agitation did much to foster co-operation among women's organizations at local level.[11] As Government ministers had feared, the concession put wind in the sails of the equal pay campaign leading in 1944 to a further backbench revolt over Government opposition to equal pay for teachers which was only quashed by resignation threats from both Bevin and Churchill.[12]

[10] Dart to Reading, 10 Nov. 1939; Reading to Dart, 16 Nov. 1939; Smieton to Dart, 20 Nov. 1939; Huxley to Dart, 23 Nov. 1939, WRVS, R10 Northwest.

[11] BIPO Poll, Oct. 1941: 84% approved; 11% disapproved. H. L. Smith, 'The Problem of Equal Pay for Equal Work in Great Britain During World War Two', *Journal of Modern History*, 53 (1981), 652, 655, 661–3; Olive Banks, *The Politics of British Feminism, 1918–1970* (Aldershot, 1993), 100–1; Brooks, *Women at Westminster*, 136–9; Alison Oram, ' "Bombs don't Discriminate!" Women's Political Activism in the Second World War', in C. Gledhill and G. Swanson (eds.), *Nationalising Femininity, Culture, Sexuality and British Cinema in the Second World War* (Manchester, 1996), 55–8; *Labour Woman* (Jan. 1941); 'Democracy in Action', *International Women's News* (May 1943).

[12] Smith, 'Equal Pay', 665–9.

Some feminists sought to raise more ambitious demands. Like the First
World War socialists who had demanded the 'conscription of riches' as a
quid pro quo for military conscription, Second World War feminists seized
on the conscription of women as an opportunity to press for comprehensive
equal rights legislation. In September 1943 the Women's Publicity Planning
Association—the main wartime co-ordinating group for equal rights activity—launched what was intended as a mass campaign for a 'blanket' bill
designed to outlaw all forms of sex discrimination. But whereas the demand
for the 'conscription of riches' had opened the way for Labour's 1918 unifica-
tion under the banner of socialism, the blanket bill campaign ran rapidly into
the sands. The comprehensive nature of the bill not only revived an old bone of
contention with Labour women over existing legislation protecting women
workers, it was also dismissed by most middle-class women's organizations,
including some of the more feminist ones, as 'wholly impractical'. The absence
of any single issue with the simplicity of the equal compensation demand
inhibited ongoing feminist mobilization, as did the untimely death in August
1944 of the moving spirit of the blanket bill campaign, Dorothy Evans.[13]

Despite the success of the equal compensation campaign women's rights
remained a divisive issue. Caroline Haslett, the founder of the Electrical
Association of Women who combined unflagging activism in the women's
movement with insider status as a trusted Whitehall adviser, urged women 'to
adopt the attitude of assuming our responsibilities rather than asking for our
rights'. It was largely in this spirit that the leaders of the main women's
organizations sought to enhance their members' influence. Although most
of the organizations involved in the WGPW supported equal compensation
and equal pay, feminist campaigning was less central to their members'
strategies of empowerment than the exercise of their skills as social leaders.
Taking responsibility, as Haslett argued, meant constructively giving 'to the
Community any gifts or talents that [we] possess' rather than attempting to
exploit the war emergency to wring concessions on women's rights.[14] For

[13] *International Women's News* (Sept. 1943; July 1944); Oram, 'Bombs don't Discriminate!',
60–3; Penny Summerfield, 'The Effect of War on the Status of Women', in H. L. Smith (ed.), *War
and Social Change. British Society in the Second World War* (Manchester, 1986), 224–5.

[14] Electrical Association of Women, Nottingham Branch, Minutes, 24 Mar. 1943, Nottinghamshire RO, DD 1357\1\4\1. According to Kathleen Halpin, Haslett was seen by other leading
women at the time as having been co-opted into the Whitehall establishment: 'more man's
woman than a woman' (Brian Harrison interview with Halpin, 16 Mar. 1977, Fawcett Library).
Born into the respectable working class, Haslett trained as an electrical engineer and founded
the EAW in 1924. As Chairman of the BFBPW she helped to form the Woman Power Committee
in 1940 to protect women's interests during the war, and was appointed to the Ministry of
Labour's Women's Consultative Committee. Walter Citrine, the TUC General Secretary, remembered her as a woman who, though 'never an ardent feminist' (in fact she had been a militant
suffragette before 1914) 'had never swerved from her high purpose of raising the social status of
women' (*Dictionary of National Biography* (1951–60)). From 1947 until her death in 1957 she
was the only female member of the Central Electricity Authority.

most publicly active women in mid-twentieth-century Britain, 'feminism' remained a deeply problematic concept. They sought empowerment less by demanding their rights as women than by embracing their responsibility as social leaders.

II

Our Towns has been widely discussed by historians as a window into the middle-class female soul in the founding years of the welfare state. Originating in a request from the WI for an examination of the 'customs and habits of a minority of town-dwellers'[15] which the 1939 evacuation had revealed so shockingly to their members, the study presented detailed evidence of the extent and causes among the urban poor of body lice, skin diseases, unsanitary habits, dirtiness of clothes and bodies, inadequate spending, feeding and sleeping habits, and juvenile delinquency. The report was produced by 'a small group of professional working women, all familiar at first hand with the conditions of poverty', supplemented by interviews with a further twenty-seven teachers, health and social workers, and public officials, all but two of them women.[16] The discussion of 'bad habits', particularly those involving excretion and menstruation, was frank and the report required of its readers 'stout stomachs and an appetite for facts, including...unpleasant' ones.[17] The authors of *Our Towns* were in no doubt that, whatever cultural misperceptions might also be involved, the accusations levelled by hostesses against the personal habits of a significant minority of evacuees were fully justified.[18] Moreover, much of the explanation of this behaviour was framed in a late-Victorian language of the 'residuum':

the 'submerged tenth' described by Charles Booth still exists in our towns like a hidden sore, poor, dirty, and crude in its habits...Within this group are the 'problem families', always on the edge of pauperism and crime, riddled with mental and physical defects, in and out of the Courts for child neglect, a menace to the community, of which the gravity is out of all proportion to their numbers.[19]

Not surprisingly some historians have seen *Our Towns* as evidence of the prevalence of a reactionary victim-blaming analysis of poverty centred on notions of the 'slum mind' and the 'problem family'.[20] In line with this

[15] Women's Group for Public Welfare, *Our Towns: A Close-Up: A Study Made in 1939–1942 with Certain Recommendations by the Hygiene Committee of the Women's Group on Public Welfare* (London, 1943), p. ix.
[16] Ibid., pp. viii, xi, 114.
[17] Ibid., p. xi.
[18] Ibid., pp. xvi, 3, 8, 30, 40.
[19] Ibid., p. xiii.
[20] J. Macnicol, 'The Evacuation of Schoolchildren', in Smith, *War and Social Change*, 24; Elizabeth Wilson, *Women and the Welfare State* (London, 1977), 138–9.

diagnosis the report laid heavy emphasis on the potential role of nursery schools—'the only agency capable of cutting the slum mind off at the root'— in breaking the inter-generational transmission of a culture of poverty by rescuing young children from the influence of their degraded mothers.[21] Other historians, by contrast, have seen the report as 'breathtakingly radical', indicating an 'astonishing' turn-round in middle-class attitudes during the early war years from blaming the bad personal habits of evacuees to blaming the urban environmental conditions that produced them.[22] The report analysed in detail and with considerable sympathy for the slum mother the obstacles to 'good home-making' created by overcrowding, inadequate sanitation and water supplies, poor facilities for cooking and food-storage; and it demanded a raft of reforms including family allowances, minimum wages, a national health service, long-term controls on the price and distribution of basic foodstuffs, and serious curbs on the freedom of landlords or other commercial interests to exploit working-class needs.[23] The most extensive study of *Our Towns* so far published stresses its ambiguity, while warning that it may be unhelpful to view it through 'anachronistic' categories of 'reactionary' and 'radical'.[24]

In fact the authors of the report were well aware of the tensions they were negotiating between cultural and environmental explanations of poverty. They warned readers not to neglect the economic causes of poverty just because defects of individual character could also be shown to be at work. At the same time they were insistent that transforming the behaviour of poor people was an educational as much an environmental challenge.[25] This belief may have reflected, in part, the authors' own claim to positions of social leadership. The purpose of the Women's Group was 'to bring the experience of its constituent organisations to bear on questions of public welfare', and this was an experience not just of observing problems but also of solving them. A remark in the report about local councillors 'dreary with complacency' reflects the frustrations often experienced by women's organizations campaigning for vigorous local action on health, housing, or the opening of nursery schools.[26] Tackling the slum mind through the class-bridging initiatives of women visitors bringing support and enlightenment to working-class

[21] WGPW, *Our Towns*, 105.

[22] Bob Holman, *The Evacuation: A Very British Revolution* (Oxford, 1995), 143, 144, 146. John Welshman analyses the ambiguity of the report, arguing that 'reactionary motives' led to 'surprising progressive conclusions': Welshman, 'Evacuation and Social Policy During World War Two: Myth and Reality', *Twentieth Century British History*, 9 (1998), 39.

[23] WGPW, *Our Towns*, pp. xviii, 43, 45 103–6.

[24] Welshman, 'Evacuation, Hygiene and Social Policy: The Our Towns Reports of 1943', *Historical Journal*, 42 (1999), 805, 807. For a similar stress on the ambiguities of the report, see G. Field, 'Perspectives on the Working-class Family in Wartime Britain, 1939–1945', *International Labor and Working-Class History*, 38 (1990), 10–12.

[25] WGPW, *Our Towns*, pp. xiv-xv.

[26] Ibid., 101–2.

mothers had long been central to middle-class notions of feminine social responsibility.[27] In this tradition *Our Towns* offered its readers an analysis of poverty which gave them a role, not only in demanding action by the state, but as agents of reform in their own right whether as professional social workers or in voluntary social service. If evacuation reminded some well-to-do people of their obligations towards the poor, this may well have done more to reinforce traditional patterns of social leadership than to lay the basis for a genuinely egalitarian transcendence of class difference.

At the heart of the analysis offered by *Our Towns* is nostalgia for a communal solidarity characterized by the 'juxtaposition of the social classes' and 'the [benign] influence of tradition'.[28] The old order, assumed to be alive and well in rural areas, had long since disappeared from the towns: 'With their great masses of people, largely segregated according to social class, they have destroyed the feudal conceptions of rights and duties without progressing to a society that is democratically integrated.'[29] At its most Utopian, 'democratic integration' would involve massive social engineering designed to put an end to both the geographical and educational dimensions of class segregation. But while the language is modern—'rapid transition to a more equal and democratic structure of society'—the central aspiration replays Victorian notions of urban squirearchy: 'such a policy would humanise the comfortable [and] acquaint them with the incredible virtues and kindliness of the working class'. While fantasizing about how 'wholesome' it would be to have 'less "social work" by the conscientious well-to-do in regions remote from their homes, and much more neighbourly visiting of people in the next street born of genuine common interests', there is no suggestion that such 'class mingling' would abolish class difference. Rather, the Utopia dreamed of for 'our' towns was one in which human sympathy would transcend such difference, enabling 'us' to exercise social leadership as 'naturally' as did our country cousins.[30] Advocacy of class mixing was not at all unusual in discussion of post-war reconstruction. Even left-wing Labour Party leaders spoke of the need 'to try and recapture the glory of some of the past English villages ... where the doctor could reside benignly with his patients in the same street'.[31] But this convergence says more about

---

[27] Ann Summers, 'A Home from Home—Women's Philanthropic Work in the Nineteenth Century', in S. Burman (ed.), *Fit Work for Women* (London, 1979); F. K. Prochaska, *Women and Philanthropy in Nineteenth-century England* (Oxford, 1980); Ellen Ross, 'Good and Bad Mothers: Lady Philanthropists and London Housewives before the First World War', in K. D. McCarthy (ed.), *Lady Bountiful Revisited: Women, Philanthropy, and Power* (Piscataway, NJ, 1990); S. Pederson, 'Gender, Welfare and Citizenship in Britain during the Great War', *American Historical Review*, 94 (1990), 992–3.

[28] WGPW, *Our Towns*, 6.

[29] Ibid., 102.

[30] Ibid., pp. xvii, xviii, 106–8, 110.

[31] Aneurin Bevan, cited in D. Matless, *Landscape and Englishness* (London, 1998), 234–5. See also Lewis Silkin, 'Creating Communities', *Social Service*, 21 (1947).

the sentimentality of some socialists—Nye Bevan in this case—than it does about the radicalism of the Women's Group.

III

Speaking at the founding meeting of the Liverpool Women's Organisations Committee in November 1939, Miss Foulkes, a delegate from the Soroptimists, declared her conviction that the key to progress was 'the formation of women's organisations into one body so that the mothers would be educated to a sense of citizenship'.[32] The problems of middle-class spinsters offering education to working-class mothers had long been acknowledged in the women's movement, and were noted in *Our Towns*, which was itself produced almost entirely by women who had chosen careers over marriage.[33] Miss Foulkes, however, may also have been referring to the education in citizenship of middle-class housewives by their more educated and outgoing sisters. By 1943, when *Our Towns* was published, the example of local co-ordination set by Liverpool had been taken up in many other places, and the WGPW promoted the book as an agenda for action by local co-ordinating groups which were themselves usually led by professional women.[34] The dynamics of female social leadership in 'our towns' tended to place upon childless professional women the responsibility for fostering the virtues of citizenship not only among working-class mothers but also among their married sisters in the middle class.

Professional women were mainly responsible for the establishment of local Standing Conferences of Women's Organisations (SCWOs), the most sustained attempt in the 1940s to co-ordinate action by women's organizations at local level. Inspired by the success of the campaign for equal compensation, the Soroptimists decided in July 1942 to encourage the formation of what they called 'Group Action Councils' at local level.[35] Caroline Haslett urged professional women to adopt 'a statesmanlike attitude', looking beyond their own self-interested concerns to make links with the far larger world of housewives and engage with issues 'that concern the

[32] Liverpool Women's Organizations Committee, Minutes, 3 Nov. 1939, WF K41.
[33] WGPW, *Our Towns*, 107.
[34] M. Bondfield, WGPW Press Statement, 30 Nov. 1943, WF A42; WGPW Newsletter (July 1944), 9, WF I7.
[35] 'Standing Conferences. The Principle of Group Action Inspired by Soroptimism', Oct. 1943; 'Group Action Councils', 1942, in WF I2; Report of Joint Conference of WGPW and SCWO, 23 June 1945, WF J2. The name 'Group Action Council' derived from the United States where British delegates attending the 1938 International Convention of Soroptimists had been impressed by research and lobbying organizations operating under this name. Elizabeth Hawes, the Soroptimist leader, had made an unsuccessful attempt to launch the Councils in Britain shortly before the war (D. Warner, 'Miss Elizabeth Hawes, MBE', n.d., WF H6).

whole mechanism of the women's world'.[36] Since the outbreak of war a number of other towns had followed the example of Liverpool where women's organizations meeting under the auspices of the influential local Council of Social Service in November 1939 had resolved to work together 'to bring about urgent social reforms that were of particular concern to women'.[37] In Leicester, co-operation in the equal compensation campaign led to the establishment of a Co-ordination Committee of Women's Organizations in May 1942.[38] The Soroptimists' initiative in July 1942 met with an enthusiastic response and within months thirty local Group Action Councils had been formed.[39]

This sudden upsurge of local co-ordination caused alarm among the parent bodies of some of the organizations concerned. The National Council of Women was worried that the new Group Action Councils would eventually spawn a new national organization rivalling its own (disputed) claims to speak for the women's organizations as a whole. Moreover it had always seen local co-ordination as one of its own functions. In some towns the new initiative was indignantly attacked as an attempt to usurp the functions of the NCW; in others the Group Action Council was seen to be succeeding where the NCW had failed.[40] The Soroptimists' attempted to be more inclusive than the NCW by insisting that the new Councils would not themselves become policy-making bodies but would have a purely consultative role: any resulting activity would be undertaken by constituent organisations acting, if they chose to do so at all, in their own names. Organizations like the Inner Wheel or the Townswomen's Guilds would, it was hoped, feel free to participate without committing themselves to joining in activities which might compromise their own non-political stances. Gertrude Horton, the

[36] *British Soroptimist* (Aug. 1942). She herself was extremely active in lobbying Whitehall on behalf of housewives, battling—without much success—to persuade Whitehall to rationalize and streamline its machinery for cajoling ordinary housewives to observe the disciplines of austerity. She did this, however, not as a representative of the housewife—she herself had no time for housework—but as a professional woman to whom the housewife was something of an irritant.

[37] *Townswoman* (May 1947); Liverpool Council of Social Service Minutes of a Meeting of Women's Organizations, 28 Feb. 1939, WF K41; 'Statement on Women's Organizations', 30 June 1942, WF I2; Report of a Meeting to Discuss Group Action Councils, 11 Nov. 1942, WF I1; Circular to Regional Officers of NCSS, 25 Mar. 1943, WF I2. The WGPW file on Liverpool (WF K41) contains copious material on the activities of the women's organizations in the city.

[38] Co-ordinating Committee of Leicester Women's Organizations, Minutes, 15 May 1942, Leciester RO, SCWO DE 3104/2; NCW, Minutes 14 Oct. 1942, WF I2; 'Group Action Councils', 1942, in WF I2; Warner, 'Miss Elizabeth Hawes, MBE'. Dora Warner—a leading figure among British Soroptimists—was the moving spirit behind the Leicester initiative.

[39] Report of the Second Meeting of the Women's Group on Group Action Councils, 27 Nov. 1942, WF I1.

[40] NCW, Minutes, 14 Oct. 1942, WF I2; Report of a Meeting to Discuss Group Action Councils, 11 Nov. 1942, WF I1; Coventry NCW, Minutes, 31 July, 25 Sept. 1942, Coventry RO, PA/1269; Coventry EAW, Minutes, 1 Apr. 1943, Coventry RO 1199.

Townswomen's national secretary, pointed out that the title adopted by the Soroptimists appeared to belie their purely consultative intentions—'the name "action" is just what we can't agree to'—and the Soroptimists found themselves explaining, somewhat absurdly, that 'a Group Action Council ... [must] not act as a Group'.[41]

Faced with these difficulties, the Soroptimists asked the WGPW to take on the role of guiding the development of the Councils in a way acceptable to all the women's organizations.[42] A new model constitution was negotiated which took full account of the Townswomen's anxieties by dropping the offending name in favour of the more neutral 'Standing Conference of Women's Organisations'; tightening up the provisions for preventing the groups taking on 'propagandist' functions; and incorporating as their leading aim the Townswomen's own commitment to the provision of a 'common meeting ground.'[43] At the same time the Women's Group established a sub-committee briefed to act as an 'advisory headquarters' to watch over the development of the new local bodies. Chaired by Lady Norman, this committee represented the Soroptimists and the Federation of Business and Professional Women (which had been associated with the Soroptimist initiative from the outset), the Townswomen, the National Council of Women, the Standing Joint Committee of Working Women's Organisations (of whose involvement more later), and the Young Women's Christian Association.[44]

The resulting structure—local co-ordinating bodies pledged not to take action in their own name and policed by a national committee on which they had no direct representation—was a curious one.[45] By the time the new arrangements were in place, in March 1943, Group Action Councils had been formed in fifty-one towns, mainly on Soroptimist initiative, and some of the women involved were indignant that their national leaders had handed authority to the WGPW without first consulting them. They were particularly resentful of a ban on SCWOs taking up national issues directly, rather than through the national headquarters of their constituent organizations.[46] After the war pressure from below forced the Women's Group to

[41] 'Group Action Councils', 1942, in WF I2; Horton to Hawes, 21 Oct. 1942, WF I2; Report of the Second Meeting of the Women's Group on Group Action Councils, 27 Nov. 1942, WF I1; WGPW, Minutes, 12 Mar. 1947, WF A1.

[42] Warner, 'Miss Elizabeth Hawes, MBE'; Harford to NCSS Regional Officers, 25 Mar. 1943, WF I2.

[43] *Townswoman* (May 1943), 123–4.

[44] 'Group Action Councils', 4 Dec. 1942, WF I2; Harford to Farrer, 15 Jan. 1943, WF I2; Warner, 'Miss Elizabeth Hawes, MBE'; Reports of Meetings to Discuss Group Action Councils, 11 and 27 Nov. 1942, WF I1.

[45] As Harford admitted to the NFBPW: Harford to Deakin, 28 July 1944, WF I3

[46] Soroptimist Club of Nottingham, Minutes, 16 Mar., 17 Apr., 15 July 1943, Nottinghamshire RO, DDSO/2/2; SCWO Sub-Committee, Minutes, 25 July 1944, WF I3; Warner to Harford, 12 May 1943, WG/I2.

allow biennial national joint conferences of SCWOs to elect half the membership of the advisory committee.[47] But the Group held the line against pressures—'latent since the beginning'—to turn the SCWOs into the nucleus of a new national organization, insisting that any move in this direction would destroy the Standing Conferences by upsetting the delicate balance between facilitating local co-operation while respecting the autonomy of established organizations.[48] This was not enough to satisfy the National Council of Women, which never reconciled itself to the existence of a rival co-ordinating organization, and eventually withdrew in 1947.[49] Despite this the device of WGPW tutelage served its purpose. By the summer of 1944 all but four of the fifty-one Group Action Councils in existence at the launch of the WGPW scheme had signed up, together with a further twenty-five new local groups. The movement peaked with over 100 affiliates during 1947, most of them in the North and Midlands rather than in Southern England. Numbers fell in the late 1940s, to seventy-six by 1951, but they picked up again during the 1950s.[50]

The activities of local SCWOs reflected the common concerns of its constituent members. The Soroptimists' draft constitution had given pride of place to the promotion of 'the economic interests of women', and in Coventry, for example, the group devoted much of its energies to a scheme to provide suitable housing for single professional women.[51] But Coventry had rather a narrow group, very much dominated by the professional women's organizations, and such sectional concerns were not normally seen as appropriate business for a Standing Conference.[52] After the war, when queues and food shortages became a subject of public agitation, some Standing Conferences found themselves drawn in, and in a number of areas branches of the militant British Housewives' League were accepted as affiliates.[53] In Coventry and Leicester the SCWOs took up equal pay campaign-

---

[47] Report of the Standing Conference Advisory Committee, 1948–1950, WF H6; SCWO Constitutiuon, 1949, WF I2; Warner, 'Miss Elizabeth Hawes, MBE'; List of local SCWOs, n.d. (?Spring 1943), WF I2.

[48] WGPW Sub-committee on SCWOs, Minutes, 18 July 1946, WF I1.

[49] *Women in Council* (Sept. 1947), 8–10; Bondfield, Statement to Membership, 24 Sept. 1947, WF G2. In some areas, however, the local NCW worked happily enough with the SCWO: NCW, North East Region, Minutes, 21 Jan. 1948, Calder Valley RO NCW 40.

[50] Harford to Hamilton, 11 Aug. 1944, WF K76; Report of the Standing Conference Advisory Committee, 1948–1950, WF H6; Draft Report on SCWOs, n.d. (?1951), WF H6; Brasnett, *Voluntary Social Action*, 109, 194–6.

[51] Coventry Soroptimists Club, Minutes, 14 Sept. 1943, 12 Dec. 1944; 21 Mar. 1946, Coventry RO, 1000/1/1.

[52] WGPW *Newsletter* (July 1944), WF I7.

[53] Leicester SCWO, Minutes, 25 June 1945, 25 Mar. 1946, LRO, DE 3104/2; Leicester SCWO, Chairman's Report for 1947–8, WF K38; Halifax SCWO, Minutes, 20 May, 28 June, 29 July 1946, 11 June 1948, Calder Valley RO, Misc. 733/1/1; *Liverpool Post* (8 Feb. 1946); Golders Green SCWO, Minutes, 25 Feb. 1946, WF K27.

ing after the war.[54] Several Lancashire Conferences were supportive of campaigning by the feminist Married Women's Association for legal protection of married women's savings.[55] The promotion of women's 'economic interests' was not, however, the main concern of the Standing Conferences: indeed the phrase itself had been omitted from the WGPW's model constitution under pressure from the Townswomen's secretary, Gertrude Horton. In October 1943, the Townswoman, commenting on the equal pay campaign, reminded members that the Guilds 'were not prepared to associate themselves with a feminist movement'; that up to half the membership would not consider itself feminist; and that the principle of equal pay could not be taken as an article of faith in the movement.[56]

The WGPW constitution stressed, not feminist self-assertion, but the pursuit of 'matters of interest to the women's organisations *and* to the city, town or district' as the prime function of the SCWOs.[57] Most groups undertook some voluntary service of their own. In Halifax, for example, the SCWO opened and staffed its own youth club, and raised the extraordinary sum of £4,500 from a market fair held in aid of the local hospital, on whose board they were campaigning to secure women's representation.[58] A favourite cause was catering for young people's (alcohol-free) leisure by setting up evening cafés or extending the opening hours of British Restaurants with voluntary labour provided by women's organizations.[59] The moral agenda underlying such activity was apparent in discussions of juvenile delinquency, the sexual behaviour of young girls, and—the single most common campaigning issue taken up by SCWOs during the war—the appointment of women police.[60] SCWOs conducted surveys of local needs and

---

[54] SCWO Sub-committee, Minutes, 21 Sept. 1945, WF I3; Leicester SCWO, Minutes, 3 Feb. 1947, LRO, DE 3104/2. On the British Housewives League, see J. Hinton, 'Militant Housewives: The British Housewives' League and the Attlee Government', *History Workshop Journal*, 38 (1994), 129–56; Elizabeth McCarty, 'Attitudes to Women and Domesticity in England, circa 1939–1955', Oxford D.Phil., 1994, 309–10.

[55] *Wife and Citizen* (organ of the Married Women's Association) (Feb. 1947), 8. On the MWA campaign, see Catherine Blackford, 'Wives and Citizens and Watchdogs of Quality: Post-War British Feminism', in J. Fyrth (ed.), *Labour's Promised Land? Culture and Society in Labour Britain, 1945–51* (London, 1995), 60–4.

[56] 'Standing Conferences', Oct. 1943, WF I2; *Townswoman* (Oct. 1943); Franklin, 'Notes for a Talk to a Mass Meeting of...Members', Aug. 1944, in PRO MAF 102 10.

[57] *Townswoman* (May 1943) (emphasis added). See also WGPW, *Our Towns are our Opportunities. Suggestions for Standing Conferences of Women's Organisations* (London, 1948), 6–7.

[58] Halifax SCWO Annual Reports, 1944, 1945, 1946, and Minutes, *passim*, Calder Valley RO, Misc. 733/1/1.

[59] WGPW *Newsletter* (July 1944), WF I7. This often had an underlying teetotal purpose—British Restaurants were not permitted to sell alcohol (Report of Birmingham and District SCWO, July 1946, WF K6).

[60] Leicester SCWO, Chairman's Report, 1948–9 and 1949–50, WF K38; Coventry Soroptimists Club, Minutes, 15 June, 14 Sept., 11 Dec. 1943, Coventry RO, 1000/1/1; WGPW *Newsletter* (July 1944), WF I7. For discussion of this moral agenda during the 1940s see

lobbied local authorities on a host of issues, including housing, transport, the provision of maternity accommodation and home helps, and the chronic shortage of public lavatories for women.[61]

IV

The Soroptimists had seen one of the main functions of Group Action Councils as pressing for the appointment of women to public bodies, thereby 'opening the door to full service in local affairs and ... training members for leadership'.[62] Although the WGPW constitution made no mention of this objective, pressing for women to be co-opted to council committees never-theless became a primary function of the SCWOs: as Irene Ward, Tory MP and chairman of the Northumberland Standing Conference, remarked: 'even the most ardent anti-feminist can hardly deny that women have a right to be associated with housing policy.'[63] Women had long been co-opted onto Maternity and Child Committees, and many SCWOs campaigned to extend this practice, especially to housing, education, and reconstruction commit-tees.[64] The Halifax Conference was exemplary in this respect, setting up a panel of women, nominated by their respective organizations, suitable for appointment to council committees, hospital boards, or the magistracy.[65] Co-option was, however, a second best. The refusal of the Halifax town council to co-opt women to its housing committee was defended by the town's leading Conservative woman (herself an alderman) on democratic grounds, and she urged women's organizations to put pressure on the political parties to select women candidates.[66] The SCWO was in fact already doing this, and as the November 1945 local elections approached constituent organizations renewed the pressure.[67] In September 1945 they

Sonya O. Rose, 'Sex, Citizenship and the Nation in World War II Britain', *American Historical Review*, 103 (1998); G. Field, 'Perspectives on the Working-class Family in Wartime Britain, 1939–1945', *International Labor and Working-Class History*, 38 (1990).

[61] WGPW *Newsletter* (July 1944), WF I7; WGPW, *Our Towns are our Opportunities*, 15; Halifax SCWO, Annual Reports, 1944, 1945, 1946, Calder Valley RO, Misc. 733/1/1; Leicester SCWO, Chairman's Report for 1949–50, WF K38; Horton to Harford, 31 Mar. 1944 on the activities of the Bristol SCWO, WF K20.

[62] 'Standing Conferences. The Principle of Group Action inspired by Soroptimism', Oct. 1943, WF I2.

[63] Ward to Harford, 5 Oct. 1944, WF I3.

[64] Annual Report of Birmingham SCWO, July 1946, WF K6; Leicester SCWO, Minutes, 14 July 1944, Leicester RO, DE 3104/2; Horton to Harford, 31 Mar. 1944 on the activities of the Bristol SCWO, WF K20. The Leeds Town Council refused to admit even a single woman to its Reconstruction Committee in 1944: WGPW Sub-Committee on SCWOs, Minutes, 10 Feb., 24 May 1944, WF I3; secretary of Leeds SCWO to Harford, 21 Jan. 1944, WF K37.

[65] Halifax SCWO Annual Reports, 1944, 1945; Halifax SCWO, Minutes, 21 Feb., 22 May 1944, Calder Valley RO, Misc. 733/1/1; Halifax NCW, Minutes, 10 Sept. 1943, 12 Sept. 1947, 16 Jan. 1948, Calder Valley RO; WGPW, *Our Towns are our Opportunities*, 6.

[66] Halifax SCWO, Minutes, 4 July, 21 Aug., 18 Sept. 1944 Calder Valley RO, Misc. 733/1/1.

[67] Ibid., 19 Apr. 1943, 6 July 1945.

went further, inviting two of their members to stand as independents. Both women were Liberals and one of them, a married businesswoman who ran a farm as a hobby and a past president of the local Soroptimists, accepted the invitation. This may have been a manœuvre designed to force the dominant party on the Council to adopt women candidates. If so it succeeded: within two weeks the Liberals had adopted her as their own candidate. The SCWO treasurer, an unmarried cashier who believed that men and women should have equal representation on all public bodies, also stood as an independent, sponsored by the Business and Professional Women. Money was collected for both candidates at SCWO meetings, and the treasurer used the meetings to recruit canvassers.[68] The SCWO also paid for an advertisement in the local paper urging women to vote for women candidates 'as far as their consciences allowed if two candidates were standing for one ward'. Both women were elected, but the SCWO's electoral intervention thoroughly upset the Labour Party, and the Liberals objected to the advertisement. The Conservatives, however, drew a different conclusion, asking the SCWO to suggest a suitable candidate to stand for them in a forthcoming by-election. Although they had come close to endorsing independent candidates in 1945, the Halifax SCWO drew back from any long-term involvement in electoral politics, resolving in January 1946 that names of suitable council candidates submitted for its panel would in future be forwarded to the appropriate political party.[69]

Halifax was not alone in confronting the issue of independent candidates. One of the first actions of the Group Action Council in Leamington Spa when it was set up at the end of 1943 had been to nominate (successfully) their own president for a vacant council position. Alerted by an anxious Labour Party, Harford warned the Leamington group against the danger of 'side-tracking the democratic methods of the country on the one hand, and of giving the impression of extreme feminism on the other'. The Leamington secretary was quick to point out that they had no such intentions and that they had already secured a council place for a second of their members, the wife of a leading local industrialist, as the nominee of the Conservative Party.[70] The Leamington action had been a product of the wartime political truce and in 1945 there appears to have been no move to put up independent candidates. SCWO leaders in nearby Coventry did discuss the possibility, but 'came to the conclusion that independent women candidates would

---

[68] Ibid, 1 Sept., 1 and 19 Oct. 1945; E. Cockcroft, 'Silver Jubilee Poems', 1948, Calder Valley RO, SOR 4/24; *Halifax Courier and Guardian* (27 Jan. 1945, 27 Oct. 1945, 3 Nov. 1945.

[69] Halifax SCWO, Minutes, 16 Oct. 1944, 19 Nov. 1945, 21 Jan. 1946, 3 Apr. 1946, Calder Valley RO, Misc. 733/1/1.

[70] Leamington Group Action Council, Minutes, 8 Dec. 1943; Toulmin to Harford, 21 Dec. 1943, 28 Feb. 1944; Harford to Toulmin 24 Feb. 1944, WF K36; SCWO Sub-committee, Minutes, 19 Jan. 1944, WF I3; SJC, Minutes, 9 Dec. 1943, LP NEC.

stand very little chance of being elected, and that at the present time women
must put up as representatives of a party'.[71] In May 1945 the SCWO leader
in Grimsby reported an anti-party mood—'we have several excellent
women, who are prepared to stand as independent candidates, but will not
join a political party'—but she was clearly asking the WGPW for backing in
resisting this pressure.[72] Darlington had also considered the possibility of
putting up their own candidate in 1945 but decided instead to launch
a Women's Municipal Campaign to mobilize support for any women candidates regardless of party.[73] In Portsmouth, where the Women's Citizen's
Association carried out many of the functions elsewhere performed by the
SCWO, the chairman's desire for the organization to sponsor an independent candidate was frustrated by the political realism of her chosen candidate
who reported in September 1945 that, while she would love to stand as an
independent, her 'enquiries all over the City from people in all walks of life'
made it clear that 'the coming elections were expected to evoke violent party
feelings and that the times might not be propitious for candidates without a
strong organisation behind them'.[74] This evidence suggests that wherever
independent electoral intervention was discussed it was rejected—with the
interesting exception of the Halifax Business and Professional Women. Most
Standing Conferences contented themselves with pressing the parties to
adopt women candidates and convening meetings at which all the women
candidates could be quizzed on policy issues, a practice recommended by the
Townswomen.[75] There was a significant strand of anti-party feeling in
English political culture—aptly summed up in Mrs Miniver's Utopian
slogan: 'neither right-wing...nor left-wing...but the wish-bone'—and
this had been apparent in opinion polls during the war.[76] The major outlet
for the non-partisan sentiments of middle-class women, however, was in the
voluntary work, campaigning and lobbying undertaken by women's organizations, and the leaders of these organizations were realistic about the
difficulties of carrying non-partisanship into the electoral arena. In
May 1945 Letty Harford warned the Grimsby SCWO that 'were the

[71] Coventry SCWO, Annual Report, Apr. 1946, WF K20.
[72] Cooper to Harford, 11 May 1945, WF K29.
[73] Darlington SCWO, Annual Reports, 1945 and 1946, Durham RO.
[74] Portsmouth Women's Citizen's Association, Minutes, 20 Sept. 1945, 8 Dec. 1948, Portsmouth RO, 1055a.
[75] *Townswoman* (May 1945), 129–31, 138; A. Franklin, 'Notes for a Talk to a Mass Meeting
of...Members', Aug. 1944, in PRO, MAF 102 10 ; 'Clubs, Societies and Democracy', *Planning*,
263, 21 Mar. 1947, 13–14. For examples of such activity in Birmingham, Leicester, Northampton, Scarborough, Blyth, and Hull see: Birmingham and District SCWO, Annual Report, 1943–
4, WF K6; Leicester SCWO, Chairman's Reports for 1948–9 and 1949–50, WF K38; WGPW
Newsletter, July 1944, WF I7, 13; Blair to King, 15 Jan., 1947, WF K 82; Johnson to King, 10
Apr. 1947, WF K34.
[76] S. Fielding, 'The Second World War and Popular Radicalism: The Significance of the
"Movement away from Party"', *History*, 80 (1995).

representatives of the different organisations to back an independent woman
candidate, it would lead to misunderstanding and people would think you
were trying to start "a woman's party".'[77] However much some might feel
themselves to be, in Patricia Hollis' words, 'tacit members of a hidden
women's party', these women knew that when it came to electoral politics
discretion was the better part of wisdom.[78]

V

The Standing Conferences mainly represented middle-class women. The
WGPW, keen to involve working-class organizations, brought the SJC
onto the advisory committee from the outset, and the SJC representative
expressed the hope that 'the reluctance of trade union and co-operative
members would be gradually overcome'.[79] But the Labour women were in
fact much more interested in restraining the SCWOs from getting involved
in municipal elections than they were in encouraging active participation
by their members: 'the SJC has taken the position', Mary Sutherland explained in 1945, 'that we would offer no objection to local branches
of our organisations participating in the Standing Conferences, while *of
course* we would not urge them to do so'.[80] The 'of course' testifies eloquently to the abiding reluctance of Labour women to involve themselves in
what would necessarily be a subordinate position in the middle-class
women's world.

Many SCWOs had no representation at all from working-class organizations. This was not for want of trying. In Leicester, where repeated invita-
tions to the working-class organizations had been refused, the SCWO
decided in 1948 to abandon attempts to persuade them to affiliate in favour
of seeking co-operation in organizing specific undertakings, such as the
impressive campaign run by the SCWO to persuade women to return to
factory jobs. A year later, however, they were again trying to talk the WCG
and the Labour Party into affiliating. Eventually this persistent pressure paid
off when the WCG decided to join. The Labour Party, however, remained
aloof.[81] This was a common pattern, with the Co-operative Guilds being

[77] Harford to Cooper, 14 May 1945, WF K29.
[78] P. Hollis, *Ladies Elect, Women in English Local Government, 1865–1914* (Oxford, 1987),
464.
[79] SCWO Sub-committee, Minutes, 20 Mar. 1944, WF I3. She was commenting on a report
that Boot and Shoe Workers had refused to affiliate to the SCWO in Leicester.
[80] Sutherland to Whyatt, 4 Mar. 1945, WF I6 [emphasis added]. From the beginning the SJC
line had been that while they would refrain from advising local groups not to join SCWOs
they would urge them to remember that their own work should come first: SJC, Minutes, 8
Apr. 1943, LP NEC; SCWO Sub-committee, Minutes, 19 Jan., 20 Mar. 1944, WF I3
[81] Leicester SCWO, Minutes, 15 May 1942, 7 June 1948, 23 Oct. 1950, Leicester Record
Office, DE 3104/3; Warner to King, 12 May, 4 June 1947, WF K38; SCWO Sub-committee,
Minutes, 20 Mar. 1944, WF I3; *Citizen* (Jan. 1948), 22–3.

rather more inclined to join than the Labour Party Women's Sections.[82] In a few areas Labour women were fully represented, but they seldom, if ever, played a leading role.[83] In Halifax the Labour Party was represented from the outset and Mrs Oxley, later to be Labour's first woman councillor in Halifax, played an active part in SCWO proceedings.[84] Nevertheless their sense of unease as participants in this middle-class public world was revealed when the Women's Section decided not to take part in the Conference's major fund-raising effort—a market fair—'in view of the fact that we can't [even] supply a stall for our own At Homes.'[85] Nor were they interested in the SCWO's other big project—the co-ordination of nominations for co-option to council committees and other public bodies, seeing this as strictly a Party matter. Following the SCWO's interventions in the local elections in November 1945, the Labour Women decided to withdraw altogether, complaining that, while they had been keen to help the organization to do 'a useful service in awakening civic consciousness and rousing a keen interest in the problems of the day', they had not joined in order:

to become part of a purely feminist organisation, which is a reactionary not a progressive outlook... [nor] to help to make the SCWO into a political machine ... We cannot remain affiliated to an organisation which poses as being non-political and then enters into the political arena.

The idea that women candidates should be supported irrespective of party was anathema to the Labour women, and the notion that there could be genuine independents on local councils simply revealed 'a complete lack of knowledge in [*sic*] the working of ... Local Government machinery'.[86] For Labour women whose access to local power depended overwhelmingly on

[82] For example, the WCG (but not the Labour Party) were affiliated in Bristol, Birmingham, Liverpool, and Lincoln: SCWO Sub-committee, Minutes, 17 Jan. 1945, WF I3; Birmingham SCWO, Annual Report, July 1946, WF K6; Liverpool SCWO, list of affiliates, 1947, WF K42; Lincoln SCWO, list of affiliates, 1949, WF K40.

[83] Golders Green, where several Labour women occupied leading positions, provides a possible exception (Golder's Green SCWO, Minutes, 25 Feb. 1946, WF K27), as does Croydon, where in 1946 the Conservatives believed that the very active SCWO was being taken over by socialists (South-east Area Conservative Women's Advisory Committee, Minutes, 10 July 1946, CPA, ARE 9/11/4; SCWO Sub-committee, Minutes, 28 Apr., 24 May 1944, WF I3; correspondence and reports in WF K24). However, a further exception, Luton— where the SCWO was being run in the early 1950s by the delegate from the WCG—was seen by the WGPW as a failing organization which demonstrated the inadequacy of working-class leadership (correspondence in WF K45).

[84] When Oxley became a councillor, however, she ceased to be active in the SCWO. Halifax SCWO, Minutes, 1 Mar., 8 Nov. 1943, 19 Nov. 1945, Calder Valley RO, Misc. 733/1/1; Halifax Labour Party Women's Section, Minutes, 2 Feb. 1943, 23 May 1944, Calder Valley RO, TU28/8.

[85] Ibid., 24 Oct. 1944.

[86] Dixon to Oakley, 21 Jan. 1946; Halifax SCWO, Minutes, 17 Dec. 1945 Calder Valley RO, Misc. 733/1/1; Halifax Labour Party Women's Section, Minutes, 20 Nov. 1945, Calder Valley RO, TU28/8.

party politics, and who were acutely aware of ways in which anti-socialists
had long hidden their party affiliations behind a 'non-political' label, the
desire of established middle-class social leaders to consolidate female influence across party boundaries could only appear as a deliberate attempt to
sabotage Labour's advance.[87]

VI

Soroptimists had hoped that their Group Action Councils would serve as a
meeting point for 'women from every type of organisation and from every
walk of life...' and Margaret Bondfield described the SCWOs as places
where 'the representatives of the business and professional women's club
will have discussions... with the trade union members or the housewife from
a church meeting or a women's guild'.[88] If the trade unionists were mainly
notable by their absence, the middle-class housewives, though present,
tended to take a back seat, and leadership remained largely with the professional women.[89] Dora Warner, a leading Soroptomist who ran the Leicester
group and who took over the chairmanship of the WGPW advisory committee from Lady Norman in 1948, complained that professional women had
been left to shoulder the burden because other organizations were jealous of
the potential influence of the Standing Conferences.[90] While this may well
have been true of working-class organizations, it was unfair as a criticism of
the Townswomen, who did what they could to persuade their members to
take the initiative: 'why leave it to one or two other organisations [i.e. the
professional women], to put the wheels in motion.'[91] But the assumptions
that Horton and Franklin themselves made about the leadership capacities of
their own members should have enabled them to answer this question.
Despite the safeguards she had written into the model constitution, Horton
remained vigilant in seeking to prevent the innocent enthusiasm of inexperienced Guildswomen being exploited by sinister forces to inveigle them
into 'propagandist' activity. In July 1943 the WGPW Executive drew up a

[87] McKibbin, 'Class and Conventional Wisdom: The Conservative Party and the "Public" in Inter-war Britain', in *The Ideologies of Class: Social Relations in Britain, 1880–1950* (Oxford, 1990); K. Young, *Local Politics and the Rise of Party. The London Municipal Society and the Conservative Intervention in Local Elections, 1894–1963* (Leicester, 1975), 186–93; Ken Young, 'The Party and English Local Government', in A. Seldon and S. Ball (eds.), *Conservative Century* (Oxford, 1994); Ball, 'Local Conservatism', ibid.; J. W. B. Bates, 'The Conservative Party in the Constituencies, 1918–1939', Oxford D.Phil., 1994, 218–19, 230 ff.

[88] WGPW, Press Release, 30 Nov. 1943, WF A42; 'Group Action Councils', 1942, WF I2.

[89] All of the nine new SCWOs formed in 1951, for example, were initiated by Business and Professional Women's Clubs or Soroptimists. Members of these two organizations also predom-inated among those enquiring about the possibility of setting up new SCWOs, with the Townswomen coming a poor third (Draft Report on SCWOs, n.d. (?1951), WF H6).

[90] Warner to Homer, 28 May 1951, WF H6.

[91] *Townswoman*, Apr. 1944; SCWO Sub-Committee Minutes, 28 Apr. 1944, WF I3.

blacklist of 'mushroom organisations' with which it resolved to have no dealings. Apart from one militantly pro-family group, the Council of Seven Beliefs, these were all 'extreme' feminist organizations, including Women for Westminster and Dorothy Evans' Women's Publicity and Planning Association.[92] Horton urged Harford to impress on the Soroptimists and the Federation of Business and Professional Women—'societies which have a reputation of being composed of sensible women'—the danger of their 'really irresponsible behaviour' in allowing their own local groups to co-operate with 'mushroom organisations'.[93] She appeared unaware that the internal structures of these two organizations would have made it quite impossible for their national leaders to impose such proscriptions on local activity, even if they had wished to do so.[94] This defensive paranoia was nicely matched by the SJC which believed that the Communist-inspired Women's Parliament needed watching as least as carefully as did Dorothy Evans. The Communist Party official responsible for the Women's Parliament found the leaders of the middle-class women's organizations much less worried about working with Communists than were their working-class counterparts.[95] Mrs Whyatt, representing the Women's Co-operative Guilds on the SCWO sub-committee, confessed that one of the main reasons why the SJC had agreed to participate was to alert middle-class organizations to the dangers represented by the Women's Parliaments, and Harford looked to the Labour women to expound these dangers whenever the occasion arose.[96] A curious alliance thus emerged between the representatives of middle-class and working-class housewives against the 'irresponsibility' of professional women in consorting freely with feminist or communist subversives. It was an alliance which spoke more of the nervousness of the housewives' leaders than the naïvety of the professional women. Despite Horton and Whyatt, the advisory commit-

[92] WGPW Executive Minutes, 15 Apr., 1 July 1943, 6 Mar. 1944, WF A1. Dorothy Paterson, who set up the Council of Seven Beliefs for the Guardianship of Family Life in order to promote women's post-war return to domesticity, opposed not only equal opportunities for women in the labour market but also their participation in political life, earning her the hostility of feminists and the mainstream women's organizations alike (*International Women's News* (June and July 1943); D. Paterson, *The Family Woman and the Feminist. A Challenge* (London, 1945); Penny Summerfield, *Reconstructing Women's Wartime Lives* (Manchester, 1998), 255–6).
[93] Horton to Harford, 3 Mar. 1944, WF A8; WGPW Executive, Minutes, 6 Mar. 1944, 30 Jan. 1946, WF A1.
[94] In Birmingham, for example, the feminist Women for Westminster held one of the five offices, despite the fact that nationally they were refused membership of the Women's Group as a 'mushroom organization' (WGPW Executive, Minutes, 1 July 1943, 6 Feb. 1945; Annual Report of Birmingham SCWO, 1943–4, in WF K6).
[95] Interview with Tamara Rust, 15 Nov. 1990. The TUC file on the Women's Parliament (TUC 292/778.29/2) is a valuable source for this under-researched organization.
[96] SJC Minutes, 9 Dec. 1943, LP NEC; Report of a Meeting to Discuss Group Action Councils, 11 Nov. 1942; Report of the Second Meeting of the Women's Group on Group Action Councils, 27 Nov. 1942, WF I1; SCWO Sub-committee Minutes, 1 June, 9 Dec. 1943 WF I1.

tee was inclined to believe that in dealing with extremists it was usually better
to co-opt than to exclude: 'such organisations will probably modify their
outlook by association with the more established organisations'.[97] The
Birmingham Standing Conference, for example, was advised to admit Communist women on the grounds that 'very often [they] have very little idea
how much is being done by voluntary organisations, nor how effective is
their work, and by joining in a Standing Conference they will learn much'.[98]
Whether or not this belief in the co-optability of Communists was justified, it
certainly revealed a spirit of confident social leadership among some of the
established women's organizations that was sadly lacking in the obsessive
attempts of leaders of both Labour women and the Townswomen's Guilds to
close down potential avenues of subversion. Given her fears about the
political inexperience of her members, Horton should not have been sur-
prised that, in general, they left the initiative to more confident and better-
educated professional women. And those who did not hang back represented
a potential threat to the style of leadership of the NUTG's own founders.
Franklin and Horton's nemesis, the Bristol doctor's wife Mary Courtney, had
acquired the experience necessary for her role in bringing them down partly
by her chairmanship of the local Standing Conference.[99]

The developments charted in this chapter owed more to the initiative of
business and professional women than to those leisured housewives whose
energies WVS was primarily designed to channel. Among both groups
of women, however, Mrs Miniver's longing for 'the wishbone' of non-
partisanship was widely shared. In the realm of electoral politics such aspirations were generally acknowledged to be Utopian, if only because they were
rejected by Labour women who saw them as a hypocritical disguise for the
promotion of anti-socialist politics. The dependency of Labour women on
the ballot box for challenging middle-class social leadership made them
understandably sceptical about the reality of non-partisanship in the associational life of middle-class women. The rhetoric of nation before party,
however, addressed a genuine duality in the attitudes of many middle-class
women, including Conservative Party members, and that is one reason why
Lady Reading was able to win her battle to revive WVS after the war. This
institutional continuity, however, disguised a major shift in the weight and
function of her organization. The post-war WVS never again functioned as

[97] SCWO Sub-committee Minutes, 24 May 1944, WF I1.
[98] In deference to the SJC the Birmingham group was advised to sound out the local Labour
Party before acting. Harford to Hayes, 9 Oct. 1944, WF K6; SCWO Sub-committee Minutes, 20
Sept. 1944, WF I1. In June 1943 the Communist Party had applied, unsuccessfully, for representation on the national WGPW (ibid., 1 June 1943). But local Communist branches were
represented on many SCWOs until 1948, when the Party appears to have lost interest.
[99] Warner to King, 4 June 1947, WF K38. See Ch. 3 above for the conflict between Courtney
and the NUTG old guard.

an instrument of middle-class social leadership in the way it had done during the war. The limits to the WVS revival were set, not so much by the hostility of Labour women or of the established middle-class women's organization, but by the declining social power of middle-class housewives in a post-war order in which voluntary service was increasingly subordinated to paid professionals employed by statutory authorities. The next chapter examines this process, with particular reference to the post-war establishment of local Home Help services, a process in which WVS played a pioneering, but ultimately rather a demoralizing, role. In the realm of personal social services, just as in the associational world discussed above, the middle-aged housewives who had gloried in their wartime status as the backbone of Britain increasingly found themselves being marginalized by their younger and better educated professional sisters.

10

Home Helps

Arguing the case for middle-class social leadership in the late 1940s Lewis and Maude warned against the profound changes in 'national life and character' that would flow from any 'final surrender to the idea that paid work is the best work'. They were especially caustic about the 'vast new body of professional social workers' being spawned by the welfare state:

The young woman, paid to do good according to a book of official rules, provided at the age of twenty-one with the loving-kindness and thorough understanding of human nature which only a social science certificate can give, is regarded as infinitely more efficient and hygienic than the voluntary worker whose lineage is derived from those Lady Bountifuls who used to dispense red flannel and thin gruel to the 'deserving' poor of the last century. The new social worker is impervious to that snobbery which was the motive behind much voluntary work, the pleasure of sitting on committees with titled people, and to that corrupting vice of charity, enjoyment of the exercise of power.[1]

Middle-class women, urged Lewis and Maude, should not allow themselves to be pushed by such parodies into retreating 'from the idea of community and the practice of leadership'.[2] These were sentiments with which Lady Reading would certainly have sympathized. It was, she insisted, not as snobbish Lady Bountifuls but as 'real people', mature women with qualities of human understanding and skills of leadership that her members would contribute to post-war reconstruction, just as they had contributed so effectively to the war effort.[3] The ongoing professionalization of social work held dangers which, she believed, had become all too clear in the United States where 'voluntary workers are completely controlled by trained and salaried officials whose professional jealousy is rapidly destroying all voluntary effort'.[4] While WVS frequently distinguished itself from other voluntary organizations by the 'professionalism' with which its work was organized,

---

[1] R. Lewis and A Maude, *The English Middle Classes* (London, 1953), 223–4.
[2] Ibid., 227.
[3] Lady Reading, 'Draft Statement on WVS', 30 Sept. 1947, WRVS, Box 204.
[4] Reading to Maxwell, 6 Aug. 1948, WRVS, A1/38 File 6; R. G. Walton, *Women in Social Work* (London, 1975), 147, 152, 181, draws the same contrast with the USA, where the drive to professionalize social work had led to a 'dramatic shift to devalue voluntary work'.

Lady Reading was at one with the philosophical guru of the philanthropic establishment, Ernest Barker, in defending 'the voluntary habit' against the technocratic rule of the expert.[5]

Despite the massive expansion of state welfare provision under the post-war Labour government, it was widely believed that there would be a continuing role for voluntary work. 'The majority of thinking people', wrote Kathleen Halpin in February 1946, 'realise that a great deal of the Socialist legislation cannot possibly be implemented without the help of voluntary organisations for some time to come'.[6] A generation of debate and experimentation had reconciled all but the most diehard to the view that the future of philanthropic effort lay in some kind of partnership with the state,[7] and there was growing evidence that the coming of the welfare state would create at least as many opportunities for voluntary social service as it displaced.[8] Nor were the virtues of voluntarism lost on the Attlee government. Wartime experience had demonstrated to civil servants the indispensability of auxiliary voluntary services.[9] Attlee himself had learned his socialism though voluntary social service, and other leading ministers, notably Herbert Morrison, were keen to stress the fundamental contribution made by volunteering both to democracy and to social welfare.[10] In 1949 Morrison urged the Chancellor of the Exchequer to confront every proposal for further state action with the question of 'whether the work could not be equally well done by existing voluntary agencies'. This was not just a question of saving money: 'keeping the voluntary spirit alive' was central to Morrison's understanding of the socialist project.[11] Even Nye Bevan, hostile though he was to those 'patchworks of paternalism' which sought

---

[5] Julia Stapleton, *Englishness and the Study of Politics. The Social and Political Thought of Ernest Barker* (Cambridge, 1994), 166–70.

[6] Halpin to Aykroyd, 8 Feb. 1946, WRVS, R2 Yorkshire.

[7] By 1942 even the Charity Organisation Society was abandoning its hostility to the pragmatic norms of the 'new philanthropy'. Jane Lewis, *The Voluntary Sector, the State and Social Work in Britain* (Aldershot, 1995), 103. On the responses of voluntary organizations more generally to the twentieth-century expansion of state welfare, see C. Braithwaite, *The Voluntary Citizen. An Enquiry into the Place of Philanthropy in the Community* (London, 1938); Margaret Brasnett, *Voluntary Social Action. A History of the National Council of Social Service, 1919–1969* (London, 1969); Keith Laybourn, 'The Guild of Help and the Changing Face of Edwardian Philanthropy', *Urban History* 20 (1993); G. Finlayson, *Citizen, State and Social Welfare in Britain, 1830–1990* (Oxford, 1994); N. Deakin, 'The Perils of Partnership. The Voluntary Sector and the State, 1945–1992', in J. Davis Smith, C. Rochester, and R. Hedley (eds.), *An Introduction to the Voluntary Sector* (London, 1995).

[8] M. Rooff, *Voluntary Societies and Social Policy* (London, 1955), 260.

[9] H. Land, R. Lowe, and N. Whiteside, *The Development of the Welfare State, 1939–45. Guide to Documents in the Public Records Office* (London, 1992), 184–7.

[10] G. Finlayson, 'A Moving Frontier: Voluntarism and the State in British Social Welfare, 1941–49', *Twentieth-century British History*, 1 (1990); D. Owen, *English Philanthropy, 1660–1960* (Cambridge, Mass., 1965), 537; *Social Service*, 22 (Sept.–Nov. 1948), 65.

[11] Morrison to Cripps, 15 Jan. 1949, in PRO, CAB 124 136.

to resist the nationalization of voluntary hospitals, was well aware of the need for voluntary work in the new health service.[12]

Voluntary organizations were valued not simply as a source of auxiliary labour, but also because they were perceived as delivering services in a flexible and kindly way, unrestrained by bureaucratic procedure.[13] Surveying the state of public opinion for Beveridge in 1948, Mass Observation reported that 'there is a demand for those qualities in administration now associated in people's minds with the voluntary services; humanity, the individual approach'.[14] Most importantly, the voluntary sector claimed a continuing role as a pioneer of services in areas as yet inadequately covered by state action.[15] Informing Lady Reading's hostility to the professionalization of social work was a belief that it was the independence of her women from local bureaucratic (or democratic) control that, together with their personal qualities of leadership and their status in the community, enabled them to take the initiative where mere employees would be condemned to follow instructions from rule-bound officials and unimaginative local councillors.[16] While the effectiveness of WVS in improvising new services for wartime emergencies appeared to vindicate this approach, as a basis for sustaining middle-class female authority in the longer term the pioneering role was problematic. In an era of relentless state expansion pioneering volunteers would tend to find themselves all too quickly superseded, as new state services staffed by professionals moved in to take control of their innovations. 'Initiation followed by disappearance', as one authority described it, was as likely to give rise to feelings of defeat as of achievement

[12] Report of Conference on Home Helps Scheme at Caxton Hall, 11–12 Nov. 1947, 44. Bevan, however, had done his best to avoid speaking to this conference (Reading to Dunbar, 15 Aug. 1962, WRVS, Box File, Wartime, Home Helps), and Kathleen Halpin claimed that Bevan's assurances had come too late to prevent the establishment of the NHS from creating havoc in the existing networks of voluntarism (Interview with Miss Kathleen Halpin, 16 Mar. 1977, Brian Harrison Tapes). Bevan took a leading role in persuading the Home Secretary, Chuter Ede, to address the long-term future of WVS (Lord President's Committee, Minutes, 7 Sept. 1945, PRO, CAB 71 19; Bevan to Reading, 18 Apr. 1946, PRO, MH 130 277; Bevan to Reading, 31 May 1948, PRO, MH 130 253).

[13] Titmuss praised WVS and other voluntary organizations for helping to transform the rest centres from the 'bleak, inhospitable' poor law institutions of September 1939 to 'good and kindly board and lodging' (R. Titmuss, *Problems of Social Policy* (London, 1950), 267–8).

[14] Lord Beveridge and A. F. Wells, *The Evidence for Voluntary Action* (London, 1949), 53.

[15] A. F. C. Bourdillon (ed.), *Voluntary Social Services. Their Place in the Modern State* (London, 1945), 7, 298, 305–6. See also Lord Beveridge, *Voluntary Action. A Report on Methods of Social Advance* (London, 1948); H. A. Mess, *Voluntary Social Services since 1918* (London, 1947).

[16] In 1947, for example, Reading complained of 'the poor municipal authority which is nervous of a band of skilled [voluntary] workers who might show them up' (Reading, Draft Statement on WVS, 30 Sept. 1947, WRVS, WVS Histories in Draft, Box 204). Local councillors sometimes shared this view. The reluctance of some local authorities in the 1950s to appoint trained staff was attributed by Eileen Younghusband to a preference for 'experienced local men and women who "know our ways"...' Eileen Younghusband, *Social Work in Britain, 1950–1975*, i (London, 1978), 41.

among the innovators.[17] This chapter tells the story of one such initiative in which WVS played a central role—the post-war emergence of local authority Home Help services.

I

Since the end of the First World War local authorities had been empowered to employ home helps to alleviate the domestic impact of childbirth and of sickness among mothers of young families. Legislation, however, was not in itself sufficient to call effective services into being. Few authorities responded, and the efforts of voluntary organizations to fill the gap were restricted by the shortage of women prepared to undertake such work.[18] Despite pressure from midwives, Labour Women, and others, little had been done by the outbreak of war to meet a need graphically documented in the 1939 report by the Women's Health Enquiry Committee on the overwork and hidden misery that characterized the daily life of so many working-class wives.[19] Wartime disruption of neighbourhood networks of mutual aid only served to emphasize the need.[20] In December 1944 local authority powers were extended to meet non-maternity cases, including the needs of the elderly, and the 1946 Health Service Act consolidated home helps as a regular part of local authority welfare provision.[21] Demoralized by twenty-five years of 'half-hearted and poorly-conceived' attempts at implementation, however, most local authorities were reluctant to tackle afresh the difficult problems of recruiting and administering emergency domestic workers.[22] This situation left the initiative with the voluntary sector.[23]

[17] Bourdillon, *Voluntary Social Services*, 7.

[18] Elaine Burton, *Domestic Work. Britain's Largest Industry* (London, 1944), 12–13. For the failure of the Leicester scheme due to labour shortages, see Leicester Standing Committee of Women's Organizations Minutes 28 Oct. 1945, Leicestershire RO, DE 3104/2. The Ministry of Labour did what it could, placing nearly 12,000 women in part-time or full-time domestic work in private households or local authority home help schemes during 1944. Elizabeth McCarty, 'Attitudes to Women and Domesticity in England, circa 1939–1955', Oxford D.Phil., 1994, 242.

[19] Martin Pugh, *Women and the Women's Movement in Britain, 1914–1959* (Basingstoke, 1992), 84; Gillian Scott, *Feminism and the Politics of Working Women. The Women's Co-operative Guild from the 1880s to the Second World War* (London, 1998), 245; *Labour Woman* (Dec. 1942); Margery Spring Rice, *Working-Class Wives: Their Health and Conditions* (Harmondsworth, 1939), 202.

[20] WVS Circular on Home Helps, 12 Apr. 1943; Report of Inter-Departmental Enquiry into Emergence Domestic Help Schemes, 17 Dec. 1945, WRVS H32 Home Helps Policy.

[21] Ministry of Health, Circular 110/46, 'Home Helps and Domestic Help', 6 June 1946, copy in WRVS H32/14 Home Helps Pioneer Scheme, Oxford; Land, Lowe, and Whiteside, *The Development of the Welfare State*, 184–5.

[22] T. MacDonald, 'WVS and Home Helps' (n.d.), WRVS, Box File, Wartime, Home Helps.

[23] Some details of wartime home help services run by voluntary organizations other than WVS are given in E. M. Howell Davies, 'A Helping Hand', *Social Service*, 21 (1947), 133–7. See also SCWO *Newsletter* (July 1944), 4, WF I7.

KING ALFRED'S COLLEGE
LIBRARY

WVS Housewives Service, set up to organize neighbourly help in blitz conditions, soon found itself providing aid to the sick and elderly in more normal times. When, in the winter of 1943, a major flu epidemic threatened to fill hospital beds needed for wounded servicemen and force women workers to desert munitions production in order to care for sick relatives, Housewives Service played a significant part in coping with the crisis.[24] It was clear to those involved, however, that good-neighbour schemes and voluntary effort would never be sufficient to meet the ongoing need for emergency domestic help.[25]

Teresa MacDonald, the energetic and ambitious organizer of Oxford WVS, had been alerted by the experience of the 1943 flu epidemic to the need for an 'organised and controlled band of charwomen' paid to provide emergency domestic help. From the outset she intended her scheme not merely to meet wartime needs but to set the pattern for the post-war evolution of home helps. A key feature of the Oxford scheme was the balance struck between voluntary effort and paid local authority employment. The leading personnel were middle-class volunteers—MacDonald herself, and a group of field workers who visited households, decided what help was needed, and supervised the home helps. These field workers also collected payments from the clients, conducting a means test if the householder objected to paying the standard rate. Clerical and administrative support were initially provided voluntarily, but MacDonald quickly persuaded the local authority to pay for this.[26] The home helps themselves were paid directly by the local authority. Although the council accepted the scheme on an experimental basis in November 1944, the elected members remained nervous about the expense involved, and had to be kept in line by the Town Clerk—another forceful character who shared MacDonald's enthusiasm from the start. MacDonald herself had a flair for publicity, and was assiduous in informing both Tothill Street and the Ministry of Health of her plans and involving them in promoting the scheme locally.[27] By August 1945 there

---

[24] WVS Chairman's Committee, Minutes, 18 Mar. 1943; Report on Local WVS participation in Home Helps Schemes, 11 Feb. 1944, WRVS, H32 Home Helps Policy.

[25] MacDonald, 'Narrative Report on Emergency Home Helps Scheme', Jan. 1944, WRVS, H32/14 Home Helps Pioneer Scheme. A report from one respectable working-class neighbourhood in Oxford concluded that while most people thought such a service would be essential after the war, they expected it to be provided with paid labour by the Local Authority, not by organizing existing good neighbourliness (WRVS H32/14 Home Helps Pioneer Scheme).

[26] However, a national survey of WVS members in 1948 found that while 388 were acting as home help organizers a further 588 were providing clerical help to the organizers, presumably in a voluntary capacity (Survey of WVS Activity, 1948, WRVS Statistics).

[27] Katherine Bentley Beauman, *Green Sleeves. The Story of WVS/WRVS* (London, 1977), 97 ff.; Report on City of Oxford and WVS Home Help Scheme, Mar. 1945, 1, 2, 41, WRVS, Box File, Wartime, Home Helps; Schuster, report of discussion at Ministry of Health, 20 Nov. 1946, WRVS, H32 Home Helps Policy; 'Narrative Report on Emergency Home Helps Scheme', Jan. 1944; 'Memo from WVS for Maternity and Child Welfare Sub-Committee', 16 Apr. 1945,

were twenty-three home helps in Oxford, serving fifty-five households each week.[28]

MacDonald's initiative in Oxford provided Lady Reading with exactly the kind of scheme she needed if WVS was to carve out a long-term role for itself in the post-war world. During the early months of the Attlee administration, WVS persuaded a joint enquiry by the Ministries of Health and Labour to nominate the Oxford Scheme as one of two model schemes to be recommended to all local authorities the other, in Lewisham, was run by the local authority without voluntary help. Whitehall encouraged local authorities to make use of the WVS, stressing the advantages of using capable, enthusiastic, and unpaid full-time organizers to overcome initial difficulties and to undertake the home visiting required.[29] Tothill Street embraced its role as nurturer of a new social service, confident that local WVS 'enthusiasm' would enable this 'delicate plant' to 'take root and thrive', and claiming that its national infrastructure made it uniquely well-fitted to the task of overcoming the parochial horizons of local authorities and spreading good practice from one area to another.[30] By the end of 1949 over 18,000 women were employed as home helps in England and Wales, all but 4,000 of them on a part-time basis. This was still a service in its infancy, with the Ministry of Health calculating that five times as many people would be required to meet the legitimate need for emergency domestic work.[31] By March 1948 WVS claimed to have been involved in initiating a substantial proportion of

Helen Smith to Reading, 30 May 1946, WRVS, H32/14 Home Helps Pioneer Scheme, Oxford; WVS, Chairman's Committee, Minutes 19 July 1945, WRVS; Report on WVS Home Helps Conference, 11–12 Nov. 1947, WRVS, WF/G12 Domestic Service.

[28] Report on City of Oxford and WVS Home Help Scheme, Mar. 1945, 39, WRVS, Box File, Wartime, Home Helps. A year later there were 40 home helps in Oxford, serving 38 families a week, WVS County Borough Organisers' Conference, Minutes, 3 Oct. 1946, WRVS.

[29] Report on Enquiry into Emergency Domestic Help Schemes, 17 Dec. 1945, WRVS, H32 Home Helps Policy; Johnston to Reading, 14 June 1945; Ministry of Health, Circular 110/46, 'Home Helps and Domestic Help', 6 June 1946, WRVS, H32/14 Home Helps Pioneer Scheme, Oxford.

[30] WVS, County Borough Organisers' Conference, Minutes 1 Oct., 3 Oct. 1946, WRVS; Report on City of Oxford and WVS Home Help Scheme, Mar. 1945, 1, 3, 5–6. In November 1947 WVS ran a national conference on Home Help schemes, addressed by Bevan, which helped to promote further local initiatives.

[31]

	Full Time	Part Time	Total
End of 1948	3,108	8,230	11,338
End of 1949	3,967	14,688	18,655

(Report on Training Course for Home Help Organizers, June 1950, WRVS, H32/17 Home Helps). For the growth of the Home Helps service from 1950 to 1980, see A. H. Halsey (ed.), *British Social Trends since 1900. A Guide to the Changing Social Structure of Britain* (London, 1988), 478.

the schemes, in 123 towns and sixteen counties, and two years later about a quarter of the 400 home help schemes in existence were run by WVS on an agency basis while WVS also provided assistance to many of the local authority-run schemes.[32] Writing to Bevan in 1949, Lady Reading argued that the pace was now being set not, as in the past, by national legislation but by local initiative: a 'social revolution in the domestic sphere' was 'upthrusting from beneath and shaping its own future'.[33]

The main agents of Lady Reading's revolution from below were leisured ladies whose continuing claim to social leadership was exemplified by their role in promoting the new social service. 'Character and an intense desire to serve', together with experience in the public sphere, were the main qualifications for the job, according to the home help organizer in Salford. Such women knew their way around civic power structures and had the confidence and connections necessary to hustle timid local authorities into implementing Whitehall's welfare agenda.[34] As social revolutions go, this was a remarkably conservative one. The Women's Co-operative Guild, like other predominantly working-class women's organizations, was identified as a source of supply for home helps; but no one thought of inviting them to the WVS's 1947 national conference on the scheme until the last moment, presumably because the conference was intended for potential home help organizers.[35] A few middle-class WVS women, like the part-time home help in Oxford who found herself helping out her former cook, do appear to have been prepared to do domestic work for their social inferiors, but such fundamental role reversals were rare.[36] MacDonald might claim that full-time home helps were being recruited from 'all classes, all kinds, typists, clerks', and that many of the part timers were 'the kind of woman who would be glad to do voluntary work but needs the extra bit of money',[37] but it was

[32] WVS, *Report of Ten Years' Work, 1938–1948* (London, 1948), 24; Report on Training Course for Home Help Organizers (June 1950), WRVS, H32/17 Home Helps; MacDonald, 'WVS and Home Helps'; Report of WVS Conference on Home Helps, 9 May 1950, WRVS, H32 Home Helps Policy.
[33] Reading to Bevan, 28 May 1949, WRVS, H32 Home Helps Policy.
[34] B. Chadwick, 'Experiences of a Home Help Organiser in a County Borough', Mar. 1949, WRVS, H32/17 Home Helps.
[35] WCG Central Committee, Minutes 11–12 Dec. 1947; Report of Inter-Departmental Enquiry into Emergence Domestic Help Schemes, 17 Dec. 1945, WRVS, H32 Home Helps Policy; WVS Regional Administrators' Conference, Minutes, 17 Dec. 1943.
[36] Report on City of Oxford and WVS Home Help Scheme, Mar. 1945, 2, WRVS Box File, Wartime, Home Helps.
[37] Report on City of Oxford and WVS Home Help Scheme, Mar. 1945, 2, WRVS Box File, Wartime, Home Helps; Report of Darlington Meeting on Home Helps, 30 Oct. 1946, WRVS, R/1/2 Darlington. The latter may account for the 808 WVS members identified in a 1948 national survey as working as home helps (Survey of WVS Activity, 1948, WRVS Statistics). In seaside towns, where competition from guest-house landladies made it impossible to obtain home helps, Tothill Street advised local WVS organizers to use WVS volunteers. WVS County Borough Organizers' Conference, 3 Oct. 1946.

clear from the outset that the 'armies of charwomen' that she envisaged would be recruited mainly from the working class.[38]

MacDonald was keen to distinguish her enterprise from contemporaneous efforts to raise the status of domestic service in general. Home helps were represented not as 'domestic drudges', but as social workers helping with any problem that arose, and as 'ordinary homely women' who could act as civilizing agents by 'passing on their own knowledge of housekeeping and family rearing'.[39] While no one was in any doubt that most home helps worked primarily for the money, organizers saw their role as trying 'to stimulate in them a sense of vocation—hard going sometimes'.[40] 'You cannot pay for the spirit of service,' declared one of WVS's more gushing public speakers, 'all you can do is to make the "token" payment to enable them to do a job they will love. The right women must be found.'[41] More mundanely, organizers were advised to look for 'the cook-general type—able to cope'.[42] Participation in this new social service offered, in the words of MacDonald's Oxford recruiting leaflet, 'A New Career for Women . . . a career corresponding very closely to that of the District Nurses, [which] . . . may in time command as much respect . . . If you take up this work you will belong to a public service in the same way as the police, school teachers and nurses are public, not private, servants.'[43] The fact that the home helps were public employees whose services were provided according to need not according to ability to pay enabled home help organizers to deploy the rhetoric of service with rather more authority than could be achieved by the organizers of the National Institute of Homemakers, whose prime purpose was to increase the supply of private domestic servants.[44]

---

[38] The lower ranks of women's auxiliary services were, MacDonald believed, substantially underemployed and would be better used doing emergency domestic service work. (MacDonald, 'Narrative Report on Emergency Home Helps Scheme').

[39] Note on 'The Oxford Scheme' (n.d.) in WRVS, Box File, Wartime, Home Helps; Report of Inter-Departmental Enquiry into Emergency Domestic Help Schemes, 17 Dec. 1945, 6, WRVS, H32 Home Helps Policy; B. Chadwick, 'Experiences of a Home Help Organiser in a County Borough', Mar. 1949, WRVS, H32/17 Home Helps.

[40] Chadwick, 'Experiences of a Home Help Organiser in a County Borough'. Wages were normally set to compete with local factory rates (Report of Inter-Departmental Enquiry into Emergence Domestic Help Schemes, 17 Dec. 1945; Report of Birmingham Home Helps Conference, 11 Oct. 1946, WRVS, H32 Home Helps Policy; Ministry of Health, Circular 110/46, 'Home Helps and Domestic Help', 6 June 1946, copy in WRVS, H32/14 Home Helps Pioneer Scheme, Oxford).

[41] Report of Darlington Meeting on Home Helps, 30 Oct. 1946, WRVS, R/1/2.

[42] Report on City of Oxford and WVS Home Help Scheme, Mar. 1945, 2, WRVS, Box File, Wartime, Home Helps.

[43] Report on City of Oxford and WVS Home Help Scheme, Mar. 1945, 15, WRVS, Box File, Wartime, Home Helps.

[44] In 1948, sensing the indefensibility of public subsidy to the training of private domestic servants, Dorothy Elliot attempted unsuccessfully to promote NIH as a rival to WVS in running local home help schemes on an agency basis (MacDonald, Report on Reports on 7th and 8th meetings of NIH Advisory Council, 15 Apr. 1948 and 30 June 1948, WRVS V131/38 National

Given the shortage of domestic labour MacDonald was worried about her home helps being enticed into private service by her more well-off clients: 'contemptible, but a constant temptation'.[45] Vera Dart, standing as a Labour candidate in the 1945 election, was not out of line with her erstwhile employer when she contrasted the home help system with the injustices of the past: 'In the old days large numbers of people were employed to look after people who did not need it, while working mothers injured their health through lack of help in the house.'[46] Despite progressive intentions, however, the WVS approach to the home help service as an opportunity for members of the urban elite to exercise social leadership in partnership with local authorities ran foul of two powerful forces in post-war Britain: socialism and professionalism.

By 1950 about three-quarters of local home help organizers were directly employed by local authorities, and it had for some time been clear that the WVS role as an agency running schemes on behalf of local authorities was under challenge.[47] Despite optimistic claims that war had transformed Labour attitudes to voluntarism, many labour local authorities remained bitterly hostile. G. D. H. Cole, drawing on the findings of the Nuffield Social Reconstruction Survey, pointed out that 'Labour Councillors, having got control of the local government, are sometimes disposed to try to use it for doing everything, and to reject as unnecessary any close co-operation with voluntary bodies which they suspect of upholding middle-class and anti-socialist views.'[48] The view that voluntary workers should never be used where the work could be done by a paid employee was widely reported at the

Institute of Houseworkers; County Organizers' Meeting, Minutes, 31 May 1948, WRVS, R6). Elliot quickly backed off assuring Reading that the Institute's initiatives on training and certification of home helps were 'in no way [intended to] encroach on the field of organisation, recruitment or administration' (Elliot to Reading, 15 June 1949, WRVS V131/38 National Institute of Houseworkers). Some of her supporters were unhappy about this, on the grounds that 'any girl who enters public service will remain there and be lost to private service...' (MacDonald, Report on the 8th meeting of the NIH Advisory Council, 30 June 1948, WRVS, V131/38).

[45] MacDonald to Reading, 14 Jan. 1946, WRVS, V131/38. See also the speech of the Wembley Home Helps Organizer, Report of Conference on Home Helps Scheme at Caxton Hall, 11–12 Nov. 1947, WRVS, Box File Wartime Home Helps; WVS County Borough Organizers' Conference, Minutes, 3 Oct. 1946.

[46] *Kent and Sussex Courier*, 22 June 1945.

[47] Report on Training Course for Home Help Organizers, June 1950, WRVS H32/17 Home Helps. In May 1948 Lady Reading told organizers that 'the main question facing us at the moment was whether WVS was going to be able to retain the running of the Home Helps Scheme, or whether this was going to be taken over by the Local Authorities' (County Organizers' Meeting, Minutes 31 May 1948, WRVS R6) 9/5/50. Report of WVS Conference on Home Helps, 9 May 1950, WRVS H32 Home Helps Policy.

[48] G. D. H. Cole, 'Mutual Aid Movements in their Relation to Voluntary Social Service', in Bourdillon, *Voluntary Social Services*, 132.

end of the war.[49] In 1946 the Sheffield's Labour council was said to be 'much against voluntary work ... they wish to put all paid people into jobs and not use volunteers unless there should be an emergency.'[50] In Hull, where the WVS leader had laid out plans to use her wartime partnership with the local Tory council as a basis of resistance to further state encroachment on the voluntary sector after the war, the incoming Labour Council made it clear in September 1946 that 'we are not going to allow a voluntary organisation to take over the welfare work of this town ...'.[51]

Equally frustrating to WVS claims to leadership was the attitude adopted by the paid home help organizers themselves. In 1948 the paid organizers set up their own association—the National Association of Home Help Organisers (NAHHO)—chaired by the London County Council's home help organizer in Westminster, Mrs Richey.[52] At first WVS attempted to infiltrate this body with its own members, but it quickly became apparent that the full timers were set on ousting the WVS ladies from any influence in their emergent profession. The NAHHO objected to the WVS role in the training of organizers, and urged the Ministry of Health and local authorities to replace WVS volunteers with paid organizers. A WVS leader who found herself the only unpaid organizer at a meeting called to set up a West Midlands branch of the NAHHO felt that the others regarded her as 'something of a blackleg!'. If so, they would not have been wide of the mark, since she viewed them with obvious contempt: 'not ... of a very educated type', of doubtful administrative ability, and interested only in improving their salaries. In contrast to social leaders like herself the paid organizers appeared to be entirely subordinate to local government officials and to have no access to policy-making: 'none of them have any influence with the committees of their Local Authorities.'[53] MacDonald took a similar view, fearing that as the paid organizers took over from WVS volunteers the future of the home help service would be determined by '*their* standard of intelligence, *their* idea of service. Unhappily they are the kind of people who

[49] Wright-Brown to Eggerton-Warburton, 5 June 1945, WRVS R10 Cumberland; WVS General Purposes Committee, Minutes, 4 July 1945; WVS County Borough Organizers' Conference, Minutes, 18 Oct. 1949, 8; S. Vachell, Wales Region Report, Jan.–Aug 1948, WRVS Regional Reports.
[50] Aykroyd to Halpin, 5 Feb. 1946, WRVS, R2 Yorkshire. The position was similar in Nottingham: Johnson, report on Nottingham, June 1946, WRVS, A1/38 File 5.
[51] Maxse to Capell, 19 Mar. 1943, WRVS, R2/1 Hull; Hull Town Clerk to WVS Regional Organizer, 17 Sept. 1946, WRVS, R2 Yorkshire.
[52] Report on Training Course for Home Help Organizers, June 1950, WRVS, H32/17 Home Helps; Beauman, *Green Sleeves*, 95–6; WVS Chairman's Committee, Minutes, 12 Mar. 1948; The Houseworker, July 1948, in TUC 292/54 76/62a; Report of Conference on Home Helps, July 1949, TUC 292/ 676/1/3.
[53] Ida M.Wilson, Report on the Meeting of Home Help Organizers at Stafford, 8 Oct. 1949, WRVS, H32 Home Helps Policy; MacDonald, Report on Quarterly General Meeting of NAHHO, 22 Jan. 1949, WRVS, H32 Home Helps Policy.

allow circumstances to shape their principles...'.[54] She sought to convince the Ministry of Health that WVS could run the schemes both more efficiently and more cheaply than local authorities, alleging instances in which full-time organizers had refused WVS help because they feared that this would obviate the need for further paid assistance and, with it, increases in their own status and salary. However sympathetic officials might be in private to WVS complaints about 'the prejudices and shortcomings of human nature', and however much Lady Reading might convince herself that she had friends in high places, the Ministry made no attempt to shore up WVS control against the encroachment of the full-time organizers.[55] Accepting that the barbarians were now in control in most localities, MacDonald saw the best strategy for defending her vision as seeking to influence developments through WVS links at national level with the Ministry of Health and the nursing profession.[56] Unless the Ministry could be persuaded to resist what she saw as an unholy alliance between small-minded local authority inertia and the merely trade union concerns of the NAHHO:

gradually trade unionism will become the dominant voice...and although trade unions are all right in their place, a great national health service is more likely to draw its inspiration from disinterested, many-sided and experienced leadership.[57]

By 1960 the WVS were involved in no more than 6 per cent of home help schemes, mainly in southern England. The last WVS-run home help scheme—in East Sussex—was wound up in 1974.[58] MacDonald's fears about the ousting of 'disinterested' social leaders from the service were realized. Moreover, the status aspirations of their paid successors proved, in this instance, as illusory as the opponents of professionalization had feared. In 1956 80 per cent of home help organizers still lacked any professional qualifications and despite the wealth of information accumulated by organizers about families in crisis they were seldom consulted by social workers.[59] In 1989 an ethnographic study of home help organizers reported a low-status group of women lacking professional identity and unable to articulate their objectives in terms that went beyond 'a largely undifferen-

---

[54] MacDonald, Report on Home Helps, 15 Nov. 1949, WRVS, H32 Home Helps Policy.

[55] Report of MacDonald's Interview with Miss Russell-Smith, 26 Nov. 1949; Reading to MacDonald, 22 June 1949; MacDonald to Reading, 27 June 1949, WRVS, H32 Home Helps Policy. See also WVS Country Organizers' Meeting, Minutes, 31 May 1949.

[56] MacDonald, Report on Home Helps, 15 Nov. 1949, WRVS, H32 Home Helps Policy. In May 1950 she urged Lady Reading to take the initiative in establishing a high-level advisory body for the home help service.

[57] MacDonald to Reading, 25 May 1950, WRVS, H32 Home Helps Policy, Sometime in the early 1950s MacDonald gave up the fight and emigrated to Australia.

[58] Beauman, *Green Sleeves*, 97. On the particularly close relationship between WVS and the local authority in East Sussex, see E2/4 E. M. Foster, report on East Sussex, (n.d., 1941?) in NCSRS, E2/4.

[59] Eileen Younghusband, *Social Work in Britain*, i. 320–5.

tiated desire to help'. Significantly the people that they felt most at home
with were the WRVS ladies delivering Meals on Wheels to the elderly.[60]

The civil servants who had identified the Oxford scheme as a model for the
development of home help services at the end of 1945 had drawn attention
to the advantages for local authorities of using WVS for the time-consuming
spade work involved in setting up schemes: 'the organising is done on a
voluntary basis until the scheme can be regarded as operating successfully as
a social service and full-time help paid by the Local Authority becomes
justified.'[61] It was within such a narrative—of voluntary work operating as
a pioneering advance guard of an expanding welfare state—that the quasi-
official 1970s historian of WVS framed her account of the post-war development of home help services: WVS stood proudly, she wrote, *in loco
parentis* to the paid organizers and was happy to yield the initiative to the
NAHHO and the local authorities.[62] Such an interpretation underestimates
the degree to which WVS leaders had sought to resist the professionalization
of the service and experienced this process, not as a triumphant vindication
of the pioneering role of voluntarism, but as a defeat for their attempt to
uphold the social leadership of leisured women as an integral part of the
emergent welfare state. Teresa MacDonald resolved the problem by emi-
grating to Australia in the early 1950s.[63] Other WVS organizers, however,
had to find ways of adjusting to the growing post-war dissociation between
voluntary work and claims to the exercise of social leadership.

Lady Reading was often at pains to stress the democratic nature of her
vision, insisting that 'character matters more than either position or possession' and that the qualities required for the effective exercise of leadership
knew no boundaries of class or status: 'what the world needs is not a few
national leaders but tens of thousands of men and women, who by sho-
uldering responsibility will set an example and be themselves the local
leaders.'[64] Declaring that 'the days of "charity" and patronage are a thing
of the past', she insisted that WVS was a classless organization eager to offer
unpatronizing service to the community.[65] She refused to institute ranks

[60] N. McKegany, 'The Role of Home Help Organisers', *Social Policy and Administration* (Aug.
1989), 23, 2. See also J. Kearney, 'The Home Help Organizer', *Health Service Journal* (July 1975).
[61] Report on Enquiry into Emergency Domestic Help Schemes, 17 Dec. 1945, WRVS, H32
Home Helps Policy.
[62] Beauman, *Green Sleeves*, 95–6.
[63] Ibid., 91.
[64] 'Faith and Character Matter Most', 1958 typscript in WRVS, Lady Reading (Misc.). See
also: 'Leadership is a great responsibility, not a thing one seeks, not a thing one is born to, but a
thing that is acquired though the medium of character built up throughout life' (Lady Reading,
Letter to WVS Members, June 1944, WRVS, R/10 North West Regional Office).
[65] Reading to Ede, 20 Sept. 1948, WRVS, A1/38 File 6. This claim is central to the account of
WVS given by its official historian, who portrays the organization as pioneering a new relationship between voluntary work and the welfare state which put an end, once and for all, to 'Old
Lady Bountiful': Beauman, *Green Sleeves*, 177.

within WVS, insisting as a matter of 'democratic principle that there is complete equality amongst us all and that it is the job that carries the rank and not the person'.[66] 'Not by the genius of the few', ran the WVS motto, 'but by the faithfulness of the many.'[67] Local leadership, Reading argued, should belong not to those 'established persons and the wives of service chiefs' who deemed themselves 'the top dogs because of their status, or the status of their husbands', but to whoever was best fitted to undertake the job in hand.[68] Writing to a WVS county organizer in 1948, Reading drew a significant parallel between changes in the domestic and the public spheres: 'We no longer tell parlourmaids, housemaids and other maids to do jobs, we go and do them ourselves, and in doing them we understand something of the difficulties of the doing and the problems that have got to be faced.' A similarly practical and hands-on approach should be adopted in public work, displacing what she described as 'the unctuous smugness of the past, where having held a committee meeting, we thought we had done everything'.[69]

There was, of course, a tension between such protestations and the fact that by and large WVS organizers were recruited from the social elites. Rhetorically, personal qualities might be privileged over social status but Reading was careful to point out that the two frequently coincided and her address was aimed far more at 'we [who] no longer [have] parlourmaids' than at women rising in the social order. The point was not to take social leadership out of the hands of established elites, but to persuade these elites to adapt their styles of leadership to a changing world. The replacement of snobbish committees with an efficiently organized service for the local authority was intended, not to put an end to the exercise of social leadership by leisured women of the middle class, but, on the contrary, to make such leadership sustainable in the planned society of the future.

Lady Reading overdid the contrast between old-style charity and the WVS approach. While 'unctuous smugness' may well have characterized many of the ladies that she met through her work in the Personal Service League in the 1930s, a readiness to undertake the humble everyday work of personal social service had long been a staple of middle-class female philanthropy. In seeking to rescue the philanthropic tradition from reductive theories of 'social control', recent scholarship has rightly stressed the dedication, courage, and self-sacrifice involved in female poor visiting.[70] Lady Bountiful was

[66] Reading to Worsley, 8 Nov. 1943, WRVS, R5 Kent.
[67] Lady Reading, speech to Annual General Meeting of the Wrens, *Wren*, 186 (1950), 3.
[68] Lady Reading, 'Draft Satement on WVS', 30 Sept. 1947, WRVS, Box 204.
[69] Reading to Judd, 28 June 1948, WRVS, R6/4 Hampshire.
[70] P. Hollis, *Ladies Elect, Women in English Local Government, 1865–1914* (Oxford, 1987), 229 and *passim*; F. K. Prochaska, *The Voluntary Impulse. Philanthropy in Modern Britain* (London, 1988); ead., 'Philanthropy', in F. M. L. Thompson (ed.), *The Cambridge Social*

characterized as much by an ethic of Christian humility and service to those less fortunate than herself as she was by her aspiration to social leadership: the two went hand in hand. There was, moreover, nothing new about Lady Reading's insistence that 'the days of "charity" and patronage are a thing of the past'. Denial of the association between voluntary work and class condescension had been central to expositions of the 'new philanthropy' since the early years of the century.[71] But the historian would be naïve to take at face value a discourse of egalitarian voluntarism which had produced so many premature announcements of the tumbling of class barriers.[72] In the 1940s 'charity work', with its associations of class condescension, was widely rejected in favour of the more acceptable term 'voluntary social service'.[73] Changing the words, however, did not necessarily change the things. The involvement of middle-class volunteers in Mother and Child Welfare Centres or in British Restaurants, it was reported from Hertfordshire, marked them as institutions to be avoided by those who valued their respectability.[74] And Reading's distaste for committees had more to do with her autocratic organizational philosophy than with any attempt at transforming her social leaders into menial workers with no greater status than their own charwomen.

The weakening of the link between voluntary work and the maintenance of middle-class authority had less to do with any democratization of voluntarism than with the consolidation of professionalism. Female middle-class authority, sustained so effectively by WVS during the war, came increasingly to rest more on professional status than on the unpaid labour

History of Britain, 1750–1950, iii, *Social Agencies and Institutions* (Cambridge, 1990); C. Jones, 'Some Recent Trends in the History of Charity', in M. Daunton (ed.), *Charity, Self-interest and Welfare in the English Past* (London, 1996), 58–60.

[71] M. Cahill and T. Jowitt, 'The New Philanthropy: The Emergence of the Bradford Guild of Help', *Journal of Social Policy*, 9 (1980); Keith Laybourn, 'The Guild of Help and the Changing Face of Edwardian Philanthropy', *Urban History*, 20 (1993); R. McKibbin, 'Class and Poverty in Edwardian England', in McKibbin, *The Ideologies of Class: Social Relations in Britain, 1830–1950* (Oxford, 1990); Elizabeth Macadam, *The New Philanthropy: A Study of the Relations between the Statutory and Voluntary Services* (London, 1934); Braithwaite, *The Voluntary Citizen*; Finlayson, *Citizen, State and Social Welfare*.

[72] As Rodney Lowe points out, state-subsidized 'new philanthropy' was throughout a matter of civil servants backing the initiatives of upper- and middle-class philanthropists, rather than putting resources directly into working-class mutual aid (Lowe, 'Welfare's Moving Frontier', *Twentieth Century British History*, 6 (1995), 374). While close attention to the whole range of meanings attributed to philanthropic exchanges by both givers and recipients can undoubtedly enrich our understanding, there is a danger in some treatments 'of loosing sight of material reality in a conflicting babble of messages and signs'. M. Daunton, 'Introduction', in Daunton (ed.), *Charity, Self-interest and Welfare in the English Past* (London, 1996), 3.

[73] Beveridge and Wells, *Evidence for Voluntary Action*, 36. On the evolution of the terminology, see also A. J. Kidd, 'Philanthropy and the "Social History Paradigm"', *Social History*, 21 (1996), 181.

[74] Dr Roper Power, 'The Voluntary Social Services in Hertfordshire' (n.d., 1942), 5, 13 in NCSRS, E2/7.

of public-spirited housewives. The women who willingly embraced the relatively humble roles fulfilled by the post-war WVS in hospitals, care of the elderly, etc., were, no doubt, sustained by Christian traditions of female service long after their access to positions of social leadership had been decisively narrowed by the growing dominance of their professionally qualified sisters. An 'undifferentiated desire to help' sustained the WVS volunteer just as it did the low-status paid home help organizer. Nevertheless past pretensions continued to haunt the organization and the image of Lady Bountiful lingered on. When, from the later 1960s, the voluntary sector entered a new period of growth, WVS appeared old-fashioned and irrelevant to the dynamics of the new voluntarism.

None of this, however, was apparent in the immediate post-war years. The positive attitude to voluntary service adopted by the Attlee government encouraged Lady Reading in her determination to promote WVS not just as a valuable addition to the voluntary sector, but as a far-sighted innovation which would provide the model—'ten years ahead of its time'—for future relations between the voluntary sector and the state.[75]

---

[75] Memo by Lady Reading, 11 Oct. 1946, PRO, CAB 124 914.

Women's Voluntary Services and the Voluntary Sector

While ministers in the Attlee Government were keen to support an ongoing role for voluntary social service in the welfare state, they had few ideas about how this might be organized. Committed to expanding the role of the state and plagued by intractable economic crisis, ministers used whatever voluntary services came to hand but they gave little systematic thought to the overall relationship between the state and the voluntary sector.[1] One issue, however, could not be avoided. Since WVS had been set up by the Home Office in 1938 explicitly in order to serve anticipated wartime needs, a decision would have to be taken on whether or not the organization would be kept in being after the war. WVS had clearly made itself useful to both local authorities and the national state, but for every friend in Whitehall WVS had enemies in the established voluntary sector who saw the organisation, with its national co-ordination, direct state funding, and absence of internal democracy, as an alien competitor incompatible with the principles of voluntarism as they understood them. For several years after the war ministers tried to evade the need to make a decision, and they did their best to transfer responsibility for accommodating Lady Reading's creation onto the National Council of Social Service which spoke for the voluntary sector as a whole. This way of avoiding the issue served mainly to highlight the fundamental incompatibility between WVS and the established organizations. But it also bought time for WVS, during which Lady Reading was able to rebuild the membership after its immediate post-war slump. Vigorously pursuing her strategy of 'mission creep', tireless in seeking out new ways of making WVS indispensable, she was eventually able to convince Attlee's ministers to face down the opposition to continued state funding of WVS voiced not only by the middle-class women's organizations but also by the Labour Women.

I

Opposition to Lady Reading's determination to keep WVS going at the end of the war was, as we have seen, widespread within the organization,

[1] D. Owen, *English Philanthropy, 1660–1960* (Cambridge, Mass., 1965), 543.

and such sentiments were even more apparent among the leaders of the established women's organizations, who, according to the first General Secretary of WVS, had originally agreed to support 'this upstart body with its Government backing...and its dictator Chairman'[2] only on the assurance that it would be closed down when the emergency was over.[3] Already in January 1945 the WI was lobbying the Home Office seeking assurances about the post-war position of WVS, and by the end of the year the WI had decided to withdraw its members from the WVS Advisory Committee. The NUTG withdrew a few months later, a move instigated by members in Hull where wartime rivalry with WVS had been particularly acute.[4] By contrast, more specialist bodies like St John Ambulance, Red Cross, and various disablement organizations tended to be supportive of WVS, which was frequently useful in providing them with non-specialist assistance.[5] Conflicts tended to arise where the WVS organized jointly or in parallel with volunteers from other generalist organizations like the WI, Townswomen's Guilds, or the Women's Co-operative Guild.[6]

Particularly resented was the privileged access enjoyed by WVS to state funds: not simply to grants-in-aid for particular projects, for which any organization could qualify, but finance for basic office and administrative expenses. Such spending was the hardest thing to raise money for from charitable donations and no other voluntary organization apart from the WVS could rely on Government for this kind of help.[7] More important than envy, however, was the fear, eloquently expressed by William Beveridge in

[2] Stella Reading, Some Recollections by her Friends (London, ?1971), 16. Mary Smieton was writing ironically.

[3] WGPW Executive, Minutes, 15 June 1943, WF A1; Brown to Reading, 22 Jan. 1945, WRVS, A1/38 File 4; Farrer to Chuter Ede, 17 Feb. 1948, PRO, HO 45 24302; in Mar. 1941 the NUTG representative on the WGPW had 'asked how other organizations worked with WVS as they were not able to'. WCG Central Committee, Minutes, 11 Mar. and 23 Apr. 1941, Hull University Library, DCW 1/11.

[4] W. B. Brown to Lady Reading, 22 Jan. 1945, WRVS, A1/38 File 4; WVS Chairman's Committee, Minutes, 25 Jan. 1945, 1 Feb. 1945, 20 Dec. 1945, 11 Apr. 1946; NUTG Executive Minutes, 27 Mar. 1946; R. K. Kelsall, Report on Voluntary Work in Hull, 4 Apr. 1942, 12, 27–9, NCSRS E2/8.

[5] Memo on 'Points Arising from Discussions between the NCSS and WVS', n.d.; and Notes on Meeting of Women's Group for Public Welfare, 11 May 1948, both in WRVS, A1/38 File 6; WVS Advisory Council, Minutes, 10 Mar. and 23 June 1948.

[6] Unfortunately for the negotiations, these were precisely the bodies which involved themselves most actively with the NCSS (Reading to Maxwell, 6 Aug. 1948, WRVS, A1/38 File 6).

[7] Extract from Minutes of WGPW Meeting, 8 July 1952 in WRVS, A1/38 File 7; Geraldine M. Aves, The Voluntary Worker in the Social Services (London, 1969), 185. The 'new philanthropy' had long been anxious to build closer links with the state, not least in order to find ways of replacing declining charitable donations with direct subventions from the Treasury. For a contemporary discussion, see Social Service, 21 (1948). Already in 1938 it was estimated that around 37% of the total income of registered charities came from the state as payment for services (C. Braithwaite, The Voluntary Citizen. An Enquiry into the Place of Philanthropy in the Community (London, 1938), 171).

his 1948 report on voluntary action, that this kind of state funding would sap the independence of the voluntary sector and, with it, one of the foundations of democratic life.[8] The WI was especially outspoken, opposing the continuation of WVS on the grounds that: 'It would be a misfortune ... if the Government were to establish and finance on a permanent footing an intermediary women's service likely to overlap with and to undermine the strength of the long-established voluntary and independent women's organizations.'[9] Two years later they reminded the Home Office that in the absence of a democratic constitution WVS could not be treated as a representative women's organization: the Government, they warned, 'should be careful to avoid sacrificing the principles of democracy for the sake of efficiency, and should do nothing which might discourage spontaneous voluntary work for the community through the many and varied channels which now exist.'[10]

Although both sides made efforts to prevent this clash of principles from disrupting everyday co-operation on the ground, Lady Reading had no time for the notion that efficiency should be sacrificed to democracy. 'There is, not unnaturally,' wrote the author of a report on WVS commissioned by Lady Reading for the Beveridge enquiry, 'a certain amount of contempt for organisations of well-meaning people who meet to talk about problems and go home without doing anything more arduous than passing laudable resolutions'.[11] Hostile criticism, in the view of one WVS leader, arose from the fact that the established organizations 'were jealous that we did not have Committees and could [therefore] get on with the work quickly'.[12] What was resented, Reading claimed, was the success of WVS in creating a disciplined service in which members were no longer merely 'individuals to be used according to local whims'.[13] Accusations that WVS was usurping work that rightfully belonged to other organizations arose, she asserted, from the tendency of her committee-ridden rivals to claim that 'they were doing a piece of work when in fact they had merely put it on the agenda to be discussed at a future meeting'.[14] In this spirit Reading fully endorsed the view of the Conservative leader Marjorie Maxse that the WGPW were

[8] Lord Beveridge, *Voluntary Action. A Report on Methods of Social Advance* (London, 1948), 10.
[9] Beveridge and Wells, *The Evidence for Voluntary Action* (London, 1949), 137–8; WVS Advisory Committee, Minutes, 27 Mar. 1946; Strachey to Chuter Ede (n.d.), circulated by the Economic Information Committee on 25 June 1947, and SCL to Morrison, 26 June 1947, PRO, CAB 124 914.
[10] Farrer to Under-Secretary of State, 2 Mar. 1949, PRO, HO 45 24302.
[11] A. MacDonald, Report for Beveridge Enquiry, Apr. 1947, 3, 3, WRVS, Histories in Draft (Box 204).
[12] WVS County Borough Organizers' Conference, Minutes, 18 Oct. 1949, 7, WRVS.
[13] Reading to Chuter Ede, 11 Oct. 1946, PRO, CAB 129 914.
[14] WVS County Borough Organizers' Conference, Minutes, 22 Apr. 1947.

'an assembly of impractical theorists', who 'have a definite antagonism against us because we want things to be done on a practical basis'.[15] WVS saw itself as an organization of caring, no-nonsense, practical women anxious to get on with the job in hand without wasting time on the speculative theorizing characteristic, they believed, of the liberal philanthropic establishment.

At the end of the war, aware that the process of discovering continuing roles for WVS would depend heavily on the imagination and initiative of local organizers, Lady Reading had formally renounced her right to issue instructions to them on the work that they should undertake, and internal circulars were subsequently sent out as suggestions rather than as orders.[16] At the same time, however, she rejected suggestions that there should be any 'changes in the Hierarchy'.[17] It was precisely the undemocratic and committee-free character of the organization which, in her view, put it 'ten years ahead' of its rivals. WVS, Reading insisted, represented 'not just one more voluntary organisation' but a new kind of volunteering adapted to the needs of the modern state. As a 'voluntary auxiliary' prepared to work under the aegis of central and local government, WVS was clearly superior to the 'hit-and-miss old-world charitable voluntary service conception', offering to the statutory authorities a means both of coping with emergencies and of integrating volunteers into the ongoing provision of welfare services 'on a much tidier basis than heretofore'. WVS was the perfect instrument for organizing voluntary work in the new interventionist order, providing an effective transmission belt for the 'translation of central objectives to the lowest level in order that the central idea can be carried through to local action'.[18] At a time when the increased flow of state welfare provision, coupled with higher taxation and the drying up of charitable funds, was threatening the very principle of voluntary service, Reading claimed that WVS had found the key to preserving voluntary action. While charitable donations would continue to play an important role in sustaining the more specialized voluntary organizations, the administrative costs involved in supplying the modern state with the armies of the volunteers that it needed could best be met from public funds: 'people should give of their muscle, their sweat and their thought, rather than of their purse'.[19] WVS should be

[15] Maxse to Reading, 3 Sept. 1947, Reading to Maxse, 10 Oct. 1947, WRVS, V/101/38 Conservative Party.
[16] WVS Chairman's Committee, 20 Sept. 1945; WVS County Borough Organizers' Conference, 1 Oct. 1945. Chambers suggested in 1954 that the prestige of Reading was such that, to all intents and purposes, a suggestion from Tothill Street was treated by organizers (whose own autocracy was unchanged) as an instruction (R. C. Chambers, 'A Study of Three Voluntary Organisations', in D. V. Glass (ed.), *Social Mobility in Britain* (London, 1954), 390).
[17] Strutt to Reading, 3 Nov. 1945; Reading to Strutt, 14 Nov. 1945, WRVS, A1/38 File 4.
[18] Memo by Lady Reading, 11 Oct. 1946, PRO, CAB 124 914.
[19] Lady Reading, 'Draft Satement on WVS', 30 Sept. 1947, WRVS, Box 204; Beveridge and Wells, *Evidence for Voluntary Action*, 140.

seen not as 'a voluntary organisation financed by the State, but [as] a State service furnished by volunteers', a 'happy experiment' which had demonstrated that financial dependence was perfectly compatible with the 'functional autonomy' necessary to the voluntary sector's role in meeting emergency needs and pioneering new services.[20] 'The days of "charity" and patronage are a thing of the past', wrote Lady Reading:

but there is in the WVS a body of women in every part of the country and of all classes who are ready and willing to carry on this new time [as against money] service to the community if the right channels for voluntary activity in the modern state can but be joined to the greatly increased flow of provision by the State.[21]

By keeping open these channels—the work of organization and co-ordination in which they had become so skilled—WVS could give women meaningful work to do on behalf of the statutory authorities, thereby fostering 'a national welfare consciousness...in the individual' and preventing the coming of the welfare state from destroying those well-springs of voluntarism which were so central to the character of the nation. 'This philosophical aspect', she added characteristically, 'is to my mind the most important'.[22]

II

Lady Reading's pleas did not fall on deaf ears. The decision of the incoming Labour Government in September 1945 to extend the life of WVS for at least two years reflected a widespread belief among civil servants that the kind of auxiliary voluntary services provided by WVS would be indispensable in the transition to peace. Pending any more permanent arrangement it was agreed that Home Office funding would continue on the wartime basis, although departments making regular use of WVS services were now required to contribute to the costs.[23]

---

[20] Reading at Organizers' Meeting in Cambridge, 31 Oct. 1944, WRVS, R4 Regional Office; Reading to Chuter Ede, 20 Sept. 1948, WRVS, A1/38 File 4. A lengthy exposition of Reading's philosophy, prepared for submission to the Beveridge Enquiry in 1947 by the husband of a WVS volunteer, argued that 'as the progressive socialisation of the state is realised' the WVS model would become the norm, rendering obsolete previous notions of voluntarism: 'it does not matter very much whether it fits into previously accepted categories or establishes a fresh norm' (MacDonald, Report for Beveridge Enquiry).

[21] Reading to Chuter Ede, 20 Sept. 1948, WRVS, A1/38 File 4.

[22] Reading to Chuter Ede, 30 Sept. 1946, PRO, CAB 129 914.

[23] Memo by Home Secretary to Lord President's Committee, 28 Aug. 1945, CAB 71 21; Lord President's Committee, Minutes, 7 Sept. 1945, PRO, CAB 71 19; H. Land, R. Lowe, and N. Whiteside, *The Development of the Welfare State, 1939–5. Guide to Documents in the Public Records Office* (London, 1992), 184–7. From April 1946 financial responsibility for local WVS offices was transferred from local authorities to central government (Sir A. Salisbury MacNalty (ed.), *The Civilian Health and Medical Services*, i (London, 1953), 231). These arrangements were renewed in 1947 and again in 1951 after ministers were advised that, despite complaints from less-privileged organizations, the amounts involved were too trivial to require

Following the initial stay of execution, Lady Reading continued to lobby for some more general assurance, explaining how difficult it was to develop new projects with local authorities in the absence of any guarantee that WVS would continue beyond September 1947.[24] Eventually, in December 1946, renewed pressure from the Ministry of Health secured a meeting of officials from interested departments to consider whether 'the organisation and tradition built up by the WVS' could be incorporated into long-term arrangements for future co-operation between statutory authorities and the voluntary sector.[25] While the officials believed that the 'maid-of-all-work' character of WVS represented 'exactly the kind of assistance the public services of the future will need', they were also convinced that it would be impossible to justify a long-term policy of singling out WVS from all the other voluntary societies for the payment of administrative expenses from public funds. The solution, they argued, was to establish a federal body broadly representative of the voluntary sector as a whole which could both recruit volunteers directly and co-ordinate work undertaken for statutory services by existing organizations. The obvious organization to undertake this task was the NCSS which had been established in 1918 precisely in order to foster co-operation between the sector and the state. The Whitehall view was that the NCSS had proved ineffective in this role and was in need, as one Treasury official put it, of 'rejuvenescence'. WVS, on the other hand, had developed the necessary machinery, but was not in a position to speak for the voluntary sector as a whole. The way forward proposed by the officials was to request the NCSS to develop the necessary local machinery in co-ordination with WVS, leading effectively to the fusion of the two organizations. This, they acknowledged, would not be easy, since it required the established organizations to accept the cuckoo in their nest, and the cuckoo to accommodate to the sensitivities of its adoptive parents.[26] However much such a rationalization of relations with the voluntary sector might appeal to civil servants and their political masters, the mixing of WVS oil with NCSS water always appeared an improbable prospect to those outside the Whitehall machine.

specific statutory authorization (Maxwell to Reading, 15 Mar. 1947, WRVS, A1/38 File 5; Memo by Home Secretary on Future of WVS, Dec. 1950, PRO, CAB 132 16 LP (50) 102; Lord President's Committee, Minutes, 12 Jan. 1951, PRO, CAB 132 17).

[24] Reading to Ede, 31 July 1946, WRVS, A1/38 File 5; Reading to Ede, 30 Sept. 1946, PRO, CAB 129 914.

[25] In December 1946 the Ministry of Food—alienated by WVS's exclusive claim to ownership of the Food Leader scheme—had been the only department to dissent from the Whitehall consensus that WVS should be encouraged to take on a co-ordinating role in the interface between the voluntary sector as a whole and government (John Strachey to Home Secretary, circulated to Economic Information Committee, 25 June 1947, PRO, CAB 124 914; A. Wilson, record of interview with Lady Hillingdon, 17 Oct. 1946, PRO, MAF 102 20).

[26] Minutes of inter-departmental meeting, 5 Dec. 1946, PRO, CAB 124 914. See also 'Note of a meeting held at the Treasury... between Lady Reading and Sir Alan Barlow', 17 Dec. 1947, WRVS, A1/38 File 5.

As the officials had feared, Lady Reading was from the start dismissive of the NCSS: 'the leading spirits of that council are too old and its reputation too poor.' Moreover she warned that any attempt by the Labour Government to force through a general rationalization of the voluntary sector, however desirable this might be in theory, would raise fears of regimentation and 'nationalization' among the established voluntary organizations. Brushing aside the difficulty of maintaining privileged access for WVS to Treasury funds, she pressed for a five-year extension of the September 1947 deadline.[27] She had a powerful ally in Herbert Morrison, who as Lord President of the Council was ultimately responsible for sorting out Government relations with the voluntary sector. Morrison was inclined to agree with Lady Reading's view of the NCSS and 'felt that there was a good case for singling the WVS out from other organisations as regards continuing Government financial assistance'.[28] Nye Bevan, who had been instrumental in securing the September 1945 stay of execution and continued to be helpful, warned Reading that talks with the NCSS were unavoidable.[29] In April 1947 the Home Secretary, Chuter Ede, acting on the advice of his permanent secretary, Sir Alexander Maxwell, announced:

arrangements have been made for consultations to take place between WVS and the NCSS . . . as a first step to exploring . . . how [WVS] can best be fitted into the general pattern of Social Service rendered throughout the country by numerous voluntary bodies, and how any financial assistance given by the Exchequer can best be used to promote those forms of voluntary work which are of special assistance to Government Departments and Local Authorities.

In the meantime existing funding arrangements would continue, and local authorities were encouraged to consider new ways in which they could make use of WVS.[30] At Lady Reading's insistence the statement made no reference to Chuter Ede's proposed two-year deadline for the completion of the new arrangements—'she would be unable to keep her workers together if there were a time limit hanging over their heads'—and omitted the clear statement of the Home Office's preferred outcome, which had been spelled out in an earlier draft of the statement: 'Under such a plan the WVS would continue as a service having special functions, but it would become an agency of a central organisation [i.e. a revamped NCSS] to which various voluntary

[27] Pimlott to Morrision, 11 Feb. 1947, PRO, CAB 124 914.

[28] Pimlott, 'Note for Record', 14 Feb. 1947, PRO, CAB 124 914. Morrison had been much impressed by WVS whilst he was Minister of Home Security during the war (MacDonald Report for Beveridge Enquiry.)

[29] Bevan to Reading, 18 Apr. 1946, Bevan to Ede, 27 Aug. 1945, PRO, MH 130 277; Lord President's Committee, Minutes, 7 Sept. 1945, PRO, CAB 71 19.

[30] House of Commons, Debates, 436, Written Answers, 133-4; WVS Chairman's Committee, Minutes, 24 Feb. 1947, WRVS.

societies would be federated,' and through which any government funds would be channelled.[31]

Although there had been some exploratory talks between WVS and the NCSS at the end of the war,[32] neither organization would have chosen to pursue closer relations had it not been for Home Office pressure. The talks were conducted between Lady Reading (together with her most senior deputies, Kathleen Halpin and Alice Johnson) and Sir William Deedes,[33] vice-chair of the NCSS, accompanied by George Haynes, the NCSS General Secretary. Deedes, who was keen to promote more systematic co-operation between Councils of Social Service and local authorities, may well have thought that some accommodation with WVS would be helpful. But he was well aware that the divergence between WVS centralism and the local autonomy prized within the voluntary sector more generally constituted a major obstacle.[34]

From the outset, Deedes' freedom of manœuvre was restricted by the attitude of the other women's organizations. Far from welcoming the prospect of the NCSS being refashioned as a more effective instrument of co-operation between the state and the voluntary sector, the leaders of the main women's organizations represented on the WGPW were intensely suspicious of the negotiations and hostile to any arrangement that might give WVS a co-ordinating role in the organization of voluntary work.[35] For once leaders of the middle-class organizations and Labour women saw eye to eye. Alice Cook, General Secretary of the Women's Co-operative Guild, had been instrumental in pushing Ede to go public on his intentions for WVS, and she saw the Women's Group as a key forum for keeping up the pressure on the Home Secretary to put an end to the privileged financial status enjoyed by WVS.[36] When Haynes tried to explain the purpose of the talks to the Women's Group in May 1947 he was met by a chorus of complaints about WVS imperialism. Reporting privately to Lady Reading on the 'bitter feeling' displayed at this meeting, one of the women present explained that the

[31] 'Future of the WVS', 15 Mar. 1947, WRVS, A1/38 File 5; Maxwell to Ede, 19 Apr. 1948, PRO, HO 45 24302.
[32] WVS Chairman's Committee, Minutes, 18 Oct., 8 Nov. 1945, WRVS.
[33] Brigadier-General Sir Wyndham (Henry) Deedes (1883–1956). He gave up a career in Middle Eastern colonial administration at end of the First World War to live in the Oxford settlement house in Bethnal Green; served as a Labour member of the LCC for Bethnal Green from 1941 to 1946 and was chair of the London Council of Social Service during the war. The philosopher Ernest Barker paid tribute to him as the man who drew him into the NCSS: 'always my prophet—a veiled prophet, a shy prophet...' (Sir Ernest Barker, 'Community Centres. Memories from the 1930s', *Social Service*, 21 (1947), 114).
[34] On Deedes' views, see A. M. Watson, 'Social Service and Civic Responsibility', *Social Service*, 22 (1948), 7; Halpin to Reading, 25 July 1947, WRVS, A1/38 File 5; Report on Meeting of WGPW, 13 May 1947, WRVS, A1/38 File 5.
[35] Report on Meeting of WGPW, 13 May 1947.
[36] Women's Co-operative Guild, Central Council, Minutes, 13–14 Mar., 25 May, 22 June, 4 Sept. 1947, WCG DCW 1/11.

delegates 'seemed quite certain that it would be their prerogative to make or break the future of WVS and that it lay with them to absorb it or not as they chose'.[37]

In this atmosphere the negotiators decided to start by gathering information about the relationship between WVS and local Councils of Social Service. Anxious to avoid stirring up further antagonism before they had any positive proposals to put forward, they carried out these inquiries as discreetly as possible and in only a small number of selected localities.[38] The results, as might have been expected, were inconclusive: in some areas co-operation was good, in others inadequate or non-existent. Apart from the obvious step of ensuring that WVS was represented on local Councils of Social Service, Deedes proposed that the Councils be encouraged to set up 'clearing houses' to which all requests by the local authority for voluntary assistance would be submitted in the first instance. While he allowed that in exceptional circumstances a local authority might go direct to WVS, and admitted that the local coverage of NCSS was patchy, his main concern was to enlist Home Office support in a drive for the universal establishment of Councils of Social Service so that they could provide the necessary machinery of co-ordination throughout the country.[39] The implication was that in any redirection of Government funds first priority should be given to universalizing the local coverage of the NCSS so that it could play the main co-ordinating role. This was unacceptable to Reading since it implied that whoever ran the local CSS would be in a position to dictate to WVS what work they could or could not undertake. She had, she claimed, been assured at the outset by the Home Office that 'any collusion ... would be in an equal partnership and under no circumstances whatsoever would WVS be put under the NCSS either as to finance or anything; in fact,' she added, provocatively, 'quite the reverse.'[40] WVS, she reminded Deedes, acted as 'an auxiliary service work[ing] direct to the Local Authority or through its headquarters to a Government Department. When requested to undertake specific jobs ... WVS Centre Organisers should notify the local Council of Social Service where it exists', but they could not be beholden to the CSS for permission to undertake the work.[41] Effective co-operation, WVS insisted, would be impossible unless the constituent organizations of the NCSS accepted that WVS 'must conduct its own discussions and make its own arrangements with Government departments.'[42] Where work commissioned

---

[37] Report on Meeting of WGPW, 13 May 1947.

[38] D. H. W. Hall to NCSS Regional Organizers, 'Women's Voluntary Services', 13 June 1947; WVS Circular to Regional Organizers, 16 June 1947, WRVS, A1/38 File 5.

[39] Deedes, 'Discussions between the NCSS and WVS', 25 July 1947, WRVS, A1/38 File 5.

[40] Reading, Report of Discussion with Deedes, 3 Sept. 1947, ibid.

[41] 'Adaptation of Memorandum Prepared by Sir William Deedes', 10 Dec. 1947, ibid.

[42] 'Memorandum on Relations between NCSS and WVS', 22 Dec. 1947, ibid.

by a Local Authority required co-operation between a number of voluntary organizations, WVS was happy for co-ordination to be provided by the local Council of Social Service 'where it exists'. Elsewhere, instead of waiting for the NCSS to achieve national coverage equivalent to that already claimed by WVS, the normal procedure would be for WVS to act as the co-ordinating body.[43]

By October 1947 it was already clear to Deedes that the 'principles and methods of work' of the two organizations were so different that no generally applicable machinery of co-ordination was likely to emerge unless the Home Office itself laid down the ground rules.[44] For several months over the winter of 1947–8 drafts were exchanged of a document designed to clarify the *modus operandi* of the two organizations, but these did more to elucidate irreconcilable differences than to provide any basis for agreement.[45] All that could be agreed was the establishment of high-level monthly meetings to exchange information and, if possible, defuse disputes between WVS and other voluntary bodies.[46] Deedes, however, rejected WVS proposals that they should experiment with arrangements for closer co-operation in a few localities, or conduct a second survey of co-operation between WVS and other organizations in areas where no Council of Social Service existed.

From the start of the negotiations Deedes and Haynes had refused to discuss the issues of principle involved with the Women's Group, arguing that until there was some progress to report the discussions were best kept secret. In November 1947 frustration at their exclusion from the talks erupted in bitter condemnations of WVS at a meeting of the WGPW executive led by a powerful combination of the WI and the WCG.[47] In January 1948 the SJC lobbied Chuter Ede, who assured them that the public subsidy to WVS was being cut back. They resolved to 'watch closely the progress of the plan for the fusion of WVS and NCSS'.[48] In February the WI reminded the Home Secretary that they had agreed to support WVS in 1938 'on the understanding that the new body was being formed for wartime purposes only'.[49] With negotiations effectively stalled during the early months of

---

[43] 'Adaptation of Memorandum Prepared by Sir William Deedes', 10 Dec. 1947, ibid.
[44] Deedes to Reading, 11 Oct. 1947, ibid.
[45] 'Note of a Meeting Held at the Treasury... between Lady Reading and Sir Alan Barlow', 17 Dec. 1947, ibid.
[46] Reading to Deedes, 13 Jan. 1948; Meeting between WVS and NCSS, Minutes, 21 Jan. 1948, WRVS, A1/38 File 6; Reading, Report of Discussion with Deedes, 3 Sept. 1947; Deedes to Reading, 11 Oct. 1947; Reading to Deedes, 25 Oct. 1947, WRVS, A1/38 File 5.
[47] Patterson to Reading, 10 Nov. 1947; Bondfield to Reading, 19 Dec. 1947, WRVS, A1/38 File 5; WGPW Executive, Minutes, 9 Dec. 1947, WF A1.
[48] Women's Co-operative Guild, Central Council, Minutes, 11–12 Feb. 1948, WCG DCW 1/11; SJC Minutes, 12 Feb., 13 May, 2 Sept. 1948, Labour Party NEC, Minutes (Harvester microform).
[49] Farrer to Ede, 17 Feb. 1948, PRO, HO 45 24302.

1948, it became increasingly clear to members of the Women's Group that the main effect of their continuing observance of the NCSS request not to campaign openly against the continuance of WVS while the talks continued was to allow Lady Reading a free run in Whitehall. It seemed to them that Reading was stringing the NCSS along while exploiting her privileged access to public funds to launch a major new recruiting campaign.[50] In April a WGPW deputation including Gertrude Horton (NUTG) and two Labour women, Alice Cook (WCG) and Nancy Adam (TUC), finally met the NCSS negotiating team, and subsequently forwarded a memorandum, drafted by Frances Farrer of the WI, outlining the principles they believed to be at stake. Uppermost in their minds was what they clearly saw as an urgent need to defend the integrity of the voluntary sector against the hybrid nature of WVS. Was it going to take its place alongside members of the Women's Group as a 'genuine voluntary organisation' or would it continue as 'an auxiliary Government Service'? If the former, they insisted, it would have to adopt a democratic constitution, and agree to avoid encroaching on spheres of action already occupied by other bodies. If the latter then it should drop the misleading word 'voluntary' from its title, and 'its work should be clearly defined, so as to in no way overlap with, or undermine, that of the free voluntary organisations'. Any suggestion that WVS might act as a co-ordinator for the work of other women's groups was firmly rejected.[51] Not everyone was happy with the WGPW statement and the representative of St John Ambulance, in particular, sprang to the defence of WVS when it was discussed at the Women's Group.[52] Nevertheless, the endorsement of such an uncompromising position by the major women's organizations can only have served to reinforce the belief of the NCSS negotiators that their differences with WVS were irreconcilable.

In March 1948 the two sides had agreed to ask Chuter Ede to rule on whether they should be talking simply about WVS/NCSS relations, or whether they were also expected to advise on the proper relations between WVS itself and the statutory authorities.[53] Reading lobbied Maxwell requesting a negative answer to the latter question: co-operation between the two bodies would be facilitated, she assured him, if Deedes was firmly told that neither the status of WVS itself, nor its internal machinery of government, were part of the negotiable issues.[54] After a delay of nearly three

---

[50] WGPW Executive, Minutes, 10 Feb., 13 Apr., 8 June 1948, WF A1; Farrer to Wall, 31 May 1948, PRO, HO 45 24302.

[51] 'Memorandum Presented to NCSS by Delegates from the WGPW' (n.d.), WRVS, A1/38 File 6; NFTG Executive, Minutes, 17 Mar. 1948; WGPW Executive, Minutes, 13 Apr. 1948, WF A1. Nancy Adam was reported as making the same point: MacDonald, 'Note on 7th Meeting of Advisory Council of National Institute of Houseworkers', 15 Apr. 1948, WRVS, V131/38.

[52] 'Rough Notes of a Meeting of WGPW', 11 May 1948, WRVS, A1/38 File 6.

[53] Reading and Deedes to Ede, 22 Mar. 1948, ibid.

[54] Reading to Maxwell, 28 May 1948, ibid.

months, Maxwell finally responded by spelling out clearly that what the
Home Office was looking for was not just an arrangement to prevent friction
and overlapping, but 'the formulation of some provisional plan for the
creation of a new national organisation serving purposes similar to
those at present served both by the National Council and the WVS'. Unless
they could deliver an outline of a future scheme within the next six weeks
Maxwell threatened either to appoint an independent committee of enquiry
or an independent chairman for the talks, a proposal he had already cleared
with the Treasury.[55] The NCSS was horrified. As Haynes told his executive,
Maxwell's new formulation went far beyond anything that he or Deedes had
ever considered either feasible or desirable, and they reiterated their view
that no progress could be made until the Government clarified its own
thinking on 'the precise nature of the status and relation to the statutory
services of WVS in the future'.[56] It was, Deedes insisted, impossible for the
NCSS to work out any plan for co-operation until it knew whether or not
WVS 'was to be regarded as a voluntary organisation in the generally
accepted sense of the term or not'. Moreover, no agreement would be
possible unless WVS agreed not to take on any new projects without
prior consultation with other voluntary organizations through whatever
joint machinery emerged.[57] Reading, on the other hand, welcomed the
proposal for an independent chairman, encouraged, no doubt, by a suggestion that the job would be given to a senior Treasury official known to share
her dim view of the capacities of the elderly men leading the NCSS. The
NCSS reaction confirmed her worst fears and she responded by again
spelling out her bottom line: any requirement for prior consultation on
new projects with an organization which was 'entirely theoretical in outlook
and works on a basis that nothing can be done except by precedent' would
fatally undermine the chief virtue of WVS: its capacity to make rapid and
innovative responses to unanticipated demands.[58]

Since its inception at the meeting of officials in December 1946 the project
of fusion between NCSS and WVS had been masterminded by Sir Alexander
Maxwell, permanent secretary at the Home Office. His retirement, aged 68,
in the summer of 1948, coming on top of the deadlocked talks, finally put an
end to the pressure for fusion.[59] Reading was delighted. Maxwell's successor

[55] Maxwell to Reading, 11 June 1948, ibid.; Maxwell to Ede, 19 Apr. 1948, PRO, HO
45 24302.
[56] NCSS Executive, Minutes, 8 July 1948, NCVO Box 154.
[57] Deedes to Maxwell, 22 July 1948, WRVS, A1/38 File 6.
[58] Reading to Maxwell, 14 June 1948; Reading to Deedes, 22 June 1948; Reading to Ede,
5 Aug. 1948; Reading to Maxwell, 6 Aug. 1948, WRVS, A1/38 File 6.
[59] Alexander Maxwell (1880–1963) had been permanent secretary at the Home Office since
1938. Samuel Hoare remembered him as possessing 'the imperturbable assurance essential to a
department of historic tradition' (*Dictionary of National Biography*, 1961–71 (Oxford, 1981),
744), which was precisely Lady Reading's problem with him.

at the Home Office, she believed, understood WVS better and had 'a more practical approach to life'. 'Although I am devoted to Sir Alexander', Reading wrote, '[he] is definitely very Old School, [and] keeps on bleating that it might be difficult for ministers to recommend that WVS should be in a "privileged position" '.[60] With Maxwell gone, and the pressure for fusion with the NCSS removed, Reading was optimistic that the time was now ripe for a new attempt to persuade Chuter Ede to accept WVS and its funding arrangements as a permanent feature of the post-war order.

III

By 1948 WVS was well on the road to recovery from its post-war decline. Previous chapters have documented some aspects of its work in the later 1940s—on food and fuel economy and in the development of Home Help services. But the range of WVS activity was far broader. Many of the wartime activities continued—national savings, salvage, the distribution of ration books, welfare work for the armed forces both at home and overseas. WVS played a major role in the resettlement of refugee Poles and in welfare work with the influx of European Volunteer Workers. Another major area of work was with the Ministry of Health, where WVS came to occupy a central position in the organization of volunteers in hospitals and services for old people—most notably the provision of Meals on Wheels.[61] A June 1948 survey of over 80,000 WVS members showed a quarter working on national savings and a similar number on various food-related schemes. Other major areas included old people (15 per cent), salvage (10 per cent), child welfare (8 per cent), and hospital work (5 per cent).[62] Although its civil defence obligations had disappeared at the end of the war, WVS remained invaluable to Government as an emergency organization organizing refugee reception, helping out at railway accidents, and, most importantly, re-mobilizing wartime volunteers during the floods of 1947 to organize evacuation, emergency feeding and clothing, and the distribution of relief funds.[63] Confident that she had seen off the threat from the NCSS and that the indispensability of her organization was now beyond question, Reading again approached the Home Secretary in the autumn of 1948 requesting that

[60] Reading to Garrett, 11 Aug. 1948. Maxwell's successor, Sir Frank Newsam, was 13 years younger (b. 1893).
[61] MacNalty, *Civilian Health and Medical Services*, 238–9. For an account of WVS work in this area, see Katherine Bentley Beauman, *Green Sleeves. The Story of WVS/WRVS* (London, 1977).
[62] Survey of WVS work, June 1948, WRVS, Box 53. This report was prepared for Bevan (Clarke to Hawton, 19 July 1948, PRO, MH 130 253).
[63] Lord Beveridge and A. F. Wells, *The Evidence for Voluntary Action* (London, 1949), 138; MacNalty, *Civilian Health and Medical Services*, 232; MacDonald, Report for Beveridge Enquiry.

the Government should make a permanent decision on the future of WVS.[64] To her intense irritation, however, she was immediately confronted with a new political hurdle.

In an effort to seize the initiative following the collapse of the WVS/NCSS talks, the SJC had drawn up precisely the kind of outline proposals for co-ordinating the work undertaken by voluntary organizations for Government Departments and local authorities that Maxwell had requested.[65] They proposed the establishment of a co-ordinating body representative of national women's organizations through which all requests for voluntary help by Government Departments would be channelled. The expenses of this body would be paid from public funds, and any grants made to particular organizations for specific pieces of work would be distributed through this committee. The national co-ordinating body would have no responsibility for voluntary work undertaken for local authorities which, the SJC argued, could best be co-ordinated by local committees of women's groups established at the instigation of the local authority concerned.

If Maxwell's fusion project had foundered on the divergent *modus operandi* of the NCSS and WVS, the SJC proposals suffered from the opposite problem—they were drafted as though there had been no previous history of voluntary/statutory co-operation at all. In the world of Labour women the assumption that Ede could start from a blank sheet may have had some plausibility: voluntary social service was not an activity to which the affiliates of the SJC had given much thought before the 1940s. No mention was made of the SCWOs, the obvious bodies for any co-ordination between local authorities and women's organizations, and the only mention of the NCSS was a token remark that care should be taken to avoid overlapping. So far as WVS was concerned, the SJC had always objected to what they saw as its illegitimately centralizing implications as an agent for Whitehall to impose its will on local authorities,[66] and their scheme went further than the Women's Group in assuming that Whitehall would cease to have any special relationship with the organization. The only place for WVS, within the SJC scheme, was as a genuinely self-financing voluntary organization, with the same right as any other women's organization to bid through the national co-ordinating committee to undertake work for Government Departments.[67]

[64] Reading to Chuter Ede, 20 Sept. 1948, WRVS, A1/38 File 4.
[65] This was done at Ede's request, after SJC leaders met him in October to find out what had happened to the WVS/NCSS talks (SJC, Minutes, 2 Sept., 7 Oct., 25 Nov. 1948, Labour Party NEC, Minutes (Harvester microform)).
[66] Sutherland to Hoare, 16 Sept. 1938, WRVS, V95/38, SJCIWO. See also Herbert Morrison cited in T. J. Crosby, *The Impact of Civilian Evacuation in the Second World War* (London, 1986), 18.
[67] SJC, Memo on WVS, Oct. 1948, PRO, CAB 124 914.

Not surprisingly Lady Reading was unimpressed by this blueprint, and she had little difficulty in showing that the proposed national co-ordinating committee would involve a quite unrealistic degree of centralization, citing a series of activities in which WVS was currently involved in which the Whitehall department concerned had no way of knowing what exactly needed to be done at local level. It was precisely the combination of local knowledge and national hierarchy embodied in WVS that made it such a valuable instrument for Whitehall. Moreover, even if Government depart ments could acquire the knowledge necessary to offer discrete bits of work to particular organizations, the ethos of many of the established women's organizations would not allow national leaders to pledge their largely autonomous local groups to undertake the work.[68] Although these were cogent arguments, Ede appears to have felt that it was politically necessary to treat the SJC scheme seriously, even to the extent of giving Mary Sutherland the impression that he would back her on ending the privileged financial position of WVS. When Herbert Morrison got wind of this he forcefully reminded the Home Secretary of an earlier discussion in which Ede had accepted 'that it was right to distinguish the WVS from other voluntary organisations for purposes of Government financial support, and that in the event of there being any difficulty about maintaining this line, you would take the matter to the Lord President's Committee'.[69] Consequently, when Ede convened a joint meeting of WVS and the SJC under his own chairmanship in February 1949, he ruled out any discussion of the financial issue. The ensuing discussion was desultory, enlivened only by an exchange between the WVS organizer for Worcestershire who reported that WVS acted as the co-ordinator of voluntary work in her county and the Home Secretary who replied that such an arrangement would not be acceptable in his own constituency of South Shields, where, much to Tothill Street's embarrassment, there had been bad feeling between WVS and the local Labour Party.[70]

One curious feature of Home Office pressure on the NCSS to negotiate a merger with WVS had been the lack of attention to the obvious gender mismatch between the two organizations. While Deedes was keen to promote his Councils of Social Service as the main clearing house for local

[68] Reading, 'Memorandum on WVS', Dec. 1948, PRO, CAB 129 914.
[69] Morrison to Ede, 24 Jan. 1949; Ede to Morrison, 25 Jan. 1949, PRO, CAB 124 914. Cook also believed that Ede had 'accepted' the SJC position: Women's Co-operative Guild, Central Council, Minutes, 10–11 Jan., 10–11 Mar. 1949, WCG DCW 1/11. It is clear from Ede's exchange of letters with Morrison that the Home Secretary was less impressed by Lady Reading's claims than the Lord President. He may well have led the SJC women to believe that they had his backing.
[70] Rough Note of Meeting held at Home Office, 4 Feb. 1949, WRVS, A1/38 File 6. For the tensions in South Shields, see Chatfield to Halpin, 20 Feb. 1946; Halpin to Reading, 21 Feb. 1946; Reading to Halpin ('I attach the greatest importance to this . . . '), 21 Feb. 1946; Halpin to Chatfield, 26 Feb. 1946; Chatfield, Report on South Shields, 4 Mar. 1946, WRVS, R1/2 South Shields.

authority relations with the voluntary sector, the WGPW, excluded from the talks, preferred to see the local Standing Committees of Women's Organisations as the natural successor bodies to WVS when, as they fervently hoped, it was closed down.[71] Ede's insistence, at the meeting in February 1949, that representatives of WVS and the SJC should meet again in 'a conference of their own at which no man should be present'[72] gave belated acknowledgement to the gender issue; but it did so at the expense of the class one. As Lady Reading had pointed out,[73] any agreement reached between WVS and the Labour Women would have little meaning in the absence of the established middle-class organizations who dominated the WGPW and its local Standing Committees. Since the failed negotiations with NCSS had scuppered any possibility of agreement with these organizations, Ede's support for the SJC initiative had little obvious purpose. Reading was hopeful that these pointless discussions would soon 'fizzle out', and indeed they did.[74]

In December 1950, reviewing the failure to get WVS to reach agreement on is future role with either the NCSS or the SJC, Chuter Ede told the Lord President's Committee that 'we must accept the fact that for the time being at any rate there is no prospect of the creation of a broadly based organisation which could be entrusted with the type of work that the WVS is now doing.'[75] The Committee agreed, noting not only that WVS 'performed efficiently a number of peacetime tasks which would be much more costly if they were carried out by public authorities', but also 'their great potential value in time of war'.[76] Although explicit reference to civil defence had been dropped from its official title in 1945, WVS had always seen the possibility of 'future warfare' as a significant reason for its continued existence.[77] By the autumn of 1950 renewed civil defence preparations, revived since the Berlin crisis in 1948, had come to constitute a substantial part of WVS activity, and this made it easier to justify the organization's anomalous financial position.[78]

[71] WGPW Executive, Minutes, 12 Mar. 1947, WF A1.
[72] House of Commons, Debates, 470, 2073, 8 Dec. 1949.
[73] Reading to Ede, 6 Dec. 1948, WRVS, A1/38 File 4.
[74] WVS Chairman's Committee, Minutes, 10 Feb. 1949; 'Memo by Home Secretary on the Future of WVS', LP (50) 102, Dec. 1950, PRO, CAB 132 16.
[75] 'Memo by Home Secretary on the Future of WVS'.
[76] Lord President's Committee, Minutes, 12 Jan. 1951, PRO, CAB 132 17.
[77] MacNalty, *Civilian Health and Medical Services*, 231; Beveridge and Wells, *Evidence of Voluntary Action*, 139; Reading to Chuter Ede, 20 Sept. 1948 , WRVS A1/38 File 4.
[78] In the summer of 1948 the WVS general secretary received a surprise visit from a senior Home Office official bringing a General in tow. War, they explained, could break out at any moment—an unannounced conventional blitzing of London could not be ruled out. The WVS should be prepared to meet this immediately; and, in the longer term, to help in training housewives on how to cope with atom bombs. Nothing, however, should yet be made public. The Cabinet, it was explained, insisted that the populace should not be given 'the slightest impression that any Civil Defence preparations are being made'. Johnson to Reading, Aug. 1948; Johnson to Hutchinson, 23 Aug. 1948 in WRVS, A1/38 File 6; WVS Chairman's Committee, Minutes, 22 June 1950, and *passim*.

When, in 1951, the Treasury tried to force cuts in the WVS grant, complaining that they were employing as many staff as during the war, Chuter Ede replied that the payments were 'a cheap insurance premium for the services we expect to receive from them in an emergency'.[79]

When Lady Reading learned that ministers had at last agreed to maintain WVS on a permanent basis,[80] she pressed for a public statement to this effect. The legal position, however, remained ambiguous. Noting that the payments to WVS still lacked any statutory basis, the Lord President's Committee minuted that legislation would eventually be necessary 'if the annual grant continued for a considerable number of years'.[81] Ministers were understandably reluctant to make an announcement that could be guaranteed to stir renewed controversy about the privileged position of WVS, deciding instead to deal with the issue in the context of a debate on civil defence planned for the autumn of 1951. The planned debate was overtaken by the general election, and it fell to the incoming Conservative Government, with full Labour Party support, finally to make it clear that WVS had become a permanent feature of the social architecture of post-war Britain.[82]

The most considered discussion of voluntarism during the Attlee years came from Beveridge, whose *Report on Voluntary Action* was published in October 1948. Beveridge, however, does not appear to have been aware of the NCSS–WVS negotiations, or to have understood the issues at stake.[83] His own proposal that the government appoint a 'Minister-Guardian of Voluntary Action' was explicitly restricted to distributing taxpayers' money to those voluntary organizations that were *not* undertaking work on behalf of government departments.[84] The idea being pressed by the Home Office on WVS and the NCSS that a new representative body should be formed through which state funding for work undertaken on its behalf could be channelled,

---

[79] Ede to Morrison, 9 Feb. 1951, PRO, CAB 124 914.

[80] WVS Chairman's Committee, Minutes, 23 Jan. 1951, WRVS.

[81] Lord President's Committee, Minutes, 12 Jan. 1951, PRO, CAB 132 17.

[82] WVS Chairman's Committee, Minutes, 14 Sept. 1951, WRVS. Reading had been expecting a statement about WVS in the anticipated Parliamentary Debate on Civil Defence. When this was overtaken by the election, Reading asked for a separate statement but all she secured was a promise from the Home Secretary to leave a note for his successor about planned announcement on WVS and Civil Defence (ibid., 27 Sept. 1951). The incoming Conservative administration lost no time in making the long-awaited announcement, a consensual decision welcomed by the Labour Party leadership (ibid, 7, 13 Dec. 1951).

[83] NCSS Executive Committee, Minutes, 29 May 1947, 20 Jan. 1949, NCVO, Box 154. For other negative judgements on this report, see Jose Harris, 'Society and the State in Twentieth-century Britain', in F. M. L. Thompson (ed.), *The Cambridge Social History of Britain, 1750–1950*, iii (Cambridge, 1990), 104; N. Deakin, 'The Perils of Partnership. The Voluntary Sector and the State, 1945–1992', in J. Davis Smith, C. Rochester, and R. Hedley (eds.), *An Introduction to the Voluntary Sector* (London, 1995), 46

[84] J. A. R. Pimlott to Morrison, 30 Dec. 1948, PRO, CAB 124 136; Beveridge, *Voluntary Action*, 150, 316–17.

flew in the face of Beveridge's conception of the proper autonomy of the voluntary sector. He fully endorsed the position, spelled out in the evidence presented to his enquiry by the Liberal Party, that, despite the obvious advantages to government of 'consulting with one organisation [rather] than with many', any such centralization was 'a modern tendency which Liberals must deplore ... [voluntary organizations] must not accept a State-planned existence. Their vitality must spring from spontaneous desire.'[85] Most leaders of the voluntary sector during the remainder of the twentieth century would wholeheartedly endorse that view.

Far from WVS pioneering the future shape of relations between the state and the voluntary sector, the organization that emerged was a curious hybrid, a one-off improvisation which spawned no imitators. The voluntary sector, and its most important post-war defender (Beveridge), had no place for WVS, and Attlee's ministers, who lacked the time and perhaps the inclination to address the issues of principle involved, supported it for strictly practical reasons. WVS found a place for itself in the post-war mixed economy of welfare not because anyone in government, or anywhere else, had planned it that way, but because ministers found it handy. As one disgruntled opponent of the organization had predicted as early as 1940: 'England never drops an institution [unless] it cannot possibly be helped.'[86]

[85] Beveridge and Wells, *Evidence of Voluntary Action*, 193.
[86] Ritchie to Reading, 21 May 1940, WRVS, R 7/5 Wiltshire.

12

Conclusion

For Elizabeth Bowen, whose 1948 novel *The Heat of the Day* brilliantly evokes the paranoid dark side of wartime unity and who hated Attlee's post-war 'nanny state', WVS represented the hollowness of middle-class pretensions to social leadership. Ernestine, the home counties WVS organizer she portrays as stereotypically bossy, interfering, and hyperactive, lacks the qualities necessary for leadership: her 'absence of human awareness was quite startling'. Introduced for the first time to her brother's lover her gaze remained emotionally empty: 'she might have been scanning a public notice to see if anything further ought to be done.' The English middle class, Bowen believed, found themselves 'suspended in the middle of nothing', quite unable to sustain or renew those bonds of paternalism and deference which, she fondly imagined, continued to flourish in rural Ireland.[1] Bowen, however, was out of joint with her times and in reality WVS represented, not the social incompetence of middle-class women, but their remarkable ability to rise to the challenges of the age, adapting Victorian values to mid-twentieth-century realities. And if, in the end, the Ernestines proved unable to rule their roosts, most of them were prepared to peck more humbly rather than beat their wings in the void.

The middle-class female associational world which had grown so strongly in the inter-war years provided, via WVS, a significant component of Britain's wartime mobilization. Established initially to bring the influence of patriotic local social leaders to bear on local authorities reluctant to prepare for war, WVS operated at one and the same time to consolidate female middle-class power and to subordinate it to the needs of the war-making state. The precise outcomes of these paradoxical dynamics varied with the local terrain. Across much of rural England WVS was simply a manifestation of existing social hierarchies. This was also true in many provincial towns, while in others WVS served to broker an accommodation between middle-class social leaders and the labour movement. Significantly, however, the Labour representatives were normally themselves of middle-class extraction,

---

[1] Elizabeth Bowen, *The Heat of the Day*, 1948 (Harmondsworth, 1962), 107, 114. On Bowen's social vision see H. B. Jordan, *How Will the Heart Endure. Elizabeth Bowen and the Landscape of War* (Ann Arbor, Mich., 1992); Adam Piette, *Imagination at War. British Fiction and Poetry, 1939–1945* (London, 1995); Gill Plain, *Women's Fiction of the Second World War. Gender, Power and Resistance* (Edinburgh, 1996).

and working-class women, although mobilized by WVS in large numbers, seldom occupied leading positions. Where they did WVS could become a site of open class struggle, as in the Durham coalfield.

WVS survived after the war because it had succeeded in convincing Whitehall that it could provide effective auxiliary services for the statutory authorities. Its hierarchical internal structure, which so offended leaders of established voluntary organizations, was crucial to its effective operation as a handmaiden of the planning state: 'an organised service with a proper chain of command', as Chuter Ede put it, on which Whitehall could rely.[2] Lady Reading insisted that her creation represented a far-sighted reworking of the relationship between the voluntary sector and the state, and one which was not only more efficient but also more democratic than the self-appointed cliques of local notables who wanted to close WVS down. The relationship between democracy and voluntarism is complex, particularly when, as was frequently the case in 1940s Britain, political and social leadership rested in different hands, with Labour controlling local government but Tory-voting middle-class social leaders continuing to predominate in associational life. Much contemporary debate about the proper relationship between statutory and voluntary services reflected such disjunctures. Where Beveridge felt impelled to defend freedom of association in civil society against totalitarian extensions of state power, Bevan, who (at the very least) had no less a passion for democracy, identified the unaccountable power of local social leaders—'patchworks of local paternalism'[3]—as a significant obstacle to the democratization of British society. The local democracy defended by voluntarists was often a democracy of elites effectively excluding most of the population: witness the horror felt by established social leaders in the Durham coalfield when election by universal suffrage was claimed as a superior qualification for leadership to wealth, property, or social status.[4] Lady Reading, unlike Bevan, was no egalitarian and her aim was not the root and branch democratization of voluntary service: rather she sought to adapt middle-class social leadership to what she assumed would be an ongoing process of state expansion. This produced an intriguing moment of convergence between middle-class female associationalism and the planning state. While the centrality of the idea of 'character' in Lady Reading's social philosophy reflected the continuing salience of late-Victorian philanthropic ideology, her willingness to subordinate the voluntary impulse to the needs of the state was anything but Victorian.

As WVS recovered in the late 1940s from its immediate post-war collapse it offered to its members a way of being publicly active, responsible house-

---

[2] Chuter Ede to Morrison, 9 Feb. 1951, PRO, CAB 124 914.
[3] F. K. Prochaska, *The Voluntary Impulse. Philanthropy in Modern Britain* (London, 1988), 85.
[4] See Ch. 6 above.

wife-citizens that stood in sharp contrast to the stridently anti-socialist consumerism promoted by Conservative Central Office. That is not to say that women necessarily felt that they had to choose between these proffered identities. There were a few who believed, with more or less enthusiasm, that the wartime planned economy prefigured an egalitarian socialist future: for them the voluntary personal social service of housewives would remain a vital corrective to the mechanical impersonality of the beehive state.[5] In general, however, WVS responses to wartime talk of the inevitability of socialism were probably more along the lines of the bemused organizer in Devon, who reacted by declaring that she could reconcile herself to a socialist future so long as 'people could still be divided into rich and poor' so that she could continue her good works.[6] By the late 1940s, in any case, belief in the inevitability of socialism had faded. Lady Reading's repeated appeals to her members to put partisan feelings to one side in order to serve in the work of national reconstruction suggest that most of her members embraced both identities, self-consciously balancing the 'persecuted victim of socialist austerity' against the 'self-sacrificing citizen-housewife'. Writing at this time, Lewis and Maude noted that while middle-class people were for ever bemoaning their powerlessness, they could not bring themselves to believe that they were not in fact indispensable to national survival: an attitude they described as 'an amalgam of dread and confidence'.[7] Lady Reading's task was to shore up the confidence, fostering among her largely Tory-voting members a capacity for constructive engagement with the social and legislative transformations of the age.

Nor was the Conservative Party itself so enamoured with the electoral rewards of anti-socialist consumerism that it lost sight of the advantages of cultivating the involvement of its members in the non-partisan world of the women's organizations.[8] Party leaders reacted with alarm to evidence that Labour women were being urged to challenge the traditional Tory monopoly in voluntary work.[9] However important the frustrated consumerism of housewives may have been to the Tories' electoral recovery, it did not replace the need for Conservative women to sustain their credentials as social leaders

[5] Kathleen Graham, 'A Survey of WVS and its Place in a Post-war World' (n.d., 1946?), WRVS, Box 204. For a more elaborated view of 'the place of philanthropy in a socialist Britain', see C. Braithwaite, *The Voluntary Citizen, An Enquiry into the Place of Philanthropy in the Community* (London, 1938), 66 ff.

[6] James McIntyre, 'Voluntary Service in Devon' (n.d., 1942?), 46, NCSRS, E2/5.

[7] R. Lewis and A. Maude, *The English Middle Classes* (London, 1953), 230.

[8] South East Area Conservative Women's Advisory Committee Executive, Minutes, 23 Nov. 1944, CPA, ARE 9/11/4. See also Maxse's views reported in Ad-Hoc Committee on Outside Organisations, Minutes, 9 Oct. 1945, CPA; South East Area WAC, Minutes, 24 Oct. 1946, CPA ARE 9/11/4.

[9] Central Women's Advisory Committee, Minutes, 6 May 1948, CPA CCO 170/1/1; North West Conservative Women's Advisory Committee, Minutes, 8 May 1948, CPA ARE 3/11/4; Joan Bourne, 'For the Community', *Labour Woman* (Feb. 1948).

by active participation in the voluntary sector.[10] During Labour's post-mortem on the 1950 election, Attlee attributed Conservative success in part to precisely this factor: 'In the smaller provincial towns, well- to-do people did a great deal of public work and they had an effect.'[11] Conservative women knew in their bones that sustaining the right to rule had more to do with taking responsibility and delivering public service than it did with the quint-essentially subaltern characteristics projected by much of the anti-austerity propaganda which the party aimed at housewives: grumbling and moaning.

Lady Reading claimed to have found the key to reconciling voluntary work and state expansion, and she was quite legitimately proud of her achieve-ment—almost single-handed—in keeping WVS going after the war in face of the hostility of the established women's organizations. But WVS did not provide a model for the future. Attlee's welfare state certainly enabled middle-class people to sustain their social dominance, but as trained professionals not as amateur volunteers, especially not the middle-aged and often rather poorly educated women who had found so much fulfilment in WVS during the war. Lady Reading made big claims about the professionalism of WVS in contrast to the rest of the voluntary sector,[12] but this should be seen as a defensive posture taken up on behalf of unemployed women whose age and educational deficiencies were ultimately to leave them on the sidelines in the emerging professional society. Some of the most effective WVS leaders were themselves career women, retired doctors or headmistresses. But the great majority were the product of late nineteenth-century separate spheres, women excluded from the opportunities offered by professional employment whose sense of themselves as public figures rested on their roles in the female associational world and the status of their menfolk. While it was remarkable how import-ant these women made themselves to Britain's war effort, this turned out to be their last stand as social leaders, not the beginning of a new dispensation. The female public world explored in this book may well have reached the apex of its effectiveness during the Second World War. In the longer term the lady volunteer as social leader had little future. The world built by Attlee and his successors belonged to precisely those processes of professionalization in the social services that WVS had tried to resist.

The professionalization of social work did not necessarily disrupt the continuities of class. Discussing an earlier phase of this development around the First World War, Angela Woollacott has pointed to the ways in which:

[10] Eastern Area Women's Advisory Committee, Minutes, 21 June 1950, CPA, ARE 7/11/2.

[11] Report of a Conference Held at Beatrice Webb House, Dorking, 20/21 May 1950, 5, Labour Party Archives, GS/DORK.

[12] Memorandum by Reading, 11 Oct. 1946; Note of Meeting Held at Treasury, 17 Dec. 1947, PRO, CAB 124 914. Lady Reading's interest in personnel management may have owed something to her work in ICI in 1929–30 as secretary to the first Lady Reading, who was an ICI director. *Stella Reading. Some Recollections by Her Friends* (London, 1978?), 7.

middle-class women drew a line of continuity between the old and new forms of feminine authority, that of authority based on class superiority. That they were able to do so is one example of the complex process of social change in which class hierarchies can be and are maintained amid radical historical shifts, such as women's admission to citizenship and professional employment.[13]

In 1938 Lady Reading had summed up the style of WVS as 'acting in the way of smoothing out difficulties'; and it was the authority accorded to their social status that enabled her followers to exercise such soothing leadership.[14] More than sixty years later the deployment of a similar graciousness by women of superior social standing remains an important supplement to more orthodox techniques. I have it on good authority that in one Midlands social service department this practice is known as 'the duchess touch'— using the (apparently) most upper-class woman in the department to sort out the more intractable conflicts with the clients. As social services grapple more or less despairingly with problems of social exclusion in a world where *noblesse oblige* has lost all purchase, 'the duchess touch' provides a faint and probably inauthentic echo of a world that has gone.

From the mid-1960s volunteering entered a new period of growth.[15] The major growth points were quite unlike the quietly auxiliary role in provision of personal social services developed by WVS. The new voluntarism centred around information and advice services designed to help clients negotiate the intricacies of welfare rights, mutual aid groups operating with little direct connection with the state, and campaigning, pressure-group activities. Organizations like the Child Poverty Action Group (1965), the Disablement Income Group (1965), Shelter (1966), and Age Concern (1971) stood in a critical, campaigning relationship to the statutory authorities quite unlike anything that WVS had aspired to. Another major innovation, the systematic recruitment of youth in voluntary work, had little to learn from WVS techniques for mobilization of middle-aged housewives.[16] Although it might be possible to view the younger women who often played a major role in

[13] Angela Woollacott, 'From Moral to Professional Authority: Secularism, Social Work, and Middle-Class Women's Self-Construction in World War I Britain', *Journal of Women's History* (Summer 1998), 103. See also Penny Summerfield, *Reconstructing Women's Wartime Lives* (Manchester, 1998), 85–8.

[14] Report of Deputation to Home Secretary from the Labour Party Executive, 14 July 1938, 11, WRVS V95 SJCWWIO.

[15] G. Finlayson, *Citizen, State and Social Welfare in Britain, 1830–1990* (Oxford, 1994), 329; Stephen Hatch and Ian Mocroft, 'Voluntary Workers', *New Society* (7 Apr. 1977), 24; Hatch, *Outside the State. Voluntary Organisations in Three English Towns* (London, 1980); Joe Sheard, 'Volunteering and Society, 1960–1990', in J. Davis Smith, C. Rochester, and R. Hedley, *An Introduction to the Voluntary Sector* (London, 1995).

[16] Maria Brenton, *The Voluntary Sector in British Social Services* (London, 1985), 38, 53; [Wolfenden] Committee on Voluntary Organisations, *The Future of Voluntary Organisations. Report of the Wolfenden Committee* (London, 1978), 20, 184–5; Joe Sheard, 'Volunteering and Society'; Hedley and Hatch, *Social Welfare and the Failure of the State: Centralised Social Services and Participatory Alternatives* (London, 1981), 24.

these initiatives as engaged in constructing new forms of middle-class social leadership, any continuities with the kind of voluntarism espoused by WVS would be complicated by the explicitly feminist underpinnings of their activity.[17] The limitless scope of personal social service meant that there would always be a demand for volunteers, and the rapid expansion of statutory services during the 1960s and 1970s served, as in wartime, to stimulate rather than to displace auxiliary voluntary service.[18] But these volunteers increasingly found themselves working under the supervision of trained professionals, and the scope narrowed for the unpaid social worker to exercise skills of organization and leadership.[19] From the early 1970s the numbers of paid volunteer organizers appointed by hospitals and local authorities expanded rapidly, leaving little space for the kinds of partnerships between statutory authorities and local social leaders which had been at the core of WVS activity in the 1940s.[20] Already by the end of the 1940s it had been becoming clear that the social leadership exercised by middle-class housewives in wartime was giving way to humble service directed by professionals.

When the new wave of voluntarism was taking off in the 1960s, WVS was widely perceived as a rather old-fashioned survival from an earlier era. Stereotypes of the bossy, interfering woman lived on, as was demonstrated by one survey of attitudes among volunteers conducted in the late 1970s:

the sort of people, posh ladies and the like, who used to come around my children's homes. They make me sick, patronising bitches. [39-year-old yard foreman who had grown up in a children's home]
I thought that this 'women's volunteering service' was for people well-off and I wouldn't be able to mix with them. [58-year-old working-class volunteer]

Younger, educated middle-class women drawn to voluntary activity were unlikely to tolerate the hierarchical character of WVS, a point made by one 34-year-old graduate mother describing her brief encounter with the organization:

---

[17] N. Deakin, 'The Perils of Partnership. The Voluntary Sector and the State, 1945–1992', in J. Davis Smith, C. Rochester, and Hedley (eds.), *An Introduction to the Voluntary Sector* (London, 1995).

[18] Brenton, *Voluntary Sector*, 26, 41–3.

[19] As one study pointed out, the numbers of women prepared to volunteer would not necessarily be increased by the appointment of professionals to organize the work: 'Part of the attraction of voluntary work may be that it provides opporunities to undertake organisational work outside the home.' Margot Jefferys, *An Anatomy of Social Welfare Services. A Survey of Social Welfare Staff and their Clients in the County of Buckinghamshire* (London, 1965).

[20] In 1962 the Ministry of Health was still stressing that recruitment of volunteers for hospitals should be done through voluntary bodies like WVS (Mary Morris, *Voluntary Work in the Welfare State* (London, 1969) 230 , 234). By the 1970s, however, both hospitals and local authorities were being urged to appoint their own paid volunteer organizers (Geraldine M. Aves, *The Voluntary Worker in the Social Services* (London 1969); Wolfenden, *Future of Voluntary Organisations*, 91, 100, 105; Brenton, *Voluntary Sector*, 44, 46).

The woman who runs the WRVS is extremely efficient; she would run a battleship very well. She would be absolutely superb. But I don't like semi-uniformed organisations; there is a definite type of person working there.[21]

Such negative reactions can only have been enhanced by the 1966 decision—taken against Lady Reading's better judgement[22]—to add 'Royal' to the organization's name. Throughout the voluntary sector the Home Office subsidy remained a continuing source of resentment, reflected by one academic's observation in 1985 that the 'establishment connections' enjoyed by WRVS appeared to give it 'an immunity from research and investigation by government departments which would dearly like to ask more searching questions about the uses to which its massive grant is put'.[23]

In many ways these negative stereotypes of WVS were unfair. The place that WVS eventually found was very different from its wartime role as co-ordinator of local networks of female social leadership. In 1982 Mrs Thatcher chose WRVS as the platform from which to declare her intention of reversing the auxiliary relationship of voluntary to statutory social service:

I believe that the volunteer movement is at the heart of all our social welfare provision. That the statutory services are the supportive ones underpinning where necessary, filling the gaps and helping the helpers.[24]

While this vision may have owed a good deal to her memories of the operation of hierarchical social leadership in inter-war Grantham, it could hardly have been more distant from the compromise between local social leadership and state expansion which Lady Reading had pursued in the 1940s. Nor was WRVS in any position to pioneer Thatcher's dream of a return to 'Victorian values', reasserting civil society against the state. Although statistics on volunteering are notoriously difficult to evaluate, there is no reason to believe that volunteering at the end of the twentieth century was any less extensive than it had been in the 1940s. In 1995 one survey claimed that nearly half of the adult population had done some organized voluntary work during the year.[25] But the numbers of people volunteering

---

[21] Roger Sherrott, 'Fifty Volunteers', in Hatch (ed.), *Volunteers: Patterns, Meanings and Motives* (Berkhamstead, 1983), 78, 104–5, 118.

[22] Note added by Mary Smieton to Elsa Dunbar, Memoir of Lady Reading, 1990, FL 7/yyy/2/2.

[23] Wolfenden, *Future of Voluntary Organisations*, 255; Brenton, *Voluntary Sector*, 64; Aves, *Voluntary Worker*, 185.

[24] Brenton, *Voluntary Sector*, 145–6. Wilson and Heath, by contrast, had both used the NCSS as the platform for expounding their Government's attitude to the voluntary sector (Wolfenden, *Future of Voluntary Organisations*, 61).

[25] Roger Tarling, 'Statistics on the Voluntary Sector in the UK', *Journal of the Royal Statistical Society* 163 (2000), 3, 255–61.

through WRVS, which stood at about 200,000 in 1950, had fallen to 160,000 by the late 1980s and 100,000 by the turn of the century.[26]

WRVS continued to undertake a wide range of activities on behalf of local authorities and central government. Its most important contributions today are in hospitals (shops, cafés, trolley services, reception and guiding services) and in services for the elderly, especially Meals on Wheels, day centres, lunch clubs, and community transport. It also remains integral to local authority emergency planning. Although funding continues to come mainly from the Home Office, nobody any longer suggests that this anomalous position provides a blueprint for the voluntary sector as a whole. In recent years, under Government pressure to move away from dependence on state funding, WRVS has started undertaking its own fund-raising. In 1999 the organization established 'a more democratic structure', perhaps rather an extravagant description of a decision to set up a national committee of thirty volunteers drawn from the regions to ensure 'that the voice of the volunteer is heard at the very top of the organisation, as well as providing training for future trusteeship of WRVS'.[27] These recent breaches of two of Lady Reading's most fundamental organizational principles—no fund-raising and no committees—suggest that whatever future may be in store for the organization it will not be that envisaged by its founder.

The continuities of class run strong in modern British history. Despite the upheavals of the first half of the twentieth century—two world wars, mass unemployment, the collapse of the Liberal Party, the mobilization of a mass labour movement, women's suffrage, the arrival of a majority Labour Government—many of the values and attitudes laid down in Victorian Britain remained intact into the 1950s. What finally overwhelmed Victorian Britain was neither the erosion of its global dominance (it took a very long time before anybody really took the measure of that), nor the rise to power of a labour movement which in so many ways embodied its own version of Victorian values, but the revolutionary dynamic of a triumphantly expanding capitalism during the global boom of the third quarter of the century.[28] Not until the impact of affluence in the 1950s was the death knell sounded for the kind of social leadership explored in this book. Despite the despair of reactionaries like Elizabeth Bowen, the Second World War had done more to sustain than to undermine middle-class social leadership. Alongside professionalization, it was consumer capitalism that did for it. By the 1960s the ethos of duty and self-sacrifice embraced by Lady

[26] Chuter Ede to Morrison, 9 Feb. 1951, PRO, CAB 124 914; WRVS website, www.wrvs.org.uk.

[27] WRVS website.

[28] François Bedarida, *A Social History of England, 1851–1990* (London, 1991), 249–52; Jose Harris, *Private Lives, Public Spirit. A Social History of Britain, 1870–1914* (Oxford, 1993), 252–3.

Reading's women came to look old fashioned. In a world which prioritized personal choice, 'character' and the publicly accountable selfhood it embodied were being displaced by more private, autonomous, and self-regarding notions of the self. Lady Reading's followers represented a generation whose dutiful lives exemplified the self-repression that their more liberated daughters were determined not to reproduce.[29] As duty and 'character' gave way to 'self-development' in the therapeutic society, and a younger generation of middle-class women eschewed self-sacrifice for feminist self-assertion, the devoted service of elderly leisured women became less a claim to social authority than a dogged upholding of self-respect against the tide of the times. Looking back one might feel some nostalgia for a world which had space for notions of self-actualization in a public sphere existing beyond mere subjectivity. The ladies from the WVS may have been working to sustain the power of their class but most of them did so unselfishly enough, believing that social leadership was the duty they owed to those less privileged than themselves. They were, perhaps, fortunate to inhabit a sphere of active citizenship that enabled conscientious people to distinguish duty from pleasure and to invest self-worth in public service rather than reducing all values to narratives of self-realization.

By the 1970s the world of 1938 had gone—a world in which Lady Reading's missionaries could walk into town and confidently expect to find a handful of leading women who would command sufficient respect to set up a new co-ordinating service for voluntary work. The ladies offering street stoves and brown paper against the bomb (and, more usefully, food, clothing, and shelter to victims of floods), meals on wheels, Derby and Joan clubs, and hospital sweet trolleys did not embody either the mainstream of social leadership or the future of voluntary work. Post-war Britain had a place for them, but it was a smaller and humbler place than WVS had occupied in wartime. During the war WVS had served as a means of adapting traditions of middle-class female social leadership to the needs of the emergency. Its post-war fate, however, demonstrated that the days in which leisure dignified by 'character' could continue to play a central role in upholding the continuities of class were numbered. Meals on wheels did valuable social work, but it hardly carried the prestige or centrality in local service provision that the more ambitious WVS organizers had aspired to during the war. The kind of woman attracted to leading positions in WVS meant that the image of Lady Bountiful long continued to cling to the organization: but the main vectors of middle-class power had moved elsewhere. The centre organizers' younger and better-educated sisters were

---

[29] Becky Conekin, Frank Mort, and Chris Waters (eds.), *Moments of Modernity. Reconstructing Britain, 1945–1964* (London, 1999), 1–21; Nikolas Rose, *Governing the Soul. The Shaping of the Private Self*, 2nd edn. (London, 1999), pp. vii–xxv; A. Giddens, *Modernity and Self-Identity* (Cambridge, 1991).

gaining authority in their own right as professionals, rather than fulfilling social leadership roles derived from the social status of their husbands.

WVS can be understood as an attempt by middle-class social leaders under threat from the expansion of professional social services to sustain and shore up traditional patterns of social authority by finding a new kind of accommodation between the voluntary sector and the state. In the short term they were remarkably successful, not only mobilizing a million women into voluntary war service under exclusively female leadership, but also in persuading the Attlee administration to face down opposition from the rest of the voluntary sector to the post-war continuation of WVS. But while WVS succeeded in establishing a permanent place for itself in Britain's post-war social services, its capacity to sustain the influence of untrained, unpaid social leaders in the face of a bureaucratized and professionalized state welfare system did not long outlive the 1940s. WVS reminds us how much Britain's wartime mobilization, led by a generation born and educated before 1914, relied on the adaptation of attitudes and behaviour patterns laid down by Victorians to the profoundly un-Victorian problems presented by mid-twentieth-century modernity—from coping with the aerial bombardment of civilians to the construction of a planned economy. During the 1950s and 1960s, however, these continuities were to be decisively broken, and Lady Reading's achievement stands as a late flowering of Victorian values, rather than as a seedbed for social progress.

Bibliography

I. WRVS ARCHIVE

(a) Envelopes

A3/38, Advisory Council, General Correspondence, 1938–62
A14/38, Home Office, General Correspondence, 1945–78
A4/39, Ministry of Information, General Correspondence, 1939–54
A11/40, Ministry of Health, General Correspondence, 1943–9
A15/40, National Assistance Board, General Correspondence, 1940–66
E1, Evacuation, Pre-Munich Plans, 1938
F1, Food, Correspondence with Ministry of Food and Education, 1943–53
F1/3, Food, Advice, 1939–51
FP3, Fuel/Power, Women's Advisory Council on Solid Fuel
M456/40, Memoranda, Voluntary Social Service Enquiry
R2, Region, Confidential Correspondence, 1941–73
R10/2/BE, Region, Bootle CB, 1938–63
V1/40, Labour Party, Women's Section, 1940–75
V3/38, National Union of Townswomen's Guilds, 1955–68
V3/40, Transport and General Workers Women's Guild, 1939–56
V4/40, Associated Society of Locomotive Engine and Firemen's Society, 1940–59
V5/40, National Union of Railwaymen, 1940–68
V7/38, National Federation of Women's Institutes, 1950–85
V10/38, British Federation of University Women, 1938–63
V12/2/38, Junior Council of London and National Society for Women's Service, 1938
V13/6/38, National Council of Social Service, Citizens Advice Bureaux, 1969
V13/2/38, National Council of Social Service, 1939
V13/4/38, NCVO, Women's Group on Public Welfare, 1946–67
V22/38, The Mother's Union, 1938–75
V51/38, Women's Cooperative Guild, 1938–57
V57/38, Application for Paid Posts, 1939–43
V95/38, Industrial Women's Organisations, 1938–51
V101/38, Conservative Party Women's Section, 1938–78
V102/38, Liberal Party, 1938–81
V107/38, National Labour Organisation, 1938–45
V111/38, Women's Division of the Liberal National Council, 1938–51
V113/38, Miss Ellen Wilkinson, 1938–40
V131/38, National Institute of Houseworkers

(b) Box Files (General)

Box 46, Press Notices, 1938–54
Box 53, Statistics
Box 53, Finance Committee, Minutes, 1945–54
Box 54, Lady Reading
Box 54, Press Cuttings, Lady Reading, 1938–41
Box 55, Press Cuttings, Lady Reading, 1942–3
Box 179, Regional Reports, Wales Region, 1939–79
Box 204, WRVS, Histories
Box 205, WRVS, Histories, Regional
Box 205, WRVS, Histories, Regional/Administration Conferences, 1940–59
Box 207, WRVS, Advisory Council, Minutes, 1938–47
Box 207, WRVS, Advisory Council, Minutes, 1948–59
Box 215, WRVS, Housewives, 1938–71
Box 240, WRVS, Chairman's Committee, 1939–51

(c) Box Files (Regional)

Box 57, Region 1, Regional Office Papers, 1939–63
Box 58, Region 1, Cumberland County, 1949–63
Box 58, Region 1, R1/2 West Hartlepool, 1938–63
Box 58, Region 1, Sunderland, 1938–63
Box 58, Region 1, Gateshead, 1938–63
Box 58, Region 1, South Shields, 1938–63
Box 58, Region 1, Darlington, 1938–63
Box 58, Region 1, Durham County, 1938–63
Box 58, Region 1, Easington, 1940–2
Box 58, Region 1, Northumberland, 1938–63
Box 58, Region 1, Tynemouth, 1938–63
Box 58, Region 1, Newcastle-upon-Tyne, 1944–63
Box 58, Region 1, 1938–41, Narrative Reports
Box 62, Region 2, Regional Office Papers, 1938–63
Box 71, Region 3, Regional Office Papers, 1938–63
Box 72, Region 3, Derbyshire, Chesterfield, Derby, 1938–63
Box 72, Region 3, Leicestershire, Leicester, 1938–63
Box 72, Region 3, Holland, 1938–63
Box 72, Region 3, Regional Organisation, 1938–44
Box 72, Region 3, Kersteven, 1938–63
Box 72, Region 3, Lindsey, 1938–63
Box 72, Region 3, Grimsby, Lincoln, Scunthorpe, 1938–63
Box 73, Region 3, Northamptonshire, Northampton, 1938–63
Box 73, Region 3, Nottinghamshire, Nottingham, Rutland, 1938–63
Box 81, Region 3, Derbyshire, Leicestershire
Box 81, Region 3, Lincolnshire, Northamptonshire
Box 81, Region 3, Nottinghamshire

Box 81, Region 4, Regional Office Papers, 1938–43
Box 87, Region 5, Regional Papers, 1943–63
Box 87, Region 5, Kent, 1938–63
Box 87, Region 5, Kent, 1943–63
Box 87, Region 5, Canterbury, 1938–63
Box 87, Region 5, East Sussex, 1938–63
Box 87, Region 5, Brighton, Eastbourne, Hastings, 1938–63
Box 88, Region 5, West Sussex, 1938–63
Box 88, Region 5, Surrey, 1938–63
Box 96, Region 6, Regional Office Papers, 1938–63
Box 97, Region 6, Bournemouth, Portsmouth, Southampton, 1938–63
Box 97, Region 6, Berkshire, 1938–60, Reading, 1938–63
Box 97, Region 6, Buckinghamshire, Dorset, 1938–63
Box 97, Region 6, Hampshire, 1938–63
Box 97, Region 6, Isle Of Wight, Oxfordshire, Oxford, 1938–63
Box 106, Region 7, Regional Office Papers, 1938–63
Box 113, Region 9, Regional Office Papers, 1938–53
Box 114, Region 9, Herefordshire, Shropshire. Staffordshire, 1938–63
Box 114, Region 9, Burton-upon-Trent, Smethwick, Stoke-on-Trent, Walsall
Box 114, Region 9, West Bromwich, Wolverhampton, 1938–63
Box 114, Region 9, Warwickshire, Birmingham, 1938–63
Box 120, Region 10, Regional Office Papers, Manchester, 1938–52
Box 121, Region 10, Cumberland, Westmoreland, 1938–48; Wallasey, 1938–63
Box 121, Region 10, Cheshire, 1938–63, Birkenhead, 1938–63, Chester, 1939–68, Stockport, 1938–63
Box 121, Region 10, Lancashire, 1938–63
Box 121, Region 10, Barrow-in-Furness, Blackpool, Bolton, Bootle, Burley, Bury, 1938–63
Box 122, Region 10, Liverpool, Manchester, 1938–63
Box 122, Region 10, Oldham, Preston, Rochdale, St Helens, Salford, Southport, Warrington, Wigan, 1938–63
Box 144, Region 8, Regional Office Papers, 1938–45
Box 144, Region 8, Glamorganshire, Cardiff, Merthyr Tydfil, Swansea, 1938–63

2. LOCAL RECORD OFFICES

(a) Barrow-in-Furness

B&PWC, BDSo/69/2/1
Emergency Committee, BDSo/7
His Majesty's Services Club, BDso/27/2
Labour Party General Meetings, Group Meetings and Executive Committee Minutes
WVS Committee, Minutes, BDso/27/1

(b) Coventry

EAW 1199/1/2
NCW PA/1269
Soroptimists' Club 1000/1/1
WRVS Deposit, PA 1753
WVS Collection, PA 705

(c) Durham

Barnard Castle UDC, File on WVS, UD/BC/186
Brandon and Byshottles UDC, UD/BB/26 and 27
Chester-le-Street, Government Evacuation Scheme, Correspondence, RD/CS/319
County Council Emergency Committee, Minutes, CC A55/1
County Durham Public Assistance Committee, Minutes, CC/A50/1
Darlington SCWO
Durham Country Labour Women's Advisory Committee, D/X 1048/4
Easington RD, ARP Committee, Minutes, RD/EA/21
Headlam, D/He/188
Headlam, Diary, D/He/36
Horden Child Welfare Centre Voluntary Committee, DX 1043/1
Labour Party, Bishops Auckland Women's Section
Labour Party, County Federation of Labour Parties, D/sho/5b
Labour Party, Durham Women's Advisory, D/sho/108
Labour Party, Easington Colliery Women's Section, DX 1048/66
Labour Party, Northern Region, D/sho/06
Moderate Party, D/MCF/1
Moderate Party, Minute Book, D/MCF/17
Moderate Party, Branch Associations, D/MCF/23
Moderate Party, Elections, D/MCF/26
Moderate Party, Press Cuttings, D/MCF /71 and 77
WI County Durham Executive, Minutes, 1937–40, D/WI/1/1/12
WI Easington Colliery, D/WI/3/92/2
WI Horden, D/WI/3/94/6
WI Organisation Sub-Committee, D/WI/1/2/26

(d) Guildford RO

Emergency Committee, BR/CTM/EM/1
ARP Committee, BR/CTM/ARP
Conservative Party, Press Cuttings, 1213/9/2
Conservative Party, St Nicholas Branch, Minutes, 1213/3/2
Conservative Party, Branley Branch, Minutes, 1213/6/2
Conservative Party, Redhill Women's Conservative Association, 353/5/6/1
Conservative Party, East Sussex Provincial Area Council, 353/7/6/1

(e) Halifax (Calder Valley)

Emergency Committee, HXM/218
Inner Wheel Club IW 1–3
Labour Party, Minutes, TU 28/1
Labour Party Women's Section, Minute Book, TU 28/8 and 9
NCW, NCW/1 & 9
North East Region NCW, Minutes, NCW 40
SCWO, Misc. 733/1/1
Soroptimists, SOR 3/19, 4/24

(f) Hull

Emergence Committee, Minutes
Good Neighbours, TYW W6
Reception Centres, TYW W2
Social Welfare Committee, Minutes
WVS, TCY/1/1
WVS, TYW W/5

(g) Lancashire

ARP Press Cuttings (Blackpool), DDX 2100/2/3
B&PWC (Blackpool)
Blackpool Borough Council ARP Committee CBBl/12/4
Citizen's Advice Bureau (Blackpool) CAB3/6 and 8
Conservative and Unionist Association Blackpool Divisional, Minutes, PLC 5/1/3
Conservative and Unionist Association Women's Section, Fylde Division, DDX 1202 1/2
Conservative and Unionist Association Women's Section, Stanley Ward No. 1, Minutes, PLC/5/12/1
Conservative Members of Blackpool Council, Minutes, PLC 5/2/1
Labour Party (Blackpool), DDX 2100/3/2
Labour Party (Preston), LAB 1
Soroptimists' Minutes (Preston), DDX 1139 1/1
WCA (Preston), DDX 1749/5 and 6

(h) Leicester

ARP Committee DE 3667/7; DE3277/37
League of Nations Union, Minutes, DE 3191/1
NCW, D58/4
SCWO, DE 3104/2 and 3
Women's Luncheon Club, DE 2509/1 and 2

(i) London (GLRO)

London CSS, Acc 1888 (uncatalogued)

(j) Nottinghamshire

Conservative Party, Nottingham South Divisional Women's Branch
Conservative Party, West Bridgeford Conservative Association, Minutes, 1937–48, DD PP2
EAW, Nottingham Branch, DD 1357/1/4/1
Girl Guides, Nottingham, DD 1663/7/2
National Council of Women, DD 748/6/1
Soroptimist Club of Nottingham, DD SO/2/2

(k) Portsmouth

NCW, 116A
War Emergency Committee, 108A/1
WCA, 1055A

(l) Sheffield

ARP Committee, Reports to Council, CA 157/1
ARP, CA 157/5 and 6
Conservative Party, Park Division Association Minute Book, LD 2210
Conservative Party, Park Division Women's Executive Committee, LD 2216
Co-ordination of Voluntary Services, 1939, CA 509/2
Emergency Committee, Minutes, CA/157/3
Social Welfare Committee, Minutes, CA 137/32
Social Welfare Committee, Draft Minutes and Papers, CA 196

(m) Southampton

ARP Committee, SC 2/3/39/1
Town Clerk's Papers, TC 195/19; SC/TC Box 72/a
Women's Conservative Association, Shirley Ward

3. PUBLIC RECORD OFFICE (KEW)

CAB 71 19
CAB 71 21
CAB 129 914
CAB 124 136
CAB 132 16

CAB 132 17
HO 186 107
HO 186 569
HO 186 657
HO 45 17580
HO 45 17635
HO 45 24302
INF 2 135
MAF 102 10
MAF 102 12
MAF 102 20
MAF 102 24
MH 130 253
MH 130 277
RG 23/126A
T 273 305

4. FAWCETT LIBRARY (NOW THE NATIONAL LIBRARY OF WOMEN)

(a) Women's Forum Papers

WGPW Executive Committee, Minutes, 1939–50, WF/A
SCWO Organisation, WF/I
SCWO Advisory Committee, WF/H
SCWO Correspondence, WF/K
Council for Scientific Management in the Home, WF/B5
Modern Home Making Committee, WF/B6
Make and Mend, WF/B7–9
Domestic Front, WF/B11–12
Relations with NCW, WF/G2
Women in the Home, WF/G4
Domestic Service, WF/G12
Hygiene Sub-committee, WF/D4
Women's Advisory Housing Council, WF/D18–19
NUTG, WF/E1
WGPW Conferences, WF/J2–3
Press Conferences, WF/A42

(b) Brian Harrison Interviews (on tape)

Bartels, Miss Olive, 27 Mar. 1976
Courtney, Mrs Mary, 1 July 1977
Halpin, Miss Kathleen, 16 Mar. 1977
Hamilton Smith, Miss E., 13 Mar. 1977

Horton, Mrs Gertrude, 21 Mar. 1977
Smieton, Dame Mary, 31 May 1977

(c) Other

Elsa Dunbar, Memoir of Lady Reading, Jan. 1990, 7/yyy/2/2
Dorothy M. Elliott, 'Women in Search of Justice' (n.d., 1969), 7/yyy 4

5. WOMEN'S CO-OPERATIVE GUILD (HULL UNIVERSITY LIBRARY)

Central Committee, Minutes, 1938–50
Annual Reports, 1943–50
Hints for Speakers, 1942–3

6. NATIONAL UNION OF TOWNSWOMEN'S GUILDS (BIRMINGHAM)

Executive Committee, Minutes, 1938–50
St Albans TWG
Reading TWG

7. MASS OBSERVATION ARCHIVE (SUSSEX UNIVERSITY LIBRARY)

TC 5/2 Evacuation
TC 32/4 Women in Wartime
TC 17/D Fuel
TC 53 Beveridge Report Surveys, 1942–7
TC 66/21 Town Survey, Worcester
Mrs P. C. Walther, Diarist 5454

8. NUFFIELD COLLEGE SOCIAL RECONSTRUCTION SURVEY (NUFFIELD COLLEGE ARCHIVES)

(a) Reports on Voluntary Social Service (1941–2)

(i) Localities
Bootle, Charles Owen, E2/16
Bristol, Gwyneth Pritchard, E2/2
Burnley, H. P. Hall, E2/27
Cumberland, E2/3
Devon, James McIntyre, E2/5

East Sussex, E. M. Foster, E2/4
Hertfordshire, Dr Roper Power and Diana Parry, E2/7
Hull, R. K. Kelsall, E2/8
Leicester Neighbours' League, E2/12 and 15
Leicester, E2/10
Liverpool CSS E2/17
Liverpool, Ian Luckie and Vera Hilton, E2/18
North Staffordshire, M. Forsyth and M. Morris, E2/34
Preston, E2/29
Yorkshire Area, E2/9

(ii) Organizations
NCSS, E12/7
NUTG, E12/9
WI, E12/8
WVS, E12/14

(b) Other

J. H. Mathews, Southampton, Nov. 1942, B3/16

9. CONSERVATIVE PARTY ARCHIVES

Ad-Hoc Committee on Outside Organisations
Central Women's Advisory Committee, CCO 170/1/1
Eastern Area Women's Advisory Committee, ARE 7/11
North West Women's Advisory Council, ARE 3/11
Report on Bootle, CCO 1/7/102
South East Area Women's Advisory Committee, ARE 9/11
Unionist Women Organisers, CCO 170/2/3
West Midlands Women Organisers, ARE 6/25/1

10. LABOUR PARTY ARCHIVES (MANCHESTER)

SJC Reports in National Executive Committee, Minutes
Mary Sutherland Papers, S23 WVS
Report of a Conference Held at Beatrice Webb House, Dorking, 20–21 May 1950,
    GS/DORK

11. TUC ARCHIVE (MRC, WARWICK)

National Union of Domestic Workers, 292/54.76
Beveridge Enquiry into Voluntary Social Service, 292/809.5

NCSS, 292/808.91/5b
Domestic Service, 292/676/1
Future of WVS, 292/821.2/1
Chester-le-Street Trades Council, 292/79c/25
Foundation of WVS, 292/883.212/8

12. NATIONAL COUNCIL OF VOLUNTARY ORGANISATIONS (LONDON)

NCSS Papers
NCSS Executive Committee, Minutes, Box 154
396/11 Press Cuttings (Midlands)
396/27 Annual Conference of Council of Social Service
396/31 CSS, Surveys
396/36 Social Service Emergency Committees
396/40 Women's Organisations (Midlands)
1757/3/1
1757/6

13. NATIONAL ASSOCIATION OF COUNCILS OF VOLUNTARY SERVICE
(SHEFFIELD)

Reports and Correspondence from various local CSS (uncatalogued)

14. IMPERIAL WAR MUSEUM

MacKay Brown, Miss George, Memoir on wartime voluntary work in Dean, North
    Bedfordshire, Oct. 1977, 78/4/1
Minute books of Lower Stratton WVS (Housewives' Service), 1941–5, Misc. 167
    (2567)

15. POLITICAL AND ECONOMIC PLANNING (BLPES)

Executive Committee, Minutes, A 13/5

16. PERSONAL PAPERS

Cherwell Papers, K247, Nuffield College Archives
Rufas Isaacs (Lord Reading) Papers, Add. MS EUR F 118/134(0), Press Cuttings
    (Lady Reading), British Library

17. PERIODICALS

(a) Local Newspapers

Blackpool Gazette
Coventry Evening Telegraph
Coventry Herald
Durham Chronicle
Halifax Courier
Hull and Yorkshire Times
Hull Sentinel
Kent and Sussex Courier
Leicester Mercury
Luton News
Midlands Daily Telegraph
Northern Echo
Portsmouth Evening News
Sheffield Star
Shields News
Southern Daily Echo
Southern Evening Echo
Southgate Weekly Herald
Surrey Advertiser
Surrey County Advertiser
Tonbridge Free Press

(b) National Newspapers

Daily Worker
The Times
Daily Herald

(c) Other Periodicals

Social Service
Social Work
Picture Post
Planning
Labour Woman
New Statesman
The Townswoman
The British Soroptimist
Wife and Citizen
Women Today
Women's International News

18. OFFICIAL PUBLICATIONS

Report on Post-war Organisation of Private Domestic Employment, Cmd 6650, June 1945
Census of England and Wales, 1931
Census of England and Wales, 1951
House of Commons, Debates

19. BOOKS AND ARTICLES

Andrews, Maggie, *The Acceptable Face of Feminism. The Women's Institute as a Social Movement* (London, 1998).
Anon., *The National Women Citizen's Association, 1918–1968* (London, 1968).
Aves, Geraldine M., *The Voluntary Worker in the Social Services* (London, 1969).
Bailey, Peter, 'White Collars, Grey Lives? The Lower Middle Class Revisited', *Journal of British Studies*, 38 (July 1999).
Ball, S., 'Local Conservatism', in A. Seldon and Ball (eds.), *Conservative Century. The Conservative Party since 1900* (Oxford, 1994).
——(ed.), *Parliament and Politics in the Age of Baldwin and Macdonald. The Headlam Diaries, 1923–1935* (London, 1992).
Banks, Olive, *The Politics of British Feminism, 1918–1970* (Aldershot, 1993).
Barnaby, K. C., *Thorneycrofts: 100 Years of Specialised Shipbuilding and Engineering* (London, 1964).
Bealey, F., J. Blondel, and W. P. McCann, *Constituency Politics: A Study of Newcastle-under-Lyme* (London, 1965).
Beauman, Katherine Bentley, *Green Sleeves. The Story of WVS/WRVS* (London, 1977).
Beauman, N., *A Very Great Profession* (London, 1983).
Bedarida, François, *A Social History of England, 1851–1990* (London, 1991).
Bellamy, J. M., and J. Saville, *Dictionary of Labour Biography*, ii (London, 1974).
Benson, John, *Prime Time. A History of the Middle Aged in Twentieth-century Britain* (Harlow, 1997).
Beveridge, Lord, *Voluntary Action. A Report on Methods of Social Advance* (London, 1948).
—— and A. F. Wells, *The Evidence for Voluntary Action* (London, 1949).
Beynon, Huw and Terry Austin, *Masters and Servants. Class and Patronage in the Making of a Labour Organisation. The Durham Miners and the English Political Tradition* (London, 1994).
Birch, A. H., *Small-Town Politics. A Study of Political Life in Glossop* (Oxford, 1959).
Black, Amy and Stephen Brooke, 'The Labour Party, Women, and the Problem of Gender, 1951–1966', *Journal of British Studies*, 36 (1997).
Blackford, Catherine, 'Wives and Citizens and Watchdogs of Quality: Post-War British Feminism', in J. Fyrth (ed.), *Labour's Promised Land? Culture and Society in Labour Britain, 1945–51* (London, 1995).

Blaxendale, John, ' "I had seen a lot of Englands": J. B. Priestley, Englishness and the People', *History Workshop Journal*, 51 (Spring 2001).

Bonham, John, *The Middle Class Vote* (London, 1954).

Bottomore, T., 'Social Stratification in Voluntary Organisations', in D. V. Glass (ed.), *Social Mobility in Britain* (London, 1954).

Bourdillon, A. F. C. (ed.), *Voluntary Social Services. Their Place in the Modern State* (London, 1945).

Bowden, S. and A. Offer, 'Household Appliances and the Use of Time: The United States and Britain since the 1920s', *Economic History Review*, 7 (1994).

—— and—— 'The Technological Revolution that Never Was. Gender, Class and the Diffusion of Household Appliances in Inter-war England', in V. de Grazia (ed.), *The Sex of Things. Gender and Consumption in Historical Perspective* (Berkeley, Calif., 1996).

Bowen, Elizabeth, *The Heat of the Day* (Harmondsworth, 1962).

Braithwaite, C., *The Voluntary Citizen. An Enquiry into the Place of Philanthropy in the Community* (London, 1938).

Brasnett, Margaret, *Voluntary Social Action. A History of the National Council of Social Service, 1919–1969* (London, 1969).

Brenton, Maria, *The Voluntary Sector in British Social Services* (London, 1985).

Broad, Richard and Suzie Fleming (eds.), *Nella Last's War. A Mother's Diary, 1939–45* (Bristol, 1981).

Brooks, Pamela, *Women at Westminster. An Account of Women in the British Parliament, 1918–1966* (London, 1967).

Burton, Elaine, *The Battle of the Consumer* (London, 1955).

—— *Domestic Work. Britain's Largest Industry* (London, 1944).

—— *What of the Women. A Study of Women in Wartime* (London, 1941).

Cahill, M. and T. Jowitt, 'The New Philanthropy: The Emergence of the Bradford Guild of Help', *Journal of Social Policy*, 9 (1980).

Cain, J. and A. G. Hopkins, *British Imperialism. Innovation and Expansion, 1688–1914* (London, 1993).

Calder, R., *Carry on London* (London, 1941).

Callcott, M., 'The Making of a Labour Stronghold: Electoral Politics in County Durham between the Two World Wars', in M. Callcott and R. Challinor, *Working-class Politics in North East England* (Newcastle, 1983).

Cannadine, D., *Class in Britain* (London, 1998).

—— *The Decline and Fall of the British Aristocracy* (London, 1990).

Carr, F., 'Municipal Socialism; Labour's Rise to Power', in B. Lancaster and T. Mason (eds.), *Life and Labour in the Twentieth Century City: The Experience of Coventry* (Coventry, 1986).

Cauter, T. and J. S. Downham, *The Communication of Ideas. A Study of Contemporary Influences on Urban Life* (London, 1954).

Chambers, R. C., 'A Study of Three Voluntary Organisations', in D. V. Glass (ed.), *Social Mobility in Britain* (London, 1954).

Clements, R. V., *Local Notables and the City Council* (London, 1969).

Cole M. (ed.), *Beatrice Webb's Diaries* (London, 1956).

Committee on Voluntary Organisations, *The Future of Voluntary Organisations. Report of the Wolfenden Committee* (London, 1978).

Conekin, Becky, Frank Mort, and Chris Waters (eds.), *Moments of Modernity. Reconstructing Britain, 1945–1964* (London, 1999).

Corbett Ashby, M., *Women's Work and Position in the State*, Interim Report of Sub-committee of Women's Liberal Federation (London, 1943).

Crick, Bernard, *George Orwell. A Life* (Harmondsworth, 1982).

Crofts, W., *Coercion or Persuasion? Propaganda in Britain after 1945* (London, 1989).

Crosby, T. J., *The Impact of Civilian Evacuation in the Second World War* (London, 1986).

Crossman, R., 'The Role of the Volunteer in the Modern Social Service', in A. H. Halsey (ed.), *Traditions of Social Policy: Essays in Honour of Violet Butler* (Oxford, 1976).

Croucher, Richard, *Engineers at War* (London, 1982).

Daunton, M. J., 'Introduction', in Daunton (ed.), *Charity, Self-interest and Welfare in the English Past* (London, 1996).

——'Payment and Participation: Welfare and State-formation in Britain, 1900–1951', *Past and Present*, 150 (1996).

Davidson, C., *A Woman's Work is Never Done. A History of Housework in the British Isles, 1650–1950* (London, 1982).

Davidson, J. C. C., *Memoirs of a Conservative* (London, 1969).

Deakin, N., 'The Perils of Partnership. The Voluntary Sector and the State, 1945–1992', in J. Davis Smith, C. Rochester, and R. Hedley (eds.), *An Introduction to the Voluntary Sector* (London, 1995).

Delafield, E. M., *Diary of a Provincial Lady* (London, 1950).

Doyle, B. M., 'The Structure of Elite Power in the Early Twentieth-century City: Norwich, 1900–35', *Urban History*, 24 (1997), 181.

Dunbabin, J. P. D., ' "The Revolt of the Field": The Agricultural Labourers' Movement in the 1870s', *Past and Present*, 26 (1963).

Dyehouse, C., *Feminism and the Family in England, 1880–1939* (Oxford, 1989).

Field, G., 'Perspectives on the Working-class Family in Wartime Britain, 1939–1945', *International Labor and Working-Class History*, 38 (1990).

Fielding, S., 'The Second World War and Popular Radicalism: The Significance of the "Movement away from Party" ', *History*, 80 (1995).

Finlayson, G., *Citizen, State and Social Welfare in Britain, 1830–1990* (Oxford, 1994).

——'A Moving Frontier: Voluntarism and the State in British Social Welfare, 1941–49', *Twentieth-century British History*, 1 (1990).

Francis, Martin, 'The Labour Party: Modernisation and the Politics of Restraint', in Becky Conekin, Frank Mort, and Chris Waters (eds.), *Moments of Modernity. Reconstructing Britain, 1945–1964* (London, 1999).

Gaffin, Jean and David Thoms, *Caring and Sharing. The Centenary History of the Co-operative Women's Guild* (Manchester, 1983).

Garrard, John, 'The Mayoralty Since 1835', in Alan O'Day, *Government and Institutions in the post-1832 United Kingdom* (Lampeter, 1995).

——'Urban Elites, 1850–1914: The Rule and Decline of a New Squirearchy?', *Albion*, 27 (1995), 583–621.

Garside, W. R., *The Durham Miners, 1919–1960* (London, 1971).

Gershuny, J., *Social Innovation and the Division of Labour* (Oxford, 1983).

Giddens, A., *Modernity and Self-Identity* (Cambridge, 1991).

Giles, J., *Women, Identity and Private Life in Britain, 1900–1950* (London, 1995).

—— and Middleton, T., *Writing Englishness, 1900–1950. An Introductory Source Book on National Identity* (London, 1995).

Glucksmann, M., *Women Assemble. Women Workers and the New Industries in Inter-war Britain* (London, 1990).

Grant, Isabel, *The National Council of Women, 1895–1955: The First Sixty Years* (London, 1955).

Graves, Charles, *Women in Green. The Story of the Women's Voluntary Service* (London, 1948).

Graves, Pamela M., *Labour Women. Women in British Working-class Politics, 1918–1939* (Cambridge, 1994).

Gunn, Simon, 'The Public Sphere, Modernity and Consumption: New Perspectives on the History of the English Middle Class', in A. Kidd and D. Nicholls, *Gender, Civic Culture and Consumerism. Middle-class identity in Britain, 1900–1940* (Manchester, 1999).

Hall, Dorothy, *Making Things Happen* (London, 1963).

Halsey, A. H. (ed.), *British Social Trends since 1900. A Guide to the Changing Social Structure of Britain* (London, 1988).

Hannah, L., *The Rise of the Corporate Economy* (London, 1976).

Harris, Jose, *Private Lives, Public Spirit. A Social History of Britain, 1870–1914* (Oxford, 1993).

—— 'Society and the State in Twentieth-century Britain', in F. M. L. Thompson (ed.), *The Cambridge Social History of Britain, 1750–1950*, iii (Cambridge, 1990).

—— 'War and Social History: Britain and the Home Front during the Second World War', *Contemporary European History*, 1 (1992).

Harrison, Brian, 'Philanthropy and the Victorians', in Harrison, *Peaceable Kingdom. Stability and Change in Modern Britain* (Oxford, 1982).

—— *Prudent Revolutionaries. Portraits of British Feminists between the Wars* (Oxford, 1987).

Harrisson, Tom, *War Begins at Home* (London, 1940).

Hatch, Stephen, *Outside the State. Voluntary Organisations in Three English Towns* (London, 1980).

—— and Ian Morcroft, 'Voluntary Workers', *New Society* (7 Apr. 1977).

Hay, D., 'Property, Authority and the Criminal Law', in D. Hay (ed.), *Albion's Fatal Tree* (London, 1975).

Hedley, R. and S. Hatch, *Social Welfare and the Failure of the State: Centralised Social Services and Participatory Alternatives* (London, 1981).

Hewison, Robert, *In Anger. Culture in the Cold War, 1945–60* (London, 1981).

Higonnet, M. R. J., *et al.*, *Behind the Lines. Gender and the Two World Wars* (New Haven, Conn., 1987).

Hinton, J., 'Militant Housewives: The British Housewives' League and the Attlee Government', *History Workshop Journal*, 38 (1994).

Hinton, James, *Protests and Visions. Peace Politics in Twentieth-Century Britain* (London, 1989).

——*Shop-Floor Citizens. Engineering Democracy in 1940s Britain* (Aldershot, 1994).

——'Voluntarism and the Welfare/Warfare State. Women's Voluntary Services in the 1940s', *Twentieth Century British History*, 9 (1998).

——'Women and the Labour Vote, 1945–50', *Labour History Review*, 57 (1993).

Hodgkinson, George, *Sent to Coventry* (London, 1970).

Hollis, P., *Ladies Elect, Women in English Local Government, 1865–1914* (Oxford, 1987).

——*Women in Public. Documents of the Victorian Women's Movement, 1850–1900* (London, 1979).

Holman, Bob, *The Evacuation: A Very British Revolution* (Oxford, 1995).

Holmes, Gordon, *In Love with Life. A Pioneer Career Woman's Story* (London, 1944).

Holton, S., *Feminism and Democracy: Women's Suffrage and Reform Politics in Britain, 1900–1918* (Cambridge, 1987).

Horn, Pamela, *The Rise and Fall of the Victorian Servant* (Dublin, 1975).

Howkins, Alan, 'Mass Observation and Rural England, 1939–45', *Rural History*, 9 (1998).

——*Reshaping Rural England. A Social History, 1850–1925* (London, 1991), 185–94.

Hyde, H. Montgomery, *Lord Reading. The Life of Rufus Isaacs* (London, 1967).

Isaacs, Susan, *The Cambridge Evacuation Survey* (London, 1941).

Jackson, Alan A., *The Middle Classes, 1900–1950* (Nairn, 1991).

Jay, Douglas, *The Socialist Case* (London, 1947).

Jeffery, Tom, 'A Place in the Nation', in R. Koshar (ed.), *Splintered Classes: Politics and the Lower Middle Classes in Inter-war Europe* (London, 1990).

——'The Suburban Nation: Politics and Class in Lewisham', in G. S. Jones and D. Feldman, (eds.), *Metropolis London* (1989).

Jefferys, Margot, *An Anatomy of Social Welfare Services. A Survey of Social Welfare Staff and their Clients in the County of Buckinghamshire* (London, 1965).

Jones, Colin, 'Some Recent Trends in the History of Charity', in M. Daunton (ed.), *Charity, Self-interest and Welfare in the English Past* (London, 1996).

Jones, G. S., 'March into History?', *New Socialist* (Jan.–Feb. 1982), 12.

Jones, Helen, *Duty and Citizenship. The Correspondence and Parliamentary Papers of Violet Markham, 1896–1953* (London, 1994).

Jones, Peter, *et al.*, 'Politics', in D. Nash and D. Reader (eds.), *Leicester in the Twentieth Century* (Leicester, 1993).

Jordan, H. B., *How Will the Heart Endure. Elizabeth Bowen and the Landscape of War* (Ann Arbor, Mich., 1992).

Kearney, J., 'The Home Help Organizer', *Health Service Journal* (July 1975).

Kidd, A. J., 'Philanthropy and the "Social History Paradigm"', *Social History*, 21 (1996).

Land, H., R. Lowe, and N. Whiteside, *The Development of the Welfare State, 1939–45. Guide to Documents in the Public Records Office* (London, 1992).

Lawrence J. and M. Taylor (eds.), *Party, State and Society: Electoral Behaviour in Modern Britain* (Aldershot, 1996).

Laybourn, Keith, 'The Guild of Help and the Changing Face of Edwardian Philanthropy', *Urban History*, 20 (1993).

Leat, Diana, 'Explaining Volunteering: A Sociological Perspective', in S. Hatch (ed.), *Volunteers: Patterns, Meanings and Motives* (Berkhamsted, 1983).

Lee, J. M., *Social Leaders and Public Persons. A Study of County Government in Cheshire since 1888* (Oxford, 1963).

Lewis, Jane, 'Gender, the Family and Women's Agency in the Building of "Welfare States": The British Case', *Social History*, 19 (1994).

—— *The Voluntary Sector, the State and Social Work in Britain* (Aldershot, 1995).

—— *Women in England, 1870–1950* (Brighton, 1984).

—— 'The Working-class Wife and Mother and State Intervention', in Lewis (ed.), *Labour and Love. Women's Experience of Home and Family, 1850–1940* (Oxford, 1986).

Lewis, R. and A. Maude, *The English Middle Classes* (London, 1953).

Liddington, Jill, *Female Fortune. Land, Gender and Authority. The Anne Lister Diaries, 1833–36* (London, 1998).

—— *The Long Road to Greenham. Feminism and Anti-Militarism in Britain since 1820* (London, 1989).

Light, A., *Forever England: Femininity, Literature and Conservatism between the Wars* (London 1991).

Lovenduski, Joni, Pippa Norris, and Catriona Burness, 'The Party and Women', in A. Seldon and S. Ball (eds.), *Conservative Century. The Conservative Party since 1900* (Oxford, 1994).

Lowe, R., 'Welfare's Moving Frontier', *Twentieth Century British History*, 6 (1995).

Luetkins, Charlotte, *Women and a New Society* (London, 1946).

Lynn, P., 'The Influence of Class and Gender: Female Political Organisations in County Durham during the Inter-war Years', *North East History*, 31 (1997).

Macadam, Elizabeth, *The New Philanthropy: A Study of the Relations between the Statutory and Voluntary Services* (London, 1934).

Macnicol, J., 'The Evacuation of Schoolchildren', in H. L. Smith (ed.), *War and Social Change: British Society in the Second World War* (Manchester, 1986).

Maggie Andrews, ' "For Home and Country": Feminism and Englishness in the Women's Institute Movement, 1930–1960', in R. Weight and A. Beach (eds.), *The Right to Belong. Citizenship and National Identity in Britain, 1930–1960* (London, 1998).

Mark-Lawson, J., M. Savage, and A. Warde, 'Gender and Local Politics: Struggles over Welfare, 1918–1939', in L. Murgatroyd, M. Savage, J. Urry, and S. Walby (eds.), *Localities, Class and Gender* (London, 1985).

Markham, Violet R., *Return Passage* (Oxford, 1953).

Marquand, D., *Ramsay MacDonald* (London, 1977).

Mass Observation, *An Enquiry into People's Homes* (London, 1943).

Massey, P., 'The Expenditure of 1,360 British Middle-class Households in 1938–39', *Journal of the Royal Statistical Society*, 3 (1942).

Matless, D., *Landscape and Englishness* (London, 1998).

McCarthy, K. D., 'Parallel Power Structures: Women and the Voluntary Sphere', in McCarthy (ed.), *Lady Bountiful Revisited: Women, Philanthropy, and Power* (Piscataway, NJ, 1990), 1, 11.

McKegany, N., 'The Role of Home Help Organisers', *Social Policy and Administration* (Aug. 1989), 23, 2.

McKibbin, Ross, 'Class and Conventional Wisdom: The Conservative Party and the "Public" in Inter-war Britain', in *The Ideologies of Class: Social Relations in Britain, 1880–1950* (Oxford, 1990).

—— *Classes and Cultures. England, 1918–1951* (Oxford, 1998).

—— 'Class and Poverty in Edwardian England', in McKibbin, *The Ideologies of Class: Social Relations in Britain, 1880–1950* (Oxford, 1990).

Men Without Work. A Report Made to the Pilgrim Trust (Cambridge, 1938).

Mess, H. A., *Voluntary Social Services since 1918* (London, 1947).

Messenger, R., *The Doors of Opportunity* (London, 1967).

Middlemas, Keith, *Politics in Industrial Society* (London, 1979).

—— *Power Competition and the State* (3 vols., London, 1986, 1990, 1991).

Morgan, K., *Against Fascism and War. Ruptures and Continuities in British Communist Politics* (Manchester, 1989).

Morris, Mary, *Voluntary Work in the Welfare State* (London, 1969).

Morris, R. J., *Class, Sect and Party: The Making of the British Middle Class, Leeds 1820–1850* (Manchester, 1990).

Moser, C. A. and W. Scott, *British Towns: A Statistical Study of their Social and Economic Differences* (London, 1961).

Oakley, Ann, *Housewife* (London, 1974).

Oram, Alison, ' "Bombs don't Discriminate!" Women's Political Activism in the Second World War', in C. Gledhill and G. Swanson (eds.), *Nationalising Femininity, Culture, Sexuality and British Cinema in the Second World War* (Manchester, 1996).

Owen, D., *English Philanthropy, 1660–1960* (Cambridge, Mass., 1965).

Parkin, D., 'Women in the Armed Services, 1940–45', in R. Samuel (ed.), *Patriotism: The Making and Unmaking of British National Identity*, ii (London, 1989).

Paterson, D., *The Family Woman and the Feminist. A Challenge* (London, 1945).

Pear, H., *English Social Differences* (London, 1955).

Pederson, Susan, *Family. Dependence and the Origins of the Welfare State. Britain and France, 1914–1945* (Cambridge, 1993).

—— 'Gender, Welfare and Citizenship in Britain during the Great War', *American Historical Review*, 94 (1990).

Perkin, H., *The Rise of Professional Society. England since 1880* (London, 1989).

Piette, Adam, *Imagination at War. British Fiction and Poetry, 1939–1945* (London, 1995).

Pinder, J. (ed.), *Fifty Years of Political and Economic Planning* (London, 1981).

Plain, Gill, *Women's Fiction of the Second World War. Gender, Power and Resistance* (Edinburgh, 1996).

Plowman, D. E. G., W. E. Minchinton, and M. Stacey, 'Local Social Status in England and Wales', *Sociological Review*, 10 (1962).

Political and Economic Planning, *Report on the British Social Services* (London, 1937).

Priestley, J. B., *English Journey* (London, 1934).

Prochaska, F. K., 'A Mothers' Country: Mothers' Meetings and Family Welfare in Britain, 1950–1950', *History*, 74 (1989).

—— 'Philanthropy', in F. M. L. Thompson (ed.), *The Cambridge Social History of Britain, 1750–1950*, iii, *Social Agencies and Institutions* (Cambridge, 1990).

—— *The Voluntary Impulse. Philanthropy in Modern Britain* (London, 1983).

—— *Women and Philanthropy in Nineteenth-century England* (Oxford, 1980).

Pugh, Martin, *The Tories and the People, 1880–1935* (1985).

—— *Women and the Women's Movement in Britain, 1914–1959* (Basingstoke, 1992).

Pursell, C., 'Domesticating Modernity: The EAW, 1924–1986', *British Journal of the History of Science*, 32 (1999).

Ramsden, M., 'Anne Lister's Journal, 1817–1840', *Halifax Antiquarian Society* (1970).

Report on Post-War Organisation of Private Domestic Employment, Cmd 6650, June 1945.

Richardson, Sarah, 'The Role of Women in Electoral Politics in Yorkshire during the 1830s', *Northern History*, 32 (1996).

Robertson, A. J., *The Bleak Midwinter: 1947* (Manchester, 1987).

Rooff, M., *Voluntary Societies and Social Policy* (London, 1955).

Rose, Nikolas, *Governing the Soul. The Shaping of the Private Self*, 2nd edn. (London, 1999).

Rose, Sonya O., 'Sex, Citizenship and the Nation in World War II Britain', *American Historical Review*, 103 (1998).

Ross, Ellen, 'Good and Bad Mothers: Lady Philanthropists and London Housewives before the First World War', in K. D. McCarthy (ed.), *Lady Bountiful Revisited: Women, Philanthropy, and Power* (Piscataway, NJ, 1990).

—— *Love and Toil. Motherhood in Outcast London, 1870–1918* (Oxford, 1993).

Rubinstein, W. D., 'Britain's Elites in the Inter-war Period, 1918–39', in A. J. Kidd and D. Nicholls, *The Making of the British Middle Class? Studies of Regional and Cultural Diversity Since the Eighteenth Century* (Stroud, 1998).

Salisbury MacNalty, Sir A. (ed.), *The Civilian Health and Medical Services*, i (London, 1953).

Samuel, R., 'The Middle Class in Britain Between the Wars', Parts 1 and 2, *New Socialist* (Jan.–Feb. and Mar.–Apr. 1983).

Savage, Mike, *The Dynamics of Working-Class Politics. The Labour Movement in Preston, 1880–1940* (Cambridge, 1987).

—— and A. Miles, *The Remaking of the British Working Class, 1840–1940* (London, 1994).

Scott, Gillian, *Feminism and the Politics of Working Women. The Women's Co-operative Guild from the 1880s to the Second World War* (London, 1998).

Scott, Joan, *Gender and the Politics of History* (Oxford, 1988).

Sheard, Joe, 'Volunteering and Society, 1960–1990', in J. Davis Smith, C. Rochester, and R. Hedley, *An Introduction to the Voluntary Sector* (London, 1995).

Sherrott, Roger, 'Fifty Volunteers', in S. Hatch (ed.), *Volunteers: Patterns, Meanings and Motives* (Berkhamsted, 1983).

Smith, A. C. H., *Paper Voices. The Popular Press and Social Change, 1935–1965* (London, 1975).

Smith, H. L., 'The Effect of the War on the Status of Women', in Smith (ed.), *War and Social Change. British Society in the Second World War* (Manchester, 1986).

—— 'The Problem of Equal Pay for Equal Work in Great Britain During World War Two', *Journal of Modern History*, 53 (1981).

Smith, Harold, 'Sex vs Class: British Feminists and the Labour Movement, 1918–1939', *Historian*, 47 (1984).

Spring Rice, Margery, *Working-Class Wives: Their Health and Conditions* (Harmondsworth, 1939).

Stacey, M., *Tradition and Change: A Study of Banbury* (Oxford, 1960).

—— E. Batstone, C. Bell, and A. Murcott, *Power, Persistence and Change. A Second Study of Banbury* (Oxford, 1975).

Stapleton, Julia, *Englishness and the Study of Politics. The Social and Political Thought of Ernest Barker* (Cambridge, 1994).

Steinberg, Marc W., 'Culturally Speaking: Finding a Commons Between Post-structuralism and the Thompsonian Perspective', *Social History*, 21 (1996).

Stella Reading. Some Recollections by her Friends (n.d., 1978).

Stott, M., *Organisation Woman. The Story of the National Union of Townswomen's Guilds* (London, 1978).

Strachey, J., *Post D* (London, 1941).

Struthers, Jan, *Mrs Miniver* (London, 1989).

Summerfield, Penny, 'The Effect of War on the Status of Women', in H. L. Smith (ed.), *War and Social Change. British Society in the Second World War* (Manchester, 1986).

—— 'The "Levelling of Class" ', in H. L. Smith (ed.), *War and Social Change. British Society in the Second World War* (Manchester, 1986).

—— *Reconstructing Women's Wartime Lives* (Manchester, 1998).

—— *Women Workers in the Second World War. Production and Patriarchy in Conflict* (London, 1984).

Summers, Ann, 'A Home from Home—Women's Philanthropic Work in the Nineteenth Century', in S. Burman (ed.), *Fit Work for Women* (London, 1979).

Tanner, Duncan, 'Labour and its Membership', in Tanner, P. Thane, and N. Tiratsoo (eds.), *Labour's First Century* (Cambridge, 2000).

—— 'Labour, 1910–31', in J. Lawrence and M. Taylor (eds.), *Party, State and Society: Electoral Behaviour in Modern Britain* (Aldershot, 1996).

Tarling, Roger, 'Statistics on the Voluntary Sector in the UK', *Journal of the Royal Statistical Society*, 163 (2000), 3.

Thane, Pat, 'Visions of Gender in the Making of the British Welfare State: The Case of Women in the British Labour Party and Social Policy, 1906–1945', in G. Bock and Thane (eds.), *Maternity and Gender Politics. Women and the Rise of the European Welfare States, 1880s–1950s* (London, 1991), 93–118.

—— 'The Women of the British Labour Party and Feminism, 1906–1945', in H. L. Smith (ed.), *British Feminism in the Twentieth Century* (Aldershot, 1990).

Thatcher, M., *The Path to Power* (London, 1995).

Thompson, Dorothy, 'Women, Work and Politics in Nineteenth-century England: The Problem of Authority', in J. Rendall (ed.), *Equal or Different. Women's Politics, 1800–1914* (Oxford, 1987).

Thompson, F. M. L., 'English Landed Society in the Twentieth Century. ii, New Poor and New Rich', *Transactions of the Royal Historical Society*, 6th ser., 1 (1991), 16–18.

Thompson, James, 'After the Fall: Class and Political Language in Britain, 1780–1900', *Historical Journal*, 39 (1996).

Thomson, Mathew, *The Problem of Mental Deficiency, Eugenics, Democracy and Social Policy in Britain, c.1870–1959* (Oxford, 1998).

Tiratsoo, N., 'Labour and the Reconstruction of Hull', in N. Tiratsoo (ed.), *The Attlee Years* (London, 1991).

Titmuss, R., *Problems of Social Policy* (London, 1950).

Trainor, R., 'Neither Metropolitan nor Provincial: The Inter-war Middle Class', in A. Kidd and D. Nicholls (eds.), *The Making of the British Middle Class? Studies of Regional and Cultural Diversity since the Eighteenth Century* (Stroud, 1998).

Wahrman, D., *Imagining the Middle Class. The Political Representation of Class in Britain, c.1780–1840* (Cambridge, 1995).

Wainwright, H., *Labour. A Tale of Two Parties* (London, 1987).

Walton, R. G., *Women in Social Work* (London, 1975).

Welshman, John, 'Evacuation, Hygiene and Social Policy: The Our Towns Reports of 1943', *Historical Journal*, 42 (1999).

—— 'Evacuation and Social Policy During World War Two: Myth and Reality', *Twentieth Century British History*, 9 (1998).

Westwood, Louise, 'More than Tea and Sympathy (Women's Voluntary Services during the Second World War in Britain)', *History Today*, 48 (1998), 3–5.

Williams, A. S., *Ladies of Influence. Women of the Elite in Inter-war Britain* (Harmondsworth, 2000).

Williams, Gertrude, *Women and Work* (London, 1945).

Williams, R., *The Country and the City* (St Albans, 1975).

Williams, W. M., *The Sociology of an English Village: Gosforth* (London, 1956).

Willmott, P. and M. Young, *Family and Class in a London Suburb* (London, 1960).

Wilson, Angus, *The Middle-age of Mrs Eliot* (London, 1958).

Wilson, Elizabeth, *Only Halfway to Paradise. Women in Post-war Britain: 1945–1968* (London, 1980).

—— *Women and the Welfare State* (London, 1977).

Women's Group for Public Welfare, *Our Towns are our Opportunities. Suggestions for Standing Conferences of Women's Organisations* (London, 1948).

Women's Group on Public Welfare, *Our Towns: A Close-up. A Study Made in 1939–1942 with certain recommendations by the Hygiene Committee of the Women's Group on Public Welfare* (Oxford, 1943).

Woollacott, Angela, 'From Moral to Professional Authority: Secularism, Social Work, and Middle-Class Women's Self-Construction in World War I Britain', *Journal of Women's History* (Summer 1998).

Worden, S., 'Powerful Women: Electricity in the Home, 1919–1940', in J. Attfield and P. Kirkham (eds.), *A View from the Interior. Feminism, Women and Design* (London, 1989).

WVS, *Report of Ten Years' Work, 1938–1948* (London, 1948).

WVS, *Report on Twenty-five Years' Work* (London, 1963).

Yeo, Eileen and Stephen Yeo, 'On the Uses of "Community": from Owenism to the Present', in S. Yeo (ed.), *New Views of Co-operation* (London, 1988).

Young, Ken, *Local Politics and the Rise of Party. The London Municipal Society and the Conservative Intervention in Local Elections, 1894–1963* (Leicester, 1975).

——'The Party and English Local Government', in A. Seldon and S. Ball (eds.), *Conservative Century* (Oxford, 1994).

Younghusband, Eileen, *Social Work in Britain, 1950–1975*, i (London, 1978).

Zeitlin, J., 'From Labour History to the History of Industrial Relations', *Economic History Review*, 40, 2 (1987).

Zweiniger-Bargielowska, Ina, *Austerity in Britain. Rationing, Controls and Consumption, 1939–1955* (Oxford, 2000).

——'Explaining the Gender Gap: The Conservative Party and the Women's Vote, 1945–1964', in M. Francis and I. Zweiniger-Bargielowska (eds.), *The Conservatives and British Society, 1880–1990* (Cardiff, 1996).

20. UNPUBLISHED THESES

Bates, J. W. B., 'The Conservative Party in the Constituencies, 1918–1939', Oxford D.Phil., 1994.

Beaumont, Catriona, 'Women and Citizenship: A Study of Non-feminist Women's Societies and the Women's Movement in England, 1928–1950', Warwick Ph.D., 1996.

Lynn, P., 'The Shaping of Political Allegiance: Class, Gender, Nation and Locality in Co. Durham, 1918–1945', Teeside Ph.D., 1999.

McCarty, Elizabeth, 'Attitudes to Women and Domesticity in England, circa 1939–1955', Oxford D.Phil., 1994.

North, D. L., 'Middle-Class Suburban Culture and Lifestyles in England, 1919–1939', Oxford D.Phil., 1989.

Index

Doyle, Barry 38
Durham Miners Association 106, 107, 113

Easington 107–32
East Anglia 94
East Sussex 165, 208
Ede, Chuter 219–29, 232
Eggerton-Warburton, Mrs 29 n. 58
Electrical Association of Women 44, 49, 180
Elliot, Dorothy 205 n. 44
Elmstead 149, 150
Ely 134
Emmet, Evelyn 93, 96, 135, 141, 150, 160, 161, 165
Essex 163
evacuation 75, 145, 147–54, 181
Evans, Dorothy 180, 195
Exeter 48

Farrer, Frances 223
feminism 9, 41, 46–7, 68–70, 179–81, 188, 189, 195
food leader scheme 168–9, 172–5
Foulkes, Miss 184
Franklin, Alice 41–2, 194
Fryer, Joan 140
fuel economy 19, 170–3, 175

Gainsborough 29
Gateshead 98
Girl Guides 53–4, 145
Glossop 36, 38
Gloucestershire 153
Gordon, Sabrina 115–17, 121, 122, 124–6, 127, 128, 131
Gosforth 134, 135, 137
Gould, Barbara Ayrton 67
Gray, Mary 138, 146
Great Yarmouth 29, 166
Grimsby 53, 191
Group Action Councils 184–90
Guildford 51, 55, 56, 80, 81

Haigh, Caroline 141
Halifax 45–6, 54, 188, 189–90, 193
Halpin, Kathleen 20, 32, 34, 199, 220
Hambro, Lady 141
Hamilton, Mary Agnes 67, 89 n. 131
Hampshire 136, 146 n. 68, 166
Hancock, Florence 28
Harford, Letty 190, 191, 195
Harlech, Lord 94, 95
Harrison, Brian 70
Harrogate 54
Haslemere 153
Haslett, Caroline 180, 184, 185 n. 36
Havelock-Allen, Lady Pamela 97–8

Hayek, F. 173
Haynes, George 220, 222, 224
Headlam, Cuthbert 106, 131–2
Hebburn 88
Hertfordshire 134, 140, 141, 143, 146, 147, 211
Higham, Mrs 164
Hoare, Samuel 67, 92
Hollis, Patricia 192
Holtby, Winifred 47
home helps 201–12
Horden 110, 112, 114, 115, 117, 118, 127
Hornyold-Strickland, Mary 136
Horton, Gertrude 41, 42, 185–6, 188, 194, 195, 196, 223
Housewives Service (WVS) 79–85, 167, 168, 169, 173, 202
housework 25–6
Howard, Lady Mable 138–9, 147
Hull 48, 50, 54, 101–3, 159, 207, 214
Huntingdon 144
Hutchinson, Miss 127, 128
Huxley, Lindsay 32, 49, 84, 94, 102, 120–1
Hyde, Pearl 86–7, 88

Inner Wheel 40
Ipswich 55

Jarrow 51
Jay, Douglas 173
Jennings, Humphrey 87
Johnson, Alice 220
Jones, Gareth Steadman 15

Kay-Shuttleworth, Rachel 50–1
Kendall 136
Kent 149, 166
Kettering 53
knitting 56–7, 58, 62, 78, 145
Knowles, Mrs 100–1

Labour Party 36, 55
  and voluntary work 68, 70–1, 206–7
Labour Women 108–9, 111
  and middle-class women's organizations 68–73
  and WVS 66–8, 70–1, 73–6, 78, 85–9, 113–32
Lambert, Sir Arthur 93 n. 13
Lancashire 162, 188
Lansdowne, Lady 136, 137
Last, Nella 23, 30, 62, 63, 64, 164
Lawson, Jack 125, 126
Lawson, Janet, 154 n.108
Leamington Spa 190
Lee, J. M. 139, 140, 141
Leeds 54, 162

Index

and uniform 33, 63
and voluntary sector 33–4, 59–61, 144–7,
  157, 161, 162, 165, 166, 168, 213–30
and working-class women 64–5, 66–9,
  77–85, 113–32, 236
Woollacott, Angela 234
Worcester 61, 62–3
Worcestershire 227
Worsley, Lady 64

York 101
Yorkshire 145, 166, 173
  East Riding 142
  North Riding 144
Young, Anthony 112, 122
Young Women's Christian Association
  186

Zweiniger-Bargielowska, Ina 9 n. 22

KING ALFRED'S COLLEGE
LIBRARY